DEBORAH FAHY BRYCESON

Liberalizing Tanzania's Food Trade

PUBLIC & PRIVATE FACES OF URBAN MARKETING POLICY 1939–1988

T0342489

in association with

JAMES CURREY
LONDON

MKUKI NA NYOTA
DAR ES SALAAM

HEINEMANN
PORTSMOUTH, N.H.

United Nations Research Institute
for Social Development (UNRISD)
Palais des Nations
1211 Geneva 10, Switzerland

James Currey Ltd
54b Thornhill Square
Islington
London N1 1BE, England

Mkuki na Nyota Publishers
P.O. Box 4246 Dar es Salaam

Heinemann Educational Books, Inc
361 Hanover Street
Portsmouth, NH 03801-3959, USA

British Cataloguing in Publication Data
Bryceson, Deborah
  Liberalizing Tanzania's Food Trade:
  Public and Private Faces of Urban
  Marketing Policy, 1939–88
  I. Title
  338.1

ISBN 0-85255-134-7 (Paper)
ISBN 0-85255-135-5 (Cloth)

ISBN 0-435-08077-6 (Heinemann Cloth)

Typeset in 10/11 pt Baskerville by Opus 43, Cumbria
Printed and Bound in Great Britain by Villiers Publications, London

Contents

VIII *Trade-Offs on Trade:*
Food Market Liberalization   182

Tables

Figures

Maps

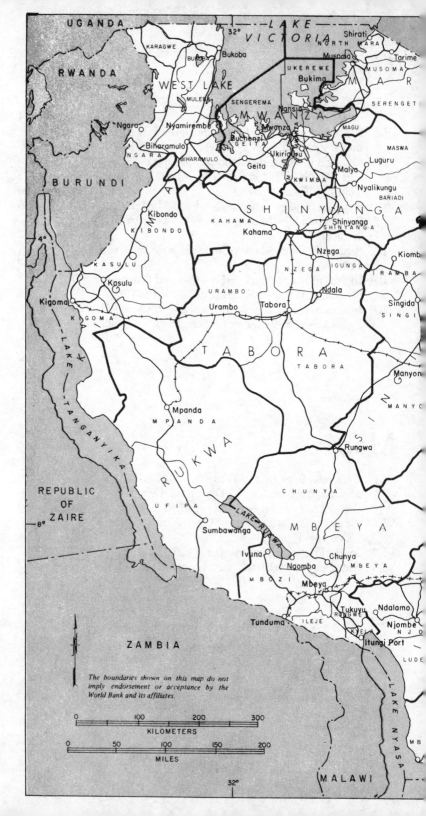

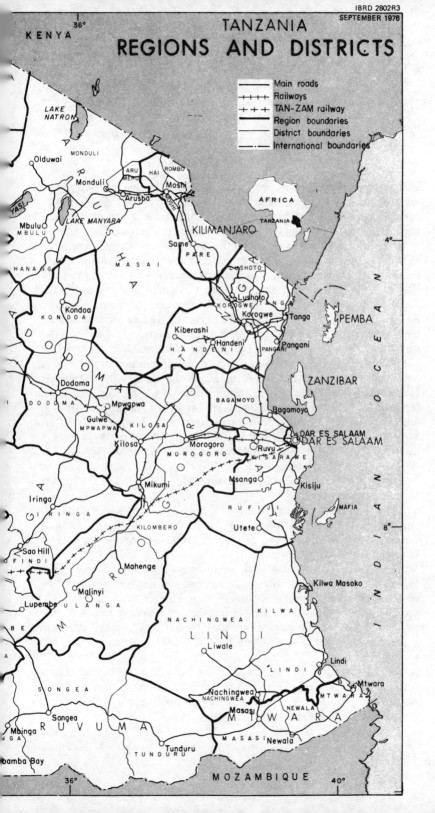

TANZANIA
REGIONS AND DISTRICTS

Main roads
Railways
TAN-ZAM railway
Region boundaries
District boundaries
International boundaries

KENYA

36°

LAKE NATRON

MONDULI

Olduvai

Monduli

ARU

MERU

HAI

ROMBO

Arusha

Moshi

Mbulu

MBULU

LAKE MANYARA

KILIMANJARO

4°

HANANG

MASAI

Same

PARE

LUSHOTO

Kondoa

KONDOA

Lushoto

KOROGWE

TANGA

Korogwe

Tanga

PEMBA

Kiberashi

Handeni

Pangani

HANDENI

PANGANI

Dodoma

ZANZIBAR

DODOMA

Mpwapwa

BAGAMOYO

Gulwe

MPWAPWA

KILOSA

Bagamoyo

DAR ES SALAAM

Kilosa

Morogoro

Ruvu

DAR ES SALAAM

MOROGORO

KISARAWE

Mikumi

Msanga

Iringa

Kisiju

IRINGA

RUFIJI

MAFIA

KILOMBERO

Utete

Sao Hill

8°

IFINDI

Mahenge

Malinyi

Kilwa Masoko

Lupembe

ULANGA

KILWA

BE

NACHINGWEA

LINDI

M

Liwale

LINDI

Lindi

SONGEA

Nachingwea

Mtwara

NACHINGWEA

Masasi

NEWALA

MTWARA

Songea

RUVUMA

MWARA

Mbinga

MASASI

Newala

NGA

Tunduru

bamba Bay

TUNDURU

MOZAMBIQUE

36°

40°

INDIAN OCEAN

AFRICA

TANZANIA

Acknowledgements

This book would not have been possible without the financial support of the United Nations Research Institute for Social Development (Geneva). Special thanks go to Cynthia Hewitt de Alcántara for her encouragement and understanding during the various stages of this project.

In Tanzania, the list of people to thank is very long indeed. The work of William Baynit, acting as survey administrator and research assistant, was invaluable. I am grateful to the survey enumerators, namely, Mwanitu Kagubila, Y.Q. Lawi, Paul Manda, Robert Mhamba and Joshua Qorro, for their concerted effort, and to the Tanzanian National Scientific Research Council. In addition to the surveyed traders and consumers, there were many people who gave information or otherwise facilitated the study. Listed by town they include: *Arusha*: Mr A.M. Sumari, Mrs C.J. Mwakalinga, and the Ward Secretaries of Kati, Ngarenuro and Levolosi wards; *Dar es Salaam*: Mr C.D. Arha, Mr T. Banda, Mr B. Bojang, Mr E.S.M. Chijoriga, Dr B. Cooksey, Prof. J. Doriye, Mr H. Gordon, Mr de Greeve, Ms J. Janabi, Mr D. Kajumulo, Mr J.A.A. Karumuna, Mr R.J. Kibushi, Ms V. Leach, Mrs Lyaruu, Mr A.S. Mlupilo, Mr M.H. Mnyamuru, Dr K. Mustafa, Mr A. Rashid, Mr Shempemba, and Mr J. Strauss; *Mbeya*: Mr M. Hombee, Mr A. Lugome, Mr B. Mwalupindi, Mr E.N.A. Mwamalumbili and Mr B. Mwambwalo; *Mwanza*: Mr P.B. Naburage and Mr J.Z. Ngussa; and *Songea*: Mr Lwoga, Mr A.B. Margwe, Mr Mkuko and Mr Msuha.

Those who kindly commented on my research methodology and draft chapters include: Han Bantje, Jorge Deutsch, Alex Duncan, Matthew Lockwood, Davis Mwamfupe, Michael Sikawa, Geir Sundet, and Peter Utting.

The shadow costs of this book weigh heaviest on my husband, John Howe, who endured my months and months of involvement with 'the traders'. This book is thus dedicated to John. Further, on the home front, the people most instrumental in seeing the book writing to completion were my son's babyminders, Madeline Gansert and Sue French. I am grateful to them for their excellent care of Nicholas, giving me the time to press on.

Special thanks go to Selina Cohen for her editing work and coping with the capriciousness of Oxford's post office. The cover design is based on the efforts of myself and John Howe as photographer, with advice from Anne Eggleton and Phyllis Ferguson.

Preface

It is necessary to give some background to the book. It was first commissioned by UNRISD in the form of a short monograph on food policy. Over the course of the project, it evolved into something bigger. The original historical material collected for the project was combined with results from two project-specific surveys of traders and consumers.

There are two ways of reading the book. For the committed student of Tanzanian marketing studies, the extremely detailed chronicle of marketing policy and trade development that unfolds over the book's eight chapters is recommended. For those with more general interests, notably those concerned with third world political economy and/or trade liberalization, Chapters 1, 2 and 8 are essential and in themselves constitute a coherent argument regarding recent market liberalization in Tanzania.

Note on UNRISD

The United Nations Research Institute for Social Development (UNRISD) was established to promote in-depth research into the social dimensions of pressing problems and issues of contemporary relevance affecting development. Its work is inspired by the conviction that, for effective development to be formulated, an understanding of the social and political context is crucial,. as is an accurate assessment of how such policies affect different social groups.

The Institute attempts to complement the work done by other United Nations agencies and its current research themes include the social impact of the economic crisis and adjustment policies; environment, sustainable development and social change; ethnic conflict and development; refugees, returnees and local society; the socio-economic and political consequences of the international trade in illicit drugs; and social participation and the social impact of changes in the ownership of the means of production.

Abbreviations

AIDS	Acquired Immune Deficiency Syndrome	OECD	Organization for Economic Cooperation and Development
APPCC	Agricultural Price Policy Coordinating Committee	ODA	Overseas Development Agency
APR	Agricultural Price/Policy Review	ODNRI	Overseas Development Natural Resources Institute
ARCU	Arusha Region Cooperative Union	PC	Provincial Commissioner
CCM	Chama cha Mapinduzi	RCU	Ruvuma Cooperative Union
CDR	Centre for Development Research	RETCO	Regional Transport Corporation
CUT	Cooperative Union of Tanganyika	RH	Rhodes House
DC	District Commissioner	SAP	Structural Adjustment Programme
DSM	Dar es Salaam	SCOPO	Standing Committee on Parastatal Organization
ERP	Economic Recovery Programme		
EWCMP	Early Warning and Crop Monitoring Programme	SDR	Special Drawing Rights
		SGR	Strategic Grain Reserve
FAO	Food and Agriculture Organization	TAG	Tanzania Advisory Group
FOB	free on board	TANSEED	Tanzania Seed Company
GDP	gross domestic product	TANU	Tanganyika African Nationalist Union
GSD	Grain Storage Department		
HBS	household budget survey	TANZAM	Tanzania–Zambia Highway
HMSO	Her Majesty's Stationery Office	TAZARA	Tanzania–Zambia Railway
IDA	International Development Association	TESCA	Tanganyika European Civil Servants' Association
ILO	International Labour Office	TFC	Tanzania Fertilizer Company
IMF	International Monetary Fund	TFNC	Tanzania Food and Nutrition Centre
KYERECU	Kysla–Rungwe Cooperative Union	TNA	Tanzania National Archives
MBECU	Mbeya Cooperative Union	TRDB	Tanzania Rural Development Bank
MDB	Marketing Development Bureau	TSGA	Tanganyika Sisal Growers' Association
NAPB	National Agricultural Products Board		
NDL	National Distributors Ltd.	UDI	Unilateral Declaration of Independence
NEC	National Executive Committee		
NESP	National Economic Survival Programme	UNCTAD	United Nations Conference on Trade and Development
NJOLUMA	Njombe–Ludewa–Makete Cooperative Union	UNDP	United Nations Development Programme
NMC	National Milling Corporation	UNRISD	United Nations Research Institute for Social Development
NMP	National Maize Project		
NUMEIST	National Urban Mobility, Employment and Income Survey of Tanganyika	USAID	United States Agency for International Development
		WASHIRIKA	the party-affiliated CUT

Kiswahili Translations

akili	intelligence	*ngoma*	dance
boma	government headquarters	*nguvu kazi*	'work is strength' campaign
Chama cha Mapinduzi	Revolutionary Party	*pishi*	small grain volume measurement
debe	grain volume measurement of approximately 17 kg.	*pombe*	beer
		posho	food ration and slang for perks on the job
dona	unrefined maize flour	*risala*	petitioning
duka	shop	*sembe*	maize meal
dukawallah	Indian shopkeeper	*shamba*	farm
kibali	permission	*ugali*	stiff maize porridge
malalamishi	complaints	*ujamaa*	familyhood
mtama	sorghum/millet	*walanguzi*	black marketeers
Mwongozo	TANU Guidelines	*wazungu*	Europeans
ndonya	grain volume measurement of approximately 0.5 kg.		

I
Introduction

Adam Smith's 'invisible hand' is more visible in some societies than others. In Tanzania the hand is faint and unsteady. The weakness of the market is part and parcel of the low level of economic development. Surplus production, notably of staple food, is not a regular feature of the economy. As a nation composed primarily of peasant farmers, Tanzania does not demonstrate a high degree of labour specialization. And, not least in the prerequisites for market development, there has been an extreme reluctance on the part of the populace to accept Adam Smith's view that:

> Whoever offers to another a bargain of any kind, proposes ... [G]ive me that which I want, and you shall have this which you want ... and it is in this manner that we obtain from one another the far greater part of those good offices which we stand in need of. It is not from the benevolence of the butcher, the brewer, or the baker, that we expect our dinner, but from their regard to their own interest. We address ourselves, not to their humanity but to their self-love, and never talk to them of our own necessities but of their advantages ... This division of labour, from which so many advantages are derived, is not originally the effect of any human wisdom, which foresees and intends that general opulence to which it gives occasion. It is the necessary, though very slow and gradual, consequence of a certain propensity in human nature which has in view no such extensive utility; the propensity to truck, barter, and exchange one thing for another.[1]

For decades, traders have been pariahs in Tanzania, accused at best of being unproductive and at worst of being super-exploitative. Their role in the nation's distribution of staple foodstuffs has been the most controversial. The purpose of this monograph is to analyse this phenomenon and the changing economic and social climate associated with world

1. Smith, A., 'The Wealth of Nations', in Abbott, L.D. (ed.), *Masterworks of Economics* (New York, Doubleday & Company, 1946), 78.

recession which has made traders' role in staple food supply more acceptable to policy-makers and the general public.

In this chapter, the strategic importance of food and food marketing in the Tanzanian economy and the rationale for vesting staple food marketing in the public sector is reviewed. Chapter II describes the recent economic crisis, the associated moral crisis of public accountability, state policy measures to counter the crisis and conflict with the IMF over the relative roles of the state and market. Chapter III provides historical background on marketing policy from the onset of the Second World War to 1973, detailing the policy changes which defined the scope of traders' activities. Chapter IV documents the establishment and performance of single-channel parastatal food marketing from 1973 onwards, and the various marketing reforms that the official marketing system has been subjected to in the 1980s. Chapter V pieces together evidence of the operation of parallel markets in the past, followed by Chapter VI's review of 1988 survey findings of 196 open market grain traders in Dar es Salaam, Arusha, Mwanza, Mbeya and Songea (Map I.1). Chapter VII discusses the results of a survey of 188 households in the above mentioned towns, revealing staple food consumer sources of supply and strategies for averting household food shortages. Chapter VIII delves more deeply into the social and economic forces behind staple food policy-making, analysing the philosophical and political underpinnings of policy stances in the transition from an overriding concern for rural community food availability to that of urban food security. Within the context of post-independence Tanzanian developmental goals, traders' present and future status is considered.

1. The Centrality of Food and Food Marketing in Tanzanian Political Economy

In 1988, the population of Tanzania was 23 million, of which approximately 80 per cent were peasant farmers who, virtually without exception, endeavoured to provision their own staple food needs. The major staple food crops consumed throughout the country in order of importance by value are: maize, rice, sorghum/millet, bananas, cassava, sweet potatoes, barley, potatoes, wheat and an assortment of more minor foodstuffs. Most Tanzanians have a heavily starch-based diet. Cereal and root crops constitute three-quarters of food consumed by weight (Table I.1).[2] The agricultural sector accounts for over half of GDP. Eighty-five per cent of crop output is contributed by peasant smallholders, the bulk of which is subsistence food production.

Historically, Tanzania has experienced a number of widespread food shortages, most severely felt in the vast semi-arid central plateau area of

2. Tanzania, Bureau of Statistics, 1976/77 Household Budget Survey.

the country. The failure of seasonal rains or locust attacks coupled with the low productivity of shifting, hoe agriculture has been the root cause of rural food shortfalls. As population growth has accelerated over the past five decades, land use has intensified and the duration of fallows has shortened. Peasant subsistence food production has had to keep pace with increasing population density amidst the introduction of export and food cashcropping. The available evidence suggests that the incidence of rural food shortages has not risen. Peasant food production has managed to keep in step with rural population growth, with the proviso that nutritional levels continue to be low, seasonal hunger is still observed in many areas, and, when the long rains fail, farmers rarely have sufficient stocks to cover their food requirments until the next rains.[3]

Even if rural food adequacy has not worsened, Tanzania's national food supply from year to year is far from secure. The proportion of the population who do not make their living from peasant farming has expanded over the years and the growth of staple food demand has naturally followed. During the 1960s and the 1970s the urban growth rate exceeded 10 per cent per annum. The country's growing reliance on food imports indicates that peasant agriculture has failed to meet the growing market demand for staple foodstuffs.

In this context, food policy, specifically, the organization of food marketing, has become a central pivot of national policy. Besides the obvious humanitarian considerations involved in trying to ensure a basic level of food consumption, economic and political imperatives are at stake. The staple foodstuffs listed above, especially maize, constitute the labour force's most essential and, in value terms, most important wage good. Food policy becomes vital to ensuring political stability.

Given the centrality of staple food supply in Tanzania in economic and political terms, it comes as little surprise that the evolution of Tanzanian food policy has been a testing ground for Tanzania's development philosophy. The dynamic interaction between the country's development philosophy and food policy will be illustrated in the chapters that follow.

2. Food Security as a State Priority

Tanzanian food policy has evolved around the principle that staple foodstuffs are 'strategic commodities'. Their strategic nature relates to the dominant place food production occupies in the economic activities of the populace. However, paradoxically, the commodity status of staple foodstuffs is not generally acceptable to the broad masses of the population who, accustomed to growing their own food, have implicit feelings about their 'natural rights' to food.

3. Bryceson, D.F., *Food Insecurity and the Social Division of Labour in Tanzania, 1919–85* (London, Macmillan, 1990).

Most tribal communities had rituals depicting the sacred, life-giving properties of staple foodstuffs. While these rituals no longer are a part of the basic education and cultural milieu of most Tanzanians, the moral economy which underlies these rituals has not entirely disappeared. One could argue that, in the minds of policy-makers and citizens alike, there is a belief that the foremost civil right a Tanzanian holds is access to sufficient food to ensure physical survival. Basic 'food entitlements',[4] in one form or another, are considered part and parcel of every Tanzanian's birthright. In this milieu, a government that transgresses these rights divorces itself from the morality of the society and could face heavy sanctions for doing so.

Traditionally, food security of the tribal community was the main criterion for judging the effectiveness of leadership. Food shortages were the most frequent grounds for a contending faction to seize power. Although the days of small tribal communities have been superseded, a subsistence ethic continues to influence the national polity. The persistence of food shortages from time to time reinforces the traditional outlook. Food supply uncertainty is not an individual threat, it is a social threat, a threat to the household, to the community and ultimately to the state. Thus staple foodstuffs are politically strategic.

Furthermore, the natural, harmonious order of the economy, society and state is, and has to be, food adequacy for all. Hence, the buying and selling of foodstuffs, in which one party sells in order to profit whereas the other party buys in order to secure his/her household's food requirements, are subject to moral scrutiny. The consumer is inherently right and the trader is always suspect.

In this context, a central issue that food policy must address is what agency and agents can be entrusted with marketed food distribution. The moral climate gives marketed staple foodstuffs an ambiguous and politically-charged status. Practicality dictates that they are commodities, but on a philosophical plane they are public goods. The colonial as well as the post-independence government faced this dilemma and each worked out policies that aimed, first, to encourage household food self-sufficiency as much as possible as a means of avoiding reliance on market supply; and, second, to ensure the supply of staple foods to the population dependent on market supplies.

In the case of the British colonial government during the period between the two world wars, the emphasis was on rural supply because urban settlement had barely surfaced. Colonial by-laws enshrined a 'food first' approach to peasant agriculture. Peasants were required to plant their food crops first before devoting time to cashcropping. Furthermore, in many areas, district authorities made the planting of minimum acreages

---

4. Term derived from Sen, A.K., *Poverty and Famines* (Oxford, Clarendon Press, 1980).

of food crops mandatory. In semi-arid regions where harvest failures were common, peasants were forced to plant drought-prone crops such as cassava.

British colonial officials took a very paternalistic view towards peasants' encounters with traders.[5] It was generally believed that the peasant would be no match for the worldly-wise trader. At the first hint of food shortage, by-laws were enacted which closed districts off to external trade. It was hoped that, in doing so, all trade speculation in staple foodstuffs would be averted to protect peasant food supplies.

The notion of a 'just price' for essential foodstuffs frequently surfaces in the literature. Colonial officialdom was intolerant of food price fluctuation. Genuine supply constraints and high transport costs, which were passed on into the purchase price or sale of food, were generally considered to be extortionate.[6]

Food policy became more complex during the Second World War as the impact of the war economy and urbanization emerged. Chapter III provides a detailed discussion of marketing policy during this period. What is significant to note, at this point, is that despite the growth of urbanization, peasant producers were not pressurized into specializing in production. Every peasant household was expected to continue to produce its own staple food requirements with resort to market supply or, at worst, state famine relief only in extreme circumstances. Cashcropping and other non-farm economic activities of the peasant households were in effect sideline activities.

Following independence in 1961, the post-colonial state continued to pursue a household food self-sufficiency policy *vis-à-vis* the peasantry. Urbanization was escalating, however, and the nation's lack of stable annual surpluses to feed the urban population was an impediment to economic development planning. Raising peasant food crop production became a central aim of the nation's rural development programme.

Post-colonial marketing policy displayed a tendency towards increasing state intervention. In the past, the move towards state intervention had

5. Bryceson, D.F., 'Colonial Famine Responses', *Food Policy* (May 1981).
6. For example, during the mid-1930s, Asian traders were accused of forming collusive rings for the market supply of food to the labour force at the inaccessible Lupa goldfield in southwestern Tanzania. Malcolm, a visiting government official sent out to investigate the situation, records that maize was being sold by traders at 230 Sh. per ton, while peasants in the closest, though geographically distant, Native Authority markets were receiving only 60 Sh. The 'normal' price for maize in other parts of the country was considered to be 140 Sh./ton. However, in his back-of-an-envelope calculations, Malcolm figured that, given the exceptionally high transport costs involved in bringing maize into the area by human porterage, the only feasible way the government could break the ring would be to transport maize down from the railhead at Dodoma to the Lupa at the cost of 250 Sh. He then recommended that the maize be sold at 180 Sh., which resulted in a loss of 70 Sh. per ton. This strategy was never pursued (Malcolm, D.W., Diary 29/11/35, RH Mss. Afr. s. 1445).

always been strongest during times of food shortage. Efforts to accommodate rising urban food demand further reinforced this tendency. Furthermore, increased state intervention in marketing was conducive to the country's socialist development philosophy and the associated proliferation of civil servants and parastatal personnel. The operation of an open market in staple food supply was, in many respects, antithetical to Tanzania's historical evolution and chosen development path. Consequently, it was viewed as a threat to basic needs provisioning of the general population.

Periods of national food shortage have often corresponded with periods of economic crisis. The situation during the Second World War exemplifies this, and it is true for the protracted economic crisis between 1979 and 1984 as well. One would therefore expect that during an economic crisis the tendency would be for state intervention in marketing to increase. Yet, from 1984 to 1988, more and more space was made for the operation of an open market in foodstuffs.

An attempt to unravel why and how Tanzanian policy-makers and consumers began to change their attitude towards open market food supply is presented in the chapters that follow. Has there been a genuine change of heart or has force of circumstances dictated the situation? To answer these questions requires delving deeper into Tanzania's political economy, its history of food marketing policy, and the nature of the recent economic crisis.

II

Post-Independence Egalitarian Goals & Economic Crisis

From 1979 through 1988, Tanzania faced a severe economic crisis which posed many obstacles to the realization of its development goals. The state agencies designated to spearhead Tanzanian socialist development, namely the party and the parastatals, were exposed to several conditions which undermined their performance. This chapter is divided into three sections: first, a review of the causes of the crisis and its extent; second, a discussion of the role of the party and parastatals; and, third, an examination of Tanzania's general policy responses to the economic crisis and the conflict that ensued between the Tanzanian state and the International Monetary Fund (IMF).

1. Levelling Down not Up

In 1967, Tanzania announced its commitment to African socialism in the Arusha Declaration. In fact, prior to this date, the egalitarian objectives of the post-independence government had already been made abundantly clear. At independence, Nyerere, leader of the major national party, TANU,[1] and president of the nation, declared a war on ignorance, poverty and disease. The strategy was one of promoting agricultural development and welfare of the peasantry over industrial growth and urban prosperity. The Arusha Declaration launched Tanzania on the road to state, rather than market-led, development. This was a pragmatic move in the face of the lack of foreign and domestic capital investment that had hitherto been experienced, as well as reflecting a genuine belief in the power of the state to achieve more egalitarian development.

In the early 1970s, the development goals were revised to embrace a

---

1. Tanganyika African Nationalist Union.

basic industries strategy. However, the declared commitment to egalitarian distribution of the fruits of independence remained. Egalitarian distribution in the Tanzanian context did not infer dispossession of a large landowning class. There was none. Amongst the African population, it was assumed that everyone's standard of living would rise, although peasant incomes, according to the development philosophy, would rise faster than those of urban dwellers. Asian traders, it was felt, had held an advantageous position in trade for too long. Their trading operations were restricted, as described in the chapter to follow, but the intention was not to dispossess them *per se*. *Ujamaa*,[2] as it was originally espoused by Nyerere, was about pulling up an illiterate rural population from a position of colonial neglect and embarking on economic and social advance under a benevolent government and progressive African one-party state.

For the first ten years of independence, Tanzanian economic performance was promising. As a nation whose foreign exchange earnings derived almost solely from the export of primary commodities, the collapse of world demand for sisal came as a severe blow to the large plantations of the coast and northeast and the economy at large. On the other hand, the export of the peasant-produced crops, namely coffee, tea, cotton and cashew, was expanding, contributing to rising exports overall and a healthy balance of payments on current account (Table II.1). The dismantling of the large bachelor-waged workforce connected with the colonial sisal plantations undoubtedly removed a potential dissent group from the political arena. The country's gross domestic product was edging upwards (Table II.2).

The tide started to change in the early 1970s. Tanzania's early attempts to develop an industrial base led to increased imports of capital goods which, together with the effects of drought in 1971/72, caused the balance of trade to become negative. Without time to recover, the oil price shock of 1973 and another more serious drought struck in 1974. Per capita food imports reached unprecedented levels and signalled the beginning of a period of food insecurity similar in many respects to the food supply uncertainty experienced under colonial rule during the Second World War. The oil price rise was a new problem, but one that was to prove just as intractable given Tanzania's heavy reliance on road transport, the country's large size, dispersed settlement and regional crop pattern.

Coinciding with the drought and the oil price rise was the party's call for peasants throughout the nation to move into concentrated village settlements rather than live in widely dispersed homesteads. Villagization, or the establishment of 'development' villages, was viewed as a stage of the

2. Nyerere, J.K., *Socialism and Rural Development* (Dar es Salaam, Government Printer, 1967), 26.

government's *ujamaa* programme. However, development villages were not *ujamaa* villages. There was no obligation to establish collective production. Local leaders could urge and indeed require this to be done, but, at the national level, development villagization was a policy aimed solely at nucleating rural settlement into villages on or adjacent to roads to facilitate the distribution of productive and social service infrastructure. It was hoped that over time the villages would progress to collective forms of production, but, initially and for the foreseeable future, their residential proximity would be used to develop economies of scale in production. Individually owned household agricultural plots were allocated, by the village party officials, contiguous to one another to form large 'block' farms. Distribution of productive inputs as well as mechanization of production was to be facilitated by the cultivation of large fields.

Many critics have slated the villagization programme as the source of Tanzania's economic decline, downplaying the adverse effects of the oil crisis and drought. It is argued that, as a move towards more socialist agriculture, it caused resentment on the part of the peasantry, stifling its initiative.

On the other hand, the 'villagization as disaster' view does not accord with the fact that there was a significant recovery in food crop production in 1977 and 1978 which was achieved by villagized peasants. The more than adequate availability of domestic staple foods and the healthy export position arising from the boom in coffee prices led the government, with the prompting of World Bank advisers, to liberalize imports. This proved foolhardy in retrospect, as the move was quickly followed by the second oil price crisis of 1979 as well as Tanzania's war with Idi Amin's Uganda. The balance of payments plunged to new depths. The country was trapped in a quicksand from which it found it impossible to extricate itself. Every move seemed to bring about further sinking.

Virtually all the economic indicators of the early 1980s show a steady downward trend. The country's terms of trade were exceptionally adverse, as a result of the continual rise in the price of oil and the consequent price increase of manufactured imports (Table II.3). Tanzania's response was to cut down on imports, which would be reduced to the barest minimum as time progressed. In 1985, the value of oil imports was 22 per cent of total imports whereas consumer goods were only 16 per cent, intermediate goods (excluding oil) accounted for 18 per cent and capital goods were 44 per cent.[3] Efforts to keep up exports under the duress of fuel and peasant incentive goods shortages were surprisingly good under the circumstances.

Nevertheless, the gap in the balance of trade persisted, in fact widened, and its knock-on effects quickly evidenced themselves in the government's

3. Figures from Customs & Excise Department and Bank of Tanzania quoted in *Tanzanian Economic Trends* 1(2), July 1988, 59.

financial position. Between 1979 and 1983, the TSh. 18,600 million cumulative deficit in current account was financed by long-term credit (57 per cent), suppliers' credit (12 per cent), exceptional financing (21 per cent) and a decrease in reserves (11 per cent).[4]

Table II.4 shows the steady increase in the government's budget deficit. Taxation was raised, particularly in the form of a sales tax. For the first time since colonial rule, a poll tax was introduced, renamed the 'development levy'. Foreign finance in the form of loans and grants fluctuated with a serious reduction in 1983/84 and a strong recovery in 1984/85, but this did not offset the alarming climb in public debt. Debt servicing increased from 7 per cent of government expenditure in 1975/76 to over 20 per cent in 1983/84.

Significantly, development expenditure declined from 40 per cent to roughly 20 per cent of total government expenditure between 1976/77 and 1987/88. Increasingly, government outlay went towards merely trying to maintain the existing infrastructure. But, as inflation climbed, real cutbacks in recurrent expenditure were occurring. For the most part these were being felt in all sectors of the economy. Table II.5 shows the expenditure by sector. It will be noticed that in proportional terms the public debt quadrupled whereas most social and productive services were halved. Other general public services increased.

The Tanzanian population was experiencing a serious decline in real incomes due to inflation and increasing taxation. Just how drastic is indicated by figures in Table II.6. The government-set minimum wage was not keeping up with increases in the cost of living (Tables II.7 and II.8).

According to formal sector statistics, urban dwellers, particularly the highly paid ones, have suffered the greatest decline in their real incomes (Table II.6). By 1985, the top salaried parastatal employees were receiving less than 10 per cent of their 1969 salary in real terms, whereas minimum wage earners' real income had been reduced to a third of its 1969 value. Available data suggest that peasants experienced comparatively less decline in income because of the large component of their income which derived from subsistence production (Table II.9),[5] but shortages of consumer goods in rural areas were acute.[6] A process of income levelling was taking place in line with Tanzanian development philosophy, but not in the direction anticipated.

4. ILO, *Distributional Aspects of Stabilisation Programmes in the United Republic of Tanzania* (Geneva, ILO, 1988), 6.
5. See ILO, *Distributional Aspects*, Table VII.
6. Bevan, D., A. Bigsten, P. Collier and J.W. Gunning, *East African Lessons on Economic Liberalization* (Hampshire, Gower, 1987), 10.

2. African Socialism in Practice: Party Supremacy, Parastatal Power and Personal Privation

The statistics cited above indicate the degree of economic decline, but they do not begin to suggest how the decline affected the Tanzanian population and to what extent economic, social and political relationships were transformed. How did the society respond to deprivation? Later chapters will consider at length the political and social consequences of the economic crisis, specifically with reference to the organization of food marketing. In this section, it is pertinent to examine the institutional environment in which the economic decline took place. Key aspects of the party and the parastatals, two of the main public decision-making institutions in post-colonial Tanzania, are reviewed as a prelude to Section 3 where the general Tanzanian policy response to economic decline is discussed.

Tanzania is a nation of peasants and bureaucrats. The hoe and the rubber stamp best symbolize the means used to achieve the country's stated development goals. Under the Germans for 30 years and the British for 40 years bureaucratic administration of the peasant population was refined. For most of those 70 years Africans were ordained to remain peasant farmers; the bureaucrats were virtually all European, whereas the Asians occupied the middle tier of the social pyramid as traders. In the 1950s, in the run-up to independence, the constrictions on Africans gaining an education were loosened. Africans were trained for positions in the civil service but not the market place.

In a country characterized by a widely dispersed peasantry at an extremely low level of technological development and served by a fragmentary transport and communications infrastructure, the 'nation-state' was an exceedingly tenuous concept. Only an anomalous group would be capable of constructing the 'imagined community' of the nation. Significantly, this group was Tanganyika's first generation of educated Africans. Their youth and foreign education did not auger well for their chances in the age hierarchy of the agrarian society. Their strongest social identification was with each other and yet their estrangement from peasant life was not so complete as to make it impossible for them to communicate with rural dwellers. They generally had a good command of Kiswahili, a language whose nineteenth century Arab caravan trading origins and Bantu base made it less foreign to most tribal language-speaking peasants than English.[7]

---

7. Anderson's description of twentieth century nationalists in the colonial peasant societies of Asia and Africa aptly corresponds to the Tanganyikan nationalists of the 1950s and their vision: 'The expansion of the colonial state which, so to speak, invited natives into schools and offices, and of colonial capitalism which, as it were, excluded them from boardrooms, meant that to an unprecedented extent key early spokesmen for colonial

There are over 100 different African ethnic groups in Tanzania so it is difficult to generalize about rural society and cultural norms. However, with the fairly low levels of agricultural surpluses and the shifting cultivation practices that prevailed, most groups evolved around egalitarian principles based on the provision of basic needs for the entire ethnic community.

The newly formed African bureaucracy that inherited the reigns of power at independence under the leadership of Nyerere believed that development could only come through transformation of peasant agriculture, but this had to be done with a peasantry which superseded its narrow local identity. Sensitive to the egalitarian values of the peasantry, Nyerere propounded *ujamaa* as a development philosophy in 1962. *Ujamaa*, translated 'kin', used the terminology associated with the narrow, local identity of the peasants, but transferred it to a national plane. The egalitarian exchange taking place amongst kin was posited as perfectly feasible, if not natural, at the level of the nation-state. The social distance between bureaucrat and peasant was to be minimized by the *ujamaa* philosophy. As far as Nyerere was concerned, for *ujamaa* to be credible to the peasantry, remuneration of those working in the bureacracy had to be kept in check. Nyerere warned two years before independence:

> The position is that our Civil Service is largely an expatriate Civil Service. What happens? We draw salaries not to suit the condition of Tanganyika at all... We have huge salaries of £2,500 and £2,700 and we take them for granted in a country of mud huts... We must not think that again year after year when we are independent we are going to come here and vote salaries. We will have to put the emphasis where that emphasis must be laid and this is raising this country, sparing every penny so that that penny produces another penny for the development of this country.[8]

2.1 The Party

Nyerere's egalitarian stance was a source of continual tension for those in the bureacracy who did not share his idealism. His views were more acceptable to the party rank and file of the Tanganyika African Nationalist Union (TANU). TANU was the nationalist organization most responsible for achieving political independence from colonial rule in December 1961.

(cont.) nationalism were lonely, bilingual intelligentsias; they had access, inside the classroom and outside, to models of nation, nation-ness, and nationalism distilled from the turbulent, chaotic experiences of more than a century of American and European history. These models, in turn, helped to give shape to a thousand inchoate dreams' (Anderson, B., *Imagined Communities* (London, Verso Editions and New Books, 1985), 127–128).

8. Nyerere, *Hansard* 34th Session, 27/5/59, 131.

The colonial state's attempt to pre-empt TANU's spread had had a significant influence on TANU's development. African civil servants were prohibited from joining the party, thereby restricting its membership to less educated Africans or those willing to give up their jobs for party work.

After independence, the ban on civil servant membership of the party was lifted. There was a tendency for government and party-appointed personnel to be interchangeable and for the functions of the two to merge. However, this tendency was being counteracted by the *de facto* assertion of party supremacy. The concept of party supremacy had strong anti-bureacratic, populist underpinnings.

The move towards party supremacy began in 1965 with the establishment of a one-party state and was reinforced by the Arusha Declaration in 1967. When a handful of parliamentarians challenged the concept of party supremacy in 1968, they were silenced in no uncertain terms and stripped of their party membership by the party's National Executive Committee (NEC).[9] Party supremacy achieved a *de jure* status through an amendment to the constitution in 1975 and was reinforced by the merger of TANU and Zanzibar's Afro-Shirazi party into Chama cha Mapinduzi[10] (CCM) and the adoption of a new constitution in 1977.

The CCM constitution lists a grand total of 19 party objectives, nebulous aims whose implementation was open to wide interpretation.[11] In practical terms, party supremacy boiled down to the following functions: mass mobilization, supervision and evaluation of government performance, and the enforcement of a socialist morality. Most importantly, the party held the inititive in major policy formulation.

Party supremacy had the effect of making policy-making a less formal process, giving Nyerere a freer hand, in his capacity as party chairman, to chart Tanzania's development strategy. During the 1960s, Nyerere increasingly introduced new policies through the NEC rather than parliament. The Arusha Declaration and the Leadership Code, which curbed asset holdings of party and government officials, were prime examples of this.[12]

9. In the parliamentary debate the second vice president, R. Kawawa, was firm: 'This Parliament belongs to TANU. That the Parliament is supreme is a colonial way of behaving... In a one party democracy the party is supreme all the way.' (Quoted in Srivastava, B.P., 'The Constitution of the United Republic of Tanzania 1977: Some Salient Features – Some Riddles', University of Dar es Salaam, Professorial Inaugural Lecture Series, No. 34, Dar es Salaam University Press (1983), 21.
10. Translated 'revolutionary party'.
11. CCM, *CCM Constitution* (DSM, Tanganyika Standard Ltd., n.d.), 4–6.
12 '[The NEC] provided Nyerere and the TANU leadership with a valued means of keeping in touch with the middle-rank leaders in the party. It was also a supplementary channel through which local political discontent and restlessness might be made known to the national leaders. It is fair to say that the meetings of the NEC tended to be orchestrated by Nyerere to maximize these advantages. His opening speech often provided the main topic, which would then dominate the NEC's discussions. He thus used the NEC to win

Because of a number of constraints in the party, Tanzanian policy orbited around the ideas and personal charisma of Nyerere.[13] The party's delegates at the national level were on the whole less educated than the parliamentarians. 'Grassroots participation' in the national party organs remained fairly spontaneous and unrestricted by set procedure and thus did not have the organizational structure or the expertise for proposing or evaluating policies in the same way as parliament.

Because of its grassroots orientation, TANU (and later CCM) became a means for the emergence of many natural leaders to elected party positions who had not been availed of the educational opportunities enjoyed by government bureaucrats. At district and branch level, their energies tended to be primarily fixed on enforcing a socialist life-style and morality. Depending on the most recent national policy directive, local party officials were in a position to influence people's actions over a wide behavioural spectrum, including where to live (villagization), what not to wear (indecent dress campaign), where and how to farm (block farm extension) and where not to shop (Operation Maduka involving the closure of private shops). The TANU Guidelines of 1971, otherwise known as *Mwongozo,* brought party activism to the workplace with its call for vigilance against arrogant and oppressive managers.[14]

Often the national party directives were vague or indirectly communicated. Not surprisingly, implementation varied a great deal spatially. Ambitious officials tended to be over-zealous, adopting the most extreme interpretation or trying to implement the policy very rapidly, causing huge disruptions to people's daily lives. Undoubtedly, in many cases people's basic legal rights were being transgressed, but, even if they were aware of their rights, few ventured to challenge party supremacy.[15] However, it must be stressed that implementation of any specific policy tended to be sporadic and haphazard. People could find loopholes and means of escaping the full force of the policy and they knew that party officials' vigorous implementation efforts were bound to subside over time.

Anderson's distinction between popular and official nationalism helps to explain the chameleon nature of the post-colonial state and the pattern

(cont.) party endorsement for his ideas and to gain directly a feel of popular reactions to his ideas. He chaired the meetings in a relaxed fashion which kept the discussion open and frank' (Pratt, C., *The Critical Phase in Tanzania 1945–68* (Nairobi, Oxford University Press, 1978), 212).

13 'The Party's supremacy...represents in effect the power of the presidency' (Goulbourne, H., 'The Role of the Political Party in Tanzania since the Arusha Declaration', in H. Goulbourne (ed.), *Politics and State in the Third World* (London, Macmillan Press Ltd., 1979), 219.

14. TANU, *TANU Guidelines 1971* (Dar es Salaam, Government Printer, 1971), 5, 11.

15. Williams, D.V., 'Authoritarian Legal Systems and the Process of Capitalist Accumulation in Africa', Paper presented at the Southern African Universities Social Science Conference, DSM (1979), 4–7.

of policy formulation and implementation. The constant vacillation between populist policy panaceas and obdurant 'toe-the-line' corrective measures reflected the desire to accomplish as much nation-building as possible in a liberal nationalist vein, but, when people, places or organizations strayed too far from the national vision as defined by TANU and the state bureaucracy, then the official approach became more disciplinary. Tanzania's peculiar blend of popular and official nationalism was an uneasy one. The national vision was extremely ambitious and the time frame for achieving it was set in years rather than the more realistic decades or centuries that other countries covering a similar path have been known to take.

For Nyerere, the main stated reason for advancing party supremacy was to mitigate the alienating effects of the inevitable spread of bureaucracy associated with development.

> However much you try to be near the people, to be constantly in their midst – and we have tried – the responsibilities of leadership, particularly now, necessitate our reducing the time we would like to be with the people... In addition, there are government protocols, some necessary and others quite unnecessary, which help to build a wall between the leader and the people thereby making the possibility of being together for longer periods remote.[16]

The general interpretation of party supremacy during the late 1960s and early 1970s was that the government would eventually merge with the party. However, in 1975 when party supremacy was legally enshrined, Nyerere countered this view. He argued that the party and government had to remain separate entities, otherwise the merger of party and government would mean the submission of the party to the government rather than vice versa. Equating the party with grassroots democracy and the government with leadened bureaucracy, which was viewed as an unwanted but none the less unavoidable by-product of the process of economic development, Nyerere saw the party as the vital check on bureaucratic performance.

The various checks included: the enforcement of the Leadership Code on all high and middle level government and parastatal employees; reviewing government planning documents; intervening in personnel disputes through the local TANU party branch at the workplace; and monitoring who ultimately would become a bureaucrat through the Musoma Declaration mature age university entry scheme which required applicants to gain party approval before being accepted by the university. Periodically, the

---

16. *Majadiliano ya Mkutano Mkuu, Tarifa Rasmi,* June 1969, 708 translated in Mwansasu, B.U., 'The Changing Role of the Tanganyika African National Union', in Mwansasu, B.U. and C. Pratt (eds), *Towards Socialism in Tanzania* (DSM, Tanzania Publishing House, 1979), 177.

party's ideological school, Kivukoni College, would send out student investigators to various ministries and parastatals to evaluate overall performance of these institutions. Their reports would be widely publicized and often be followed up with remedial action at the insistence of the party. The 1981 CCM Party Guidelines reinforced this supervisory role.[17]

2.2 The Parastatals

Indisputably, the party's biggest supervisory challenge was keeping an eye on the parastatals. The rapid proliferation of parastatals resulted in the extension of parastatal operations into most facets of Tanzanian commerce and industry by the 1980s.

Parastatal ownership dated back to the colonial period when the railways, harbours, posts, telecommunications and airlines were run as East African government corporations. The crop marketing boards set up during the 1950s were also parastatals. After independence, the parastatal sector expanded into banking to facilitate the mobilization of domestic capital with the establishment of the National Bank of Commerce. During the 1960s, foreign investment was not forthcoming to the extent hoped for. This, in combination with the private sector's reluctance or inability to invest in large infrastructural and industrial projects, made parastatals an attractive option for the government. Furthermore, the government's attempts at planning the economy, it was thought, would be enhanced by the expansion of the parastatal sector. In 1965, the National Development Corporation was formed and quickly diversified its interests in manufacturing, trade, agriculture and tourism.

In the years that followed, parastatal assets steadily expanded while the number of parastatals proliferated at a comparatively faster rate, as large firms were broken down into smaller, more manageable units. By 1981 Tanzania had almost 200 parastatals.[18]

Coulson identifies three broad roles that the parastatals were expected to play: first, to limit the transfer of profit out of the country; second, to invest in productive sectors, especially industrialization; and, third, to provide productive infrastructure in transport, construction and power generation.[19]

Table II.10 shows parastatal enterprise growth between 1966 and 1986. Parastatal employment increased on average by 12 per cent per annum during that period. Parastatals were expected to be profit-making. In terms of access to credit and resources, they received preferential treatment.

17. Mlimuka, A.K.L.J. and P.J.A.M. Kabudi, 'The State and the Party', in Shivji, I.G. (ed.), *The State and the Working People in Tanzania* (London, Codesria, 1986), 80.
18. It should be noted that when one includes the district development corporations and other small firms the total count is doubled to 400.
19. Coulson, A., *Tanzania: A Political Economy* (Oxford, Clarendon Press, 1982), 274.

However, a great deal of their operations were at the behest of government directives which did not give primacy to profit. According to the Tanzania Audit Corporation, in 1985, 165 of 354 parastatals had net losses. Semboja's comparative study of parastatal and private industrial firm performance indicated that private firms out-competed parastatal firms in terms of the output–labour ratio by a factor of two.[20]

Each parastatal had a parent ministry, a board of directors, and a general manager. General managers were appointed by the president who usually chose on the basis of names recommended by the minister concerned. El-Namaki comments that:

> As a result of the heavy politicized nature of the state and the lack of properly trained personnel to man professional and technical posts the process of selection and promotion of top level technocrats in Tanzania tends to be strongly influenced by factors other than sheer professional competence. Although there are no established channels for that selection, as it mostly follows an informal pattern based on contacts and personal knowledge, considerations of political commitment, ideological orientation and patriotic pretentions weigh heavily on the government's decision.[21]

In 1981 a reform was introduced, requiring vacant chief executive posts to be advertised nationally, stipulating that the Board and the minister interview prospective candidates before handing a short list to the president.

Three main types of men were selected as general managers. Many were politicians.[22] George Kahama, for example, the corporate empire-building general manager of the National Development Corporation, had distinguished himself in TANU during the independence struggle. The politician managers were influential people who usually had extensive contacts with high level government and party officials throughout the country which could be advantageous to parastatal operations. However, they tended not to have training in business management. By the early 1980s, it was claimed that general managers' posts were often used as a dumping ground for troublesome politicians.[23]

The second category, the professional managers, who had received

20. Semboja, J., 'The Parastatal Study: Analysis of the Qualitative and SCOPO Data', University of Dar es Salaam, July 1987; Msambichaka, L.A., S.M.H. Rugumisa, and J.J. Semboja, *The Role of the Public Sector in Development – Tanzania*, Economics Research Bureau, University of Dar es Salaam, June 1985.
21. El-Namaki, M.S., *Problems of Management in a Developing Environment: The Case of Tanzania (State Enterprise between 1967 and 1975)* (Amsterdam, N. Holland Publishing Company, 1979), 45.
22. Shivji, I., *Class Struggles in Tanzania* (DSM, Tanzanian Publishing House, 1975), 9.
23. Moshi, H.P.B., 'Adequacy of Control in Tanzania's Public Enterprises', *Public Enterprises*, 5(1) (1984), 34.

training either abroad or at the University of Dar es Salaam, were becoming more numerous over the years as educational opportunities expanded. Because of rapid promotion, they tended to be quite young and inexperienced for the amount of responsibility they shouldered.

Finally, there were the expatriate managers who were part of a foreign management agreement connected with the setting up of a parastatal, or, alternatively, they were hired on an individual basis.[24] In all cases, their employment was seen as a temporary stop-gap measure until suitably-trained Tanzanians could be found, particularly since their salaries were considerably in excess of those of Tanzanians of similar rank.[25] Although many of them were highly qualified, their effectiveness was hampered by difficulties in settling into a new environment, their unfamiliarity with local circumstances, and the short duration of their contracts.[26] Over time expatriates in management positions were replaced with Tanzanians. None the less, some of the older less qualified Tanzanian managers were eager to keep expatriates in key advisory positions, to subvert the promotion prospects of more qualified juniors who might otherwise pose a threat to their positions if they rose too high. Expatriates were often considered useful for their neutrality. They were not in a position to play office politics in a way that an up-and-coming Tanzanian university graduate might.

These three categories of personnel applied to the various managerial positions under the general manager as well. It should be noted that the shortages of suitable candidates for managerial positions frequently led to positions being left vacant.

It is difficult to generalize about the character of non-managerial employees of the parastatals since they were both blue and white collar workers, the predominance of one or the other depending on the type of parastatal. The industrial and agricultural parastatals employed many manual workers.

The position of parastatal employees was considerably strengthened by measures directed at increasing worker participation. In addition to the role of party branches in protecting workers' interests, a 1970 presidential directive called upon all parastatals to set up workers' councils, which would consist of workers and management meeting together. In effect, workers' representatives were being accorded advisory rather than

24. Carvalho, V.N., 'The Control of Managing Agents in Tanzanian Parastatal Organizations with Special Reference to the National Development Corporation', *Eastern Africa Law Review*, 5(1) (1977), 84-115.

25. For example, in 1974 an expatriate's basic salary could be up to 50% more than a Tanzanian's occupying the same position, in addition to a gratuity of 25% of his earned income and 10% home leave allowance (El-Namaki, *Problems of Management*, 205).

26. Temu, P., 'The Employment of Foreign Consultants in Tanzania: Its Value and Limitations', *African Review* 3 (1) (1973), 69-84.

decision-making functions. Hyden interprets this move as an effort at 'reducing the influence of capitalist practices in the parastatal management'.[27] The reluctance of parastatal managers to support worker participation policies is reflected in the fact that by 1984 only 60 per cent of the parastatals had set up councils.[28] In any case, the older workers' committees, consisting entirely of worker members rather than the management/worker councils, were the instigators of the workers' unrest and management lock-outs during the two years following *Mwongozo*, before the state clamped down on the workers' initiative.[29]

In the wake of *Mwongozo*, party supremacy was at issue in the workplace; managers feared worker criticism and the possibility of labour disruption. *Mwongozo* had given workers considerable scope to challenge not only managers' malpractices but also commandism and arrogance. Obviously these traits were very open to interpretation. Many managers hesitated to take decisive action *vis-à-vis* workers; and it was widely believed that this had a negative effect on workers' productivity.[30]

Managers who succeeded in striking up an understanding with the workers' leadership were relatively untroubled by charges of commandism. Manager promotion of party representatives beyond their educational and skill qualifications, placing them in a position of occupational insecurity and dependency in the enterprise, was very functional. In this way, many workers' councils were neutralized.

Shivji argues that the workers' councils were too 'top-heavy with bureaucrats' to be an effective vehicle for worker participation.[31] By 1984, the party was more preoccupied with worker indiscipline than with participation. Addressing a symposium of 400 chief executives of parastatals, the CCM secretary general, Rashidi Kawawa, was reported to have 'lashed at managers who failed to discipline their employees for fear of being blamed'.[32]

27. Hyden, G., *Beyond Ujamaa in Tanzania*, (London, Heinemann, 1980), 158.

28. *Daily News*: 'Ministry reviews Civil Service Act', 13/7/84.

29. Mihyo, P.B., *Industrial Conflict and Change in Tanzania* (DSM, Tanzania Publishing House, 1983).

30 Hyden interprets workers' work apathy as a direct result of the abandonment of 'capitalist management' in the wake of *Mwongozo*. 'For most wage-earners work was the price you paid for urban residence and access to its amenities. It was not something honoured in itself. Only the sanctions imposed by capitalist management had made many workers accept this obligation... [R]equests for time off to visit sick relatives, or loans for emergency needs in the family, were made with less constraint, because many workers expected such favours to be granted now that the capitalist concern for profit had been officially condemned' (Hyden, *Beyond Ujamaa*, pp.160–161). I would argue that *Mwongozo* probably facilitated this direction, but it was the decline in the purchasing power of urban wages which was the main motive force.

31 Shivji, *Class Struggles*, 132.

32 *Daily News*: 'Kawawa stresses discipline', 31/1/84.

Initially, the incentive pay structure in parastatals was based on the rationale that parastatal salaries had to be competitive with those in the private sector. However, as the private sector shrank in size and young parastatal and civil service personnel were recruited from the same pool of university and technical college graduates, who had studied with government bursaries and were obligated to work for the government in an assigned place for five years, the differential between the civil service and parastatal employees seemed iniquitous to all but the parastatal employees themselves. When the Standing Committee on Parastatal Organization (SCOPO) was formed in 1967, one of its first tasks was to bring parastatal remuneration in line with that of the government civil service. Furthermore, the Leadership Code, originally applicable only to members of parliament and civil servants, was extended to senior personnel in the parastatals. Throughout the 1970s there were complaints of inadequate incentives because of the rigidity of the pay scales and the enormous gap between expatriates' and nationals' salaries. In 1979, SCOPO bowed to pressure and allowed parastatals more flexibility in setting salaries.[33]

Knight and Sabot, comparing salary levels in Tanzania and Kenya, note that the Tanzanian public sector salaries were significantly more compressed relative to the private sector and there was more evidence of overmanning in Tanzania, a feature that Kim also points to in his study of parastatal performance.[34] None of these authors go on to examine the effects of declining real salary and wage levels on labour productivity during the inflationary 1970s and 1980s (Table II.6).

As indicated in Table II.6, real income declined rapidly at all wage levels during the late 1970s and the 1980s and was especially marked at the top salary levels. As real income declined financial irregularities and corrupt practices became more and more prevalent. At all levels of staff, parastatal resources were being used for personal gain. There was favouritism in allocating parastatal goods and services. Public vehicles were utilized for private business. Nepotism in hiring was not uncommon.[35]

33. Directive No. 40, 'Salary Structure for Parastatal Organisation' cited in Mwapachu, J.V. *Management of Public Enterprises in Developing Countries: The Tanzania Experience* (New Delhi, Oxford & IBH Publishing Co., 1983).

34. Knight, J.B. and R.H. Sabot, 'Public Sector Pay and Employment Policy and the Rate of Return to Education', Revised Draft (February 1985); Kim, K., 'Enterprise Performance in the Public and Private Sectors: Tanzanian Experience', *Journal of Developing Areas* 15(3) (1981).

35. *Daily News*: 'Nepotism is rampant – MP', 27/6/81; 'Kawawa denies nepotism', 28/6/81; 'the Prime Minister cautioned yesterday that the question of nepotism was complicated and added that the mere fact that two or more relatives worked in one institution did not prove nepotism...people were employed on merit and that a Government institution would not hesitate to employ two brothers or sisters who were experts in different fields' ('PM discounts nepotism claims', 30/6/81). More candidly, the principal secretary in the Ministry of Labour 'deplored the habit of providing training opportunities on family and friendship basis even if such people qualified for those opportunities' ('Train workers, employers told', 28/2/84).

Funds were misappropriated or embezzled and records were falsified. A large proportion of the parastatals had accounts permanently in arrears. In the absence of up-to-date audited accounts, 'unprofessional' practices on the part of parastatal staff were smokescreened and it made the intervention of national regulatory agencies difficult.

The poor productivity and lack of financial control led to widespread losses in the parastatal sector. Repeatedly the government stated its intention to close down loss-making parastatals, yet the liberal granting of bank overdrafts continued.[36] Between 1973 and 1982 commercial bank lending to parastatals involved in agricultural produce marketing rose from 31 to 61 per cent of total lending. As of 1982, none of the most important agricultural marketing and production parastatals had up-to-date accounts. A Ministry of Finance spokesman attacked crop authorities saying 'they were experts in making budgets while their reports of accounts were in arrears'.[37]

Interestingly, over time as parastatal debt default began to result in failure of parastatals to pay supply bills, pressure for inter-parastatal financial accountability built up to the point that some parastatals were refusing to supply others with vital goods or services until accounts were settled. This placed the government in a dilemma, since it had advocated that parastatals pay by cheque to reduce direct loss of funds and corruption, whereas creditor parastatals tried to insist on cash payments in advance of delivery.[38]

The declining professionalism in the parastatals was glaringly apparent because of the parastatal sector's high visibility in the economy in terms of provisioning goods and services and the growing numbers employed in parastatals. Not only was the Tanzanian consumer adversely affected by the poor economic performance of the parastatals, but the parastatal sector's mounting bank overdrafts and government subsidies were a drain

---

36. *Daily News*: 'Public firms told: Credit no panacea for poor performance', 12/12/80; 'Repay loans – Treasury', 19/9/84; 'Losing firms warned', 8/11/85; 'Loss-making institutions should go', 20/5/85.
37. *Daily News*: ' Accounting standards poor', 16/3/85. In 1982 the latest audited accounts were as follows with their 1980/81 profit/loss listed in brackets in millions of Tanzanian Shillings: 1977: Tanzania Sisal Authority (–34.8), Coffee Authority of Tanzania (+10.1), National Milling Corporation (–470.0); 1978: Cashewnut Authority of Tanzania (–23.5), Tanzania Cotton Authority (–5.3), National Food Corporation (–0.2);1979: General Agricultural Products Export Corporation (–20.3), Tobacco Authority of Tanzania (–128.5); 1980: Tanzanian Pyrethrum Board (–9.6), Tanzanian Tea Authority (–18.2), Sugar Development Corporation (+2.6).
38. *Daily News*: 'Seminar stresses use of cheques', 21/9/84; 'Nyang'anyi warns on invoices', 30/11/83; 'Power Cuts Campaign: Institutions owe TANESCO 350m/–', 7/4/84; 'NDC, Dabco assets to be seized?', 16/9/84; 'Operation power cut tomorrow', 13/1/85.

on the Tanzanian taxpayer and were causing inflation in the economy as a whole. Newspaper reports of the parastatals' predicament proliferated. Whether the parastatals were considered villains or victims of the national economic crisis, it was becoming more and more widely held that something had to be done to address the situation. The party and government's exhortation that parastatals follow stricter business procedures and become more accountable was not enough.

3. Policy Rectitude and Reform

In the early stages of the economic crisis there was a great deal of debate concerning whether or not the crisis had been caused by domestic policies or by a hostile international market. As the crisis proceeded it became impossible to disaggregate the cause and effect relationships between these two sets of factors. If and when one was weighted against the other, it was to justify avoidance or acceptance of IMF conditionality. In fact, the Tanzanian government sought assistance from the International Monetary Fund (IMF) at an early stage in 1979. In July of 1980, a major programme was negotiated for a three-year stand-by facility. This agreement collapsed five months later because Tanzania exceeded the ceiling on the domestic budget the IMF had imposed. For the following six years, there was continuous lack of agreement on loan conditionality. The IMF conditions were viewed by the government, particularly by Nyerere, as economically punitive and politically unacceptable.

3.1 Government's Initial Reaction

Soon after the collapse of IMF support, the government initiated the National Economic Survival Programme (NESP) which set a TSh. 6000 million export target that all government ministries and parastatals were obliged to pursue. It quickly became apparent that government exhortation was not enough and the goal was unrealistic. With the assistance of a World Bank Tanzania Advisory Group (TAG) and in the expectation of gaining external finance, a Structural Adjustment Programme (SAP) was devised and launched in 1982. This programme distinguished between crisis management and structural adjustment. The former involved getting inflation under control and restoring levels of productive activities through the procurement of external funds. The structural adjustment component was directed at restoring the growth momentum and reducing dependence on external support.

The assumption that external finance would be forthcoming to underpin SAP proved naïve. Throughout its implementation, the IMF withheld support, demanding higher rates of devaluation than the government was undertaking. Between 1981 and 1983, two small devaluations took place which cumulatively, when measured against the US dollar, amounted to 50 per cent, but this was not considered enough by the IMF (Table II.11). Bilateral foreign aid increased but not enough to turn the tide. Increasingly over time, donors were putting pressure on Tanzania to come to terms with the IMF, sometimes making future aid contingent on it.

Despite the limbo-like status of SAP, it is recognized as the breeding ground for a new economic realism. Like NESP it was directed at drastically improving export performance. In addition, it set out to effect major cutbacks in public spending. Parastatals were targeted for a major overhaul. The 1983 Hamad Commission recommended the complete disbandment of a number of poorly performing parastatals, the replacement of crop authorities with marketing boards and various cost-cutting measures, including the retrenchment of approximately 20,000 employees between 1984 and 1986. More generally, the central government budget was reduced in real terms. Table II.5 shows that cutbacks were quite evenly distributed between sectors. Government expenditure on basic needs, i.e. education, health and water supply, did not receive disproportionately large cuts until the second half of the 1980s.

The government's development budget steadily declined as revenues became increasingly inadequate to fund recurrent costs, let alone development. To maintain the mere fabric of the health and education sector, foreign aid was used to cover recurrent costs more and more. It was generally conceded that the goal to provide all households with clean water within 4 km of their home was, with only 38 per cent coverage in 1983, unattainable for the foreseeable future. On the other hand, in terms of the provision of primary schools, Tanzania succeeded in achieving a 99.7 per cent enrolment in 1983, having set out in 1976 to achieve universal primary education. On the health front, performance was similar to that of water supply: 40 per cent of all villages were reported to have health facilities in 1984.

Productive sectors did not register any positive growth under SAP. Agricultural producer prices rose in real terms, slightly more for food crops than export crops despite the aim of maximizing export crops. The spread of improved agricultural input usage was severely hindered by the poor state of up-country roads and the financial straits of the parastatal and government sources of supply. Industrial performance under SAP sank to new depths. With capacity utilization averaging 30–40 per cent some factory closures became imperative.

The government's intention to carry out large-scale retrenchment was not implemented. A clear policy on redundancies was never worked out. What retrenchment was done was sometimes contested by the affected workers through the Permanent Labour Tribunals and often the workers were reinstated.

Wages were held constant. The minimum wage was kept at TSh. 600 despite rapid inflation (Table II.7). The hardship this imposed on wage earners, however, was intended to be offset by the retention of the large consumer subsidy on *sembe* (maize meal), the country's major staple food. Pay differentials continued to collapse. On the overall general decline in incomes, the ILO commented: 'In ILO experience there have been few international parallels. Indeed, declines of a much smaller magnitude have sometimes been associated with much social unrest.'[39]

3.2 Party-style Corrective Campaigns

Frustration was vented in the form of official campaigns against groups that were designated as perpetrators of economic decline. The National Economic Sabotage campaign, launched in early 1983, targeted traders as *'walanguzi'* (black marketeers). Hint of the campaign came in late 1981 when an extraordinary CCM party congress was held which called for legislation to combat acts of economic sabotage and corrupt practices.[40]

Prior to the initiation of the campaign, district government officials frequently fined traders for selling goods above controlled prices. In January 1982 the Minister for Trade stated that industries could only sell their commodities to national trading companies, regional trading companies and other institutions permitted in writing by his ministry. Those who violated this ruling were liable to fines of up to TSh. 100,000 and/or imprisonment of up to 14 months. Instructing local licensing authorities carefully to scrutinize all trading licence applications and renewals, he did not mince his words: '[G]reed on the part of some industrialists and unscrupulous businessmen created a thriving ground for commodity racketeers... the crackdown on bogus traders must continue.'[41] The Minister for Information and Culture, addressing the business community in Dar es Salaam at a Lions International convention, alluded to Asian traders when he called on: '[A]ll good citizens of Tanzania to wage battle against unfair and illegal business practices responsible for unnecessary hardships to the people ... the current difficulties in Tanzania were a test of "good citizenship".'[42] In regions bordering Kenya, the police were getting active in arresting suspected smugglers. Suspicion against traders built up, culminating in Nyerere's address in April 1983 when he warned: 'We are going to overthrow the racketeers' regime. We have only one Government – the CCM Government.'[43]

39. ILO, *Distributional Aspects*, 34.
40. *Daily News*: 'Party launches 19 Guidelines', '21/1/82.
41. *Daily News:* 'Distribution to be monitored more closely', 15/1/82.
42. *Daily News:* 'Fight illegal trade', 15/2/82.
43. *Daily News:* 'Surrender goods, money', 9/4/83.

The CCM party secretary general quickly followed with a speech in Mwanza in which he announced that CCM leaders and members who failed to expose racketeers would face severe measures.[44] The Anti-Economic Sabotage campaign entailed the arrest of hundreds of suspected hoarders and the seizure of their goods and money. They were held under presidential detention orders. The rationale underlying their arrest and detention was that they were engaged in illegal activities which were unproductive and wealth-begetting. The egalitarian objectives of the state as well as regulated distribution of consumer goods were considered to be threatened by the *walanguzis'* activities.

The party, government and police were involved in the crackdown. The party secretary general threw the gates open to mass participation by urging all party members to become active in identifying 'racketeers': 'Party branches in residential areas, industries and work places know who these racketeers and economic saboteurs are. They must expose them without sympathy.'[45] The campaign was launched by presidential order with the enactment of the Economic Sabotage Act that was scheduled to remain in effect for one year and was then extended by the president for an additional six months.[46] To curb the over-zealousness of implementers of the campaign, as well as putting a stop to actual theft of goods on the part of thieves posing as campaign activists, the inspector-general of police had to intervene and stipulate search procedures.[47]

A month after the initiation of the campaign, 1057 people had been arrested. They consisted of licensed traders (over 60 per cent), traders without licences (roughly 30 per cent), parastatal employees (4 per cent), civil servants (2 per cent), as well as one party employee and one member of parliament.[48]

The campaign continued, albeit at a lower pitch, for the rest of the year. Meanwhile a 12-member tribunal was established for the hearing and conviction of 'economic crimes'.[49] By the beginning of 1984, 1745 cases had been filed with the National Anti-Economic Sabotage Tribunal. Many of the accused were detained in custody for a number of months awaiting trial.

44. Maliyamkono, T.L. and M.S.D. Bagachwa, *The Second Economy in Tanzania* (London, James Currey Ltd, ESAURP – Heinemann Kenya, 1990). p. xii.
45. *Daily News*: 'Fight sabotage, branches told', 13/4/83.
46. Regional commissioners recommended that the legislation be made permanent (*Daily News*: 'Sabotage Legislation: RCs form advisory body', 8/2/84; 'Nyerere renews lease', 2/4/84).
47. *Daily News*, 'Police chief issues search conditions', 15/4/83.
48. *Daily News*; 'Crackdown nets 1,057', 22/4/83.
49. The tribunal included four judges and eight others, mostly politicians. They tried 372 cases, making 212 convictions as of 3 February, 1984 (*Daily News*: 'Police files 1,745 cases', 3/2/84). It was rumoured that some members of the judiciary were critical of the contents of the Economic Sabotage Act. It is significant that trials did not take place in the ordinary courts of law.

The trials revealed that there were many excesses on the part of officials who did not adhere strictly to the law, particularly with regard to the disposal of impounded goods.[50] On the part of the accused, many were found to have large stores of essential goods, deemed as 'hoarding', and/or were holding large amounts of money which, it was felt, were not commensurate with the scale of their official businesses. At the beginning of February 1984, of the 1745 cases filed, 580 were withdrawn by the prosecution, 17 were referred to ordinary courts of law, 732 were still pending and 372 had been tried by the Tribunal, 57 per cent resulting in convictions. Sentences usually ranged between two and eight years imprisonment.[51]

Signs that the campaign was losing steam came in March 1984, when the government released 264 of the 296 detained on suspicion who were not taken before the Tribunal. The prime minister commented that: 'the Government trusted that the one-year detention period was harsh enough as a punishment'.[52] In July 1984, permanent legislation against economic crime, which transferred jurisdiction from the Tribunal to the High Court, was debated in parliament. The bill was passed unanimously. In the debate some members of parliament heavily criticized the original act for its transgression of civil rights, since accused did not have the right to apply for bail and could not employ defence counsels.[53] The contents of the new bill implied the assertion of legal restraint with a shift of power in determining cases brought under the court from the Minister for Home Affairs, acting on the advice of the inspector-general of police, to the Director of Public Prosecution.[54]

A party NEC member offering an overall assessment of the campaign maintained that the protracted war had restored public confidence in the party and government bearing fruits in some parts of the country where 'fair distribution of essential commodities' was introduced.[55] Two Tanzanian economists' assessment of the campaign differed:

It helped to focus attention on the real problems of the country, and convinced the Government that the shortage of consumer goods was not mainly due to hoarding. The crackdown scared off new entrants to the second economy [black market]... On balance the crackdown

50. In some cases, the property was transferred to the government Regional Trading Company shops (*Daily News:* 'Arbitrary property seizure condemned', 9/4/84; 'Produce accused, Tribunal orders', 25/1/84).
51. *Daily News:* 'Police files 1,745 cases', 3/2/84.
52. Technically, all those detained under the Economic Sabotage Act were supposed to have their cases filed within 60 days of their arrest (*Daily News:* '264 sabotage suspects freed', 16/3/84; 'Police files 1,745 cases', 3/2/84).
53. See Shaidi, L.P. 'Trade Liberalization and the Law' in *Taamuli* I (1 and 2) (1990), 49, for a detailed discussion of the Act's disregard for civil rights.
54. *Daily News:* 'MPs block Bill', 26/7/84; 'Bunge passes sabotage Bill', 27/7/84.
55. *Daily News:* 'Tribunal jails 531', 18/12/84.

reinforced faith in the legitimacy of the state and its ability to deal with illegality.

However, it may also be argued that the targets aimed at were not always hit accurately. Not only did the crackdown open the door to the conduct of personal vendetta and the waste of public resources, but the draconian measures trumpeted so loudly landed tiddlers, but failed to catch the big fish. Maybe there were no big fish, for such activities did not exhibit any form of organization.[56]

Another campaign that met with more mixed reaction on the part of the general public was *nguvu kazi*.[57] This entailed rounding up people in towns suspected of not having any formal employment. Unlicensed market vendors were included. According to Campbell, 'the official line was that the [economic] crisis was created because many in the urban areas were not doing "productive" work, but were depending on subsidies from the state in the form of subsidized *sembe*'.[58] The Human Resources Deployment Act empowered the government to return these people to their home areas or to send them to the sisal plantations which were chronically short of labourers. Thousands were arrested and rusticated. However, it is believed that a large proportion of them absconded and returned to their urban residences. While some of the public hailed the exercise as the only way to clear the towns of 'idlers', others saw it as futile and heavy-handed.[59] Many, after all, were directly affected by having members of their family removed.

3.3 *The Technocrats' Turn: Major Policy Shifts*

The campaigns provided a political distraction but did not succeed in bringing about any reversal in the country's poor economic performance under the SAP. Enigmatically, as the anti-economic sabotage trials proceeded, the Ministry of Planning and Economic Affairs was preparing a policy on private sector investment, clarifying where private investment would be encouraged. The Ministry of Planning and Economic Affairs and the Treasury were staffed by personnel with a technocratic outlook. They were grappling with what response should be made to the continued deterioration of capital infrastructure, renewed pressure to accept IMF conditionality, growing external debt and threat of seizure of assets. In June 1984 they produced a budget which, from the perspective of the IMF, was a budget of appeasement. It included a 26 per cent devaluation,

56. Maliyamkono and Bagachwa, *Second Economy*, xvii.
57. Translated 'work is strength'.
58. Campbell, H. 'The Politics of Demobilization in Tanzania: Beyond Nationalism' in *Taamuli* I (1 and 2) (1990), 64.
59. Bryceson, D.F., 'Food and Urban Purchasing Power: The Case of Dar es Salaam, Tanzania', *African Affairs* 84 (337) (1985), 520.

the removal of the *sembe* subsidy, and the introduction of an 'own-fund' account to allow Tanzanian residents with foreign exchange to import goods without questions asked about the source of the foreign exchange. Nyerere maintained that these measures had to be taken whether or not they were demanded by the IMF, stressing that 'the major difference between Tanzania and the IMF was not the demands advanced ... but the extent to which those demands should be stretched'.[60]

For Tanzanian consumers, the removal of the *sembe* subsidy was mitigated by the increase of the minimum wage from TSh. 600 to TSh. 810 (Table II.7). On the minus side, parents were required to pay fees for their children's secondary school education, and a development levy was imposed on all individuals above the age of 18. The development levy was intended to provide support for the recently reintroduced local government councils.

The devaluation and the measures curbing the operation of Tanzania's welfare state preceded Hassan Mwinyi's election to the presidency in October 1985, Nyerere having declined a sixth term of office. Under Mwinyi, regular, moderate adjustments of the exchange rate took place. Between February and June, the Tanzanian shilling devalued from 16 to 32 TSh. against the US dollar (Table II.11). The 1986 budget placed a ceiling on public sector borrowing and credit expansion. Mwinyi gave the parastatals a two-year ultimatum to get themselves on a financially sound basis. These measures set the scene for the final reconciliation of Tanzanian and IMF differences and the signing of an agreement in September 1986. Following another 25 per cent devaluation, Tanzania was granted an 18-month stand-by credit facility of SDR 64.2 million and debt rescheduling with the Paris Club (OECD governments). The IMF agreement unleashed aid grants worth US $363 million in 1986 in comparison with US $193 million in 1985. Interestingly, the IMF component of Tanzania's structural adjustment was very small, approximately 10 per cent.

The government's sectoral priorities and minimum import requirements were set out in a new Economic Recovery Programme (ERP) initiated in June 1986. The main criteria for resource allocation were:

- rehabilitation of critical areas of the economy which have been inadequately maintained due to the prolonged shortage of foreign exchange
- provision of key recurrent inputs ... in order to increase productive efficiency, and the availability of basic consumer goods
- completion of ongoing investment projects where relatively small additional resources would enable the project to become operational
- improvement of social services (especially health and education) as basic necessities and as minimum incentives for a productive population.[61]

60. *Daily News*: 'Separation of powers temporary', 7/5/85.
61. Tanzania, *Economic Recovery Programme* (DSM, May 1986), 21.

Specific measures of the ERP included the depreciation of the Tanzanian shilling by an average monthly rate of 3.7 per cent in nominal terms and 1.8 per cent in real terms to the US dollar with the aim of eliminating the over-valuation of the shilling by the middle of 1988. Efforts were made to base foreign exchange allocations to the industrial sector on economic performance. The 'own-funded imports' scheme allowed individuals with private access to foreign exchange to import a wide variety of products. A freeze on new recruitment to the public service and more checks on parastatal finance were imposed. The government enforced ceilings on bank lending by parastatals, although many of the marketing cooperatives were unable to keep the costs of their operations within these limits.

Interest rates rose dramatically. Commercial loan lending rates were between 27 per cent and 29 per cent. Price control, which originally covered more than 400 categories of goods, was reduced to only 24 categories, with further reductions planned. Power and fuel prices rose substantially. Agricultural pricing policy aimed to set producer prices at 60 to 70 per cent parity with FOB prices. Steps were taken to give private traders a legitimate role in the staple food trade.

Tanzania's annual growth of GDP rose from minus 2.4 per cent in 1983 to plus 3.9 per cent in 1987 (Table II.2). It should be noted that, with an annual population growth rate of 2.8 per cent, the growth of GDP per capita remained negative until 1986. The achievement of a 4 to 5 per cent annual growth rate of GDP in the medium term was envisaged by the World Bank in June 1986.

3.4 National Economic Outlook in 1988

It is clear that the inflow of capital and rescheduling of debt under the first 18-month stand-by credit facility provided a vital breathing space for Tanzania's beleaguered economy. Nevertheless, as of mid-1988, recovery was far from being a reality or even a certainty for the future. There were, however, some hopeful signs. The inflationary impact of devaluation was not as bad as expected (Table II.8). This was probably due to the fact that two successive years of good food harvests were experienced (1986/87 and 1987/88) which, since food accounts for such a large part of the consumption basket (66 per cent by value), helped to keep the cost of living down. Furthermore, it was believed that general price levels had already adjusted to the parallel exchange rate prior to devaluation. Another welcome surprise was the size and persistence of the own-funded imports. Estimated to be reaching levels as high as US$ 400 million per annum, available data suggest that they constituted about one-third of total imports. They proved to be more significant in volume than import support from donors.[62] However, their incredible persistence strongly hints that there was a steady stream of illicit and untaxed trade in goods and services from Tanzanians going abroad.

On the minus side, Tanzania's debt service ratio of 50 per cent in 1987 was considered far too high. Through the signing of the agreement with the IMF, the debt rescheduling provision had automatically reduced Tanzania's debt service ratio from 80 to 60 per cent the year before.

The major worry was that targets of 15 per cent annual export growth and 5 per cent annual import growth were not being realized. Tanzania's export performance did not register any significant improvements and the deficit in the balance of payments on current account continued to widen. Exports had been 44 per cent of the value of imports in 1981–84 and were only 31 per cent in 1985–87. The export sluggishness was attributable to a number of factors: many of the export crops were perennials rather than annuals, so that there was a lag of a few years between farmers' first responding to improved price incentives and actual output. Official market infrastructure, discussed in detail in Chapter IV, was in a state of disarray in many areas of the country, making it difficult for the producer price incentives effectively to reach the farmer.

Lack of improvement in real wages led to the raising of the minimum wage in 1988 to TSh. 1260, and those employed in the civil service received a slightly higher sum of TSh. 1370 (Table II.6). Rent and transport allowances were introduced for those resident in Dar es Salaam.[63]

In November 1988, the second stand-by agreement with the IMF was signed. This involved another major devaluation of 27 per cent (Table II.11). For some months the government and IMF could not agree on the conditionality, but eventually the government conceded to the devaluation, whereas the IMF eased up on its demands for reform of grain marketing.

The issue of lifting marketing controls on staple foodstuffs, more than any other, was a testing ground for just how far the Tanzanian government was willing to reply to the IMF's insistence on 'freeing market forces'. As has already been argued, the country had a long legacy of government intervention to ensure national food security. The country's socialist development strategy involved parastatal management of food marketing. The role of the state versus the market in staple food marketing was highly contentious with vested interests weighted in favour of the state. The next two chapters trace official marketing policy from the Second World War to the present revealing the problematic nature of marketed food supply, the constraints on expansion of the market, why traders were considered exploitative and why government acceptance of the IMF's marketing reforms was a very tall order.

62. 'Trade Liberalization', *Tanzanian Economic Trends*, 1 (1) (April 1988), 29.
63. *Tanzanian Economic Trends*, 1 (2), 9.

4. Summary

This chapter has reviewed the dimensions of the economic crisis which had engulfed Tanzania since the late 1970s. This crisis thwarted the government's development goals and brought about a severe deterioration in the quality of life for all segments of the population. State personnel experienced extreme demoralization as the result of a drastic fall in their real wages. Their professional performance declined accordingly.

In the 1980s, the party-led Anti-Economic Sabotage campaign cast traders and businessmen in the role of perpetrators of economic crisis. The government tried to retain a socialist policy orientation. The NESP and SAP were efforts to resuscitate the economy with cutbacks and exhortation. Tanzania's terms of trade, however, worsened and it proved impossible to continue without external finance.

Substantial financial assistance could only be had by conceding to IMF demands. Thus, the government gradually started scaling down its development goals and adjusting its strategy in line with IMF pressure to liberalize the economy. From 1984, the direction of reform was unmistakably that of IMF-style market liberalization. The reforms were introduced without the fanfare that accompanied Tanzania's previous rural development policies.

As I argue in Section 2, executive power has grown over the years as a result of the combination of (1) the president being both leader of the government and party; (2) the assertion of party supremacy; and (3) the relatively less formalized decision-making structure and procedures in party policy formulation. In President Mwinyi's first term of office, the presidency and chairmanship of the party were no longer held by one person.[64] Nyerere retained his role as party chairman. None the less, executive decision-making continued to be central to many of the reforms that took place.

It is surprising that government concessions to IMF liberalization proceeded without more public outcry. There were many vested interests at stake. The jobs of parastatal employees were at risk. Certain reforms, notably the removal of the *sembe* subsidy, risked undermining people's support for the government and the CCM's credibility as a populist mass party. But interpreting public reaction to liberalization, specifically food marketing liberalization, cannot be done in the absence of an understanding of the historical context in which the marketing reforms took place. Chapters III and IV trace the evolution of government food policy and public response.

64. In 1985, before Nyerere stepped down from the presidency he suggested that the separation of party and government powers at the apex should be temporary because the 'adoption of the new system in which the presidency and Party chairmanship are held by separate personalities, might cause problems in future... If they are at logger heads, you are in deep trouble...This is not the area where you separate powers; they must be under one cap' (*Daily News*: 'Separation of powers temporary', 7/5/85). In May 1990 Nyerere announced his intention to give up the party chairmanship.

III

Marketing Made Difficult: Food Supply Fluctuations & Marketing Policy 1939–1973

At the onset of the Second World War the national market in staple foodstuffs was relatively limited. Demand had grown alongside the expansion and contraction of the sisal industry which employed tens of thousands of male African migrant workers. The market stimulation of domestic supply had been very slow. Both the subsistence nature of peasant food production and the extremely fragmentary road and rail network in the country had held back response. Reliance on Kenyan maize imports had emerged early during the inter-war period. Until independence, Asian traders serving as retailers and produce marketing agents were the backbone of the staple food market. In this chapter, the characteristics of Asian trading operations are described and the nature of state intervention during the food shortages of the Second World War is examined. The third section reviews the post-war reorganization of the national staple food market with the establishment of the colonial government's Grain Storage Department and the eventual re-emergence of an open market. The fourth section, which deals with the changes that took place during the last years of colonial rule and the decade after independence, focuses on the displacement of Asian traders by the staple food marketing board and African cooperative societies.

1. The Asian Trading Network

An 1887 census enumerated a mere 1751 Indians, mostly traders, residing along the Tanganyikan mainland coast, and another 3086 Indians in offshore Zanzibar, the capital of the Omani Sultanate's ivory and slave trading empire.[1] Under German colonial rule between 1891 and 1919 Asian traders were considered vital to the promotion of peasant commodity

---

1. Honey, M.S., 'An Economic History of Asians in Tanzania and Zanizibar c.1840–1940', Ph.D. thesis, University of Dar es Salaam (1982), 52–53, 103.

production. Immigrants settled increasingly on the mainland, venturing into up-country areas rather than residing in Zanzibar.[2]

Under British colonialism they continued to establish shops in the larger rural settlements throughout the country, and dominated the retail trade. The first decade of British colonial rule was marked by substantial immigration with the population growing at the rate of 9.5 per cent. By 1931 there were 23,422 Indians. Over the next two and a half decades the population growth rate slowed to an average of 4 per cent, reaching a total of 65,461 Asian residents in 1957.[3]

Most Indian immigrants could trace their origins back to Gujarati villages and a tradition of trade. For a generation or more their families had lived in urban areas like Bombay and Karachi before immigrating to East Africa. Business evolved around the mutual obligations of the patriarchal joint family.[4]

In Tanganyika, the immigrant was usually absorbed as an assistant in a small retail shop of a close or distant relation, working at a very low salary for a period of months or years. If an apprenticed shop attendant showed diligence and commercial flair, he received credit assistance from his family sponsors to establish a *duka*[5] in an up-country locality. Prior to its establishment, he might return to India to marry, bringing back a wife who would assist him. After several years of hard work and with some luck he might succeed in expanding his business to operate as a sub-wholesaler in a town. He might eventually go on to wholesaling or commercial specialization in Dar es Salaam. Throughout his career, he would derive credit and cooperation not only from his extended family but also from the members of his religious sect.[6]

Tanganyikan Asians represented a wide array of religious beliefs. The majority were Shi'a Muslims. Amongst them the Ismailia Khojas were the most organized. Their incomes were subject to annual levies; a percentage of the funds so collected went to the Aga Khan, while the rest was channelled back to them in the form of credit schemes and communally-owned schools and hospitals. The other Muslim sects, the Ithnasharis and Bohras, as well as the Hindus, Sikhs, Jains and Goans, also had strong communal ties and funded schools and educational services. The solidarity of the Asian communities strengthened business activity, provided meeting places for the exchange of trade information and helped to ensure the

2. Mangat, J.S., *A History of the Asians in East Africa c. 1886–1945* (Oxford, Oxford University Press, 1969), 93–94.
3. Tanganyika, *Report on the Census of the Non-African Population taken on the night of 20/21st February, 1957* (DSM, Government Printers, 1958).
4. Defined as a man and wife, their sons' families and any unmarried daughters, frequently living under the same roof.
5. Translated 'retail shop'.
6. Ghai, D.P. and Y.P. (eds), *Portrait of a Minority, Asians in East Africa* (Nairobi, Oxford University Press, 1970), 11.

fulfilment of obligations and the recovery of loans between members of the community.[7]

Asian *dukawallahs*[8] settled with their wives and children in the numerous up-country towns, most of which were under 5000 in population, no larger than villages of the present day. Only the Sikhs, trading hides deep in Masailand, led a nomadic existence like their clients and did not subject their wives to a rural life.[9] Often the *dukawallahs* lived in the vicinity of the district administrative or sub-district headquarters, but they tended not to mix with the Africans or the Europeans, forming very cohesive social units amongst themselves, especially amongst members of their own religious community.

There were a few towns that the *dukawallahs* considered too remote. Some of the marginal producing districts could never attract Asian traders' permanent settlement. For example, Buha district, a labour reserve area in the far western part of the country still did not have a resident Asian trader by the early 1950s.[10]

Wherever the *dukawallah* settled, he became a primary node in a wider Asian trading network. There were three ways in which he could be associated with a wholesaler and the higher levels of the trading network: he could be a salaried employee acting as manager of the *duka*, he could be self-employed but obtain all his supplies on credit from the wholesaler and sell all his purchased produce to him, or, alternatively, he could be entirely independent with only an *ad hoc* trading arrangement with the wholesaler.

While the *dukawallah* plied his family and communal ties for reasonable credit terms, credit was, none the less, a major constraint. Banking facilities were largely absent in rural areas and in any case most *dukawallahs'* businesses were too small to get bank credit. The standard 90-day credit for piece goods that the supplier offered was essential. When suppliers' credit dried up during the Depression many *dukawallahs* could not manage to carry on.[11] The wholesaler practice of extending credit in the form of cash and commodities against a future crop was convenient for both parties, but had the effect of putting the wholesaler in a position to drive a hard bargain.[12]

7. Desai, R.H., 'Afro-Asian Relationships in Small Towns', in East African Institute of Social and Cultural Affairs (ed.), *Racial and Communal Tensions in East Africa* (Nairobi, East African Publishing House, 1966), 98.
8. Translated 'shopkeeper'.
9. Bharati, A., 'A Social Survey', in Ghai, D.P. and Y.P., *Portrait*, 29.
10. Leslie, J.A.K., Rhodes House Mss. Afr. s. 1516, 16 (1950–54).
11. Honey cites TNA SMP 20673, Letter from Indian Association, Mwanza to Honourable Secretary, Indian Association, Dar es Salaam, stating that the number of shops dropped from 800 to approximately 520 within the Mwanza area between 1931 and 1933 as a result of credit contraction and the effects of new marketing legislation which undermined aspects of traders' produce buying (Honey, 'Economic History', 426–427).
12. Economist Intelligence Unit, *A Survey of Wholesale and Retail Trade in Tanganyika* (London, 1962), 124.

The *dukawallah's* trading activities had to be adapted to a number of 'facts of life'. First, their peasant clients had extremely low purchasing power and made most of their purchases immediately after the harvest when they had cash in hand. Second, due to the extremely high cost of transport, return loads were vital to keeping the expense down. Under these circumstances, Asian produce buying became the pivot of the *dukawallah's* business. The retail of consumer goods was secondary and combined naturally with buying produce, for peasant customers had to sell their produce to get cash to buy consumer goods. Trade was highly seasonal, based on the agricultural season and the availability of transport. Road transport virtually ground to a halt during the rainy season.

Purchase prices on most articles were determined through bargaining. This practice seems to have been the basis of most peasants' distrust of Asian traders. Often the *dukawallah's* purchase of the peasants' produce was combined with negotiations on the sale of consumer goods. Peasants frequently felt they were being short-changed in both. Bargaining was the way in which the Asian trader reconciled the continuous fluctuation in the supply of goods. This, however, was a perspective that the peasant did not share. On certain food items, notably sugar and maize meal, the notion of a 'just price' reigned. Few *dukawallahs* dared to bargain up its price. Instead they operated with very low margins on these items. Other consumer goods, however, had a significantly higher margin, in effect subsidizing the low margin goods. On the whole, margins were fairly trim. Using family labour in the shop, not spending much time or money on bookkeeping meant that overhead costs were low.[13]

The divide between Asians and Africans was not just economic; culturally and socially there were vast differences. The language barrier was bridged to the extent that most Asian traders spoke enough Kiswahili or local African tribal languages for trading purposes. But a working knowledge of the language was not combined with sufficient commonality of interests to induce Asians to seek business partnerships with Africans. Some *dukawallahs* hired African itinerant traders to hawk piece-goods and various consumer items in slow-moving lines with high profit margins at local markets deep in the countryside.[14] After the Second World War, Africans returned from military service abroad were increasingly opening shops, usually in remote places, with a narrower range of commodities and often with only a quarter of the stock of Asian retailers. They had to compete against an extremely cost-effective Asian marketing network.

The *dukawallah* was directly instrumental in determining the well-being of the peasant both with regard to his monetary crop proceeds and the expense incurred in obtaining his household's purchased needs. But the

13. Economist Intelligence Unit, *Survey*, 127, 172.
14. Hawkins, H.D.G., *Wholesale and Retail Trade in Tanganyika: A Study of Distribution in East Africa* (New York, Frederick A. Praeger Publisher, 1965), 70.

dukawallah was far from a free agent, being merely at the end of a long series of market determinations with very little room for manoeuvring. *Dukawallahs* harboured the dream of rising from rags to riches and displayed merchant capitalist accumulative behaviour of an extreme form, sacrificing most of their own material comfort in ceaseless skimping and saving. Virtually none of the immigrant Asians came to Tanganyika with any capital. A handful of them achieved outstanding financial success in their Tanganyikan businesses, having worked their way up from a *duka*.[15] But the average *dukawallah* was extremely remote from prosperity, let alone a bonanza, as the following story told from the haughty heights of a former district colonial officer suggests:

> My Indian neighbours ... consisted of three or four shopkeepers who had their stores near the courthouse at Tarime. They traded cotton goods, soap, matches, beads, and other knickknacks for the various local products. They were a poor lot ... they just grubbed away at their sixpence ... living in the same squalor and discomfort whether the season was good or bad, with numerous dirty and rickety children, fated, I suppose, to grow into Indian 'duka wallahs' themselves. They lived in terror of the Kuria,[16] and plagued us with complaints of theft, murder and general insecurity and with demands for Police protection...[we] refused on the good grounds that ... [we] only had four policemen for the whole district...[They were advised] to get a good watchman. If they shared the expense of his salary it would not come to more than 5 Shs. a month each. They protested that it would ruin them, but finally agreed... But the thefts continued... So yet another deputation came to the Boma.[17] 'Didn't you get a night watchman?' 'Oh yes, we got a night watchman.' 'And doesn't he raise the alarm?' 'No he never raises the alarm.' 'Produce him.' The night watchman was produced. As a commercial proposition, I suppose he must have been most satisfactory since the Indians would probably pay him next to nothing. But as a night watchman he had serious drawbacks; he was a well-known half-wit, both deaf and dumb.[18]

Colonial officials tended to regard Asian traders with a mixture of disdain and distrust. The colonial state was concerned with regulating Asian traders' produce buying and eliminating barter transactions.[19] Hence, during the inter-war period, there was a profusion of trade

15. Allidina Visram, the oft-cited example, built up an extensive network of *dukas* and other businesses beginning in Bagamoyo in the 1880s (Mangat, *History*, 77–78).
16. Refers to the local tribe.
17. Translated 'district headquarters'.
18. Sillery, A., Rhodes House Mss. Afr. s. 1749, 169–170.
19. The colonial state believed that barter transactions would prevent peasants' monetary payment of the poll tax as well as making the peasant more open to unequal exchange.

legislation. In 1923, a cluster of ordinances were passed, the most important being the Restriction of Credit to Natives Ordinance which aimed to protect the peasants' productive holdings from money lenders by circumscribing the use of land or other forms of wealth as collateral. The Profits Tax and Trade Licensing Ordinances were efforts to keep tabs on merchants by requiring them to keep their ledgers in English or Swahili rather than Gujarati. These two ordinances sparked a 54-day strike by Asian traders; shops throughout the country were closed. Over time, these ordinances proved impossible to enforce and were repealed. A 1928 Markets Ordinance introduced restrictions on trade outside designated trading centres. The criticism from traders and sisal estate managers, concerned with ensuring a steady food supply for their plantation labourers, was that this legislation involved peasants carrying their produce much further to markets and estate managers travelling longer distances to make purchases, taking the place of the trader who was usually best equipped and most willing to act as a producer transporter.[20] In response, the governor exempted peasant maize sales from the 1928 Market Ordinance, restricting the ordinance to export crops rather than food crops.

In 1932 legislation was passed that gave government the power to award monopoly produce buying rights to individual trading firms, to restrict produce buying to specified Native Authority markets, and to restrict the number of itinerant traders.[21] The Cooperatives Society Ordinance was also passed in 1932, but for the next two decades remained largely unimplemented, except in a few coffee and tobacco-producing areas. The power to award monopoly produce buying rights to individual trading firms resulted in produce buying of certain crops in a few key areas being put in the hands of large European or Asian firms. It was soon found that this measure engendered large overhead costs, particularly acute in the European firms which were not relying on cheap family labour for trading activity and ultimately often led to reduced prices for peasant produce.[22]

In 1937, the Legislative Council did not allow a bill to be passed that would have given the state the power to declare any agricultural product a regulated product. But, once the bill was redrafted and restricted to coffee, it was passed. Significantly, a produce board with powers to impose levies was established for the first time under this legislation.[23]

20. Brigadier-General Boyd-Moss, *Hansard*, 3rd Session, 17/12/28, 38; Mr. Chitale, *Hansard*, 8th Session, 6/11/33, 33.
21. Refers to the Trade Licensing (Amendment) Ordinance, the Markets (Amendment) Ordinance and the Itinerant Traders (Amendment) Ordinance.
22 Provincial Commissioner, Tabora to Chief Secretary, 13/10/30, TNA SMP 10138; McCarthy, D.M.P., *Colonial Bureaucracy and Creating Underdevelopment: Tanganyika, 1919-1940* (Iowa, Iowa State University, 1982), 90.
23 Native Coffee (Control and Marketing) Bill, 1937, *Hansard*, 11th Session, 19/10/37, 296.

In effect, all of this marketing legislation constricted rather than controlled Asian merchants' interaction with African producers. Given the small number of British colonial officials in the districts to police trade, there was no way it could have been otherwise.

2. The Second World War and Food Marketing Controls

Suddenly, with the outbreak of the Second World War, Tanganyika's marketed food demand climbed to unprecedented heights. Net imports of the staple grains,[24] averaging roughly 190 tons per year between 1930 and 1939, indicated that demand persistently exceeded domestic supply. The war brought many thousands of new consumers who were reliant on the market purchase of staple foodstuffs and this was an additional strain on the structural deficit. Several thousand refugees from German occupied parts of Europe and prisoners of war were sent to Tanganyika. In addition, having formerly been a German colony, there were many German settlers whom the British colonial state interned. But the largest number of new consumers consisted of Africans who were military recruits stationed in Dar es Salaam, urban migrants, and labour conscripts sent to work on settler farms and plantations that were designated as centres for the production of 'strategic exports' for the war effort.

While the demand for marketed food increased, the number of grain producers declined. The expansion of the African wage labour force by the removal of more male labour from the peasantry brought about the concurrent increase in purchased maize consumers and a decrease in potential maize producers. German settler farmers, who at the outbreak of the war numbered several hundred, were removed from their agricultural holdings. Besides producing sisal, coffee and tea, many had been commercial grain producers, particularly of maize and wheat. Finally, several British settler farmers served in the military forces during the war, leaving the management of their farms to a wife or another trusted adult.

Despite the strain on the local food supply, the Tanganyikan state did surprisingly little over the first three years of the war. Most new policies were restricted to the sphere of distribution rather than production or consumption. Retail prices for foodstuffs were fixed as part of wartime controls. The director of agriculture was appointed the food controller within an Economic Control Board[25] set up under new Defence

24. 'Staple grains' defined as maize, rice, sorghum/millet and wheat.
25. The Economic Control Board was composed of an East African War Supplies Board that had responsibility for the foodstuff requirements of the military and the East African Civil Supplies Board which coordinated British East Africa's (Kenya, Tanganyika and Uganda) import, export and commodity control under wartime conditions.

Regulations. Under the food controller, commodity controls and price fixing were decided on a locality-specific basis. District officers, guided by the food controller's policies, were assisted by district food control committees made up of three official members and five non-officials, often traders, who advised on local conditions.[26] But in 1941 these committees were scrapped and food control was centralized in the Economic Control Board. Indians complained that there were no Asian members on the Board to represent their trading interests. The state argued that commodity and price information had to be kept secret to avoid speculation.[27] The retail prices of most basic foodstuffs were controlled. The Prices of Goods Bill (1940) was intended to check profiteering by setting a fine of Sh. 2000 or a three-month gaol sentence.

Mindful of food supply difficulties that could ensue for agricultural employers, the state fixed the wholesale free-on-rail price for maize meal in Arusha, Moshi, Kilosa and Morogoro in 1940.[28] The fledgeling European wheat industry was given a boost with some 1940 legislation that established a wheat marketing board and wheat growers' associations. The bill made it possible for orders to be served on wheat growers of specified classes and areas to market their wheat through the board, which was to be aligned with Kenya in the event of a need to export.[29] Wheat was a far less developed settler commercial crop than maize and this legislation gave the European farmers the organizational structure around which the industry could be developed.

With the exception of the Sale of Wheat Bill and some alienation of land on temporary leases not exceeding five years, the Tanganyikan state restrained itself from actively supporting European producers' interests over those of African peasants.[30] Peasant agriculture was in fact bolstered by the posting of 400 new African agricultural instructors, whose training was admitted to be rudimentary, but who were none the less anticipated to be a vital addition to a chronically understaffed Agricultural Department.[31] Peasant agriculture seemed to be managing reasonably well despite rather poor rain and the absence of thousands of young men who had been conscripted into the wage labour force or military service. There

26. President's Address, *Hansard*, 14th Session, Part II, 19/12/39, 35.
27. E.C. Philips, *Hansard*, 16th Session, 11/12/41, 93.
28. 'Maize Price Fixed', *Tanganyika Standard*, 15/1/40, TNA SMP 28259/8.
29. The fear was that, given Tanganyika's lack of comparative advantage in wheat production, export would involve heavy losses to the state, if a very low world price prevailed (The Sale of Wheat Bill (1940), *Hansard*, 14th Session, 18/3/40, 157-172).
30. Tanganyika was governed by the British under a League of Nations mandate. The mandate put restrictions on land alienation to non-Africans and required that the Tanganyikan government administration submit an annual report to the Permanent Mandates Commission on the economic and political well-being of the African population.
31. Director of Agriculture, *Hansard*, 17th Session, 10/12/42, 92.

were exceptionally high export levels of rice between 1940 and 1942, a great deal going to satisfy military requirements.

However, the colonial state faced mounting pressure from European grain farmers to give them a helping hand. During the 1930s, a nucleus of European settlers established mechanized commercial maize production in the northern part of the country around Kilimanjaro. Their yields averaged 8–10 bags an acre per year which was comparable with the yields achieved by uncapitalized peasant producers in an extremely good year. The settlers, arguing that their production was vital to the maintenance of territorial food supply, persistently petitioned the colonial state for government support along the lines that existed for European grain producers in Kenya. Specifically, they wanted protection against the competition of African maize surpluses that appeared on the market in good harvest years. They complained that, due to lack of storage and rapid deterioration of grain because of the climate, they were forced to sell their maize immediately after the harvest to Asian traders at low prices.[32] The colonial state, in the name of preserving the principles of free trade, refrained from intervening.

During the early war years, it was Kenyan settler grain production, rather than Tanganyikan peasant production, that threatened Tanganyika's European maize producers. Throughout the 1930s, European food farmers in Tanganyika had tended to play the role of little brother following in the footsteps of stronger brethren in Kenya. The war changed this. Kenya's traditional maize export markets were closed because of a shortage of world shipping space. Brotherly relations became strained as the Tanganyikan state's 'open door' trading policy allowed cheap Kenyan wheat and maize imports to pour in unimpeded. Tanganyikan European settlers demanded state protection for their less well-established maize and wheat industries.

In November 1941, the entry of the United States into the war engendered major restructuring in the world economy and triggered a price boom for agricultural commodities. East African grain production became an important source of supply for the Middle East. The Kenyan state responded by guaranteeing producer prices to its farmers. The Tanganyikan state followed suit. In January 1942 producer price regulation was introduced, ostensibly to eliminate the extremely low maize prices Tanganyika's European farmers had experienced as a result of the dumping of Kenyan maize surpluses over the previous two years.[33] However, since other outlets for Kenyan maize had opened up, it no longer posed

---

32. Note on Governor's interview with W. Nicol, Chairman, Tanganyika Maize Growers' Association, 4/8/36, TNA SMP 19533.
33. Memorandum for Standing Finance Committee, 'Guaranteed Prices for Foodstuffs to ensure Maximum Production', 29/12/41, TNA SMP 30157.

such a threat and a domestic producer price rise was probably inevitable without official prodding.[34]

Price control involved the setting of guaranteed minimum prices for maize, wheat, rice, sesame, groundnuts and beans.[35] In addition, European farmers were encouraged to form non-native farmers' district production committees that could serve as the settler farmers' self-governing and planning bodies to liaise with the state. Two committees were established in 1942, the Moshi District and the Arusha District Production Committees. They marked the organizational beginnings of a strong settler lobby that was to persist until independence.

While the setting of producer prices for food crops in 1942 was a clear encroachment on the principles of free trade that the state had held to, it was not until 1943 that the state reversed its policy and became highly interventionist in the staple food trade. In that year, drought was experienced in many parts of the country, causing extreme distress in Central Province. Famine was a frequent occurrence in the semi-arid Central Province; however, its occurrence during wartime posed particular difficulties. The situation was compounded by the fact that the drought affected Kenya as well, cancelling its usefulness as a supply fallback. Assisted by the Colonial Office, the Tanganyikan adminstration scoured the Allied world for a source of grain supply and shipping space. After an abortive attempt to get wheat from Argentina, Australia came forward with sufficient, albeit expensive stocks.[36]

Thereafter, with the rationale of avoiding another such situation and building up an adequate and reliable domestic supply, the colonial state adopted the Kenyan approach of showering support on European capitalized grain production. This involved giving planting bonuses, loans and guaranteed producer prices. Furthermore, settlers were availed of African labour through the government's labour conscription.

In the realm of food marketing, Asian traders were increasingly constrained. The East African Cereals Pool was established during the crisis of 1943 to facilitate the import of grain from overseas and equitably to distribute supplies between the territories of British East Africa. Thereafter, it assumed responsibility for organizing grain movements between the countries. The state's early policy had been to leave produce buying to private traders, awarding exclusive rights for basic foodstuff produce buying only in the event of failure on the part of traders. In 1943 this policy changed. Produce control was introduced, which entailed grains

34. It has been argued for Kenya that price control was opportunely introduced to restrain prices that would otherwise ride the crest of the world commodity price boom. This argument could apply to Tanganyika as well (Anderson, D. and D. Throup, 'Africans and Agricultural Production in Colonial Kenya: The Myth of the War as a Watershed', *Journal of African History* 26(4) (1985), 335.
35. Tanganyika, Department of Agriculture Annual Report 1942, 1.
36. Public Records Office 852/428/17600/Part II.

like maize and sorghum being bought and sold solely at appointed selling places.[37] Only persons holding permits could purchase and move grain from one district to another. Distribution was not helped by the shortage of lorries that the Economic Control Board was doing its hardest to rectify.

The urgency of ensuring wartime food supply led the colonial state to act on its suspicions and edge Asians out of the food trade, or more correctly to edge a lot of Asians out of the trade and have the remainder act as state approved marketing agents. The select few were generally well-established merchants who were thought to be trustworthy. Their small number was probably just as important as who they were in that a limited number could be subjected to closer scrutiny. Ever since the 1923 traders' strike, state supervisory checks had been contentious. Wartime commodity and price controls which were routinely introduced in almost all Britain's colonies finally gave the colonial state its chance to gain the upper hand.

However, traders who were not approved had the transport facilities, storage and skills to carry on with business. A black market in maize first appeared in the Northern Province in 1944. Asians were immediately implicated. It was generally believed that Asian traders, endowed with lorries and geographically dispersed family trading networks, controlled the black market. Asians were indignant about the charges levelled at them, but at the same time were adamant that the controls should be removed.[38] Prices in the black market were high, a reflection of the scarcity of the goods, as well as the costs of risking detection.

In the official market, staple foods sold at controlled prices. Under tight supply conditions, food rationing was introduced into the two major towns, Dar es Salaam and Tanga. As efforts to restrict supply to only those who were bona fide town residents proceeded, the government took measures to guarantee adequate food supply to civil servants. This was prompted by concern with the gap that was developing between the civil service's stationary wage levels, due to wartime austerity, on the one hand, and the inflationary rise in the cost of living, on the other. To prevent loss of morale, cost of living allowances were instituted, which were differentiated according to race. The aim of the Cost of Living Relief Committee was to maintain the standard of living of civil servants at a pre-war level.

The Tanganyika European Civil Servants Association disputed aspects of the way European allowances were calculated, specifically the tapering of allowances at higher incomes,[39] as well as being critical of the amount

37. 'Notes of a Meeting held at Government House at 11 a.m. on Friday, the 26th December 1941 to consider the fixing of prices to be guaranteed by the East African Governments for Agricultural Products for Military Requirements', TNA SMP 30157/1.

38. Rhooda to Chief Secretary, 26/9/46, TNA SMP 34927; Minutes of 2nd Meeting held at Chief Secretary's House, 4/12/46, TNA SMP 35085; Indian Chamber of Commerce to Chief Secretary 24/6/48, TNA SMP 35085.

39. Letter to Editor from C.S. Sayce, *Journal of the Tanganyika European Civil Servants Association* (TECSA), 37 (January 1944), 26.

accorded African civil servants.[40] European allowances could not exceed 25 per cent of the officers' salaries and were only awarded to bachelors earning £318 or less and married men with salaries of less than £644. Asian allowances were calculated on the same basis with the salary ceilings set at £120 and £252 respectively. Africans, on the other hand, received Sh. 2/50 plus a food ration if they earned less than Sh. 60 a month. Africans complained about the mixed cash and food form of their allowance and stated that they preferred to receive it all in cash, which the government paternalistically ruled was nutritionally inadvisable.[41]

In view of the low wages and migrant nature of the African population in Dar es Salaam, own production of staple foods on the part of urban households was common. Evidence of this comes from an inquiry set up in 1939 to investigate the availability of land in the immediate environs of Dar es Salaam for cultivation by the unemployed whose growing numbers were viewed by the state as potentially dangerous.[42] Ever since Dar es Salaam was founded in the 1860s, the low-lying valleys had been used for rice and coconut cultivation.[43] Maize and cassava were grown on higher ground. Freehold for Africans and non-Africans had been allowed under German law, but non-Africans were tending to buy up the native freehold, thereby reducing Africans to a tenant or squatter status. Non-privatized land did exist. The inquiry examined 7000 acres of Crownland within a five-mile radius from the city centre. Only 950 unoccupied acres were identified for settlement by the unemployed. Approximately 1200 acres were unsuitable for agriculture and the rest was being cultivated by an estimated 500 people living in the city who went out daily to farm. In addition, squatters had built over 900 huts on the land and cultivated adjacent shambas.[44] The local Zaramo[45] Native Authority, with the jurisdiction to grant usufruct rights for the cultivation of annual crops on the area's Crownland, was not in control of the situation. Most of the African cultivators, as non-Zaramo immigrants, disregarded their lack of

40. 'The award should rest upon the same basis for all races and although it may be outside our province to comment on the allowance given to the African we feel that he is perhaps the hardest hit of all by the increases in prices and that he is deserving of much greater assistance than he has so far received' (Letter from TECSA to Government, 22/5/45, *Journal of the TECSA*, 39 (March 1946), 22.

41. Minutes of a Meeting of the Sub-Committee of the Cost of Living Committee, 2/5/44, TNA Acc. 61/295/2/2.

42. 'The position is grave and requires drastic remedies. It is only the Native's intense "communism" that has saved us from riots so far' (McCleery, H.H., 'Extent and Conditions under which Natives are occupying Land in the Outskirts of Dar es Salaam', Rhodes House Mss. Afr. s. 870, 4).

43. Bryceson, D.F., 'A Century of Food Supply in Dar es Salaam: From Sumptuous Suppers for a Sultan to Maize Meal for a Million', in Guyer, J. (ed.), *Feeding African Cities* (London, Manchester University Press, 1987), 158.

44. Translated 'farms'.

45. The tribe indigenous to Dar es Salaam.

usufruct rights and planted permanent crops like fruit trees and coconut palms. Frequently they had fallen into debt with non-natives, notably Arabs, and been forced to mortgage their farmland in spite of laws prohibiting debt collection from Africans.[46]

Cultivation on the outskirts of Dar es Salaam was primarily of a subsistence nature. It, along with direct farm supplies from the up-country homestead derived from the labour of relations or the urban worker himself, was a vital part of African urban household food supply. There is no way of knowing the extent of such contributions to total household food requirements, but McCleery, the district officer investigating Dar es Salaam land usage, held them to be the primary source of supply, with wages being spent on non-food items. This would accord with the African demand for the cost of living allowances to be dispensed in the form of money rather than food.

The war ended but territorial food insecurity continued. An international grain shortage and high world market prices for grain prompted the colonial government to continue food commodity controls and the civil service cost of living allowances. Cost of living allowances were revised annually. In 1948 new wages and conditions of service were instituted following a Salaries Review Commission.[47]

State policy was aimed at keeping prices of basic foodstuffs as low as possible. When it was anticipated that Tanganyika would have to continue to import large quantities of maize in 1947 as it had done in the preceding year, at a price that was far in excess of locally produced maize,[48] the government decided to cover the loss of £400,000 with a cess on employers of £172,000 and an increase of non-native poll tax rates to generate £77,000.[49] As it happened, however, the harvest in 1947 was better than expected and only a tenth of the originally budgeted amount was required, so the cess was refunded.[50]

Essentially, during the late 1940s wartime agricultural policies were continued, but with heightened government material support and emphasis on mechanization in the name of achieving adequate domestic grain production to fulfil the country's requirements. The main objective was to avoid grain importation under the then high world market prices for grain. Subsidies to non-native farmers averaged over £60,000 per annum between 1946 and 1948.[51] European planting bonuses and guaranteed

46. McCleery, 'Extent and Conditions', 28–41.
47. Tanganyika, Labour Department Annual Reports 1946, 15;1947, 21; 1948, 73.
48. The local producer price for maize was Sh. 13/50 per bag, whereas the cost of importing maize was Sh. 35 ('Memorandum on the Food Subsidization Fund', Chief Secretary, 20/11/46, TNA SMP 35085).
49. In 1946, over £600,000 was spent on food imports (Chief Secretary to all Provincial Commissioners, 11/12/46, TNA SMP 35085).
50. Member for Finance, Trade and Economics, Hansard, 24th Session, 30/11/49, 56.
51. Memorandum No. 92 for Executive Council, 'Grain Prices and Price Guarantees', August 1949, TNA SMP 38804.

minimum return acreage payments were primarily for maize.[52] Sisal plantations, where a major share of marketed maize was consumed, were expected to be self-supporting as far as possible in food production. In 1947, they were offered a bonus of Sh. 11 per bag for maize grown for the exclusive use of their labour.[53] But, with high sisal export prices prevailing, sisal growers had strong reservations about the policy.[54]

The state's efforts to ensure food security led to the formulation of a four-year food plan, covering 1946–50, which had as its main aim territorial food self-sufficiency. The plan involved the continuation of government price fixing and controlled marketing with exclusive trading rights granted to particular Asian traders by the Economic Control Board.[55] The government attempted to clamp down on the black market by prohibiting the sale of maize to any purchaser other than the Economic Control Board or its agents. According to the committee which recommended such action:

> It was realised that ... [this measure] ... would lead to strong representations on the part of the small Indian shop owner who, in many cases, had performed this purchasing heretofore, but it was held that no sympathy could be extended in this direction because such traders had to a large extent been responsible for the present predicament in which Government now found itself, and the extensive black marketing which was annually on the increase. Moreover, even though this trade was taken from this type of shop owner, there were still other sources from which he could obtain his livelihood.[56]

Settler food producers were disgruntled in 1946 because producer prices for food crops did not afford them the returns that were enjoyed by export crop producers.[57] Accusing the state of allowing a bloated

52. List of Payments in respect of Guaranteed Minimum Returns', n.d., TNA SMP 31886.
53. 'Food Subsidy Bill Passed', *Tanganyika Standard*, 17/1/47, TNA SMP 35085.
54. 'My Association will protest against any "Order to Plant", being made by Government on those estates where production of food crops merely means a waste of seed material and labour owing to the soil, climate and weather conditions being unsuitable for economic planting of these crops' (Tanganyika Sisal Growers Association (TSGA), Secretary to Director of Agricultural Production, 20/8/46, TNA SMP 30626). In 1949, the TSGA claimed that very few estates that planted maize would harvest more than 25% of their requirements due to the crop failure (TSGA to Member for Agriculture, 23/5/49, TNA SMP 30626).
55. 'Minutes of Meeting held at the Chief Secretary's House ... on 22/1/47 to consider Producer Prices of controlled Produce', TNA SMP 31301/III.
56. 'Minutes of Second Meeting of Select Committee on Food Production, Prices and Subsidies at Chief Secretary's House', 4/12//46, TNA SMP 35085.
57. They argued that the maize producer price of Sh. 13/50 per bag was calculated on the basis of an average yield of 10 bags per acre which was achieved only on the best land with the most diligent farming practices, and should be Sh. 23 per bag instead to allow the government agreed profit of Sh. 50 per acre (F.J. Anderson, *Hansard*, 20th Session, 25/7/46, 198–203).

margin of Sh. 18 between the producer price of Sh. 13/50 and the retail price of Sh. 31/50, with over half going to the Economic Control Board, they demanded that the producer price be raised to Sh. 23. Black marketeering of African-grown maize gave peasant producers higher returns than theirs, they complained. Not forsaking the aim of minimizing food costs to the consumer, the state raised guaranteed producer prices to a compromise level of Sh. 17/50.[58] There was an additional hidden incentive to non-natives in the form of a bonus for 10-bag railhead deliveries.[59] Prices were set on a fixed free-on-rail basis, so that producers in remote Mbeya and Njombe were afforded the same returns as others.[60] However, settler food farmers continued to feel cheated and pushed for higher prices each year.[61]

> The contention of the maize farmers in the Northern Province of Tanganyika is that they are not prepared to subsidise any longer the producers of export crops and others who are making fortuitous profits owing to causes beyond their control by supplying them with maize at prices which may be regulated as 'cut' compared with the cost of imported maize.[62]

In between the low yielding years of 1946 and 1948, the 1947 harvest was fairly successful. The inability of the prevailing marketing organization to handle such fluctuation quickly surfaced. A glut of maize appeared in the remote Southern Province, where appointed traders were refusing to purchase at the controlled prices because transport costs were too great.[63] Southern Highlands producers, in an area ecologically suited to grain production but distant from the major areas of demand, feared the same thing happening to them.[64]

58. The maize producer price was raised to Sh. 17/50 per 200 lb. bag in 1947 with the stipulation that all maize had to be sold to the Economic Control Board ('Food Subsidy Bill Passed', *Tanganyika Standard*, 17/1/47, TNA SMP 35085; 'Minutes of a Meeting held at the Chief Secretary's House to consider Producer Prices of Controlled Produce', 23/1/47, TNA SMP 35085).

59. European producers invariably had their own means of transport whereas African producers did not.

60. Despite the higher transport cost, maize from the Southern Highlands was still Sh. 7 cheaper per bag than that imported from Kenya and way below international import parity ('Maize Prices', Director of Agriculture, 25/10/48, TNA SMP 38804).

61. Arusha District Production Committee to Member for Agriculture and Natural Resources, 28/10/50, TNA SMP 38804.

62. Memorandum for Executive Council on Maize Prices in relation to those for Export Group, 1948, TNA SMP 38804.

63. Tanganyika, Department of Agriculture Annual Report 1947, 106–108.

64. 'We are aware that Government could not care less whether Iringa grows maize for export to the Central Line or not: it costs too much, in normal times to carry it there' (Member of Legislative Council, Iringa to Director of Agriculture, 12/11/49, TNA SMP 39114).

3. Tightening the Reins then Letting Go: Grain Storage and Market Decontrol

In 1949, not deterred by criticism of state management of food marketing, the colonial government decided to replace the Economic Control Board's food marketing with a newly created Grain Storage Department (GSD). The GSD, it was hoped, would systematize transport and marketing throughout the country by creating more grain storage capacity. In so doing, the aim was to even out the wild fluctuations in the grain supply market which resulted from climatic change from year to year, magnified by the selling habits of a subsistence-producing peasantry. Generally a peasant household sold little or no grain in bad or average years whereas the full surplus following a good harvest was disposed of through the market. The sale of individual peasant household surpluses cumulatively added up to a very large amount, which the transport and storage infrastructure of the country could not absorb. The GSD was, in effect, setting out to 'bronco-bust' the Tanzanian grain market.

As luck would have it, 1949 was an extremely severe drought year. The GSD devised a highly complicated staple food pricing structure to accommodate conflictual aims during that year. They wanted, on the one hand, to supply famine-exposed peasants with subsidized food and, on the other hand, to charge employers of fed labour the full costs of foodstuffs.[65] This entailed dual pricing. Furthermore, distinctions were drawn between employers of labour in deficit as opposed to surplus food producing provinces.[66] The former were charged higher prices to cover transport costs and the greater imported maize component. It was stipulated that all maize had to be purchased through the GSD. Many employers resented the arrangement, particularly the Lake Province mining enterprises, which argued that this disrupted their longstanding marketing arrangement with the local peasantry who had settled there and started growing maize with their encouragement.[67]

In 1950, the GSD abandoned dual pricing and instituted a geographically-zoned price structure. The Lake Province mines and employers in remote areas were allowed to circumvent the GSD and make local purchases of staple food crops with the permission of the Provincial Commissioner.[68]

65. Member for Finance, Trade and Economics to Director of Grain Storage, 20/1049, TNA SMP 39114.
66. Tanga, Eastern, Lake and Western Provinces, Dar es Salaam and Tanga Townships were classifed as deficit areas (Member for Finance, Trade and Economics, Memorandum No. 73 for Executive Council, 'Prices of Maize to Employers of Fed Labour', 14/6/49, TNA SMP 39114).
67. Tanganyika Mining Association to Chief Secretary, 6/6/49; Geita Gold Mining Co. Ltd. to Department of Economic Control, 30/8/49, TNA SMP 39114.
68. Director of Grain Storage to Member for Finance, Trade and Economics 22/3/50 and Member for Finance, Trade and Economics to Director of Grain Storage, 3/4/50, TNA SMP 39114.

All grain bulked into amounts weighing 3-tons or over was deemed a commercial quantity and had to be sold to the Department. In this way, GSD buying operations were restricted to buying grain from large-scale farmers and licensed traders in bulk at railheads (Figure III.1). This allowed private entrepreneurs room to buy smaller amounts in addition to their functions as millers and retailers. Their trading margins, however, were restricted by the controlled price at which the GSD purchased grain from them, by the price at which it was sold back to them, and by the ex-mill and retail prices specified by the district commissioner through powers delegated to him by the price controller under the 1951 Price Control Act. Controlled prices varied regionally depending on local handling and transport costs.

The GSD, which was expected to be a break-even operation, was itself hemmed in by externally-determined prices. Its objective of encouraging territorial self-sufficiency in grain production was posited on the fact that the costs of production and transport of East African supplies were below import parity. From 1953 onwards, the cheapening of international supplies resulted in the cost of domestic supplies being positioned between export and import parity. Exporting local supplies was to prove as expensive as importing foreign ones. Pricing policy, aimed at matching local supply with market demand, was therefore critical to the sound management of the Department. None the less, the extreme fluctuation of domestic supplies, as shown in Table III.1, was to prove the GSD's undoing.

The GSD did achieve its aim of increasing storage capacity to 40,000, which was 80 per cent of its target. Despite the size of its operations, a reasonable level of efficiency was maintained. GSD stocks were continuously assessed with detailed attention to stock loss. During 1953 and 1954, only 956 bags of grain disappeared, at a net loss of £1600 out of a total turnover of £3,900,000.[69] Furthermore, trade and milling mark-ups remained quite modest.[70] None the less, the GSD was continually under attack.

Complaints about the guaranteed high level of producer prices were most frequent from 1953 onwards. Employers of plantation labour were especially critical of the prices they had to pay to feed their labourers knowing that international grain prices were declining. On the other

---

69. Eight staff members were dismissed and one was surcharged (Acting Member for Agriculture and Natural Resources, *Hansard*, 29th Session, 2/12/54).

70. The mark-up for a kg of maize in Northern Province in 1955 was reported as: GSD into-store price – Sh. 0/44; operating and overhead charges margin – Sh 0/07 (16%); milling margin – Sh. 0/03 (7%); wholesale and retail margin – Sh. 0/03 (7%); retail maize meal price – Sh. 0/57 (30%) (Member for Agriculture and Natural Resources, *Hansard*, 30th Session, 10/6/55, 422); note that in the sisal producing areas the mark-up was reported to be over 43% with an into-store price of Sh. 0/42 and retail maize meal price of between Sh. 0/60 and Sh. 0/70 (A.L. LeMaitre, Tanga, *Hansard*, 30th Session, 12/5/55, 231).

hand, large-scale settler grain farmers felt that turn-about was fair play and reminded plantation owners that they had had to suffer low prices during the commodity boom of the early 1950s when sisal and coffee exports flourished.[71] It was also felt that the extension of the GSD's buying operations to the Southern Highlands, where transport costs were very high, was subsidizing the producers there at the expense of everyone else.[72]

In this climate, the 1955 East African Royal Commission delivered its blast to government agricultural marketing policy, challenging the *raison d'être* rather than the operations of the GSD.

One of the most untoward consequences of a subsistence economy is the recurring danger of a failure of the basic food supply due to droughts, pests, diseases and other natural causes. The absence of a modern system of distribution, the long distances separating populated or cultivable areas, and the inability of the subsistence economy to produce regular marketable surpluses by specialized production without risking a food shortage at critical periods of the year, have led the indigenous populations to seek security by clinging to their customary methods of production ... in the policies which they [the East African governments] have adopted they have been unduly influenced by the fears and practices of the indigenous populations, and by encouraging district, regional and even territorial self-sufficiency they have perpetuated the cause of the evil which their measures were intended to combat, namely the system of self-sufficiency itself. In their anxiety to achieve security in the matter of food supplies they have tended to regard the ordinary mechanism of the market as an obstacle to the solution of their difficulties rather than as a solvent of the problem ... this philosophy of restriction of production in order to achieve self-sufficiency in food supplies underlies the whole of the state-controlled marketing system.[73]

The Department of Agriculture raised objections:

The attainment of self-sufficiency in staple foodstuffs is a policy adopted by this territory in consultation and agreement with our neighbours in the early years of the war. It has continued unchanged ever since. It is not a policy which can be followed intermittently. It is not a suit of clothes which can be taken off and put away when not required and then brought out and put on again as and when necessary. It is a policy which must be followed consistently if it is to achieve success, and I

71. B.J. Wallis, Northern Province, *Hansard,* 30th Session, 12/5/55, 231.
72. O.B. Soskice, Unofficial Member, Dar es Salaam, *Hansard,* 27th Session, 24/11/54, 101; I.C. Chopra, Mwanza, *Hansard,* 28th Session, 26/11/53, 81.
73. Great Britain, Colonial Office, *East Africa Royal Commission 1953–1955 Report* (London, HMSO, 1955), 65–67.

would therefore urge that the most careful consideration should be given to the possible consequences before this policy is abandoned or even modified to any major degree.[74]

Although the Department of Agriculture was reluctant to abandon the goal of territorial self-sufficiency, this hesitation was overshadowed by events. In 1955/56, Tanganyika experienced a massive grain harvest. The department had a surplus of 110,000 tons of maize/*mtama*[75] compared with preceding years when deficits had been as high as 95,000 tons and surpluses had never gone beyond 25,000 tons (Table III.1).[76] Due to low international prices for grain, the export of the surplus caused a loss of over £1 million. The government immediately decided to disband the GSD, which naturally was met with the disappointment of the settler grain farmers and the delight of plantation interests.[77]

In 1957, legislation for the control of all grain markets was lifted, with the exception of wheat.[78] The government retained a small grain reserve which never exceeded 5000 tons as an insurance against the occurrence of famine.[79] Traders managed the country's grain supplies unimpeded by state controls, other than the stipulation that sales should take place in Native Authority markets and be subject to a market cess. It was estimated, however, that over 75 per cent of produce sales circumvented the Native Authority markets.[80]

For six years grain marketing reverted into private hands. Although over two-thirds of licensed traders were Africans, by 1961 their participation in the grain trade was restricted to retailing small amounts. Asian merchants controlled the grain trade in their capacity as produce buyers, wholesalers, brokers and millers.

74. Member for Agriculture and Natural Resources, *Hansard*, 30th Session, 13/5/55, 342.
75. Translated 'sorghum/millet'.
76. Tanganyika, GSD, Annual Report July 1956–July 1957 (DSM, Government Printer, 1957), 12–14.
77. Tanganyika National Farmers' Union Correspondence, Record of a Joint Production Committee Meeting held at Arusha, 25/2/55, Rhodes House Mss. Afr. s. 1222, 40–41.
78. Restrictions on wheat were retained due to the close coordination between Tanganyika's and Kenya's wheat distribution policies and the government's desire to keep foreign wheat imports in check and safeguard local production. But local pressure groups did not view it that way. European wheat farmers and African nationalists alike opposed the Wheat Industry Bill of 1959 seeing it as a piece of legislation that furthered Kenyan farmers' interests to the detriment of Tanganyika. The government, however, maintained that the legislation was necessary to support local production, to rationalize milling and to prevent over-reliance on wheat consumption to the detriment of other staples that Tanganyika could more readily produce (J.D. Shah, Eastern Province, *Hansard*, 32nd Session, 31/5/57; Commissioner for Commerce and Industry, *Hansard*, 33rd Session, 5/6/57, 554–557; Wheat and Wheat Flour Policy Debate, *Hansard*, 34th Session, 14/10/58, 18–27; Wheat Industry Bill debate, *Hansard*, 34th Session 9/6/59, 530–548).
79. Tanganyika, Department of Commerce and Industry, Annual Reports 1957–1960.
80. International Bank for Reconstruction and Development, *The Economic Development of Tanganyika* (Baltimore, Johns Hopkins Press, 1961), 72.

In conjunction with the growth of urban food demand and the loosening of government marketing controls, large-scale Asian produce buyers specializing in foodstuffs began to dominate the regional grain trade. In the absence of telephones and good transport conditions, staple foodstuff produce buyers had to operate on a fairly big scale with a substantial capital outlay, storage capacity and ability to withstand financial risk. Many became millers. They were likely to be oligopolistic and even monopolistic, with only one or two buyers operating in most areas.[81] While they made profitable returns, they none the less did not serve to inflate the trading margins due to the economies of scale they achieved and their avoidance of the fixed capital costs of buying posts. They reduced overhead costs by relying on a network of small *dukawallahs* to serve as collecting agents. The *dukawallahs* were remunerated through a salaried or credit arrangement.[82]

It was the grain wholesalers and brokers in Dar es Salaam who acted to balance the flow of trade from supply areas with the rate of territorial consumption. They set price levels that cleared the market and arranged for exports and imports in relation to internal demand and differences between territorial and international prices (Figure III.2).

Producer prices were considerably lower than the artificially high level set by the GSD. Wholesale and retail mark-ups remained moderate.[83] The Economist Intelligence Unit's 1962 report identified staple food margins as low in comparison with other product lines and in comparison with other countries.[84] The reasons for this included the fact that staple foodstuffs were fast-moving items and that they sold at conventional price levels; the 'just price' criterion was firmly in place in the free market.[85]

Producer and consumer prices varied regionally depending on the cost of transport. There was virtually no government regulation except in the form of the Transport Licensing Authority which affected rail rates and the number of road transporters competing for business. Decontrol of ex-mill prices had taken place for everything except wheat flour. Most of the grain trade took place on a cash basis. If wholesalers gave any credit to retailers it was usually limited to 30 days. There was a market pre-harvest seasonality to grain demand in most rural areas as opposed to the steady

81. The Southern Province had the most pronounced monopolistic buying arrangement (Economist Intelligence Unit, *Survey*, 173).
82. Hawkins, *Wholesale and Retail Trade*, 99.
83. The wholesale mark-up for basic foodstuffs at 2–3% was cited as 'probably the most competitive in the whole distribution system' (Economist Intelligence Unit, *Survey*, 133–139, 145, 175).
84. Kriesel *et al.* give a price breakdown for maize at Iringa between 1957 and 1963 (inclusive). The average producer and retail prices were Sh. 0/28 and Sh. 0/39 respectively, representing a 39% mark-up (Kriesel, H.C. *et al.*, *Agricultural Marketing in Tanzania* (East Lansing, Michigan State University, 1970).
85. Economist Intelligence Unit, *Survey*, 127.

annual demand of the towns and plantations. Consumers bought direct from mills as well as through retail outlets.[86]

The major challenge to Asian grain marketing came in the form of political opposition rather than economic competition. During the 1950s the African cooperative movement was expanding very quickly in the cotton and coffee-producing zones of the country. The cooperatives gave the independence struggle much of its impetus and constituted an active threat to Asian marketing. Part of the criticism that the cooperative movement levelled at Asian traders related to the 'closed shop' nature of Asian marketing. Nationalist leaders exhorted Africans to take the Asian traders on in their own game. Addressing a large gathering of peasants in Newala district in 1956, Nyerere admonished: 'While you are out dancing at an *ngoma* or drinking beer, the Asians are burning their lights in the back of their shops, improving themselves. If you got together and bought a lorry instead of bicycles, you could all be as rich as Indians.'[87]

In the lead up to independence, the Asian trader could not afford to view the relinquishing of his position to an African in the same manner as a European career civil servant could. The Asian trader's family extended back several generations in East Africa; Tanganyika was the limit of his working experience. In contrast, the colonial officer's stay in Tanganyika was a career option, which if disrupted was in personal terms annoying but did not harbour the same degree of material threat to income and property.

Despite the lack of training and capital, African farmer/traders' businesses were mushrooming during the 1950s. Their one advantage over Asian *dukawallahs* was that they were not subject to the delimitation of their operations to trading centres. This avoided an expensive building premise, thereby reducing overhead costs and lowering the scale of viable stock turnover. But there were also disadvantages in siting one's business in a village, particularly one's home village. It was difficult for the trader to separate his trade from material obligations to kin and neighbours and personal feelings often took precedence in the bargaining encounter.[88] Selling by the heap rather than accurately measuring quantities and treating all money returns as profit rather than distinguishing between gross and net profit contributed to the frequent liquidation of African trading enterprises.[89]

One rung up from the village-based farmer/trader was the aspiring African trader/transporter. Up-country transport had been almost entirely in the hands of Asian firms until the early 1950s when a few African farmers-cum-traders started purchasing lorries and buses. The inauguration

86. Economist Intelligence Unit, *Survey*, 134, 147.
87. Quoted in Leibenow, J.G., *Colonial Rule and Political Development in Tanzania* (Nairobi, East African Publishing House, 1971), 229.
88. Leslie, J.A.K., *A Survey of Dar es Salaam* (London, Oxford University Press, 1963), 137.
89. Wright, F.C. *African Consumers in Nyasaland and Tanganyika* (London, Her Majesty's Stationery Office, 1955), 54.

of a Transport Licensing Authority with the powers to issue public and
private carriers' licences in 1957 revealed fierce rivalry and resentment
between Asians and Africans in up-country transport. The Transport
Licensing Ordinance was supposed to reduce 'uneconomic competition'
and ensure the safety and regularity of up-country transport services for
the customer. Both Africans and Asians opposed the bill, fearing that it
would be used to delimit their transport activities for the benefit of the
other. As it turned out, the Authority's policy was to view with favour all
African applications that were supported by sufficient facilities and
finance.[90] The hitch was that most African transporters were severely
under-capitalized and found it extremely difficult to compete against well-
established Asian transporters.[91] Africans usually obtained second-hand
vehicles on hire-purchase schemes. When they failed to make the
repayments on schedule, as frequently happened, their vehicles were
repossessed. This problem continued after independence as well. In 1966
hire-purchase schemes were declared illegal only to be reinstated again
three years later upon popular demand. Gradually the number of African
private transporters increased, but their businesses tended to be small-
scale and fragile.

But the death blow to Asian grain marketing did not come from African
private traders. State marketing again surfaced. During the independence
celebrations, a drought hit the country, bringing famine to the central
regions. Consumer prices for staple foodstuffs rose, causing a surge of
popular resentment against Asian traders. The newly installed African
government, suspicious of private traders whatever their complexion, and
eager to pay its political debt to the cooperatives, acted quickly.

4. Africanization of Grain Marketing: National
Agricultural Products Board/National Milling
Corporation/Cooperatives, 1963–1973

In 1963, the National Agricultural Products Board (NAPB) was established
as a marketing board for maize, rice, wheat, cashewnut and oilseeds. The
NAPB was obliged to provide purchasing services throughout the country,
to buy all the produce that was offered to it, and to keep a famine reserve
stock for distribution to needy areas. Tables III.2 and III.3 show NAPB

---

90. Hofmeier, R., *Transport and Economic Development in Tanzania* (Munich, Weltforum Verlag,
1973), 156; Tanganyika, *Transport Licensing Authority 1956–1957 Annual Report* (DSM), 8;
Siyovelwa (Iringa), *Hansard*, 36th Session, 22/5/61, 242.
91. In 1965, the total number of African public carrier vehicles was 1218 and non-Africans
1792. The number of vehicles operated per Public Carrier Licence was: Africans 1.2
and non-Africans 2.2 (Hofmeier, *Transport*, 334).

purchases and sales. The 1964 Agricultural Products Board Act gave the NAPB powers to regulate sales, transport, storage and processing as well as to fix minimum prices at any stage of the marketing process.

The NAPB attempted to control the full gamut of prices from producer to consumer, but, given the variation in cooperative unions' and societies' collection performance, this proved impossible. In the years that followed, the NAPB's exercise of control was restricted to fixing into- and ex-store prices, set on the basis of projected costings which had to be first approved by the Agricultural Price Policy Coordinating Committee (APPCC) of the Ministry of Agriculture and ultimately the Economic Committee of the Cabinet. Producer prices were to be the residual of the into-store price once cooperative union and society costs were deducted. Town councils and regional and area commissioners authorized by the price controller in the Ministry of Commerce and Industry set maximum retail prices. The strategic political importance of food pricing is clearly evident in this price-setting arrangement. At its two extremes, producer and consumer prices were determined by local political pressures whereas the highest level of collective governmental decision-making, the Cabinet, was instrumental in setting the NAPB's price levels rather than leaving them entirely to the NAPB.[92]

As under previous trade regimes, the licensing of retailers continued. The licensing of millers was reinstated. The NAPB issued milling licences on the recommendation of an area commissioner and the commissioner for cooperatives. In the 1960s local authorities were very stringent about allocating of licences to private millers; they were obviously influenced by the cooperative unions' investments in milling.[93] In 1967, the Arusha Declaration brought about the nationalization of the country's large urban-based mills, which were then amalgamated to form the National Milling Corporation (NMC).

While the NAPB's single channel marketing strongly resembled the GSD system, there were a number of significant differences (Figure III.3). The NAPB's system aimed at more all-encompassing government control. The maximum amount of grain that could be traded and transported by private individuals was only four bags (360 kg.) rather than three tons. Whereas the local produce buying agents under the GSD had been mostly licensed private traders, under the NAPB they were almost exclusively cooperatives. The GSD's into- and ex-store prices had generally been

---

92. Furthermore, the management of the NAPB took a political twist when Chief Fundikira, a strategic TANU supporter during the nationalist struggle, was appointed as chairman in 1962. During the following year amidst his oppositional stance to government legislation on land tenure and the one-party state, he was arrested for accepting bribes as NAPB chairman. This was seen as a political arrest and he was quickly acquitted (Bienen, H., *Tanzania: Party Transformation and Economic Development* (Princeton, Princeton University Press, 1970), 60).

93. Kriesel *et al.*, *Agricultural Marketing*, 24.

region-specific. The NAPB's were pan-territorial, giving an implicit transport subsidy to the more far-flung regions.[94]

The 1960s were to see private milling, which had been primarily Asian, gradually replaced by the cooperatives at the local level and by the NMC in the major towns. Wholesale distribution of milled products passed through the cooperatives, or, in Dar es Salaam, the National Distributors Ltd, a subsidiary of the Cooperative Union of Tanganyika. Transport of produce was about the only aspect of the trade that remained primarily in private hands. Few marketing cooperatives had vehicles of their own, for there were too many organizational difficulties if they did. Specialized transport cooperatives were not proving to be successful.[95]

The NAPB's objectives were the same as those of the GSD: price stabilization and national food security. Like the GSD, the NAPB's main difficulty was to remain financially viable while maintaining domestic prices in isolation from world market prices. When surplus domestic production occurred, it invariably meant a financial loss in the process of exporting, which the government had to cover.[96]

Several authors have criticized the NAPB for failing to achieve its objective of temporal and spatial price stabilization, or, alternatively, they have questioned the validity of the goal in view of the extremely low producer prices offered.[97] The NAPB set a pan-territorial into-store price but the price that the producer received varied a great deal from place to place and over time depending on the administrative performance and clientage practices of local cooperative unions and societies.[98]

During the 1950s, the expansion of the cooperatives had taken place on the basis of export crop marketing. Previous attempts to extend cooperatives' operations into food marketing had largely failed.[99] With the founding of the NAPB, the government gave the cooperatives a clear entry into food crop marketing, appointing cooperatives rather than Asian merchants as procurement agents. The Cooperative Union of Tanganyika (CUT), the unions and primary societies formed a three-tiered system.

94. Helleiner, G.K., 'Agricultural Marketing in Tanzania – Policies and Problems', Economics Research Bureau Paper 68.14, University of Dar es Salaam (1968), 22.

95. Hofmeier, *Transport*, 161.

96. The export loss fund amounted to: Sh. 103.50/ton in 1965, Sh. 60/ton in 1966 and Sh. 50.33/ton in 1970 (Kriesel *et al.*, *Agricultural Marketing*, 26–27).

97. Helleiner, 'Agricultural Marketing', 21–24; Livingstone, I., 'Production, Price and Marketing Policy for Staple Foodstuffs in Tanzania', Economics Research Bureau Paper 71.16, University of Dar es Salaam (1971), 3; Temu, P., 'Marketing Board Pricing and Storage Policy with Particular Reference to Maize in Tanzania', Ph.D. thesis, Stanford University (1975), 108, 194.

98. For a discussion of clientage practices in cooperatives see Bryceson, *Food Insecurity*, 155–159.

99. In 1956/57 when the deregulation of the grain trade opened the way for Asian competition in produce buying, Asian traders' offer of higher grain producer prices led to cooperative members' widespread defection in Iringa and North Mara (Tanganyika, *Annual Report on Cooperative Development 1956*, 6–7; 1957, 2).

The role of the NAPB, as a crop marketing board, was to purchase crops from the cooperative unions and provide extension advice to them.

Leadership in the cooperatives was provided mainly by farmer/traders, who generally had a strong rural base as well as a certain amount of influence in the local town. The viability of the cooperatives revolved around the commodity price paid to peasant producers (Table III.4). The main determinants of the peasants' price level were, first, the international market price for the commodity; second, the efficiency of marketing board personnel; third, the extent of central and local government taxation; and, fourth, the efficiency and honesty of cooperative staff at union and society level. In terms of the latter, besides lack of adequate training on the part of cooperative staff and the small, under-optimal size of many cooperative society and union operations, performance depended on the extent of the acceptable *posho*[100] deductions taken by the staff and committee along with the socially unsanctioned deductions, in other words, peculation. Temu's study of marketing margins suggests these factors combined to produce very high marketing mark-ups and consequent low producer prices. Between 1964 and 1973, the average cooperative mark-up throughout the country was a full 48 per cent of the average producer price for maize, whereas the marketing board margin was only 25 per cent. He thus identifies the cooperatives as the 'villain' of inflated marketing costs.[101] René Dumont was more scathing:

> Since 1962, and because of the cooperatives, the prices paid to the producers have greatly fallen. At Lushoto, a ton of maize, bought at Shs. 440/- by the Marketing Board, only brings the producer Shs. 220/-. *We have never seen anywhere in the world, such high deductions* [Dumont's emphasis] reaching half the value of the product...The reasons for such bad management seem to us so numerous that it seems difficult to classify them in order of importance. Certainly *lack of honesty* and incompetence seem amongst the more serious.[102]

Economic commentators felt that the cooperative margin was excessively large compared with the services performed and there was duplication in union and NAPB functions.[103] Total mark-ups were considerably greater than those prevailing in the 1950s under either the Grain Storage Department or Asian marketing.[104]

100. Literally translated 'food ration', referred to various allowances that were taken from cooperative funds and considered part of cooperative personnel's entitlement.
101. Temu, 'Marketing Board Pricing', 81, 95.
102. Dumont, R., *Tanzanian Agriculture after the Arusha Declaration* (Dar es Salaam, Ministry of Economic Affairs and Development Planning, 1969), 50.
103. Temu, 'Marketing Board Pricing', 190, 198; Dumont, *Tanzanian Agriculture*, 50.
104. The average maize mark-up in 1963–1969 in Iringa region was 77%. In 1967/68 the cost break-down for a kg. of maize NAPB ex-store was as follows: producer price – Sh. 0.30; cooperative society costs – Sh. 0.0547 (18%); cooperative union costs – Sh. 0.0507 (17%); NAPB costs – Sh. 0.1532 (51%); NAPB ex-store price – Sh. 0.5590 (86%).

Peasant disenchantment with the cooperatives began in the 1960s, especially in relation to food crop prices.[105] It is likely that most peasants had only a vague awareness of the international prices for export crops, and therefore remained relatively unaware of the size of the marketing margins during the 1950s. As cooperative marketing extended to food crops in the 1960s, there was a heightened consciousness of price because the margins for food crops were glaringly obvious. Peasants not only sold food crops, they sometimes had to buy food if a seasonal shortage occurred. The gap between producer and consumer prices outraged them. Low producer prices led many to sell their food crops in parallel markets rather than to the cooperatives.[106] Furthermore, producers received an initial payment at the time of crop purchase for some crops and were promised a second payment if there was money left over from cooperative society receipts at the end of the season. The likelihood of a second payment largely depended on the efficiency of cooperative staff and alerted peasants to the injustices, in their eyes, of the cooperative marketing system.

Similarly, economic analysts considered urban consumer prices to be far too high.[107] There was growing concern that urban consumer demand was not increasing in consonance with the rate of urban migration. The discrepancy was attributed to the widespread incidence of an illicit market in grain. Lack of demand in addition to over-supply was seen to be the root cause of the NAPB's difficulties. There was a tendency on the part of some policy decision-makers to give more priority to stabilizing consumer prices than producer prices. With the NAPB's over-abundant stocks of maize in 1968, the Ministry of Agriculture proposed lowering the into-store price to deter farmers from producing grain, but the NAPB's Executive Committee did not comply and the 1969 into-store price

(cont.) It should be noted that in 1967/68 the NAPB ex-store price was Sh 0.52/kg. maize, resulting in a deficit of almost four cents per kg. and that the retail price for maize meal in Dar es Salaam was Sh.0/79 representing a 164% mark-up (Kriesel *et al.*, *Agricultural Marketing*, 28, 38); Temu calculated the average maize mark-up between producer price and NAPB ex-store for the country as a whole (1964–1973) as 85% with a year-to-year range of 69% to 103% (Temu, 'Marketing Board Pricing', 81).

105. Kriesel *et al.* estimate that the proportion of the final sales value of maize going to producers dropped from 76% to 48% between 1956 and 1969 in Iringa (Kriesel, *Agricultural Marketing*, 38). Ellis calculates that, by 1970–72, peasant producers were receiving 45% of the sales value at cost for staple grains and 67% of export crops' sales value (Ellis, F., 'Agricultural Marketing and Peasant–State Transfers in Tanzania', *Journal of Peasant Studies* 10(4) (1983), 225).

106. In Temu's 1972 survey of farmers in six regions of Tanzania, 96% of the respondents to the question of why they sold on the parallel market gave low producer prices as their primary reason (Temu, 'Marketing Board Pricing', 157).

107. Kriesel *et al.* identified the urban price of maize meal as intolerably high and blamed it for the need for a high minimum wage, commenting: 'It is ironic that retail prices for maize in Tanzania are among the highest in the world' (Kriesel *et al.*, *Agricultural Marketing*, 35, 107).

remained at the 1968 level despite lack of approval.[108] In 1970, the price dropped.[109]

The NAPB was trapped in a vicious cycle. The wide official margins were traced back to the inflated costs of the cooperatives, the NAPB's need for a special fund to cover losses arising from its import and export of grain and the implicit transport subsidies that distant regions received. The NAPB was completely unable to limit the primary procurement costs of the cooperatives and the wide fluctuations of its stocks. When the cooperatives exceeded their approved margins, the NAPB had to cover the cost.[110] Over-supply was frequent. Storage and export costs were financially draining, and led to widening margins and the fuelling of the parallel market, which undermined demand for NAPB products and further contributed to over-supply. By the early 1970s the situation was becoming untenable.

However, the problem of a public glut of basic foodstuffs has to be kept in historical perspective. The predicament facing the NAPB would have been enviable to past and future policy-makers wrestling with Tanzania's food shortages. The NAPB's financial losses were tied up with food surpluses, not deficits. Livingstone is of the opinion that some of the loss arose from the NAPB's poor stock management, with unnecessary export and import following each other in rapid succession from year to year, or even within the same year.[111] The NAPB lacked an information-gathering system to monitor harvests in the regions, which would have been necessary to make accurate judgements about future stocks. Furthermore, it failed to keep up-to-date financial accounts and so no one was sure of the agency's exact position.[112] The NAPB had to resort to government subsidy in its first years to cover export losses and then again in the late 1960s.[113] This was a drain on public revenues, deflecting finance from development projects and affecting the taxpayer adversely, but the NAPB's operational difficulties did not undermine the population's confidence in a secure food supply. There were no serious food shortages in the country, even though peasants were growing increasing amounts of cash crops.

108. Bryceson, D.N.M., 'Price, Production and Marketing Policies for Maize', Paper No. 60 of 1968, submitted by the Minister for Agriculture and Cooperatives, MDPC/A.50/26/4, n.d.
109. Kriesel *et al.*, *Agricultural Marketing*, 27.
110. For example, in 1966/67, the NAPB distributed Sh. 4.3 million to cover union losses (Kriesel *et al.*, *Agricultural Marketing*, 28).
111. Livingstone admits that it is easy to make such judgements with hindsight (Livingstone, 'Production', 9–38).
112. Helleiner reports that in 1968 the NAPB had not published any accounts since 1964/65 (Helleiner, 'Agricultural Marketing', 34).
113. Kriesel *et al.*, *Agricultural Marketing*, 38.

5. Summary

At first glance the array of government marketing policies which materialized between the Second World War and the early 1970s appear as a tangle of contradictory measures designed to undo the policies immediately preceding them. It would be an over-simplification to analyse the changes as merely a volley between state control and unfettered market forces. The colonial and post-colonial states were mainly concerned with food security (in the form of guaranteed food availability) and stable producer and consumer prices. The extent to which the state intervened in marketing organization largely depended on whether food security was felt to be under threat. The various marketing structures that characterized the period do not represent a stark dichotomy between state control and the 'free' market. Rather they were solutions tailored to particular circumstances, displaying a range of policy options *vis-à-vis* food security objectives, the relative ordering of consumer and producer demands, centralization versus decentralization of marketing organizational structure, and import reliance versus domestic self-sufficiency.

Even during the periods of more active state intervention in food marketing, for a number of reasons the state stopped far short of eliminating the operation of the market completely. First of all, in the event of shortfalls or gluts of national production, Tanzania participated in the world market for rice, wheat and particularly maize. The costs of local production and transport of grain to the main consuming centres fell between export and import parity prices. In the event of a good or bad harvest, recourse to foreign import or export of grain brought about greater financial expense, and, if extreme, could jeopardize the viability of the state marketing agency that had to shoulder the financial burden. Second, unofficial markets always emerged when the state-controlled market failed to provide for its clientele's needs. This failure took a number of forms. There was the failure to provide timely purchase of farmers' produce, thereby forcing farmers to resort to lower prices from illegal traders; there was the failure to sell adequate amounts of produce to consumers, which made traders sell their foodstuffs at higher prices and, finally, excessively wide margins created a parallel market, which could operate on narrower margins.

This chapter has discussed the organization of Asian grain trading during the colonial period. Trading networks, intertwined with community and family connections, provided vertical integration for all trading functions from import/export in Dar es Salaam to buying and selling in remote rural areas. The central pivot of the trading network was the rural-based *dukawallah*. Holding the lowliest position in a well-defined career structure, he dealt directly with peasants, combining produce marketing and consumer sales, operating with negligible overheads, using family labour.

The Second World War provided the colonial state, which had always been suspicious of Asian traders, with grounds for imposing numerous restrictive controls over Asian traders. The controls were strengthened with the founding of the Grain Storage Department in 1949. Price controls, producer and consumer subsidies and food rationing were all deployed, aimed at retaining the status quo and racially differentiated consumption patterns against the onslaught of a world war and international grain shortages. Through the years, the impact of state intervention favoured consumers, i.e. European employers of 'fed labour' and then European grain producers. European farmer lobbies representing the two factions had arisen in this period to exert pressure on the government. State controls involved very complicated pricing arrangements aimed at being consistent with production and transport costs. Meanwhile the policy towards Africans was premised on household food self-sufficiency. There is evidence that many African urban households resorted to agricultural production on the perimeter of the town during this period.

Independence brought a relatively abrupt end to Asian grain produce buying with the founding of the National Agricultural Production Board. Under its infrastructural umbrella, the establishment of more and more cooperative societies and their purchase of grain from peasant producers was pursued. During the nationalization of various industries following the 1967 Arusha Declaration, the National Milling Corporation was organized from the amalgamation of several urban-based private grain mills. Peasant producers obliged to market their grain through the cooperatives, NAPB and NMC were subject to price formations that were heavily influenced by the state. Increasing margins between producer and consumer prices caused peasants in some areas to seek black market outlets. None the less, the cooperatives, incorporating localized rural clientage relations, were instrumental in the expansion of peasant marketed grain production through its provision of productive inputs and market facilities. However, the state was impatient to eliminate the inefficiencies of the cooperatives and to hasten the rate of expansion in peasant commodity production. For this reason cooperatives were doomed.

IV
State Regulation
of Staple Food Supply
1973–1988

During the mid-1970s a number of extremely ambitious policies were implemented. In 1973, the villagization programme was launched and over the next four years approximately 60 per cent of the rural population were moved into villages.[1] Once settled in villages, people were to be availed of improved educational and health facilities, as well as better agricultural extension and agricultural inputs. The main thrust of villagization was to increase yields and total marketed output. The states's development goals were not restricted to the rural areas. The Third Five Year Plan announced a basic strategy for industries which led to a dramatic increase in industrial investment on the part of the state. In this atmosphere of optimism, it was decided that agricultural marketing, particularly staple food marketing which was so strategic to national economic development, should be placed more firmly under state control. The NAPB and the cooperatives were dispensable.

The first section of this chapter discusses the state's attempts to promote increased domestic staple food production in the aftermath of villagization. The remainder of the chapter documents the rise and fall of single channel, government parastatal marketing under the National Milling Corporation (NMC), and the fall and rise of the cooperatives during the same period. Government thinking switched from the position that strict single channel marketing was the only way, to a belief, or rather a hope, that the solution was for cooperatives to operate in conjunction with the NMC.

1. Restructuring Peasant Production

Increasing domestic production and marketed supply of food was a necessary precondition for successful industrialization and attendant urbanization. As state policy aims, their importance was reinforced by the

---

1. It is estimated that 9,100,000 people were moved (Nyerere, J. K., *The Arusha Declaration Ten Years After* (DSM, Government Printer, 1977), 41.

drought, domestic food shortages and massive food imports of the mid-1970s. With a sense of urgency and confidence in its own organizational capability, the state embarked on a number of measures.

1.1 Villagization

The villagization campaign began in 1973. For the next three years, millions of peasants physically moved to new household sites in nucleated village settlements, abandoning the traditional habit of living in widely dispersed homesteads. The aim of the villagization policy was to modernize peasant agriculture rather than collectivizing it into *ujamaa* villages.[2] The state sought to eliminate the low-yielding, shifting agriculture of the peasantry and to introduce the use of fertilizers, insecticides and improved seeds. Through a carrot and a stick approach, peasants were told they had to move but, in doing so, they would be provided with highly desired health and education services, and a comprehensive market and productive infrastructure.

Relatively rich peasants as well as the middle and poor ones were subject to the dictates of the villagization 'operations' carried out by regional government and party officials. As a result, considerable social and economic levelling took place. Although the rich peasants were by no means eliminated, the inconvenience of having their residence moved, the restrictions placed on the amount of land they could farm and the general supremacy of the village chairman and council in allocating resources represented a setback to them.[3]

Many of the rich peasants were active in the cooperative movement. The strengthening of village government and the clear chain of command from party and government officials at national, regional and district levels down to the village leadership marked a reorientation of local power away from the cooperatives.

The new villages were usually sited along the main roads, sometimes with little regard for the suitability of the soils and proximity of water sources. In fact, since so many of Tanzania's roads were built on higher altitudes to avoid drainage problems, siting villages along the roads tended to cause a systematic distancing from the more fertile valley soils.[4]

2. Bryceson, D.F., 'Household, Hoe and Nation: Development Policies of the Nyerere Era', in Hodd, M. (ed.), *Tanzania after Nyerere* (London, Pinter Publishers, 1988), 44.
3. Kjaerby, F., 'Agricultural Productivity and Surplus Production in Tanzania: Implications of Villagization, Fertilizers and Mixed Farming', Discussion Paper, University of Dar es Salaam (1979), 20. However, in some cases the elected village chairman was a rich peasant which mitigated decisions against that group (Friis-Hansen, E., 'An Assessment of Changes in Land Tenure and Land Use since Villagisation and the Impact of the Development of Peasant Agricultural Production in Tanzania', Centre for Development Research Report, Copenhagen (May 1986), 17.
4. Kjaerby, F., 'Villagization and the Forms of Agricultural Production in Hanang', Centre for Development Research, Copenhagen (1985), 3–5.

By 1978, the government estimated that 86 per cent of the population lived in 7768 villages compared with only 809 villages recorded in 1969.[5] A 'critical mass' of 250 households or more was sufficient for the village to be registered as a corporate unit under the 1975 Village Act.[6] The village council, composed of 26 elected members, was vested with the power 'to do all acts and things as are necessary or expedient for the economic and social development of the village' as well as 'plan and coordinate the activities of and render assistance and advice to the residents of the village engaged in agricultural, horticultural, forestry or other activity or industry whatsoever'.[7] The registered village functioned as a multi-purpose cooperative, largely displacing the role of the marketing cooperative.

Village collective farms were encouraged by party and government officialdom, but it was left to the initiative of village leaders to organize. Not all villages had collective farms and those that did tended to be small when measured in terms of per capita acreage.[8] More common was the 'block farm' where peasants cultivated individual plots which were contiguous.[9]

The government's attempt to supervise village production took several forms. Villages were required to devise work timetables which would 'enable regional heads to know, supervise, guide and evaluate work being done by villagers in order to achieve better results'.[10] Beginning in 1978, the post of village managers was created with the aim of providing on-the-spot supervision in the technical aspects of agricultural production.[11] Besides the difficulties the government had in filling these positions, village managers tended to resent their postings to the rural areas and consequently were not highly motivated.[12] Overall, attempts to organize peasant economic life through the village government were hampered by the inadequate

5. Statistics from Prime Minister's Office, Dodoma (1978) cited in Ngware, S.S.A., 'Emerging Trends after Villagisation', Paper prepared for ILO/JASPA, DSM (1981), 7.
6. According to the 1978 census, the Tanzanian mainland had 7990 villages with an average of 365 households per village (Tanzania Bureau of Statistics, *Population Census*, IV, DSM (1983)90).
7. Villages and Ujamaa Villages Registration, Designation and Administration Act 1975, Part II 12 (1).
8. For example, in Tibaijuka's sample of 13 villages in Iringa, Mbeya and Ruvuma, on average adults only cultivated 0.14 acres communally (Tibaijuka, A., 'An Economic Survey of Village Projects in Iringa, Mbeya and Ruvuma Regions, 1979', Economics Research Bureau Paper 81.3, University of Dar es Salaam (1981), 20.
9. Block farms constituted one-third of all cultivated area in a 1977/78 sample of Kigoma villages (Loft, M. and J. Oldevelt, 'Developments in Peasant Agriculture in Kigoma Region during the Post-Villagisation Years', Economics Research Bureau, University of Dar es Salaam (1981), 39.
10. *Daily News*: 'PM calls for work timetables', 4/5/77.
11. *Daily News*: 'Government looks for village managers', 10/2/78.
12. McCall, M. and M. Skutsch, 'Strategies and Contradictions in Tanzania's Rural Development: Which Path for the Peasants?', in Lea, D.A. and D. Chaudhri (eds), *Rural Development and the State* (London, Methuen, 1983), 258; Ngware, 'Emerging Trends', 57.

managerial and accountancy skills of the village leaders, and their failure to identify with the higher echelons of the government and party bureaucracy.[13]

1.2 National Maize Project

A national maize production programme developed alongside villagization. Preceding villagization, under the state's smaller *ujamaa* village programme, in 1971/72 newly formed *ujamaa* villages in Iringa region received free agricultural inputs and tractor ploughing services from the government. This constituted an attempt to establish quickly collective socialist maize production to counteract the small group of rich peasants in nearby Ismani, who had surfaced as successful commercial grain producers with a 'capitalist' orientation.

The following year a Tanzania Rural Development Bank project worth TSh. 1.8 million was initiated for the communal farms of 30 villages to cover the costs of improved seeds, fertilizers and tractor ploughing. But the net results were not encouraging. The average yield on the communal farms was a low 600 kg./ha., whereas peasants were achieving 870 kg./ha. on their private plots. Mohele attributes this difference to a shortage of efficiently organized labour on the communal farms.[14] Furthermore, the maize crop's response to fertilizers was not promising, with less than 5 per cent of the farmers in the area being accustomed to using them. The returns from maize sales from communal farms would have covered only 32 per cent of the total debt. After much pressure the villagers pledged to repay approximately 16 per cent of the debt. The programme was henceforth discontinued.[15]

Undeterred, the government launched the National Maize Production Programme in 1973/74, which it linked to the villagization programme. Aimed at assisting newly formed villages, it involved the free distribution of improved inputs in 13 regions, using the cooperatives as distribution agents. Input delivery problems quickly surfaced. Furthermore, lack of motivation on the part of the extension staff and inadequate research data made it virtually impossible to formulate valid planting recommendations in different areas.[16] The programme was replaced by the World Bank-funded National Maize Project (NMP) in 1975. The input packages were

13. Moore, M.P. and P. Stutley, 'Smallholder Food Production in Tanzania', DSM, Report to SIDA and the Government of Tanzania (1981), 64.

14. Mohele, A.T., 'The Ismani Maize Credit Programme', Economics Research Bureau Paper 75.2, University of DSM (1975), 9.

15. Mohele, 'Ismani Maize', 3–23.

16. Following the government's 1972 decentralization policy which strengthened regional government to central ministries, agricultural extensionists were directly accountable to regional government rather than the Ministry of Agriculture which limited the possibilities for technical updating of their advice to farmers.

somewhat refined, involving the introduction of three graduated input packages into suitable maize growing areas in ten regions.[17] The packages were initially offered with a 50 per cent subsidy to be reduced over time. The project was administered by a central project servicing unit within the Ministry of Agriculture.

At the conclusion of the first phase of the NMP in 1979, roughly 10 per cent of Tanzania's villages had participated, but the results were far from encouraging. Again the extension services performed badly. Expensive inputs had been applied where rainfall was too low, and where soils were unresponsive or already adequately fertile. Often the inputs had been delivered late. Peasant labour time constraints and crop prioritization frequently led peasants to disregard the recommended input application procedures. Repayment of the loans, all of which had no interest charges, was none the less riddled with default.[18]

The programme was revamped. The number of regions covered was reduced to the six most suitable ones for maize production in the country. In view of the problems experienced in credit recovery, as well as the fact that if the provisioning of inputs was to continue credit could no longer be interest free, the Tanzania Rural Development Bank was given responsibility for the programme. Input delivery continued to be extraordinarily difficult, especially at the time of the war with Amin's Uganda during the late 1970s.

At the completion of the project in 1982, approximately 50 per cent of the TSh. 51 million loans and interest accumulated between 1975 and 1980 were unpaid.[19] The project's total costs were estimated at TSh. 307 million ($38.1 million) apportioned between: the IDA (57 per cent), the Tanzanian goverment (29 per cent), the Arab Bank for Economic

17. The input packages were: (1) improved husbandry and the use of composite seeds to increase yields of maize (assuming a base yield of 1100 kg./ha.) by 400 kg.; (2) the use of triple superphosphates and sulphate of ammonia fertilizers with the use of hybrid seeds rather than composite seeds in high altitude areas to increase yields by an additional 700 kg./ha., totalling 2200 kg./ha.; (3) additional usage of sulphate of ammonia fertilizer and further replacement of composites with hybrids to maximize yields at 2700 kg./ha. The regions were Arusha, Dodoma, Iringa, Kilimanjaro, Mbeya, Morogoro, Rukwa, Ruvuma, Tabora and Tanga.

18. Fortmann, L., 'An Evaluation of the Progress of the National Maize Project at the End of One Cropping Season in Morogoro and Arusha Regions', USAID/Tanzania (1976), 8–21; Due, J.M., *Costs, Returns and Repayment Experience of Ujamaa Villages in Tanzania, 1973–1976* (Washington DC, University Press of America, Inc., 1980), 101; *Daily News*: 'Maize project faces problems', 17/12/77; 'Poor research fails maize plan in Arusha', 3/2/78; 'TRDB loan terms are too severe', 17/3/78; 'Peasants "don't want" fertilizer', 20/1/79.

19. Interview with Mr Urasa, Director, National Maize Project, 26/12/83; Urasa, 'National Maize Project Report', mimeo (DSM, December 1983); Bryceson, D.F., 'Second Thoughts on Marketing Cooperatives in Tanzania', Plunkett Development Series 5 (1983), 23–27; *Daily News*: 'TRDB loan recovery: Legal organ proposed', 5/1/81; 'TRDB stops loans to maize growers', 13/1/82.

Development in Africa (13 per cent) and the farmers (10 per cent). The project's visible impact was concentrated in Ruvuma and Mbeya where marketed maize more than doubled and in Rukwa where it quintupled (Table IV.1). Yields in Rukwa were recorded as high as 4 tons/ha. Overall, however, yield increases were disappointing. It was estimated that average yields had increased to 1500 kg./ha. as opposed to the 2700 hoped for.

Clearly, there was a need to refine the technical package and tailor it for various local soil and weather conditions, which would require painstaking research and extension work. Furthermore, the technical package had to be better adjusted to peasant cash and labour budgets. The transition from financially unencumbered subsistence production to production bearing financial investments and risks was at the root of the peasants' inability to repay their loans. When peasants took credit for capitalization of their production the returns to peasant labour were jeopardized, even though the potential for increased output was greater. A peasant operating on a very small scale with family survival at stake often bore risks that were higher than his or her potential gains and the unreliable input delivery and crop purchasing system introduced an additional risk element.

1.3 Changes in Peasant Agriculture

The domestic constraints, which impeded the execution of the state's programme for peasant agriculture, combined with formidable exogenous factors, namely, the undermining force of Tanzania's declining terms of trade, the skyrocketing price of oil and its deleterious effect on the country's transport system. Under the circumstances, did the state's frontal programme to modernize peasant agriculture bring about any positive results?

Tanzania is a geographically diverse country so it is difficult to answer the question for the nation as a whole. However, Kjaerby has identified two salient regional tendencies, which have evolved from the the state's differentiated success in developing and delivering improved inputs for staple food production.[20]

The south and southwest, particularly the Southern Highlands, had historically held considerable commercial agricultural potential but had been marginalized by poor transport connections. It was this region that responded most positively to the state's rural development programme. This was made possible by a dramatic improvement in transport infrastructure. The TAZARA railway and the TANZAM highway, completed in the early 1970s, linking Zambia to Dar es Salaam's port, opened a corridor for the transport of goods. This was followed by the construction of an all-weather tarmac road from the TAZARA railhead at Makambako

20. Kjaerby, F., 'Scratching the Surface: The Tanzanian Tractor Fiasco, the Undiscovered Oxenization Boom and the Drag on Mixed Farming', Draft, Centre for Development Research, Copenhagen (November 1984).

to Songea in the extreme south. None the less, distances were still great from the southern regions of the country to Dar es Salaam. The state marketing agencies' pan-territorial producer pricing policy in effect gave the area a transport subsidy and a real incentive to sell its produce on the official market.

The southern regions of Iringa, Mbeya, Rukwa and Ruvuma benefited from the National Maize Project and became the National Milling Corporation's main supply areas, earning them the label 'the Big Four'.[21] These regions were rewarded for good performance by greater than average government and foreign donor technical and financial assistance. They were the closest thing that Tanzania had to model 'modern farming' areas, dependent on timely delivery of fertilizers and hybrid seeds.[22] Maize quickly edged out other staple crops. But, to get adequate supplies to these regions, the parastatal Tanzania Fertilizer Company and TANSEED continuously had to surmount the inefficiencies of Dar es Salaam harbour, TAZARA railway, the shortage of delivery lorries and their own internal managerial problems.[23] The villages furthest away from regional distribution centres suffered the most from lack of input supply and favoured access was common.[24] Farmers used whatever inputs they could get hold of regardless of whether or not they fulfilled the recommended specifications.[25]

In the more northern parts of the country, different circumstances prevailed. Commercialized peasant agriculture had been established for a longer time. Cotton and coffee production registered a dramatic decline and food production probably increased, but official marketing statistics do not provide evidence of the latter (Table IV.1). The proximity of the Kenyan border and the huge food deficit area of Sukumaland and the cities of Mwanza, Arusha and Moshi led commentators to conclude that a fairly large parallel market in staple foodstuffs, notably maize, was operating.[26]

The government's fertilizer and improved input supply coverage was

21. Rasmussen's 1980/81 study of six villages in Iringa and Njombe districts found 90% of the farmers using biochemical inputs. Annual cropped land planted to maize rose from 32% in 1973 to 74% in 1979/80 (Rasmussen, T., 'Commercialised Maize Production among Smallholders in the Southern Highland, Tanzania', Centre for Development Research Project Paper 86.3, Copenhagen (February 1986) 8–9); Mgeni, B.C., 'Diffusion of an Agricultural Innovation: Hybrid Maize in Njombe District', M.A. Thesis, University of Dar es Salaam (1978).
22. These four regions received 59% of all distributed fertilizer between 1978 and 1980 (Moore and Stutley, 'Smallholder Food Production', xi).
23. *Daily News*: 'TFC rushes fertiliser to regions', 10/8/79; 'Order seeds in time, regions told', 25/7/80; 'TFC hits snags', 17/4/81; 'More fertiliser reaches Songea', 28/1/84; 'Peasants struggle for fertilizer', 16/2/84; 'Tanseed to meet Iringa demand', 14/5/84.
24. Rasmussen, T., 'The Green Revolution in the Southern Highlands of Tanzania', Centre for Development Research Project Paper A85.7, Copenhagen (1985), 15.
25. Friis-Hansen, 'An Assessment', 125.
26. Moore and Stutley, 'Smallholder Food Production', 20; Schneider-Barthold, W., 'Farmers' Reactions to the Present Economic Situation in Tanzania with Respect to Production and Marketing', German Development Institute, Berlin (June 1983), 18.

inadequate. Recommended modern farming practices were relatively out of reach. The nucleated village settlements were experiencing an acute land-use crisis, for continuous cropping of the same fields depleted the soil fertility, which would have previously been remedied by shifting agricultural practices. Kjaerby argues that peasants resorted to agricultural intensification, notably the widespread adoption of ox-cultivation, manuring, maize mono-cropping and labour and land-intensive forms of animal stockfeeding.[27] Increased yields were not likely under the circumstances. Positive effects of government agricultural development attempts were not in evidence. Kjaerby was led to hypothesize that: 'It tends to be the pressure of crisis which does the trick of intensification (unless the pressure is too overwhelming as in the Sahel), rather than the accidental or government/aid-induced peasant option towards a more "rational" economic opportunity.'[28]

2. State Order and Market Disorder: The National Milling Corporation

The disbandment of the National Agricultural Products Board and elevation of the National Milling Corporation (NMC) from an urban-based state milling complex to a single channel state marketing agent for staple foodstuffs arose out of the state's continuing preoccupation with achieving food security and ensuring stable producer and consumer prices. The immediate intention of the policy was to eliminate wide marketing margins by removing the involvement of inefficient agencies. Through the introduction of a pan-territorial producer pricing policy and the directive that the NMC could bypass inefficient cooperative unions and purchase directly from the cooperative societies,[29] it was felt that the marketing chain would be simplified. Working backward from milling, the NMC's activities would cover the NAPB's former sphere of control as well as that of the cooperative unions. Market rationalization was pursued through the principle of single channel marketing.

The pivotal importance of into- and ex-store pricing under the NAPB was replaced with a far more ambitious price-setting arrangement. Pan-territorial producer prices, cooperative society and union margins were all

27. It should be noted that the government became concerned about the detrimental consequences of over-dependence on fertilizers in the early 1980s and started promoting ox-cultivation and leguminous fallow crops, especially 'marejea' (*Crotalaria*) which could be used as animal fodder and soil fertilizer (*Daily News:* 'Crotalaria: Cheap fertilizer for peasants', 10/4/80; 'Encourage compost manure – PM', 28/2/81; 'Nyerere opens Agro-Conference: Africa urged to use local resources', 14/2/84).

28. Kjaerby, 'Scratching', 11.

29. Tanzania, MDB, 'A Strategic Grain Reserve Programme for Tanzania', II, Dar es Salaam (November 1974), 31.

fixed. The cooperatives, in effect, became the mere executing agents of NMC parastatal marketing.

Without cooperative autonomy in price determination, it was thought that cooperative clientage practices and financial leaks at the local level could be kept in check. National government and party leadership were of the opinion that, at this time of intensified development effort, it was necessary to eliminate the many cooperative middlemen whose localized interests were an impediment to national development. Since independence, the cooperatives' significance to the national economy was seen in terms of Africanizing the market, providing a rich source for government taxation and serving as a structure for achieving government crop production targets. With respect to the former, the cooperatives had outlived their purpose; Asian market competition had been supplanted by African state regulated produce trade. As regards government taxation, the national leadership felt that the inefficiencies, peculation and bloated margins of the cooperatives thwarted their utility. Furthermore, cooperatives were seen to be bungling the provision of food marketing services and, since staple foods were strategic commodities, this could not be tolerated. Their days were numbered. Villagization had made it possible for the government and party to focus on the newly installed village leadership, using the village rather than the cooperative society as the primary unit for peasant mobilization.

The NMC quickly grew into the largest government marketing parastatal, absorbing the NAPB and many former cooperative staff. By 1978, personnel numbered 4200, a third of these based in Dar es Salaam. Apart from the management at the top, the staff was mostly uneducated and poorly trained. The majority had obtained their positions through long service in the NAPB or cooperatives, rather than through formal schooling.[30]

Operationally, many of the NMC's policies and procedures were characterized by bureaucratic expediency rather than tried and tested ways of managing food marketing, pan-territorial pricing being the prime example of this. Similarly, produce grading tended to be forsaken, with adverse consequences for product quality, consumer choice and likelihood of impurities and insect infestation in storage.[31]

At the outset, the NMC faced a number of obstacles. It was under-capitalized and, in taking over from the NAPB, had inherited its large bank overdraft. The transfer of responsibility took place just before drought caused nationwide food shortages. Before the NMC had time to assess its position,

---

30. 82 per cent of the staff had no formal training (Tanzania, MDB, 'Report on Investigation into the Financial and Operating Position of Kilimo Crop Authorities: NMC', DSM (1979), 10, 79.
31. Canadian International Development Agency (CIDA), *Report of the Wheat Sector Study Team Tanzania 1977*, Manitoba Pool Elevators (1977), 142–145.

it was being called upon to distribute famine relief in the rural areas.

Meanwhile, food demand in the towns grew very rapidly as urban migration accelerated. Trying to satisfy urban food demand, specifically that of the capital, Dar es Salaam, became the NMC's major focus as the years unfolded (Tables IV.1 and IV.2).[32] To do this, grain importation increased significantly (Tables IV.3).

After the completion of the villagization operations and the passage of the 1975 Village Act, the party's National Executive Committee unilaterally abolished local cooperative societies in May 1976. The NMC's staple food procurement had to be pursued directly with village governments. This represented another step towards 'simplifying' the marketing chain, while at the same time producing a gigantic, unwieldy set of operations for the NMC headquartered in Dar es Salaam. From village to central mill, the NMC had control. Distribution at wholesale level was in the hands of the government's Regional Trading Companies up-country, whereas in Dar es Salaam the National Distributors Ltd., another parastatal, served in that capacity. The only role for private traders in staple food marketing was at the retail level.

As a strategic parastatal in charge of national food security, the NMC's policies were largely a result of external government decision-making. Frequently, the NMC's assigned tasks and procedures did not match its actual operational capabilities. This predicament will be analysed in relation to village produce buying, pan-territorial procurement, pricing and transport, food relief, urban food shortages, parallel food markets and NMC staff and financial performance.

2.1 Village Produce Buying

The NMC's produce buying at village level had serious shortcomings. First of all, under the 1975 Village Act, registered villages functioned as multi-purpose cooperatives. Dealing with village governments rather than the erstwhile cooperative societies meant that the NMC had far more buying points to cover. Villages numbered 7768 by 1978, whereas each marketing cooperative society had represented a larger area encompassing two to four villages.

Unlike the other crop parastatals, the NMC was instructed to make advance payments to the village governments for its purchase of staple food crops. The intent was to counter the farmers' bitter experience of the co-operatives' late payments and to discourage farmers from selling foodstuffs

---

32. Contributing to this tendency was the fact that the Regional Trading Companies distributed grain in the regions. Because they received little or no extra remuneration for sale of grain in the rural areas, the bulk of regional supplies, an estimated 80% was sold in the regional towns (Keeler, A. *et al.*, *The Consumption Effects of Agricultural Policies in Tanzania*, Sigma One Corporation, USAID (1982), 73.

in the parallel market. But to work effectively an advance payment system required judicious estimates of marketed crops as well as detailed accounting of issued payments. Village governments were paid 9 cents/kg. for their role as NMC buying agents, but their execution of the task was seriously flawed. With a dire shortage of accounting expertise, documentary evidence of crop purchases and money disbursements tended to be fragmentary, if not misleading. For example, at the end of the 1978/79 buying season, village cash advances worth TSh. 110.2 million were still outstanding.

The vast majority of villages did not have bank accounts. Payments had to be made in cash, making theft and the more casual leakage of funds very common. Financial loss through mismanagement and theft occurred at various points. NMC personnel absconded with funds,[33] village officials siphoned funds[34] and robberies *en route* from NMC regional headquarters to village buying posts by thieves necessitated police escorts in many areas, thereby raising marketing costs.[35] In 1978, the amount reported stolen from village cash advances was TSh. 2 million.

In the years immediately following the 1976 dissolution of the co-operatives, the NMC seemed to be succeeding in providing payment on delivery and keeping the parallel grain market in maize at bay with record level purchases arising from abundant harvests (Table IV.1).[36] However, this situation altered very suddenly when the Ugandan war erupted. During the 1979/80 buying season, government and private transport was commandeered, which seriously impaired the NMC's ability to collect produce. Meanwhile, the second oil shock caused a deterioration in Tanzania's balance of payments. Shortages of essential consumer goods such as soap, cooking oil and batteries, let alone more expensive items like cement, corrugated iron roofing and bicycles, became so severe that peasants' crop sales lacked follow-up incentives. It was in this vacuum that a parallel market in staple foodstuffs, notably for maize, started coalescing on a scale significant enough to become a problem for the NMC's purchasing operations.[37]

2.2 Pan-territorial Procurement, Pricing and Transport

The NMC was obliged to buy all staple food crops offered to it throughout the country at set pan-territorial prices. This policy was one of the most financially draining imposed on it.

33. *Daily News:* 'NMC man on theft charges', 23/12/78; 'Morogoro', 15/8/81; 'NMC funds diverted?', 8/2/82.
34. *Daily News*: 'Crop purchases: Better system planned', 30/6/79; 'Party team probes NMC', 2/10/79; 'Dodoma', 11/9/79.
35. Tanzania, MDB, 'Review of Crop Buying Arrangements 1976/77', DSM (February 1977), 4.
36. Tanzania, MDB, 'Crop Buying Arrangements', 1.
37. *Daily News*: 'Mbeya middlemen deprive NMC of rice', 30/10/79; 'Middlemen cheat peasants', 31/5/80; 'Middlemen cash in on NMC vacuum', 16/10/80.

Transport had always been difficult in Tanzania, but was particularly so during the 1970s. Over the decade transport infrastructural investment and maintenance declined as a result of decentralization budgeting and the economic crisis. Although rail was the cheapest mode of transport over long distances, serious mismanagement, technical problems, lack of spare parts and the breakup of the East African Railways and Harbour Corporation impeded a smooth flow of traffic, halving the traffic load of agricultural commodities between 1974 and 1978. Only 25 per cent of the grain crop tonnage offered to the Tanzania Railways Corporation was actually moved.[38] The rail line between Dar es Salaam and Kigoma was antiquated, limiting traffic and causing frequent derailments, whereas the TAZARA railroad was new, but suffered from lack of trained staff and under-utilization. Designed for a capacity of 2.0 million tons per year, its peak load was only 1.3 million tons in 1978, declining to 0.9 million tons in 1979.

The majority of food crops were transported by road. The trunk and feeder roads were subject to deterioration by overloaded lorries. Potholes often reached gigantic proportions before adequate funds and road works personnel could be mustered for their repair. The poor state of the roads led to increased wear and tear on vehicles, whereas the availability of spare parts and tyres seriously declined. These factors, in addition to the growing prevalence of petrol rationing, kept demand for road haulage of crops in excess of supply.

In 1975, the country's lorry fleet totalled about 13,000 vehicles, of which 3000 were publicly owned. Mismanagement of the publicly-owned lorry firms exacerbated the road transport problem. UMITA, the national road haulage corporation, folded in April 1977. Teeteko, a cooperative union transport firm operating in the southern regions, went bankrupt in 1980.[39] Although the NMC had a lorry fleet of about 200, an estimated 25 per cent of it was grounded at any one time. With insufficient NMC vehicles, especially at the peak of the buying season, the haulage of most procured food crops was done by hired private transport, the rates of which varied widely depending on road conditions, vehicle type and capacity, outward versus return load, and the local availability of fuel and spare parts. Between 1969 and 1979 road haulage rates increased by 150 per cent on average, reflecting the effects of the oil crisis and inflation.[40]

Food crops, as low-value bulky commodities, were extremely sensitive to transport costs. The NMC's transport difficulties were more extreme than those of most other crop parastatals. It was transporting the bulk of

---

38. Only 10% in the case of maize (Tanzania, MDB, 'The Inter-regional Transport of Major Agricultural Commodities in Tanzania', R5/79, DSM (1979), 22–24.

39. *Daily News:* 'UMITA a lesson: Plan to improve road links', 10/4/77; 'TEETEKO closes business', 30/1/80.

40. Tanzania, MDB, 'Inter-regional Transport', 32–43.

its tonnage to the coast, notably Dar es Salaam, the major centre of food demand, but food crops were grown everywhere and the pan-territorial pricing system served to encourage the geographical specialization of marketed food production in an inversion of von Thunen's concentric rings. The most distant areas, namely Ruvuma, Rukwa and Mbeya, were producing the greatest amounts of marketed food crops. In 1978/79 the overall weighted average cost of transporting maize between the NMC's regional godown and the central mill was estimated at TSh. 211 per ton, approximately 12 per cent of the *sembe* [41] retail price. But Ruvuma and Rukwa's transport costs were TSh. 650 and 470 respectively. [42] These regions accounted for only 12 per cent of the NMC's maize purchase in 1978/79, but by 1982/83 they were 52 per cent of the total (Table IV.1).

Criticism of the expense of the pan-territorial pricing policy and the evocation of the principle of comparative advantage led the government to revise the policy but not in the direction that economists hoped for. [43] Higher prices were set for the regions most climatically suited to maize production which included the 'Big Four' regions in the extreme southern part of the country.

The NMC's pricing policy, like that of the NAPB, was externally-determined. The Cabinet's Economic Committee was free to overlook the well-researched price recommendations of the Ministry of Agriculture's Marketing Development Bureau and set prices according to its perception of 'fair' incentive prices for producers and 'just' prices for the fulfilment of the consumers' basic staple food needs. The economic feasibility of the resulting squeezed marketing margins, within which the NMC was bound to operate, was not the main concern of the political decision-makers.

The food crisis spurred the government into raising peasant producer prices for food out of their hitherto stagnant level (Table IV.4). Prices for the famine-reserve crops (cassava, millet and sorghum) were increased on a par with the preferred cereals, maize, rice and wheat. The latter had an assured urban market, whereas the former ended up as surplus stocks, for which the NMC found it difficult to find adequate storage and which it eventually had to export at a considerable financial loss. [44] The increase in food prices succeeded in bringing about a notable supply response in food crops, but probably had the additional unintended effect of contributing

41. Translated 'maize meal'.
42. Tanzania, 'Inter-regional Transport', Appendix 14, 49.
43. Ndulu, B., 'The Impact of Inter-regional Transport Subsidy Policy on Commercial Supply of Food Grains in Tanzania: The Case of Paddy and Maize', Economics Research Bureau Seminar Paper, University of Dar es Salaam (November 1979); Tanzania, MDB, 'An Analysis of Regional and Seasonal Price Options for Maize in Tanzania', DSM (November 1980).
44. Tanzania, MDB, 'Agricultural Price Policy Review', Dar es Salaam (1979), 43.

to the reduction in peasant export crop production, since the relative prices for export crops declined.[45]

The combination of the staple food producer price rise, the transport subsidy and the existing over-valued Tanzanian currency exchange rate led the costs of the NMC's domestically procured maize, rice and wheat to supersede import parity as well as export parity.[46] It was considerably cheaper for the NMC to purchase imported maize shipped to Dar es Salaam, the main centre of demand, than to purchase and transport domestic maize.[47] The fact that the NMC got supplies on concessional aid terms reinforced the cost difference.

Consumer pricing policy revolved around the objective of ensuring the basic nutritional needs of urban, low-income earners at affordable prices. In effect, the *sembe* price was subsumed under the government's minimum wage policy.[48] Between 1975 and 1983, the minimum wage rose by less than 60 per cent while the cost of living increased by 300 per cent (Tables II.7 and 8). The price of *sembe* was kept extremely low as a compensating measure. Until 1984, the price of *sembe* in relation to the minimum wage was such that a day's wage purchasing power measured in kilograms of *sembe* never slipped below 7 kg. Thus, no more than three months' wages were required to buy sufficient maize supplies for a year for an average household of two adults and three children.[49] In 1985, purchasing power of the minimum wage declined to 3.4 kg./day and, in 1986, to 2.0 kg./day.

The low price for *sembe* forced the official NMC marketing margin for maize to become extremely compressed and artificial. Maize marketing margins between producer and *sembe* consumer price were: 309 per cent from 1964/65 through 1972/73, 110 per cent between 1973 and 1980 and a mere 37 per cent between 1980 and 1984.[50] The *sembe* subsidy, i.e. the difference between the NMC's actual margin and the official margin, contributed a major share of the NMC's spiralling bank overdraft. By 1984, the overdraft had reached crippling dimensions. The government, under pressure from the IMF, raised the price of *sembe* by 320 per cent, which largely removed the subsidy (Table IV.5). Not surprisingly, the

45. Ellis, F., 'Agricultural Marketing and Peasant–State Transfers in Tanzania', *Journal of Peasant Studies* 10(4) (1983), 225.

46. Tanzania, MDB, 'Proposals for Staple Food Prices under the Structural Adjustment Programme', DSM (1983), 8; Tanzania, MDB, 'Price Policy Reviews' (1980), 46 and (1977), ii.

47. For example, in 1982/83, imports were 30% cheaper than local maize (Kaberuka, D., 'Evaluating the Performance of Food Marketing Parastatals', *Development Policy Review* 2 (1984).

48. Bryceson, D.F., 'Food and Urban Purchasing Power', *African Affairs*, 84 (337) (1985), 518.

49. Assumes the FAO standard for a starch-based diet: 180 kg. grain consumed per annum per adult. Children are assumed to be consuming 90 kg.

50. Bryceson, D.F., *Food Insecurity and the Social Division of Labour in Tanzania* (London, Macmillan, 1990).

minimum wage was raised at the same time, but by only a token 35 per cent (Table II.7). Dar es Salaam, the major centre of consumption, won the special concession of having its *sembe* price raised only to TSh. 6/60 rather than TSh. 8/00 per kg. on the grounds that Dar es Salaam relied on imports that were cheaper than up-country supplies.[51]

The post-1973 official grain mark-ups of rice and wheat dropped only slightly below their pre-1973 level, quite unlike the much smaller mark-up for *sembe*, which, of course, was decreed by policy, hiding the much larger margin with which the NMC actually operated (Table IV.6). Thus, to the extent that *sembe* supplies actually met demand, the *sembe* subsidy succeeded in ensuring basic food adequacy for lower income groups in urban areas, disregarding the costs. Furthermore, through its pricing policy, the government managed to tip consumer demand more towards maize which was a cheaper staple and less import-reliant than wheat and rice.[52]

2.3 Food Relief

Emergency food distribution was an additional source of financial loss. The NMC was continuously on call to provide famine relief wherever the Prime Minister's Office requested. Rural food shortages were widespread between 1974 and 1976. The NMC's famine relief was carried out in a fairly *ad hoc,* 'we'll manage somehow' manner. Impromptu decision-making and lack of attention to accounting paperwork led to insufficient documentary proof of deliveries. As a result, the NMC was underpaid despite the government's previous promise of full reimbursement. Likewise, at the time of the Ugandan war, the NMC had to provide the army with its staple food requirements, with the promise of later payment, which had not yet materialized as late as 1982.[53]

2.4 Urban Food Shortages

Market demand for food was concentrated in the urban areas, particularly Dar es Salaam. Urban growth was proceeding at the rate of over 10 per cent a year. The NMC could not keep up with the demand and urban food shortages became more frequent. It directed its efforts towards keeping maize in adequate supply so that *sembe* shortages were less frequent than those of rice and especially of wheat.

In the face of a growing discrepancy between supply and demand, the NMC sales became increasingly focused on Dar es Salaam. In the mid-1970s, Dar es Salaam accounted for a third of all NMC sales. Ten years

51. Tanzania, MDB, 'Price Policy Review', I, DSM (1984), 28.
52. Wheat consumption fell when the government abruptly raised the price of flour in November 1973 (CIDA, *Report,* 129).
53. Tibenderana, H.K., 'The Factors affecting Tanzania's National Milling Corporation's Performance (1968–1981)', M.A. thesis, University of Dar es Salaam (1982).

later, the amount was more than half, which was disproportionately greater than the percentage of the total national urban population Dar es Salaam represented. In comparison, the second and third largest towns, Mwanza and Tanga, representing 6.7 per cent and 6.2 per cent of the urban population, accounted for only 2.8 per cent and 2.5 per cent of NMC's total maize sales in 1983/84. The same pattern pertained to NMC rice and wheat sales. Insufficiency of supply to Dar es Salaam harboured a greater threat to political stability.[54] By 1984, however, NMC distribution was falling far short of Dar es Salaam requirements as well. In this context, Nyerere appealed to Dar es Salaam regional government authorities to bypass the NMC and 'shoulder the responsibility of feeding the city themselves and look for supplies from producer regions in the country.'[55]

In 1983, urban food shortages were especially acute, prompting the government to introduce a party-supervised rationing system in Dar es Salaam. Ward party secretaries were put in charge of collecting staple foodstuffs from the National Distributors Ltd for their areas which were then allocated to local retailers according to the size of the population each retailer served. Households were issued with ration cards that entitled them to 0.5 kg. of staple grain per capita per day. Initially, the system was hailed as a great improvement. However, over time people got more and more disillusioned with the retailers who were not adhering to the system and the ward party secretaries who were not bothering to supervise it properly.[56]

2.5 Parallel Markets

Maize, rice, wheat, cassava, millet, sorghum and beans were scheduled for control under the NMC Act of 1975. The Act stipulated that a private individual's sale of these crops could not exceed 30 kilograms. The transport of grain by individuals for household use was restricted to 100 kg., though this amount was subject to variation and revision by regional authorities' orders. Penalties for breaking the law included a fine of TSh. 5000, imprisonment of up to one year and seizure of the grain.[57] Despite these deterrents, unofficial parallel marketing sprang up and intensified in various places as staple food shortages spread. On the parallel market dried maize sold at roughly twice the price of controlled *sembe* and rice was two and half times more expensive than NMC rice on average in

54. With regard to NMC supplies to urban areas, Nyerere admitted in a nationwide speech that 'Sugar and sembe ... bothered him most especially in DSM which was very different from places like Musoma. The shortage of the two items in DSM caused quite a stir...' (*Daily News:* 'Mwalimu on food situation: no need to panic', 16/12/79).
55. *Daily News:* 'Mwalimu tells Dar: Get down to business', 19/4/84; 'NDL explains food shortage', 25/4/85.
56. *Daily News:* 'Dar distribution snags explained', 12/6/84; 'Check food leakages – Machunda', 10/2/84; 'Distribution is the problem', 16/1/84.
57. Keeler, A., 'A Preliminary Report on the Parallel Market for Grains in Tanzania', MDB, Dar es Salaam (March 1983), 1.

1983 and 1984.[58] Keeler reported parallel market prices for maize in the Lake Region which were 303 per cent greater than the official price in 1979–81 and 101 per cent greater for rice.[59] Virtually no parallel market produce price data existed until 1986, so it is impossible to compare official and unofficial margins. A more detailed discussion of the nature of the parallel markets follows in the next chapter. It suffices here to point out that there was a growing incidence of parallel marketing, particularly in maize, from 1979 onwards. The NMC's acute transport problems during the Ugandan war led to crops in many areas not being procured in time.[60] Thereafter, NMC buying performance did not improve and economic conditions and harvests were never conducive to farmers willingly returning to selling their crops to the NMC if parallel market outlets were at hand.[61] Kilimanjaro and Arusha were most notable in this respect. Between 1978/79 and 1981/82, their NMC maize sales as a proportion of total sales dropped from 38 to 4 per cent (Table IV.1). The NMC's maize procurement more than halved. The 'Big Four' regions assumed the lead as NMC suppliers at that time.

2.6 Staff Performance and Financial Deficit

As everywhere else in Tanzania, NMC staff pay packets were subjected to the assaulting force of inflation. This tended to create apathy on the part of staff and management, who were frequently engaged in other productive activities outside their salaried employment.[62] In some cases these circumstances led to corruption. NMC staff, after all, were strategically placed with their control over highly valued food commodities and large sums of money. Commodity distribution and financial irregularities were not uncommon.[63]

The NMC and other crop parastatals were criticized for having over-

58. The proportion by which parallel market prices exceeded the controlled price for rice ranged between 21% and 268% in 1983 and 45% and 281% in 1984. Parallel market dried maize exceeded the *sembe* price by a wider spread of 0% to 344% in 1983 and −36% to 191% in 1984 after the removal of the *sembe* subsidy (Tanzania, MDB, 'Monthly Marketing Bulletin', December 1982–December 1984).
59. Keeler *et al.*, *Consumption Effects*, 81.
60. *Daily News*: 'Bid to save Tabora crop', 7/9/79; Campaign to save crops', 2/10/79; 'Storage, transport hamper NMC operations', 14/12/79; 'Buy crops fast – call', 27/7/80.
61. *Daily News*: 'Tons of maize get spoilt', 6/9/81; 'Pay now, NMC told', 10/3/81; 'Pay peasant promptly', 6/6/81; 'Mbeya NMC blames villages', 16/11/81; 'Shinyanga plans food transport', 18/1/84.
62. The Marketing Development Investigating Team found: 'Currently if a staff member does not do what is asked of him, i.e. figures requested are not submitted, no action seems to be taken. The system grinds to a halt' (Tanzania, MDB, 'Financial and Operating Position', 11).
63. For example, in 1977/78, stock losses were estimated at 16.8% (TSh. 148.6 million); 7.5% due to deterioration and 9.3% from stock disappearance (Tanzania, MDB, 'Financial and Operating Position', 27, 32). A comparable figure under grain storage management was 1.7% loss *en route* from source of supply to retailer and 0.4% loss due to insect infestation (Acting Director of Grain Storage, 31/1/51, TNA SMP 35181).

centralized management, which, it was argued, had created innumerable difficulties with respect to transport, stock monitoring and coordination of purchasing activities, as well as resulting in a lack of staff supervision and increased opportunities for corruption.[64] It is impossible to ascertain whether or not peculation and inefficiency were greater under single channel marketing than under cooperative buying, for, without proper accounts, the NMC's actual operational costs cannot be known. None the less, Ellis, on the basis of existing figures, calculated that in 1970–1972 producers received 45 per cent of crop sales value at cost and 38 per cent in 1978–80.[65] Ellis attributes the decline to the NMC's lack of financial supervision, its bureaucratization and increased fixed overheads. Late produce buying, haphazard storage of crops, inadequate maintenance and frequent breakdown of mills characterized the NMC's operations.

The net result of the NMC's operational difficulties and the government-imposed welfare-oriented polices was a spiralling bank overdraft. In 1973/74, the overdraft stood at TSh. 286.5 million, rising to TSh. 524 million in 1976 and an astronomical TSh 2,300 million in 1981, heading the league of parastatal overdrafts.[66] The NMC's accounts were in complete financial disarray.[67] It was obvious that its actual marketing costs vastly exceeded the margins delimited by government price controls, but no one could give precise figures. Audited accounts were in arrears by several years. Besides the usual problem of insufficiently trained accounting staff, the NMC had had to decentralize its accounting system to branch level, which led to even less supervision and uniformity in accounts.

In the five years between 1978/79 and 1983/84, the NMC was reported to have received TSh. 10,600 million out of a total TSh. 12,000 million in subsidies allocated to agricultural parastatals.[68] Increasingly over the 1980s government policy was directed at reducing parastatal costs and staffing. The NMC responded by cutting down on hired vehicles and laying off 687 workers.[69] It was recognized, however, that economizing reforms were not enough; major structural changes had to take place.

3. Revival or Survival: Cooperatives/National Milling Corporation Tandem Buying

In 1981, a government investigating committee suggested that the NMC

64. Keeler, A., *et al. Consumption Effects*, 35.
65. It should be noted that the comparable figures for export crops were 67% and 43% (Ellis, 'Agricultural Marketing', 222–225).
66. Coopers and Lybrand Assoc. Ltd., *Grain Storage and Milling Project*, DSM (1977).
67. *Daily News*: 'NMC accounts books "in mess"', 26/5/84.
68. *Daily News*: 'Crop bodies got 12bn/– subsidy', 29/10/84.
69. *Daily News*: 'NMC cuts down costs', 5/3/84; 'NMC lays off 687 workers', 19/1/85; 'Well done NMC', 20/1/85.

be decentralized. The task force of high-level Tanzanian professionals appointed to look into the viability of this proposal, rejected it, fearing that decentralization would engender an expansion of staff and bureaucracy.[70] Instead they supported an alternative line of thinking which involved reinstating marketing cooperatives to handle regional produce buying. The Cooperative Bill, which was passed in parliament in 1982, was intended to be implemented gradually as cooperative unions and societies were slowly re-established. Primary produce buying would be handed over to the cooperatives, leaving the NMC to deal with bulk buying from the cooperative unions, milling, monitoring of the national food supply situation, managing a strategic grain reserve and, when the need arose, provisioning famine relief.

3.1 Reinstating Cooperative Marketing

The decision to reinstate cooperatives was not as sudden is it appeared to be. Banished, as a blot on the countryside, in 1976, the cooperative movement had not entirely disappeared. Its three-tier structure had been left partially intact. The cooperative unions and societies were disbanded, leaving the apex organization, the Cooperative Union of Tanzania (CUT), with little *raison d'être* other than to oversee a sprinkling of wholesale and retail establishments that were under the aegis of the cooperative movement.[71] The party, ever vigilant to extend its influence, stepped in. In 1978, CUT was made a party-affiliated organization called WASHIRIKA.[72]

As NMC marketing operations floundered, there was mounting popular pressure, supported by the party, for the government to do something. Ironically, the party's NEC, which had abolished cooperatives in 1976, took the initiative a mere four years later in deciding that they must be reinstated. In October 1980, the government appointed a 22-man commission to look into how the cooperative unions should be revived. The former secretary general of the CUT was appointed the committee's chairman along with 12 other members who had been former cooperative officials.[73] In June 1981, the prime minister announced to parliament that the government had accepted the committee's report. In the months that followed both the government and party were involved in planning the mechanics of reintroducing the cooperatives. A detailed study by van Cranenburgh reveals that veiled disagreement broke out between those stressing the importance of the cooperatives' economic viability, notably civil servants and former cooperative leaders, versus those who favoured

70. *Daily News*: 'NMC task force meets on Tuesday', 25/7/81.
71. For example, the National Distributors Ltd, the main Dar es Salaam wholesale agent for grain, was owned by the Cooperative Union of Tanganyika and the National Milling Corporation.
72. Translated 'cooperative members'.
73. *Daily News*: 'Cooperatives revival', 23/10/80.

using the cooperatives to further the party's objectives of socialist village development.[74] The legislation resulting from their deliberations represented a compromise between the two lines and contained many ambiguities.

Meanwhile, the 1982 National Agricultural Policy drafted by Simon Mbilinyi, the then principal secretary of the Ministry of Agriculture, lent further weight to the reinstatement of cooperatives in its criticism of the over-centralization of marketing parastatals. This document suggested the promotion of inter-regional trade in food commodities to relieve NMC distribution constraints.[75]

Thus, with the forces of party and government behind it, the Cooperative Bill was passed by parliament in May 1982. In the same session of parliament, a number of other bills were passed which amounted to startling revisions of the rural organizational framework that had been shaped during the 1970s. Surprisingly these bills did not seem to attract much public attention. The 1975 Village Act, the cornerstone of Tanzania's villagization policy, was unanimously repealed and in its place a bill for a local government system, reminiscent of what had prevailed in the 1960s, was passed.[76] Adjoining legislation, which empowered local governments to raise levies and devise by-laws for the enforcement of levy payment, sparked heated debate, but was eventually passed.[77] All of this legislation had a common theme, namely, the central government's willingness to transfer responsibility for service provisioning to local governments and cooperatives, thereby relieving the parastatals and central ministries of tasks that they could no longer operationally or financially maintain.

The decision to reinstate the cooperatives appears to be a case of convergence of interests of party activists and government technocrats. The party activists were always on the look-out for a chance to engage in institution-building, or in this case institution restoration, as a means of generating populist sentiment in their favour. The decline in the NMC's marketing services, which was a source of peasant dissatisfaction, was a predicament begging party intervention. Government technocrats, on the other hand, were responding to the economic crisis. Groping for a solution to spiralling marketing costs, cooperatives were the only possibility at hand that rang true to national development objectives.

In this delicate balance between party zeal and technocratic stabilization, the compromise was tenuous. A legislative amendment in 1985 made cooperative membership voluntary, pleasing old school cooperativists. However, the subsequent issuing of Party Guidelines on the Cooperatives

74. van Cranenburgh, O., *The Widening Gyre: The Tanzanian One-Party State and Policy towards Rural Cooperatives* (Delft, Holland, Eburon, 1990).
75. Tanzania, Ministry of Agriculture, 'Tanzania: National Food Strategy', Second draft (June 1982).
76. *Daily News*: 'Village Act to be repealed', 28/4/82; Mongella tables councils bill', 30/4/82; 'Civil Service bill passed', 3/5/82.
77. *Daily News*: 'MPs criticize Finance Bill', 30/4/82; 'House passes Finance Bill', 1/5/82.

chose to define voluntary as 'belief in producer cooperatives and *ujamaa* and self-reliance', from which few Tanzanians would dare to disassociate themselves publicly.[78] Contrary to the original legislation, which stipulated that primary cooperative societies would be formed from two or more villages, these guidelines backed the principle that each village should be constituted as a cooperative. From the perspective of viable produce marketing, there were few individual villages with enough marketed produce to achieve economies of scale in cooperative marketing. Furthermore, the 1987 CCM Party Ordinary General Conference ruling that primary societies should be multi-purpose and serve as centres of cooperative production in accordance with the *ujamaa* tradition diluted the organizational effort given to marketing still further. Thus the conflict between party rulings and the cooperative legislation left the criteria for establishing cooperatives open to wide interpretation. In fact, regional cooperative officials tended to ignore the 'supremacy' of the party decision and opt for multi-village societies with greater economic viability.[79]

Slowly, the cooperative unions were re-established. At the end of 1986, there were 24 regional[80] cooperative unions and 2048 primary cooperative societies. In the two years that followed only one more cooperative union was formed but the total number of primary societies mushroomed to 6537.[81] Originally, the cooperatives were placed back under their previous parent ministry, the Prime Minister's Office, which had for so long been the ministry most responsive to party calls for rural mobilization, notably villagization. However, with the implementation of the Local Government Act, a new Ministry of Local Government and Development of Cooperatives was formed.

In 1988, the crop marketing boards, except for the National Milling Corporation, were handed from the Ministry of Agriculture to the Ministry of Local Government as a means of consolidating the cooperatives' relationship with the marketing boards. In the past, when a technical service was placed in a non-technical rural development ministry, the provisioning of the technical service tended to deteriorate through a decline in technical expertise.[82] The fact that the National Milling Corporation was not included in the transfer to Ministry of Local Government

---

78. CCM 1985, '*Ushirika wa Uzakshaji Mali*', Party Directive, unofficial translation by S. Makilla, University of Dar es Salaam, quoted in van Cranenburgh, *Widening Gyre*, 170.
79. Van Cranenburgh, *Widening Gyre*, 176.
80. It should be noted that in some cases there was more than one regional cooperative in a government region: for example, Iringa region had the Iringa Regional Cooperative Union and NJOLUMA.
81. *Sunday News*: 'PM urges education for co-op members', 18/9/88.
82. The prime example of this occurred when, under the decentralization and villagization policies, agricultural extension agents were placed under the Prime Minister's Office rather than the Ministry of Agriculture. In so doing, extension services were severed from research, thereby undermining the quality of extension advice to farmers.

could be read as an indication of the importance the government continued to attach to the NMC's operations. The NMC was still critical to government food security planning and it therefore remained in the Ministry of Agriculture, where it was more accessible to the government's economic planners than to the party activists.

3.2. Operational Difficulties

Cooperative buying began in 1985/86. At their launching, the cooperative unions were endowed with many of the NMC's regional assets and avoided having to assume any of its liabilities. The marketing chain resembled what had prevailed under the NAPB (Figure III.3). The cooperative union, through its primary societies, purchased produce which was then, in the case of the staple foodcrops, sold to the National Milling Corporation, at a fixed into-store price. The into-store price varied from region to region, being set after the cooperative union had submitted its costs estimates and the ensuing tug-of-war between the NMC and the cooperative union over shares in the overall marketing margin was resolved.[83] Frequently, the into-store price was set at a level that the cooperatives knew would incur a deficit for them.[84]

83. For example, Iringa Cooperative Union's costings for a kg. of maize were as follows (note society/union's maize mark-up is in brackets):

	TSh.
Producer price	8.200
Society Levy	.380
Union Levy	.650
Transport	1.050
Bags & Twine	1.020
Cash Insurance	.025
Handling	.050
Fumigation	.030
Crop Insurance	.043
Shrinkage	.229
Interest	1.343
Local Authority	.200
Stamp Duty	.060
Cooperative Society & Union Costs	5.079 (62%)
Total Union Costs	13.279
vs. Official Into-Store Price	11.279 (38%)

Source: Tanzania, MDB, 'Annual Review of Maize, Rice and Wheat 1987', DSM (1987), 64.

84. For example, in 1987/88, NJOLUMA, a relatively efficient cooperative union in Iringa, asked for an into-store price of TSh. 13.78/kg., which, with a set producer price of TSh. 8.20, afforded a margin of TSh. 5.58. They were granted an into-store price of TSh. 12.31, which gave them a 33% margin, rather than the requested 40%. With this margin they expected a deficit. The previous year with a 35% margin they had managed to break even, whereas during the first year of operation they had had a deficit of TSh. 124 million (Airey, T., D.F. Bryceson and J. Howe, 'Interim Evaluation of the Songea–Makambako Road', Report submitted to the Ministry of Communications and Works under assignment by the Overseas Development Administration, London (July 1989), 50).

From the time of their re-establishment, the cooperative unions were plagued with operational problems. A shortage of qualified personnel, confusion over the redistribution of assets from the crop parastatals, lack of sales outlets and escalating marketing costs prevented a smooth start.[85] Transport and crop finance were the cooperatives' most serious constraints. The relative unavailability and high cost of transport constantly plagued the unions. It was estimated in 1986 that on average a $100 worth of maize had $68 worth of imported inputs which went largely on transport costs.[86] Most unions had some lorries but their numbers fell far short of what was needed to move the purchased crops. This necessitated hiring private transport. However, given the very high demand for transport, most private sector transporters were in the habit of charging higher rates than the government-set inter-regional and intra-regional transport rates. Naturally, the transporters tried to avoid contracts with cooperatives offering them the official rate. The Ruvuma Cooperative Union, which dealt primarily in maize, provides an extreme example of the likely consequences. In 1986, after a good harvest, there was a 'maize mountain' in Songea town as maize piled up that could not be transported to Dar es Salaam because of the unavailability of willing transporters at the fixed government transport rate. There was an even greater problem getting transporters to pick up crops in villages and bring them to Songea. The transporters argued that the official rates were entirely unrealistic in view of the very bad state of the rural roads and the consequent wear and tear on their vehicles. Thus, in late September, the union had only managed to collect 25 per cent of the harvest and a mere month and a half remained before the onset of the rains. As in the preceding year, the cooperatives had to launch an emergency campaign, which involved the government authorities issuing orders to commandeer transport both within and outside the region to come to the rescue of the union.[87]

Cooperative crop finance was no less problematic. Cooperatives needed cash to purchase the village crops. Credit was normally channelled from the National Bank of Commerce through the NMC to the cooperative unions. Relations between the NMC and the cooperative unions became increasingly strained over the issue of credit. The NMC was chronically late with its payments to the cooperatives, which led either to late purchase by the cooperatives or to the peasants having to accept promissory notes for their produce. Alternatively, the cooperatives made their purchases with direct bank credit which, due to the NMC payment delays, resulted in huge interest charges being levelled on them.[88] Since the 1986 agreement

85. Sym, J., *Food Security and Policy Interventions*, Tinbergen Institute/Centre for Development Planning, Erasmus University, Rotterdam (November 1990), 133–4.
86. Tanzania, MDB, 'Annual Review of Agricultural Marketing 1988', DSM (1988).
87. Airey *et al.*, 'Songea–Makambako Road', 51.
88. *Daily News*: 'Nsekela outlines Co-ops loan problems', 28/9/88.

with the IMF, interest rates had increased drastically.[89] Furthermore, bank credit ceilings were imposed on the insistence of the IMF and this threatened the continuation of cooperative buying. Over 60 per cent of national bank credit was allocated to produce buying.[90] The NMC's bank overdraft problem, which was greatly alleviated by the removal of the *sembe* subsidy, began to assert itself with renewed strength. Due to extremely good harvests in consecutive years, the supply situation had reversed itself. By 1987, the NMC was forced to export maize (Table IV.3). As in the final days of the Grain Storage Department, the NMC staggered under the financial loss incurred from its maize exports. The 1987/88 average into-store price was 6.4 times greater than export parity. This gave the IMF an additional rationale to press for a further major currency devaluation. It was estimated that a loss of TSh. 2800 million was incurred on export by early 1988. The NMC's total losses in 1987/88 amounted to TSh. 3700 million and cumulatively the NMC's debt was estimated to have reached the dizzy heights of TSh. 12,000 million.

Besides debt, the abundance of maize produced an embarrassing situation for the NMC and the government. Having championed the cause of the urban working class for so long with cheap *sembe*, the NMC found itself selling maize to consumers at a price higher than the private traders. In 1986, the government planned to set the retail price for *sembe* at TSh.16.80, but this would have been so glaringly high relative to the open market price that they lowered it to 12.20/kg. However, the average into-store price paid to cooperative unions was 12.31/kg. Still worse, the cooperative unions' average costs were estimated at 14.31/kg.[91] The consumer subsidy had crept back into the political economy of national food supply.

The situation was exacerbated by the fact that the government's guaranteed producer prices were higher than those of the open market. Cooperative/NMC purchases increased dramatically almost everywhere, especially in northern areas where peasants had become accustomed to selling their grain to private traders. The cooperatives and NMC were obliged to purchase all grain that was offered to them, even though the NMC was only too aware that the consumer market was saturated.

The NMC and the cooperative unions were both deeply in debt and at odds with each other. The government planners were struggling to keep a lid on the situation, while the IMF was demanding that stronger liberalization measures be taken to cure Tanzania of the NMC affliction once and for all.

3.3 'Cooperative' Peasant Producers

While the political tempest raged in the capital, the countryside remained

89. Interest rates were 22% in May 1987.
90. Tanzania, MDB, 'Agricultural Marketing 1988', 6.
91. Tanzania, MDB, 'Annual Review of Maize, Rice, and Wheat 1987' DSM (1987), 53.

relatively calm. Peasants were enjoying the mere hint of prosperity that a succession of good harvests brings to agricultural producers. Food was plentiful and most households had some cash in hand. Since the availability of consumer goods was so limited, cash holdings did not change their economic opportunities or political outlook. They had grown accustomed to limited consumer supply. According to the Afro-Aid survey of cooperatives in four northern regions, even late payments from cooperatives for their crops was something to which they were resigned. They had, after all, the option of selling their produce to private traders. The survey indicated that peasants viewed the cooperatives quite favourably because, on occasion, they had been the channel of distribution for some highly desired consumer goods, e.g. bicycles, iron roofing, clothes and sugar at reasonable prices. This had resulted from a decision by several aid agencies to provide incentive goods through the cooperatives.[92] Overall, the interviewed peasants were far more concerned with the availability of goods *per se* than with prices. They were keen for their cooperative society to be multi-purpose in nature and to have a retail shop.

By a ratio of two to one respondents said that prices for consumer goods were higher in private than in cooperative shops. (Cooperative retail activities are the exception rather than the rule, however.) *More than nine out of ten respondents* [*sic*] said they would like their consumer goods to be channelled to them through the unions to the society retail outlets. Nevertheless, a large majority of respondents (85%) said they preferred *agricultural implements* to reach them through private traders. This probably reflects (1) a realistic appraisal of the reliability of private vs cooperative supplies, and (2) a popular perception that private traders make extortionate profits at the expense of customers. Society shops were also preferred as regards the speed of services (compared to private shops!) and the courtesy with which customers are treated.[93]

At the level of cooperative unions, the survey revealed that the difficult financial straits that most unions faced did not deter them from an expansionist outlook. Union leaders in the Arusha, Mwanza, Shinyanga, Tabora, Mara, Kagera and Kilimanjaro regions were keen to provide new services primarily related to livestock raising, and bus and lorry transport. They desired more autonomy from the marketing boards with respect to taking over the marketing board's responsibilities, exporting their own crops and retaining the foreign exchange. In relation to CUT, some

92. Afro-Aid and BUMACO, 'Co-operative Policy and Development on Mainland Tanzania: Results of a Survey of Primary Society Members and Union Management on the Present Organisation and Future Needs of the Co-operative Movement' (DSM, June 1988), 18, 22.
93. Afro-Aid and BUMACO, 'Co-operative Policy', 18.

expressed the view that CUT should be owned by the cooperative unions, making it a representative apex organization free of CCM party control.[94] Party control extended down to the union level itself, with the party NEC's Central Committee nominating candidates to contest chairmanships of individual unions.[95]

Local autonomy was an old theme in the cooperative movement. National leaders were eager to be benefactors of the cooperatives and have their support, but it was clear that the cooperatives were expected to be subservient to national development objectives and policy making. The year 1976 was testimony to that.

Mismanagement and peculation were other features that quickly resurfaced in some of the unions. The Ruvuma cooperative leadership was suspended in October 1988 for having presided over loss-making amounting to TSh. 770 million. Ruvuma union thefts were valued at over TSh. 43 million. Morogoro and Dodoma unions suffered thefts of crops and cash by cooperative employees as well, which amounted to TSh. 1.2 million and 29.4 million respectively.[96]

3.4 Reforming the Reform

It was the longstanding and highly visible NMC debt, rather than co-operative losses, that the IMF harped on, threatening that if nothing were done about it the structural adjustment programme would have to be stopped. The Tanzanian government's own agenda was to identify the problems that had arisen from grafting the cooperatives onto the NMC marketing system and devise remedial measures. A small five-man government task force was appointed with these terms of reference in August 1986. Its composition was weighted towards a national economic policy perspective rather than rural mobilization concerns. The chairman was from the Marketing Development Bureau (MDB) of the Ministry of Agriculture, an agency that had been central to agricultural pricing policy for over a decade. The two-man secretariat also hailed from the MDB. The other members were representatives of the Ministry of Finance, Planning and Economic Affairs, the Ministry of Industries and Trade, the Ministry of Local Government and Cooperatives, and the CUT. Therefore only two of the five members were directly associated with the cooperatives.

The committee's recommendations, released in June 1987, defined the

---

94. Afro-Aid and BUMACO, 'Co-operative Policy, 28–29.
95. *Daily News:* 'CC nominates co-op candidates', 6/10/88.
96. *Daily News*: 'Government suspends Ruvuma co-op leadership', 31/10/88; 'RCU Manager suspended', 15/9/88; '24/– million coffee stolen at Mbinga', 26/10/88; 'Juma tells co-ops be honest', 22/10/88; 'Morogoro Union staff charged with theft of 1.2m/–'; 'Theft robs CRCU of 26.7m/– crops', 26/8/88.

cooperative unions as 'the backbone' of the food distribution system.[97] The recommendations revolved around restructuring the NMC to become a 'buyer of last resort', leaving the cooperatives to conduct day-to-day grain produce buying and wholesaling. Again the theme of cutting out unnecessary intermediaries to streamline marketing and reduce costs came to the fore. This time it was the NMC's turn to be labelled expendable.

The recommendations included the elimination of pan-territorial fixed prices. Floor producer prices and ceiling consumer prices were to be set from region to region. There would be no need for into-store prices because the cooperative unions would no longer be selling to the NMC on a regular basis. The NMC would, however, make purchases on behalf of the government for a Strategic Grain Reserve of 150,000 tons, just over half of which would be stored maize and the rest would be on hand in the form of cash for grain purchase when required.

The task force acknowledged that the activities of private traders were useful in creating a competitive atmosphere in food marketing for cooperative unions. However, the activities of private traders were to be confined to buying the surplus. They were not to be given the right to buy directly from peasants. They could buy produce from the cooperative unions, but otherwise their inter-regional trade was to be restricted to that done upon the request of the cooperative unions. In November 1987, the Ministry of Agriculture together with the Ministry of Local Government and Cooperatives issued a joint statement banning private traders' purchases from peasants.[98]

Steps taken to implement these recommendations came in a piecemeal fashion, but most of them were implemented to a greater or lesser degree during the 1988/89 marketing season beginning in July 1988. They constituted major reforms, which were hurriedly implemented in view of the concurrent government negotiations with the IMF over the second phase of the structural adjustment programme. This phase was already overdue as a result of the negotiating parties' opposing views on devaluation. It should be noted that the trader and household surveys, whose findings are reported in the next two chapters, took place in this policy milieu.

The MDB admitted that 1988/89 procurement proceeded under 'some confusion with regard to the exact marketing arrangements for food crops'.[99] This was the first year the NMC no longer served as a guaranteed outlet for the cooperative unions. Phrased more positively, the unions were

97. Tanzania, Ministry of Agriculture and Livestock Development, 'Food Distribution System in Tanzania with Special Reference to Institutional Functions, Inter-regional Trade, Pricing and Cost Reductions' (DSM, June 1987).
98. *Daily News*, 21/11/87, as cited in Kiondo, A., 'The Nature of Economic Reforms in Tanzania', in *Taamuli* I (1 and 2) (1990), 32.
99. Tanzania, MDB, 'Annual Review of Agricultural Marketing 1988' (DSM, 1988), 23.

free to buy and sell food crops to any customer at any price. There was, however, a floor producer price which influenced their costings. The NMC was expected to act only as a commercial buyer and seller of food-crops. Its purchases were slated to take place in regions where transport prices were moderate and therefore economically viable, namely Iringa, Mbeya, Dodoma and Arusha.[100]

None the less, welfare and egalitarian considerations were not to be swept aside entirely. The 'high transport cost' regions of Ruvuma and Rukwa, whose recently established commercial grain specialization was seriously jeopardized by the new policies, were assured that the NMC, acting as the government's agent, would purchase 40,000 tons from them to fill the country's Strategic Grain Reserve. Furthermore, it was recognized that, since floor producer prices had been set for maize, paddy, wheat, sorghum, millet, cassava and beans, the NMC had to remain on call as the 'buyer of last resort'. The government, it was promised, would reimburse the NMC for any additional cost resulting from its price support role for maize. The cooperative unions were expected to develop appropriate strategies for the other less strategic crops.[101] In September 1988 it was officially announced that, due to its reduced purchasing role relative to the cooperatives, the NMC planned to close a number of regional branches and depots.[102]

4. Summary

The ambitious nationwide rural development programme the state embarked on in 1973 combined the party's voluntaristic rural mobiliza-tion with the government's organizational follow-up based on technocratic goals and parastatal intervention. Villagization was a social and economic upheaval from which, judging from marketed grain output, the countryside recovered surprisingly quickly (Tables IV.1 and IV.2). Following the abolition of cooperatives in 1976, between 1977 and 1979 official marketed grain purchases reached unprecedented levels, but the over-extended NMC none the less managed to cope. The year 1979, however, was a turning point, with a large proportion of the country's government and private lorry fleet being commandeered for the war in Uganda. The NMC failed to buy all the crops offered to it because of the lack of transport. Meanwhile, the second oil shock hit, which sent transport costs rocketing. These events destabilized NMC operations and the national economy as a whole.

100. Finally in September 1989, private traders were officially allowed to buy direct from farmers.
101. Tanzania, MDB, 'Agricultural Marketing 1988', 24–25.
102. *Daily News*: 'NMC to close some regional branches', 24/9/88.

The ensuing economic crisis made Tanzanian government welfare concerns, most notably the population's food security, much more critical and undermined the performance of the parastatals charged with executing the welfare measures. The NMC's operations were plagued by lack of transport and a staff too demoralized to handle single channel marketing throughout the country.

In 1982 the government quietly admitted that the NMC had become over-centralized through the passage of legislation reinstating the cooperatives. In keeping with a well-established pattern of policy formulation, the party had taken the initiative in putting forward the idea of reinstating the cooperatives. The plunge was taken and the government tried to operationalize the measure through a process of trial and error. Reinstating the cooperatives was a nationalist solution, representing the convergence of attempts by party activists and government technocrats to create a solution outside the IMF's dictates.

In 1988, after functioning for three years, the cooperatives had done nothing to improve the finances or operations of the country's grain marketing. Corruption had started to reappear. Accountancy skills in the cooperatives were in short supply and wistful attempts to keep costs within realistic bounds had resulted in the setting of totally unrealistic margins. In 1987, the maize consumer price was TSh. 0.10/kg. less than the cooperative into-store price. The finances were even more askew given that the cooperative into-store price, i.e. the price at which the NMC purchased maize from the cooperative union, did not cover: first, the actual costs of the cooperatives which were roughly TSh. 2 in excess of the into-store price; second, the NMC's wholesale costs; and, third, retail costs. In 1987/88, the mark-up between the producer price and the *official* cooperative into-store price in Iringa was 38 per cent (see footnote 83), which was slightly more than the 35 per cent cooperative mark-up prevailing in Iringa under the NAPB in the 1960s (see Chapter III, footnote 104). However, the *actual* mark-up in 1987/88 was 62 per cent. This represented a very marked deterioration in marketing efficiency over 20 years. The disguised high mark-ups caused huge financial losses, which the state eventually paid for, either through a conscious subsidy or through enormous bank overdrafts and their inflationary consequences. Cooperative losses amounted to TSh. 561.3 million between 1984 and 1988.[103] The unions' debts climbed to precipitous heights. The Department of Mass Mobilization and Political Propaganda of the party was moved to express 'shock over the huge debts cooperative unions owe the banks' and

103. According to the Ministry of Local Government, Community Development, Cooperatives and Marketing quoted in *Tanzanian Economic Trends* 2 (3–4), 93.

directed six of the worst offenders to pay their debts within three months or explain why they could not do so.[104]

Further marketing policy reforms implemented at the time of this study accorded the NMC the status of 'buyer of last resort' in an attempt to reduce the NMC's debt. However, the issue of the cooperatives' debt was skirted. Would the national bank continue to loan cooperatives cash advances that they had no hope of repaying?

Fragmentary evidence suggests that the reinstatement of cooperatives and the party's role in this measure registered some success politically. Peasants were reasonably happy with cooperatives as a channel for the occasional distribution of consumer goods. As far as peasants were immediately concerned, the economic fallibility of the cooperatives, i.e. their lack of efficient marketing services, was forgivable as long as private traders were at hand for produce buying.

The party and government faced a dilemma. The private trader had gained a measure of acceptance, not because his prices were 'just' but because he was offering a service in the absence of one or in the presence of a seriously deficient state-provisioned one. The state therefore could not easily crack down on the grain trader without jeopardizing the state's populist stance. On the other hand, the open grain market was making a mockery of the government's marketing margins and putting the continuation of cooperative marketing in serious peril. For many party activists, the open market was a political affront. Officially, private traders were only recognized in terms of the services they rendered to the cooperatives. In reality, private traders gained economic power day by day. Traders, however, were politically mute. The Tanzanian state's main contender in the policy arena was a vociferous IMF.

104. By October 1989 outstanding union debts were: Nyanza (TSh 5250 million debt), Shinyanga (TSh 3440 million), Ruvuma (TSh 1570 million), Mara (TSh 1450 million), Mbeya (TSh 1340 million), Kagera (TSh 1270 million) and Tabora (TSh 120 million) (quoted in *Bulletin of Tanzanian Affairs*, No. 35, January 1990, 12).

V

Traders' Journey from Black to Parallel to Open Markets

The only recent emergence of African grain traders as a recognizable social category and economic force has been largely conditioned by government policies towards private trade. This chapter reviews some of the precedents for the development of African grain trading, tracing the sporadic appearance of traders over the past four decades, before analysing the rush of African grain trading activity during the first three years of market liberalization. Using an institutional approach[1] the evolution of the open market during the 1980s will be highlighted in Dar es Salaam and four up-country towns, namely, Mwanza, Arusha, Mbeya and Songea. The methodology used to survey private traders in these towns during the 1988/89 marketing season will be explained as background to Chapter VI's review of the survey findings.

1. Evolution of African Private Trading in Grain

1.1 Pre-colonial and Colonial Trade

Records indicate that African producers exchanged grain for other foodstuffs, animal products, or valued goods like iron, salt or copper in pre-colonial times.[2] Exchange took place between cultivators and pastoralists and between different ecosystems, especially in Rift Valley areas where elevation created different crop zones. No doubt, the vast majority of African trade was based on proximate, local differences in

1. See Mackintosh, M., 'Abstract Markets and Real Needs', in Bernstein, H. , B. Crow, M. Mackintosh and C. Martin (eds), *The Food Question* (London, Earthscan Publications Ltd, 1990), 47.
2. Alpers, E.A., 'The Coast and the Development of the Caravan Trade', in Kimambo, I.N. and A.J. Temu (eds), *A History of Tanzania* (Nairobi, East African Publishing House, 1969); and Iliffe, J., *A Modern History of Tanganyika* (Cambridge, Cambridge University Press, 1979), 18–19.

resources and production. As a consequence of long distance ivory and slave trading in the 19th century, production and exchange of food expanded at staging points on regular caravan routes. Chiefs tended to be the brokers in this trade, which drew upon tribute labour and seasonal grain surpluses. The market, in a sense, came to the producing locality.[3] Associated with this was a predilection for the young men of these areas, notably the Nyamwezi, to seek a life of travel as porters.

When the caravan trade collapsed and agricultural commodities and motorized transport became the basis of commerce under German and British colonial rule, Asians assumed an ever greater role in bulking and marketing produce, displacing African participation in long distance trade. Only the Chagga of Kilimanjaro displayed strong entrepreneurial tendencies and succeeded in edging out Asian commodity traders in their home area.[4] Increasing landlessness was a driving force behind their commercial initiatives. Elsewhere individual Africans ventured on speculative travels hoping mainly to barter to advantage.[5]

The sporadic appearance of the so-called 'black market' during the British colonial and post-colonial periods testifies to an African response to price incentives. An illegal black market in grain developed within the context of the marketing controls first introduced during the Second World War. In 1946, it was reported that farmers in the districts adjacent to Dar es Salaam were indignant about the road blocks that prevented them from freely selling their produce.[6] However, the local Native Authority felt otherwise: 'Native Authority of Uzaramo is very keen to ensure that controlled produce grown in the area of its jurisdiction is not poured into the "bottomless pit" of the Township. Black market prices are so attractive that there is a strong temptation to oversell, resulting in District food reserves being reduced to a dangerously low level.'[7]

With the relatively poor harvests of the late 1940s culminating in the

3. Koponen, J., *People and Production in Late Precolonial Tanzania: History and Structures* (Finland, Monograph of the Finnish Society for Development Studies No. 2, 1988), 236–37.

4. Von Clemm, M. 'People of the White Mountain: the Interdependence of Political and Economic Activity amongst the Chagga in Tanganyika with Special Reference to Recent Changes', D.Phil. thesis, Oxford University (1962); and Arens, W. 'Change and Development in a Tanzanian Community', in Skar, H. (ed.), *Anthropological Contributions to Planned Change and Development* (Gothenberg, Acta Universitatis Gothoburgensis, 1985), 59.

5. See Wright, M., *Lords and People in South Rukwa* (forthcoming).

6. As a means of alleviating the urban food shortage, however, bona fide residents of the township who cultivated crops on the perimeter of the city were allowed to bring in their whole harvest by special permit and relatives were permitted to enter the town with a few *pishis* of paddy, cassava, maize and sorghum (Information Officer to Member of Agriculture and Natural Resources, 24/12/48, TNA SMP 13044; 'Dar es Salaam and Uzaramo Farmers are Forbidden to Sell their Crops', *Kwetu*, 16/7/48, TNA SMP 31555/1; *Zuhra* Vol. I, 10/9/48, TNA SMP 31555/1).

7. DC, Uzaramo to PC, Eastern Province, 18/10/48, TNA SMP 13044.

severe drought of 1949, the black market spread. It was reported to be especially prevalent in Kilosa and Moshi districts.[8]

African participation in the black market was conditioned by the fact that very few Africans, apart from chiefs, had their own personal means of motorized transport which would have enabled them to transfer large quantitites of food from a rural source to a centre of food demand. Using public transport to move food was subject to inspection and easy detection. Pearson describes a group of about 60 men who carried sacks of grain onto the railway platform at Moshi station destined for black market sale in another district. The railway traffic inspector immediately pounced on them, inspected their sacks of maize meal and confiscated them on behalf of the Economic Control Board.[9] It appears that African participation in the unofficial food market, therefore, more often took the form of waged employment for Asian traders or, alternatively, small-scale petty trading on their own account of a transient nature. On the other hand, pastoralists with pack animals were in a position to transport larger consignments without detection. The colonial authorities suspected the pastoralist Masai and WaArusha of widespread black marketeering in the north of the country.[10]

1.2 Post-colonial Trade

With the improved harvests of the 1950s and the eventual re-introduction of a free trade in grain, the black market evaporated. Its reappearance in the 1960s was the result of the heavily delimited, yet loophole-ridden, ban on the private grain trade under the NAPB/cooperative marketing system. All commercial sale of grain was prohibited, except for retail sales by the producers themselves, or other retail agents, to consumers for domestic consumption. Anyone was free to transport up to 360 kg. of grain for their own household use. These clauses were intended to allow for the continuation of traditional local farmer markets as well as to give producers enough leeway to supply the staple food needs of their spatially dispersed extended households. In effect, the clauses gave the so-called 'black market' room to manoeuvre.

Various agricultural economists of the time commented on the incidence of the black market. Helleiner stated that 'there already exists a vast illegal maize (and paddy) marketing system since the compulsory nature of the present marketing [controls] is unenforceable'.[11] Kriesel *et al.* noted that 'To cope with growing illegal movements of maize and other

8. Acting Produce Controller, Economic Control Board to Chief Secretary, 25/7/46, TNA SMP 34927.
9. Pearson, N., 'Trade Unionist on Safari, 1949', Rhodes House Mss. Afr. s. 394.
10. Financial Secretary, *Hansard*, 19th Session, 14/12/44, 50.
11. Helleiner, 'Agricultural Marketing', 31.

scheduled commodities, the action agencies have increasingly needed to call in the Tanzania Police Force and at times contingents of the Peoples' Defense Force.' They pinpoint the bad weather of 1969 as the instigating force for the expansion of the black market in maize.[12] Odegaard, on the other hand, in an exhaustive study of regional cooperative pricing of agricultural commodities, hesitatingly observed that an illegal market in grain 'probably exists'.[13]

Whereas most agricultural economists attested to the existence of an unofficial market, only Temu ventured to quantify it. According to the Ministry of Agriculture's statistics the marketed production of maize between 1966 and 1971 averaged 25 per cent of total production, of which marketed maize bypassing the NAPB accounted for only 21 per cent of marketed maize. Temu challenged these figures, arguing that the Ministry of Agriculture had grossly underestimated total maize production in the country. On the basis of the 1969 Household Budget Survey and the 1971 Agricultural Census data, he argued that national maize output was double the Ministry of Agriculture figures. He then went on to assume, without offering any substantiation, that approximately 29 per cent of production was marketed and unofficial maize sales accounted for 70 per cent of marketed production.[14] Since there was no way of measuring total unofficial sales his very high estimate cannot be proven or disproven.

Temu conducted a survey of black market maize prices at 32 different market places in four regions between April and June 1972 during a below average harvest year following a drought year. He found that the median black market prices received by farmers in Kilimanjaro were 93 per cent higher than cooperative producer prices in Kilimanjaro, 96 per cent higher in Arusha, 329 per cent in Tanga and 58 per cent higher in Mara.[15] He concluded that the character of the black market was mainly one in which the agents were able to operate within the wide margins of cooperative buying and selling prices, what he termed a 'second degree black market'. In some cases, a 'third degree black market' arose whereby a supply shortage existed and black market prices to farmers and consumers were considerably above the cooperatives' selling price while the NAPB/cooperatives experienced a shortfall of supply relative to consumer demand. There was no occurrence of a 'first degree black market' in which prices were below cooperative buying prices as a result of the cooperatives' failure to purchase maize from farmers (see Figure V.1).[16]

12. Kriesel et al., Agricultural Marketing, 25–31.
13. Odegaard, K., 'A Study of Agricultural Producer Prices, their Interrelationships and Impact on Agricultural Marketing in Tanzania, 1962–1972', mimeo (DSM, Office of the Prime Minister and Second Vice-President, April 1974), 45.
14. Temu, 'Marketing Board Pricing', 38–47, 172.
15. Temu, 'Marketing Board Pricing', 141–44. It should be noted that he questioned the validity of the Tanga data.
16. Ibid.

Temu does not discuss who the black market agents were or how they organized their trade. The reader is left with the impression that black market traders were ubiquitous, but mysteriously unidentifiable. Black market agents became the 'holy ghosts' of Tanzanian grain marketing. Prices signalled their existence and agricultural economists assumed their ubiquity on the basis of belief rather than proven fact.

Under the parastatal marketing system of the NMC, illegal grain sales continued but their status in Tanzanian political economy became contentious. Economists rejected the label 'black market' and switched to terms like 'informal marketing' and 'parallel marketing'. The Marketing Development Bureau (MDB), an FAO/UNDP-funded agricultural market monitoring unit established within the Ministry of Agriculture in the early 1970s, generated a deluge of reports on grain and price movements over the decade, never referring to 'black markets'. On the other hand, government and party politicians, at national and local levels, continued to view unofficial grain marketing as illegal profiteering that had to be eradicated.

According to the MDB's annual reviews of grain marketing, parallel marketing in rice began to take off around 1970 and received a big boost in 1974 when the NMC doubled its consumer price for rice while producer prices remained low. This large official margin provided the opportunity for a 'second degree' unofficial market to spread. In 1979 the MDB estimated that only 50 per cent of marketed rice and paddy went through the NMC, an estimate that rose to 66 per cent the following year.[17] In contrast, parallel marketing in maize was not considered widely prevalent during the mid-1970s. Maize producer prices were raised following the disastrously low maize harvest of 1974/75 to encourage farmers to grow and sell more. NMC purchases of maize in 1977/78 and 1978/79 broke all records (Table IV.1). The tide turned in 1979 when poor weather in Arusha, hitherto a major supply region for the NMC, and a severe disruption to NMC purchasing following the commandeering of vehicles, spares and fuel for the war effort in Uganda, caused farmers to market their maize through unofficial channels. A 'first degree' unofficial market in maize developed in areas which were not reached by NMC purchasing activities. Thereafter, the first degree parallel maize market quickly slid into a second degree status as NMC marketing services were fully restored and official margins grew to exceptionally bloated proportions. In all probability the drought and extremely bad harvest of 1981/82, which caused serious maize shortages in the country, marked the beginning of a 'third degree' parallel market. In December 1982, when the MDB first started recording parallel market consumer prices,

17. Tanzania, MDB, *Price Policy Recommendations for the 1980–81 Agricultural Price Review: Cereals* (APR) (DSM, September 1979), p. 27; MDB, *1981–82 APR: Maize, Rice and Wheat*, 16.

parallel prices were definitely considerably in excess of official prices (compare Table IV.4 with Table V.1).

Despite the relatively recent expansion of maize parallel marketing, the MDB estimated that, of the 25 per cent of maize production that was marketed in 1983/84 and 1984/85, 75 per cent went through parallel markets. No justification was given for this extremely high figure. Estimates for rice were 50 per cent sold, of which 80 per cent was unofficially marketed.[18]

During the first half of the 1980s, economists tended to be generally of the opinion that the parallel market was very extensive and made several inferences regarding the market's competitiveness. For example, Rasmussen, using 1983–85 MDB price data, argues that there was 'a quite well-functioning market' between Southern Highland surplus maize areas and Mwanza/Shinyanga with spatial equalization of profits and no extra black market profit. None the less, he observed that parallel market margins were far in excess of the NMC's official margins because of the abnormally large profits accruing to transporters as a result of the shortage of lorries.[19] Using the unit import price of maize in dollars and converting it to local currency on the basis of a parallel market exchange rate, as a proxy for parallel market maize prices, Keeler plotted NMC purchases against the differential between official and estimated parallel producer prices. He claims that one-quarter of the variance could be attributed to weather and the rest to prices. This would infer not only that the parallel market was very widespread, but that it was also achieving arbitrage with the world grain market.[20] Odegaard argues that the smuggling of grain across Tanzania's borders was possibly so extensive that the Ministry of Agriculture's high production estimates, which many economists found improbable, were correct.[21]

The best evidence to date upon which to evaluate the parallel market's efficiency is the Marketing Development Bureau's monthly parallel market consumer price data collected for more that 30 towns and settlements beginning in December 1982. I used these data to test for market integration. If markets are integrated one would expect that the movement of

18. Tanzania, MDB, *1983 APR: Maize, Rice and Wheat* and *1984 APR: Maize, Rice and Wheat* (DSM, 1983 and 1984).

19. Rasmussen, T., 'The Private Market for Maize in Tanzania – A Preliminary Analysis', CDR Paper D.85.13, Copenhagen Project (1985), 8–14.

20. However, the years with the highest differential between parallel and official prices are the years of very good harvests and vice versa (Keeler *et al.*, *The Consumption Effects of Agricultural Policies in Tanzania*, Sigma One Corporation, USAID (1982), 87–89) and would thus be expected to coincide with a larger NMC uptake. Therefore, it would be impossible to disaggregate the effects of good harvests and parallel market prices.

21. Odegaard, K., 'An Analysis of the Food Market in a Dual Market Structure: the Case of Maize in Tanzania', Arne Ryde Symposium, University of Lund, Sweden (August 1983), 18–20.

prices in one market would be similar to that in another, particularly in contiguous areas.

Table V.3 gives the results of monthly inter-market price correlations using Spearman's rank correlation coefficients. Southworth *et al.*, using this method to study price integration amongst 16 Ghanaian markets, got first quartile correlation scores at 0.85–0.89 for maize and 0.75–0.79 for rice wholesale prices. They concluded that market integration was high with a significant degree of spatial integration.[22] In contrast, the Tanzanian data with a much larger sample of consumer prices gave low but significant first quartile results of 0.25–0.29 for both maize and rice. Spatial arbitrage was not even remotely achieved in Tanzania's maize and rice parallel markets. Others had already observed the absence of temporal arbitrage and attributed it to lack of storage.[23]

Maps V.1 and V.2 show the areas of highest significant price correlations. Interestingly, the highest correlations were not necessarily between contiguous markets. The pattern for maize is very different from that for rice. The results suggest that the Southern Highlands, notably Njombe and Mbeya, were the points of origin for the parallel maize market as well as Arusha and Mbulu. One possible interpretation is that demand emanated from a central axis extending along a line from Lushoto, to Singida, Tabora, Urambo with Kigoma exerting a very strong pull. It is likely that Kigoma, situated on the shores of Lake Tanganyika, served as a major centre for maize smuggling to neighbouring countries. The rice market seemed to originate in the northwest and to a lesser extent in Upare (near Tanga) and Mbeya, serving the towns of the northern, lake and central zones. Southeastern parts of the country were noticeably absent from the parallel rice market. The rice market had higher second and third quartile price correlations and fewer negative correlations than maize, which might be related to the fact that the bulk of marketed rice production in the country had been traded in parallel markets for a longer time than maize, resulting in a more coherent market. Such low correlations for maize cast doubt on the MDB's estimate of 75 per cent of marketed maize passing through parallel markets between 1983 and 1985.

The relative lack of spatial arbitrage can be interpreted in a number of ways. Either the market was extremely disorganized or it was very mono-polistic, although the two are not mutually exclusive. The shortage of transport was undoubtedly a critical determinant in both explanations. In the absence of detailed information on parallel market agents and their

22. Southworth, V. Roy, W.O. Jones and S.R. Pearson, 'Food Crop Marketing in Atebubu District, Ghana', *Food Research Institute Studies* 17(2) (1979), 189; see also a similar study of Nigerian commodity markets: Jones, W.O., *Staple Food Crops in Tropical Africa* (New York, Cornell University, 1972), 140.

23. Tanzania, MDB, *1984 APR* (DSM, 1984), 9; Rasmussen, 'Private Market', 6.

mode of operation during 1982–85, it is impossible to make definitive statements about the nature of the market. Given the history of Tanzanian grain marketing, i.e. its many years of state regulation, the parallel market was at a formative stage during the first half of the 1980s. Monopoly, if it existed, would be a reflection of newness rather than entrenched mercantile interests.

There were five likely categories of parallel marketing agents at this time: first, the remaining Asian merchants based in urban areas;[24] second, comparatively less experienced African entrepreneurs with transport or trading businesses headquartered in Dar es Salaam and some of the large towns;[25] third, local private African or Asian millers[26] and transporters;[27] fourth, parastatal and government employees whose official work took them to rural locations;[28] and, fifth, young primary school leavers disenchanted with farming who engaged in petty trade and, in the border areas, often specialized in smuggling food in exchange for consumer goods or foreign currency.[29]

With the extreme shortage of transport in the country,[30] a lot of maize and rice were moved out of the rural areas in 'by the way transport', i.e. if a transporter/lorry driver or state agent was in the area and had an empty vehicle on his return trip he would fill it if he could.[31] This could

24. They were primarily involved in retail trade and small industrial workshops.
25. A category of people that very little is known about in terms of their social origins and the nature of their businesses.
26. Only about one third of the country's milling activities were carried out by parastatals (i.e. NMC and the National Agricultural Farm Corporation). Approximately 25% of all villages had mills owned jointly or privately for maize. There was an extensive network of private rice mills, many Asian-owned, through the country (Tanzania, MDB, 'A Review of the Production and Marketing Arrangements for Maize, Paddy and Wheat with Particular Reference to the Milling Sector', II, DSM (1972), Appendix 5).
27. Approximately 75% of the country's lorry fleet was in private hands.
28. Government and parastatal employees could use parallel marketing as a way of supplementing their salaries (Keeler, 'Preliminary Report', 10).
29. Kjaerby, F., 'Scratching the Surface: The Tanzanian Tractor Fiasco, the Undiscovered Oxenization Boom and the Drag of Mixed Farming', Draft, Centre for Development Research, Copenhagen (November 1984), 15; Keeler, 'Preliminary Report', 13.
30. The first half of the 1980s was a period of frequent petrol shortages. Vehicle spare parts and tyres were perpetually in short supply. Deteriorating roads caused a reduction in the survival rate of lorries. The National Institute of Transport estimated that lorries with over 4 tons capacity numbered 8300 in 1983, down from 16,000 in 1971 (World Bank, 'Tanzania Programme for Transport Sector Recovery: The Transport Sector Donors' Conference: Technical Working Papers', Arusha (December 1987), Annex 2, 1).
31. 'Much of the flow of grains into district and even regional centers, is done in a small-scale informal way. The expense of transportation, however, forces this trade to use vehicles and fuels efficiently. Many cars and trucks on other business carry a sack or two of grain as well. There are enough farmers with reason to go to town and enough town residents with friends or relatives in peripheral areas to account for a large part of this trade' (Keeler et al., Consumption Effects, 78).

in part account for the great volatility of parallel market consumer prices.

In contrast, where annual surpluses of grain occurred very regularly, it was worthwhile for more organized buying and transport facilities to be provided, most likely by local millers and/or transporters, possibly in association with urban-based African entrepreneurs, Asian merchants or even high-ranking government/parastatal personnel. Such organization explains the greater market integration between the well-known surplus-producing areas like Njombe, Iringa, Arusha and points along the main east–west road artery of the country, i.e. Morogoro, Dodoma and Singida, destined ultimately for Mwanza, Tanga and Dar es Salaam (Map I.1).[32]

Rasmussen's study of parallel price margins for maize between Njombe and Mwanza did not reveal black market profits.[33] This suggests that gatekeeping fees at road blocks were fairly minimal, hinting at the possibility that the parallel market agent's costs were reduced by an officially authorized *kibali*[34] rather than the necessity of offering a bribe at each checkpoint. There is, however, another way of interpreting these 'reasonable' margins. They could have harboured a substantial degree of subsidy resulting from the participation of government/parastatal personnel who utilized state-owned fixed capital. By using official transport they would not have been liable to gatekeeping fees to the degree that a private individual would have been.

The economic and social relations behind the 1982–85 price data are open to speculation. The results of the tests for market integration do not suggest a very coherent market, particularly for maize. Yet both economists and politicians were of the opinion that the unofficial market in these two commodities was very widespread, while differing about the morality of it. Economists viewed the 'parallel market' as a logical outcome of the country's official price structure and supply situation. Politicians, on the other hand, grew continually more ill at ease with the 'black market', eventually declaring war on it.

1.3 Government Policy towards Private Grain Trading in the 1980s

The Anti-Economic Sabotage campaign initiated in April 1983 focused on *walanguzi* ('black marketeers') generally. Those seized were mostly listed as 'businessmen' by occupation and were charged with hoarding basic foodstuffs like maize and rice, beans, cooking oil, sugar and dozens of non-food items such as soap, cigarettes, cooking pots, hoes, medical

32. For example, Ali Mpore was an African entrepreneur reputed to have a large specialized two-way trade in cooking oil from Mwanza and food crops from Arusha (*Daily News*: 'Government names 6 more saboteurs', 13/4/83; Keeler *et al.*, *Consumption Effects*, 78).
33. Rasmussen, 'Private Market', 8–14.
34. Translated 'permission'. Written authorization by someone in a responsible party or government position allowing the holder to be exempted from normal procedures.

supplies and drugs, tyres, motorcar spare parts and exportable goods like cardamom, coffee, sisal rope, ivory trophies and gemstones in addition to foreign exchange.

Two factors prevented the campaign from becoming a clampdown on all parallel market grain traders. First, the focus was on catching the 'big fish' in the belief that the businesses of smaller *walanguzi* would automatically dry up through lack of supply.[35] The hunt for international border smugglers was of special concern. Since evidence suggests that so much of the unofficial trade in maize and rice was done ubiquitously on a part-time basis in relatively small amounts, such an amorphous, moving target was not readily incorporated in the campaign. Second, in line with previous rulings on the limits of control over the movement of grain, the Prime Minister's Office announced during the course of the campaign that anyone could legitimately have in their possession or transport five bags of foodstuffs of 100 kg. each.[36] This helped to correct some over-zealous enforcement of the campaign. In one extreme case a man had been arrested at a Dar es Salaam bus stop with one bag of maize and charged with suspected theft.[37] None the less the party secretary general exhorted vigilance against 'food smugglers' and there were certain towns where the crackdown on the unofficial grain trade was especially pronounced.[38] Officials in Njombe, a major surplus maize area gave food traders a one month ultimatum to stop selling their goods at illegal prices.[39] Mwanza, where the campaign had first been announced by the party secretary general, was considered to be, in the words of one member of the Anti-Economic Sabotage Tribunal, a place where heavy sentences had to be given because 'smuggling was rife in the lake zone'.[40] As a deficit maize area, its parallel market grain traders were subject to watchful scrutiny and arrest.[41]

It is impossible to determine how much the Anti-Economic Sabotage Campaign affected parallel market grain traders compared with other traders. The Human Resources Deployment Act described in Chapter II, which was very pointedly directed at 'unproductive' hawkers and small traders, undoubtedly hit retail grain traders very hard, though no statistics are available to prove this. This category of trader had been extremely vulnerable for almost two decades. The Price Control Acts of the late 1960s had set fixed retail prices for the basic staples of *sembe*, rice, wheat and bread. In 1973, with the establishment of single channel parastatal

35. Maliyamkono, T.L. and M.S.D. Bagachwa, *The Second Economy in Tanzania* (London, James Currey Ltd., 1990), xiv.
36. *Daily News*: 'Mbilinyi clarifies on food movement', 2/3/84.
37. *Daily News*: 'Food corruption', 7/4/84.
38. *Daily News*: 'Kawawa warns food smugglers', 7/6/84.
39. *Daily News*: 'Njombe', 24/2/84 and 30/4/84.
40. *Daily News*: 'Ugandan smuggler jailed in Mwanza', 12/9/84.
41. *Daily News*: 'Two jailed in Mwanza', 20/1/84.

grain marketing, the issuing of urban trading licences to self-employed traders was abolished. In 1976, a campaign very similar to the Human Resources Deployment Campaign had involved the militia in attempts to rout out 'unproductive' elements in the urban area who were then sent back to their home areas. Thus, the 1983 Human Resources Deployment Act did not represent a new policy departure. Many of the small traders who were seized and rusticated reportedly flocked back.[42] A hardy lot, their losses probably amounted to no more than a few weeks' earnings as opposed to the 'racketeers' who spent months in preventive detention.

Amidst the implementation of these campaigns, Tanzanian economists, notably those working at the University of Dar es Salaam, were vocal advocates of less state control of the market. At a workshop to discuss economic stabilization policies, they criticized official producer prices for being too low and called for the removal of the *sembe* subsidy and the increase in incentive goods in rural areas.[43] They did not have long to wait. Just as the Anti-Economic Sabotage Campaign eased up, the government started introducing a succession of liberalization measures. The new budget in July 1984 included removing the *sembe* subsidy and raising official producer prices to become floor prices. The prime minister had already ordered that road blocks to stop the inter-regional transport of grain be removed.[44] In 1986, the government removed the controls from all prices except those of 12 essential commodities. The year 1987 brought the lifting of all restrictions on the transport and movement of food grains by the private sector, limitations on the role of the National Milling Corporation and the liberalization of inter-regional trucking rates.[45] In 1987, private traders were allowed to purchase maize and rice from the regional cooperative unions[46] and the following year the National Milling Corporation became a legitimate source of supply for them as well.[47]

Despite these liberalizing measures, the restrictions and stigma on traders were not completely removed. At the end of 1988 they were still not allowed to bypass the cooperative unions and societies and buy directly from producers.[48] The legacy of traders as pariahs could not be removed at the stroke of a pen and there was often confusion on the part of traders, officials and the public at large as to what national policies currently did and did not allow. Officials in many regions and districts, defensive about the performance of the cooperatives, were not enamoured

42. *Daily News:* 'Lindi', 28/2/84.
43. *Daily News:* 'Call for more "incentive goods"', 23/2/84.
44. *Daily News:* 'Mbilinyi clarifies on food movement', 2/3/84.
45. Kydd, J. and V. Scarborough, 'Liberalisation and Privatisation in Sub-Saharan African Food Marketing: A Survey of the Issues', ODNRI mimeo, (December 1988), Table 1.
46. *Daily News:* 'Private traders can sell cereals', 29/10/88.
47. *Daily News:* 'Traders can now buy food from NMC', 2/1/2/88.
48. This was rescinded in September 1989.

with the activities of private grain traders. Thus, as trade liberalization proceeded, the veil over who the traders were and how they managed their businesses was not lifted. It was still safer for a long-distance trader to pose as a producer selling his own stocks, and for stationary wholesalers and retailers to be cagey about prices and profit margins. It was in this context that the author undertook a survey of urban staple food traders.

2. Grasping for 'Grains of Truth': 1988 Staple Food Trader Survey

2.1 Survey Methodology

In an effort to shed some light on private traders' agency in staple food sales in different parts of the country, a survey of traders dealing primarily in maize and rice was undertaken during October and November 1988 in five towns: Dar es Salaam, Mwanza, Arusha, Mbeya and Songea. The objective was to collect basic information on trading activity in the open market as a means of identifying different patterns and scales of staple food trading operations and different categories of traders.

A random survey was not attempted because neither the total population of traders nor their location and movements were known beforehand. It was assumed that, because the market was in formation and very amorphous, it was better to aim for a qualitative study of traders and their marketing chains. Any pretence at random sampling either by selection from lists of licensed traders or specified locations would have been representative of only certain types of traders and would ultimately have led to partial findings under the guise of quantitative rigour.

The five towns were selected on the basis of their status as deficit or surplus supply areas in maize and rice. Six university social science graduates and post-graduates, who either originated from the study area or were long-time residents, served as survey enumerators.[49] Their knowledge of their home town and their rapport with the local residents was critical to the sampling and the interviewing. Each enumerator was asked to use his judgement in identifying articulate respondents and selecting traders who represented a cross-section of different scales and patterns of trading operations. Starting at the town's central staple food market and radiating outwards, enumerators interviewed different types of staple food traders along the marketing chain with the ultimate aim of

---

49. A suitable native-born Songean was not found, but the enumerator assigned to Songea was able to rely on former school contacts and acquaintances from the area for detailed background information.

getting a well-rounded picture of the structure and content of the open market in staple foodstuffs for their town. Between 30 and 35 African traders were interviewed in each up-country town using a standardized questionnaire that had been pre-tested in Dar es Salaam. Dar es Salaam's trader sample numbered 69; 68 were African and one was Asian. The results of the questionnaire were supplemented by the enumerators' daily entries in their research diaries, which recorded observations while conducting the interviews as well as the findings of interviews with officials and other key informants.

Due to the possible sensitivities of the traders, the questionnaire was designed to avoid pointed questions about earnings and profit margins. Respondents were not obliged to give their names. The enumerators had to gain research clearance from the municipal authorities and market masters and, on occasion, the market master introduced the enumerator to a group of traders. Traders, in fact, sometimes insisted on seeing the researcher's official clearance papers before answering questions. However, the enumerators avoided being associated with officialdom and stressed at the outset of the interview that they were researchers interested in getting a general picture of trading activities, rather than being concerned with individual traders' businesses *per se*, in the hopes of allaying any fears the traders may have had about tax investigation or future detrimental repercussions on them. Generally, enumerators had no difficulty getting the traders' consent to be interviewed, with the exception of Mwanza, where the traders were especially guarded and this is reflected in the verity of their answers to the questionnaire. The interviews were usually conducted at the site of the respondent's trading activities, so that the answers to the questionnaire could be compared with observed practices. Overall, the traders' responses to the interviews were surprisingly open.

Biases in the survey methodology include an over-representation of retailers and market-based legitimate licensed traders. This is because sampling began at markets, which were the easiest places to find additional traders. The *in situ* retailers were the readiest at hand for interviewing and had time to answer questions. Identifying wholesalers was more difficult. Finding and questioning mobile produce supplying intermediaries, who were merely visiting the town for the purpose of delivery and sale, required ingenuity. None the less, the enumerators made a conscious effort to be as comprehensive as time allowed in interviewing different categories of traders.

All the survey enumerators were male and a sexual bias crept into the selection of traders in some towns. None of the 69 traders interviewed in Dar es Salaam were female. Historically there has been a relative absence of women in the produce market trade in Dar es Salaam and other coastal towns influenced by Islam. However, recent studies suggest that this pattern is beginning to erode.[50] This is not revealed in the trader survey. In the up-country towns, where women's role in produce trade has traditionally been more observable, women were well-represented in the sample.

Finally, because emphasis was placed on constructing a picture of the marketing chain and identifying traders' roles and functions with respect to the chain, less attention was accorded to the details of individual traders' costs and profits. Traders' finances are discussed in more depth in the work of Gordon and Scarborough.[51]

2.2 Survey Timing and Localities

The survey was conducted during the latter half of October through November 1988. Generally by the end of October approximately 70 per cent of maize and rice and 90 per cent of paddy have been purchased; at the end of November this figure is over 80 per cent of maize and rice and 95 per cent of paddy.[52] Thus, the timing of the interviews allowed the questions to ascertain the traders' overall estimation of the 1988/89 marketing season as well as to elicit information about the trading activities that were continuing to take place, albeit at a slackened pace.

The 1987/88 harvest being marketed was considered to be slightly above average with respect to maize. Maize growing conditions had been good in the western parts of the country and moderate elsewhere. Average conditions for paddy production prevailed as well (Table VI.8). Because the three preceding years had had very good harvests, with record output in the previous year, the supply of maize and rice was considered more than adequate.[53] It is interesting to note, however, that market sales to the cooperatives/NMC were markedly reduced following the 1987/88 harvest (Table IV.1), whereas rice sales were slightly up (Table IV.2). Maize sales tend to fluctuate more widely due to the character of maize. Any decline in maize production will be amplified in maize sales. The NMC had exported maize in the previous year and exports, albeit at a reduced level, continued in the survey year. Rice, on

50. Maliyamkono and Bagachwa, *Second Economy*, 43, and Tripp, A.M., *Defending the Right to Subsist: the State vs. the Urban Informal Economy in Tanzania* (World Institute for Development Economics Research of the United Nations University, Working Paper 59, August 1989).

51. See Gordon, H. 'Open Markets for Maize and Rice in Urban Tanzania: Current Issues and Evidence', mimeo, DSM (November 1988) and Scarborough, V. 'The Current Status of Food Marketing in Tanzania', mimeo, Wye College, UK (March 1989).

52. Tanzania, MDB, *1980–81 APR: Cereals* (DSM, September 1979), pp. 8 and 27.

53. FAO/Kilimo, *Food Security Bulletin for June 1988* (DSM).

the other hand, was being imported both commercially and as food aid.[54]

As in previous years, the lack of vehicles and planning made it difficult for the cooperatives to transport their purchases out of the regions. Maize piled up at Arusha and Songea, while paddy stocks at Mwanza were so large that, in January 1989, the Ministry of Agriculture declared that efforts should be made on a 'war footing' to mill the paddy and move it to Dar es Salaam, where a rice shortage was looming.[55]

All five survey localities were urban areas. Since the Second World War urbanization has been the motor force underlying the growing commoditization of staple foods in Tanzania.[56] The process of commoditization has been very uneven with respect to supply; some rural areas have been climatically suited to generating marketable grain surpluses on a regular annual basis, some do so erratically and others barely cover the needs of the local peasant population in a good harvest year. Staple food demand and market conditions in Tanzania's urban centres can be similarly differentiated. By the end of 1985, some towns had emerged as significant centres of demand on the open market.

The relative strength or weakness of the open market in towns was determined by a combination of factors, namely: population size, the degree to which the NMC had managed to supply purchased staple food requirements, the agricultural potential and land availability of the surrounding hinterland and local trade policies regarding the operation of open food markets and taxation of traders. In selecting the survey sites, Dar es Salaam, Mwanza, Arusha, Mbeya and Songea were chosen to represent a wide spectrum of variation.

3. Open Market Development in the Survey Towns

3.1 Dar es Salaam

Dar es Salaam, Tanzania's largest city, is almost ten times as big as the second largest city, Mwanza (Table V.4).[57] It has served as the country's

---

54. Exports/Imports in Tons:

Year	Maize Exports (Commercial)	Rice Imports (Commercial)	(Food Aid)
1987/88	84,609	47,692	32,769
1988/89	31,888	3,683	26,491
1989/90	32,399	0	22,152

Source: USAID, 'Tanzania: Food Needs Assessment 1990/91' (DSM, October 1990).

55. Tibaijuka, A., 'Grappling with Urban Food Insecurity in the Midst of Plenty: Government Launches "Operation Okoa Mazao", Tanzania Economic Trends 2 (3 & 4) (October 1989/January 1990).

56. Bryceson, Food Insecurity, 160–178.

57. See Bryceson, 'Century of Food Supply in Dar es Salaam' for an expanded discussion of Dar es Salaam's history and food supply.

main port throughout this century and until recently was its official capital.[58] A major share of the national wage labour force and industrial development is concentrated here. The density of settlement and the unsuitability of the coastal climate and soils for extensive maize production has made Dar es Salaam's grain deficit position dwarf that of other towns. The NMC increasingly catered to Dar es Salaam residents' maize, rice and wheat requirements at the expense of up-country towns.[59] Dar es Salaam accounted for 70 per cent of NMC *sembe* sales in 1983/84, compared with only 30 per cent in 1974/75. Headquartered in Dar es Salaam and reliant on Dar es Salaam-landed imports for a substantial part of its supply, the NMC could distribute to Dar es Salaam at relatively low cost. Furthermore, Dar es Salaam's population constituted the largest concentration of educated and economically powerful individuals in the country, exerting a political presence of which the government was ever conscious.

The spate of bad harvests from 1982/83 through 1984/85 caused NMC maize purchases to fall far short of demand (Table IV.1). Heavy grain imports did not preclude the widespread incidence of urban food shortages in which Dar es Salaam was affected (Table IV.3).[60] Although the NMC's supply to Dar es Salaam remained high at roughly 125 per cent of city needs and constituted 60 per cent of national NMC supplies in 1984/85, it was was not enough (Table V.5).[61] It is evident that households in other parts of the country looked to their Dar es Salaam relations for help with supply as their farm and market sources dried up. A rationing system was introduced in the city involving divisional and ward party officials in grain distribution to retail outlets on the basis of population quotas, despite a lack of accurate population data. Charges of inequitous distribution soon followed.[62] Meanwhile government and party officialdom made numerous calls for urban residents to start farming in Dar es Salaam's perimeter areas.[63]

58. The decision to move the capital to Dodoma came in 1973, but Dar es Salaam remains the *de facto* capital.

59. Bryceson, D.F., 'Urban Bias Revisited: Staple Food Pricing in Tanzania', in Hewitt de Alcántara, C. (ed.), *Real Markets: Essays on the Political Economy of Food Pricing and Marketing Reforms*, special issue of the *European Journal of Development Research* (December 1992).

60. A spokesman for the Ministry of Agriculture pointed out that 60% of food imports were grants, while 54% of annual food imports were consumed in Dar es Salaam (*Daily News*: 'Farming needs more foreign funds – MP', 29/6/84).

61. *Daily News*: 'Dar food supply stable – Mhaville', 31/12/83; 'City to get more 'sembe'', 27/3/84; 'Distribution affects Dar food situation', 4/6/84; 'NDL explains food shortage', 25/4/85.

62. *Daily News*: 'Leaders warned on food permits', 7/1/84; 'Distribution is the problem', 16/1/84; 'Check food leakages – Machunda', 10/2/84; 'Dar distribution snags explained', 12/6/84.

63. *Daily News*: 'Food growing', 6/5/84; 15/1/85; 'Dar valleys for distribution', 15/1/85; 'Cultivate Dar valleys – Hamad', 23/2/85.

63 Daily News: 'Massive Win for Mwinyi', 2/11/85. In 1985 there were approximately 11

In 1985 there was to be an election. Nyerere had decided not to run again and the CCM had nominated Ali Hassan Mwinyi to take his place. Despite the grim economic circumstances surrounding the election, 92 per cent of the 5.1 million votes cast nationally favoured Mwinyi's ascent to the presidency.[64] Dar es Salaam's affirmative vote was also 92 per cent, with the percentage of registered voters slightly higher, at 76 per cent compared with the national average of 63 per cent. The turnout of registered voters at both levels was roughly 75 per cent. Tanzanian presidential elections had produced affirmative votes in the low nineties for a decade and a half so it is difficult to gauge just how popular Mwinyi was as a candidate. However, the vote can be read as a good reflection of the party's continued ability to mobilize the populace along the lines of traditional consensual politics.

On a practical level, Mwinyi's ability to win popularity amongst the Dar es Salaam population was soon put to the test. As NMC supplies dwindled over the course of 1984 and 1985, a parallel market in staple foodstuffs became more and more evident. National Distributors Ltd. (NDL), the parastatal wholesaler in grain for the city, acknowledged the shortage of supply from the NMC, but was opposed to unofficial sales. So too, the parastatal management of the city's central market, Kariakoo, repeatedly stated that all staple foodstuffs must be sold through it.[65] Dar es Salaam's regional party secretary came out firmly against the parallel market.[66] In an address to NDL employees he stated that he had 'reports that NDL had enemies who wanted, for selfish reasons, the distribution of essential foodstuffs to be left to private hands'.[67] The Dar es Salaam City Council was opposed to 'uncontrolled' private trade rather than private trade *per se*. It stepped up its efforts to provide licences for and allocate stalls to petty traders in the city's recognized market centres.[68] Over the course of the following year, traders were subjected to round-ups by the City Council with the stated purpose of keeping the city clean and netting poll tax defaulters.[69] The City Council was even more condemnatory of the growing wholesale trade in staple foodstuffs at several locations on the perimeter of the city, which evaded its control. The City Council director warned that persons involved in:

64. *Daily News:* 'Massive win for Mwinyi', 2/11/85. In 1985 there were approximately 11 million adults eligible to vote, 6.9 million were registered voters. The turnout of registered voters was 74%.
65. *Daily News:* 'Kariakoo buys more staples', 9/7/84; 'City Council plans to license petty traders', 17/3/85.
66. *Daily News:* 'Dar tightens distribution of food', 25/2/84
67. *Daily News:* 'Dar to spend over 500m/-', 27/4/85.
68. *Daily News:* ' City Council plans to license petty traders', 17/3/85.
69. *Daily News:* 'Dar es Salaam', 19/6/84; 'Hawkers blame City Fathers for failing them', 7/11/86.

The carrying out of wholesale business of food items from up-country, at places other than the Kariakoo Market ... would be taken to court... [B]esides denying the Kariakoo Market its fees, [this trade] also endangered the lives of people and was a source of filth and an eyesore to the city... [Citing] Manzese area where ... the main Morogoro road has been locked by lorries unloading food ... the congestion of businessmen buying the items, endangered the lives of people.[70]

In contrast, national leaders were starting to make murmurings in favour of the parallel market. When Prime Minister Salim Ahmed Salim officiated at the handover of the Kariakoo Market Corporation to the Dar es Salaam City Council he stated that the handover would help the Dar es Salaam Development Corporation to 'improve efficiency and expand market services to other parts of the city,' but, he added, 'other wholesale markets operating outside the complex on the outskirts of the city ... [should] ... continue with their business to ensure that people are not inconvenienced in getting their provisions'.[71]

Nyerere, as the National Party chairman, called for measures to assist the food stall trade, since 'such businesses were normally operated by the poorer members of the society and that [any] decision to close down their business affected their livelihood'. [72] Mwinyi entered the fray with a decisive step. If the expanding wholesale grain market at Manzese was causing traffic congestion and accidents it should be moved rather than abolished. A plot of land was identified a short distance off the main Morogoro road at Tandale and by presidential decree an open space wholesale market was sanctioned in 1986. Tandale had no physical infrastructure besides weighing scales. On the other hand, overheads were exceptionally low for Tandale traders because they were not subject to any municipal taxation and few had licences. As long as they enjoyed President Mwinyi's protection, they were free from the City Council's trading regulations and exactions.

Tandale quickly asserted itself as the city's main wholesale market for maize and rice. Its location just off the main road connecting Dar es Salaam with the northern and eastern parts of the country made it convenient for up-country lorries to off-load their food cargo before proceeding into the city. Furthermore, this had obvious advantages for drivers who were transporting food items on their own account in their employers' lorries.

Grain retailers flocked to Tandale for supplies. During the period of contracting NDL distribution of NMC supplies of maize and rice to retail shops, open market grain traders took over consumer supply, selling in

70. *Daily News*: 'City Council plans to license petty traders', 17/3/85.
71. *Daily News*: 'City takes over Kariakoo Market', 27/10/85.
72. *Daily News*: 'Don't close food stalls – Mwalimu', 1/2/86.

open-air food stalls in the cities' numerous fresh produce markets at Tandika, Ubungo, Chang'ombe, Yombo, Temeke, Kinondoni, Mwenge and Kisutu. Generally they held licences costing TSh. 500 a year and paid a market levy fee of TSh. 200 a month to the City Council.

At the time of the survey in October–November 1988, the new organizational structure of maize and rice distribution centring on Tandale wholesale market was well-entrenched.

3.2 Mwanza

Mwanza is Tanzania's second largest town and the seat of trade and industry of the northwestern lake region. As road and rail connections between Dar es Salaam and the more central parts of the country deteriorated and shortages of consumer goods increased during the 1970s and 1980s, Mwanza's location on the shores of Lake Victoria facilitated closer trading ties with Uganda and Kenya. Not infrequently, the Tanzanian press reported cases of highly sought after consumer goods produced in Mwanza town, such as soap, cooking oil and textiles, not reaching national distribution channels. It was generally assumed that they filtered to neighbouring countries.[73]

Historically, the railway line (completed in 1928) connecting Mwanza with Dar es Salaam facilitated the growth of Mwanza as a cotton entrepôt (Map I.1). Mwanza's cotton was a major national export, which gave impetus to the African cooperative movement's development into a central political force in the nationalist struggle for independence during the 1950s. Cotton dominated peasant cash-cropping activities in Mwanza region. Mwanza town's agricultural hinterland has long been a food deficit area. This is due to the climate as well as the peasants' specialization in cotton production and is especially true for maize. Surpluses of rice, however, are produced and exported from the area in good harvest years.

The NMC has not had a record of continuous attentiveness to Mwanza town's food requirements. Table V.5 shows that, in the first few years of the NMC's operations as a single-channel marketing parastatal, its supplies to Mwanza were nearly adequate. In the bumper harvest years of 1977 and 1978 NMC supplies dropped drastically and reached a low of only 25 per cent of estimated town needs during the war with Uganda in 1979. A serious drought was experienced in Mwanza and Shinyanga regions in 1980/81, which prompted NMC supplies to rise. Much of this, however, would have been consumed in the affected rural areas. Thereafter supply fulfilment stayed at roughly a quarter of estimated urban needs. Thus, from 1977 onwards Mwanza town effectively fended for itself. Part of the reason for this seeming

---

73. *Daily News*: 'Tribunal jails', 7/2/84; 'Two jailed in Mwanza', 20/1/84; 'Saboteur jailed six years', 17/12/84.

neglect obviously lies in the transport costs the Dar es Salaam-headquartered NMC would incur in supplying such a distant locality. Furthermore, the NMC had very little produce buying presence in the region. Mwanza was well-known as a producer of surplus rice. This is evidenced by the fact that as much as 21 per cent of NAPB paddy and rice purchases had emanated from Mwanza in the late 1970s (see Table III.3). But the NAPB's successor, the NMC, was unable to capture this supply. From the outset of NMC buying, in 1973, paddy prices were unattractive, with a large gap between the producer price and the official retail price. Producers preferred to mill their paddy and sell it privately.[74] Thus a parallel market was operating at an early stage (see Map V.2). Its driving force was rice, but parallel market traders seeking markets for Mwanza's rice were undoubtedly instrumental in finding sources of maize supply to cover the town's deficit.

Objectively, with official NMC maize supplies to the town falling far short of requirements and the hinterland incapable of generating maize surpluses, one might logically deduce that private maize traders in Mwanza were a necessity regardless of antagonistic national policies. It is thus surprising to see evidence of town officials actively discouraging private trade right up to 1988. Traders faced punitive levels of taxation and fees. At the time of the survey, traders with market stalls were charged TSh. 6000 a year for a licence, the same amount as a shopkeeper paid. A hawking licence was TSh. 900. In addition traders were expected to pay TSh. 5000 income tax on an annual basis, a municipal table tax in the market of TSh. 500 a month and Municipal Council fees of TSh. 100 per bag traded. Most traders preferred to do business outside the Municipal Council markets in an effort to evade some if not all the tax and licensing burden.

Traders in Mwanza were actively dissuaded from procuring supplies in the surrounding rural areas. Trading licences, they were told, only applied to town and they could be fined if caught trading outside. As a result, wholesalers and retail traders who procured in the rural areas posed as producers, and often went to the lengths of getting a letter from a village party official stating they were residents of the village. The gap between official policy and reality in Mwanza made it extremely difficult to delineate clear divisions of function in the marketing chain.

Mwanza has several markets in which trade in maize and rice is very much in evidence. They can be divided into two types: municipal markets and open space markets. The former includes the Central Market, Kirumba and Mabatini, whereas the latter embrace Mitimirefu and Nyamanoro maize markets, Rwagasore rice market and Makongoro. The municipal markets also have open spaces where traders' fees are lower.

74. Tanzania, EWCMP, 'The Situation of Grains and Cassava Marketed through Official Channels in Tanzania' (DSM, June 1979), ii.

Other markets, which were not sampled in the survey, are Mikuyuni, Igogo, Nyakato and Igogo.[75]

The Central Market, Mwanza's largest market, is located near the bus stand where producers and poseur producers arrive with grain commodities. Not surprisingly, wholesaling activities are found primarily on the perimeter of the Central Market. Mabatini and Rwagasore are conveniently situated near rice milling machines. In general, producers rather than traders mill paddy for sale as rice. This pattern dates back to the 1970s when it became more profitable for producers to circumvent the NMC by milling their own paddy and selling rice directly.[76] However, in Mwanza, where electricity cuts are frequent, causing mills to shut for days on end, this practice has distinct disadvantages for peasant producers eager to minimize their stay in the town. Most rice retailers buy their rice supplies at Mabatini market.

3.3 Arusha

Arusha is Tanzania's ninth largest town. Its hinterland is a grain surplus area, producing maize as well as wheat. Mechanized wheat production was pursued by large-scale settler farmers during the colonial period and, more recently, under state farm management. A few highly influential large-scale capitalized African farmers also grow wheat in Arusha and, increasingly over the last decade, maize for parallel market sale.[77] Their ownership of tractors, lorries, pickups, shops and hotels has given them economic options not enjoyed by the vast majority of Tanzanian peasant farmers.

Until 1980, Arusha region's maize sales to the National Milling Corporation were in excess of those of most other regions (Table IV.1). Drought and the increasing prevalence of parallel markets in grain caused this to change, although a recovery of official maize sales was experienced in the late 1980s, when harvests were extremely good and prices in the open and official markets were equalizing.

Historically, Arusha town was a settlement servicing the consumer needs of European settlers and African farmers. Despite its small size it has a noticeable industrial base producing processed foods and textiles. Its largest factory is the General Tyre Company. Before its demise, the East African Community had its headquarters there. The physical infrastructure from that period has enabled Arusha to serve as a major

75. See Scarborough, 'Current Status of Food Marketing' for further description of Mwanza markets.
76. Tanzania, MDB, *1980–81 APR: Cereals* (DSM, September 1979), 30.
77. Raikes, P., 'The Development of Mechanized Commercial Wheat Production in North Iraqw, Tanzania', Ph.D. thesis, Stanford University (1975) and Kjaerby, F., *Peasants ahead of the State? – Agricultural Intensification and Peasant Production under Crisis Conditions in Northern Tanzania*, CDR, Copenhagen (January 1984).

international conference and tourist centre, second only to Dar es Salaam. Coffee plantations occupy much of the immediate hinterland surrounding Arusha town, which precludes the wide incidence of peri-urban agriculture.

In contrast to Mwanza, until the mid-1980s NMC supplies to Arusha were relatively generous. The extremely high percentage of need fulfilment in 1974 took place during a period of severe drought and rural famine, with much of the supply thus destined for rural consumers. Similarly in 1979 and 1980 drought hit Arusha. Apart from those two interludes, NMC supplies fluctuated consistently between 65 and 95 per cent of Arusha's estimated maize, rice and wheat requirements. Like Dar es Salaam, between 1983 and 1985 NMC fulfilment of Arusha's grain needs was halved. In the case of Arusha the jolt to consumers and traders was less extreme for a number of reasons. First, because supply from the NMC had never matched Arusha's needs in good harvest years, consumers were accustomed to depending on non-NMC supplies. The 1984 removal of the consumer maize subsidy would have given them a further incentive to rely more heavily on these sources. Second, the presence of commercially-minded capitalized farmers and, in normal to good harvest years, Arusha's position as a grain surplus region led to the emergence of parallel marketing of maize by Arusha-based traders to deficit regions of the country, notably Mwanza, Shinyanga and Dar es Salaam. When NMC supplies dwindled in Arusha town, trading experience in parallel marketing was not lacking. Similarly, as a result of traditional and more recent developments in the cash-crop economy, the region had a well-developed matrix of farmers' markets and better than average transport infrastructure, facilitated by the operation of many private lorries and buses.

The Arusha Municipal Council opted for a moderate level of trade taxation. In addition to a licence fee, traders were subjected to a monthly market fee of TSh. 500 for a shaded market stall and TSh. 300 for an unshaded area of the market. Alternatively, at the town's two main markets, those who were not trading on a regular basis were charged a market entrance fee by revenue collectors of 10 per cent of the official consumer price on the commodities they sold. Traders had to pay a market entrance fee of TSh. 10 a day at other markets. Many traders, however, managed to avoid licensing and taxes by conducting their business at the town's main bus stand or by street hawking. They were resented by those who were paying the fees.

The Arusha Municipal Council was keen to collect fees and taxes but stopped short of banning traders from procurement outside the municipality. Arusha's relatively rich agricultural hinterland, regional network of farmers' markets and good transport from the town to the outlying rural areas would have made it extremely difficult to enforce a ban on traders' rural procurement direct from farmers and from local rural markets. Interestingly, this situation led to the relative absence of wholesale and intermediary traders in the town. Retailers could easily travel 10–15 km. outside Arusha or beyond to one of the non-taxed farmer markets, where supplies could be purchased direct from peasant producers or from wholesalers who catered for distant territorial markets. Maize supplies destined for Mwanza, Shinyanga or Dar es Salaam rarely passed through Arusha town, where municipal council fees would have increased marketing costs.

3.4 Mbeya

Moving southwards to the Southern Highlands, Mbeya is Tanzania's 'economic miracle'. During the colonial period settler farmers of the region clamoured for a railway or tarmac road to enable them to export food and cash-crop surpluses that they were certain Mbeya region could provide. In the absence of markets for peasant-produced commodities, Africans, notably the Nyakyusa, migrated to the nearby Lupa goldfield or distant Rhodesian and South African mines. The infrastructural bias accorded to the northern part of the country's cash-crop economy continued until after national independence. Ironically, it was an international crisis in 1965 which gave the impetus for economic take-off in Mbeya. Neighbouring Zambia's urgent need for a transport corridor to the sea for its copper exports, following UDI in Rhodesia, instigated the building of the TAZARA railway and the TANZAM highway with Chinese and American assistance respectively. Both were completed in the mid-1970s.

Mbeya town, situated on the road and proximate to the railway line, experienced a meteoric rise in population, growing at the rate of 18 per cent a year between 1967 and 1978. It now ranks fourth in the urban hierarchy (Table V.4). Industrial production of agricultural implements and cement has been established, but the town's economic activities mainly centre on infrastructural support to the region's agriculture. With high and reliable rainfall in the region, food harvests tend to be less erratic than many other parts of the country, making exportable surpluses of maize, rice and bananas a regular feature.

The benign neglect by Mbeya officials of trade controls stands in marked contrast to the policies of the other surveyed towns. Trading licences cost TSh. 1500 but very few staple food traders had them. Many of the markets did not belong to the municipality, so traders were not obliged to get a licence. There were no monthly market fees charged at any of the markets. The peripatetic revenue collectors who roamed the market collecting bag levies managed only spotty coverage. In any case, traders were not accustomed to displaying their full stocks and would keep bags on reserve in their houses or storage areas not far from the marketplace. Thus large sales were often arranged at the market but were actually completed at a storage site away from it. These practices were well-known to the authorities. The officials interviewed felt that there was more need for control but that 'traders will be traders' and will always manage to evade control. Significantly, none of the Mbeya traders in the survey complained about a licensing and/or tax burden, in marked contrast to the other towns.

This pragmatic, almost pro-trade, attitude on the part of Mbeya officialdom pre-dates IMF-instigated market liberalization and relates to particular features of Mbeya region. The Zambian border is only about 100 km. from Mbeya town and the region is made up of a variety of different agricultural zones produced by altitudinal variation of the Rift Valley. Traditionally, local trade between areas in what were to become Tanzania and Zambia was very pronounced, given the ethnic similarities of the people on both sides and the advantages of exchanging agricultural products from different ecological zones. Much of this local trade was carried out by women.

The Nyakyusa, the ethnic group now demographically dominant in Mbeya town, were never known as traders in the way that the Chagga of Kilimanjaro were. However, over the course of the last few decades, like the Chagga, the Nyakyusa have experienced land pressure in their fertile tribal homelands. Migration to nearby Mbeya town and commodity trading comprise a handy alternative to agriculture. The completion of the TANZAM highway and the TAZARA railway reinforced this tendency. It was soon clear that Mbeya's prosperity for the foreseeable future rested on long-distance trade in staple foodstuffs, notably rice, maize, bananas and Irish potatoes and few officials wanted to stifle the trade boom for the sake of revenue collection. Leadership in Mbeya is dominated by the immigrant Nyakyusa rather than the indigenous Safwa, whose agriculture and past labour history were less outward directed than those of the Nyakyusa. Finally, unlike Mwanza, Mbeya region did not have strong historical ties with the cooperative movement. A village study in Rungwe indicated that some elements of the village population were apathetic, if not antagonistic, to cooperatives.[78] Many rural farmers, often women, were developing off-farm trading activities on their own account.

The pattern of staple food trade in Mbeya town was a derivative of the larger inter-regional commodity marketing network that embraced the region's rural areas and channelled food products in an easterly direction towards Dar es Salaam, northwards towards the food-deficit Lupa goldmine of Chunya and westwards towards Zambia. Perhaps because Mbeya officials adopted a more *laissez-faire* attitude towards trade, Mbeya

78. Mbilinyi, M., 'Co-operative Organisation in Isange Village', in Koda, B. *et al.*, *Women's Initiatives in the United Republic of Tanzania* (Geneva, ILO, 1987), 30.

town played a more direct part than Arusha town in inter-regional trade. As in Arusha, local farmer markets were well-developed in Mbeya region's rural areas and bus services and lorry transport were reasonably good. Farmers could take their produce to the farmer market nearest their home, to the mills and markets of Mbeya, or they could bypass the town and go to roadside markets. The largest market in Mbeya town, Mwanjelwa, was on the main road. Other town markets included Soko Kuu, Soko Matola and the Mabatini rice market located next to the mill. Small neighbourhood retail markets consisting primarily of women selling rice outside their houses, for example, Sinde, also existed. Maize, banana and potato markets tended to be situated in convenient locations for inter-regional trade and were therefore of a more roadside and railway line nature. They include some markets on the perimeter of the town, such as Isanga bus stop to the north on the way to Chunya, Ilomba and Uyole to the south at the Tukuyu and TANZAM road junction, and Iyunga, the TAZARA railway station to the west on the way to Mbalizi and Zambia.

3.5 Songea

In the extreme southern part of Tanzania near Mozambique is Songea town, which ranks fifteenth in the urban hierarchy (Table V.4). Though relatively small, Songea recently experienced a growth spurt. At 10 per cent per annum, it had the most rapid population growth rate of all the regional towns in the inter-censal period between 1978 and 1988. Its growth was associated with the British-financed tarmac road, which went from Makambako on the TAZARA railway line through mountainous stretches of the Southern Highlands to Songea. With the completion of the road, the vast, relatively sparsely populated and primarily peasant subsistence-producing areas of Ruvuma region had a means of getting their goods to market.

Ruvuma region asserted its surplus maize-producing potential under the government's pan-territorial pricing policy, which began in 1973. However, throughout the 1970s and early 1980s the NMC incurred huge transport costs in purchasing maize from Ruvuma. The new road reduced these costs.[79]

Songea has no industries. It has experienced what might best be described as state-led development through benefiting from fertilizer subsidies between 1973 and 1983 and the pan-territorial maize pricing of the NMC. Because its growth was nurtured by the state and parastatals, it is not surprising to find that the official maize market was dominant in Ruvuma region until 1988. In a 1987 ODA survey of household

79. Airey, T., D. Bryceson and J. Howe, 'Interim Evaluation of the Songea–Makambako Road', Report submitted to Overseas Development Administration, London (July 1989).

production in villages located on and off the Songea–Makambako road, only 12 per cent of marketed maize was sold to private traders in on-road villages and 5 per cent in off-road villages in Songea District.[80]

Crop buying was performed solely by the NMC between 1973 and 1984. With the reinstatement of cooperative buying in 1985, the Ruvuma Cooperative Union (RCU) was in charge of village crop procurement, selling its supplies to the NMC. There was a mutual dependence between the two agencies. Being physically remote from consuming markets, the RCU was happy to off-load its procurement on the NMC. Similarly, the NMC was reliant on Ruvuma as a stalwart maize supplier, as other maize-producing areas started getting involved in the open market. This cosy relationship between the NMC and RCU had several hitches. One of them was that the RCU was known to be a poorly managed cooperative. Historically, the RCU had been founded to market tobacco. Tobacco as a high value to weight crop could withstand the high transport costs and was marketed in relatively small manageable quantities. The RCU's experience in tobacco did not prepare it for the marketing rigours of Ruvuma's maize boom. Farmers complained of late buying and late payments. Maize mountains appeared in Songea as the availability of transport failed to keep up with procurement. Emergency transport measures had to be taken. The regional government commandeered vehicles to get maize transported out of the region virtually every year. With the lifting of government controls on inter-regional transport rates in 1987, private transporters were more willing to transport long-haul maize, but they complained that the government-controlled transport rates for intra-regional transport did not cover the costs of operating their vehicles over Ruvuma region's extremely bad feeder roads. As a result, local transporters were reluctant to invest in vehicles with payloads of 10 tons or under, making their fleets unsuitable for village procurement purposes.[81]

The problems of RCU/NMC crop transport, however, were superseded by financial exigencies during the 1988/89 crop buying season at the time of the trader survey. Government investigations revealed theft, corruption and mismanagement on a huge scale in the RCU, leading to the loss of almost TSh. 750,000 million. In late October 1988 the entire Executive Committee of the union was suspended.[82] Meanwhile, facing large debts and threats of revocation of bank credit under IMF stringency measures, the NMC was forced to announce that it would restrict its buying from regions with high transport costs and a long way away from Dar es Salaam. Ruvuma region was given an NMC purchase quota of only 10,000 tons. The region was no longer the national government's bonny baby. The baby had been thrown out of the cradle and had to start scrambling

80. Airey *et al.*, 'Interim Evaluation', Annexes, Survey Table 2 & 3.
81. Airey *et al.*, 'Interim Evaluation', pp. 24–28.
82. *Daily News*: 'Govt suspends Ruvuma co-op leadership', 31/10/88.

for markets for the 1988/89 maize harvest. The harvest was bountiful and peasant farmers' cash income depended on the sale of their maize surpluses.

The Songea Town Council's trader taxation and licensing fees were comparatively heavy, with a TSh. 4000 licence and a TSh. 300 monthly market fee or daily fee of TSh. 10. The licensing fee had been imposed for the first time in 1986 and had met with protest from traders, many of whom dealt in such small quantities of produce that the cost of the licence would have precluded the continuation of their businesses. Thus the Songea Town Council had backed off and did not require small-scale maize retailers, most of whom were women, to hold a licence. At the time of the study, there were only 48 licensed traders in Songea.

Songea town had four small neighbourhood retail markets with a handful of traders at Lizaboni, Ruvuma ward, Bombambili and Manzese, but Songea's Central Market was the main site for maize trading activities and rice retailing. Maize from Songea's hinterland was usually delivered to the Central Market, either by peasant producers themselves who had found some means of transport or headloaded it to town, or by intermediary buyers, often young men who made purchases in the villages and used a hired lorry, Land Rover or tractor for transport. Rural transport was at a premium because the region's roads were very bad and there were relatively few buses and heavy goods vehicles. Furthermore, a rural network of farmers' markets was not as well-developed as in the other regions under review since the lack of variation in the cropping pattern and subsistence nature of most peasant production did not encourage local market development. Thus, procurement was based on direct knowledge of village supplies and/or good contacts. The recent immigration of so much of the Songea town population from the surrounding countryside facilitated marketing.

4. Summary

Fragmentary evidence shows, not unexpectedly, that African staple foodstuffs were being traded between agricultural producers in different ecological zones during the pre-colonial period. As the colonial order expanded, wage labour generated large numbers of consumers dependent on market purchase of staple foods. It was Asians rather than Africans who grew in prominence as commercial food traders.[83]

Food exchange patterns between African peasant producers of different localities continued during the colonial period, although there is very little

83. See Bryceson, *Food Insecurity and the Social Division of Labour*, Chapter 10.
84. Gulliver, P.H., 'The Evolution of Arusha Trade', in Bohannan, P. and G. Dalton (eds), *Markets in Africa* (Chicago, Northwestern University Press, 1962).

documentation on it.[84] In the realm of inter-regional food commodity trade, state controls on food trading during the Second World War and its aftermath created a 'black market'. African participation in the black market was apparent in a number of places.

More comprehensive marketing controls following the introduction of cooperative marketing in foodstuffs during the colonial period was associated with the persistence, if not the spread, of the so-called black market. Under the single-channel parastatal marketing system of the NMC and the bad harvests of the mid-1970s, the expansion of illegal grain marketing was suspected. Economists, taking a pragmatic view, dubbed it the 'parallel market', whereas politicians were indignant about its persistence in the face of state attempts to squash it. For over a decade the state actively sought to stamp out the parallel market. It was only under pressure from the IMF and the financial disarray of the NMC that state policy began to be more tolerant of private trading and gradually steps were taken to remove state trade controls, giving birth to the 'open market'.

The degree and form of economic liberalization differed from one locality to another. Government officials at the national level took the policy initiative, but many national party activists and regional and municipal government and party officials displayed a lack of eagerness. Suspicious of private traders and defensive about the interests of the newly-reformed cooperatives, they expressed their reluctance to accept the changes through contradictory public statements and slow implementation of the market liberalization reforms. Examining the evolution of policy changes in Dar es Salaam, Mwanza, Arusha, Mbeya and Songea does, however, reveal that the hesitancy of local officialdom was slowly breaking down under the duress of revenue needs. The reinstatement of local government policy and the pinch of IMF-enforced cutbacks in national expenditure made it imperative for regional and municipal authorities to find new sources of revenue to fund local expenditure. The licensing of traders and the imposition of various market fees and levies were, from 1985 onwards, considered an important source of local revenue, so much so that in some towns it appears that it bordered on undermining the 'honest' traders who submitted to the various exactions, while creating a subterranean level in the open market composed of various types of traders who managed to circumvent local government revenue collection.

Thus, the open market was hesitantly opened by less than eager government and party officials. Furthermore, in many places, the so-called open market had a shadowy edge.

VI
Traders &
Urban Food Markets

Having reviewed the historical and political context in which market liberalization arose during the mid-1980s, the principal actors can be introduced. The results of the survey of staple food traders I conducted in October–November 1988 will be used to explore various trader characteristics and the organization of their trading activities. This chapter concludes with a consideration of the interaction between Tanzania's open and official food markets.

1. Surveyed Traders in 1988

Using the methodology outlined in the previous chapter, 196 traders were interviewed. Because the survey sample was not randomly selected, it cannot be claimed that the findings are representative of the entire food trading community. The survey's sampling procedure and background investigations were aimed at discerning major patterns, tendencies and interactions between emerging groups of traders.

1.1 Starting to Trade

Roughly 60 per cent of the traders sampled had started trading during the implementation of the new liberalization policies between 1984 and 1988. In Mbeya, however, 90 per cent of the men had started trading before 1984 as opposed to 48 per cent in Arusha, 38 per cent in Dar es Salaam, 33 per cent in Mwanza and only 14 per cent in Songea. Women were less likely to have started before 1984: 50 per cent in Mbeya, 30 per cent in Arusha, 20 per cent in Mwanza and 14 per cent in Songea. This pattern might suggest that women found the pre-1984 trade controls more intimidating than men. After 1984, many housewives, particularly in Mwanza, facing the effects of inflation on their household budgets embarked on staple food trading as a means of supplementing their household income.

A comparison of the ages at which traders began trading in the pre- and post-1984 periods does not reveal any striking differences. Nor does the origin of trading capital in these two periods differ markedly (Table VI.1), though the percentage of male traders deriving their starting capital from previous salaried employment increased in the 1984–88 period in Dar es Salaam, Mwanza and Arusha. Given the large number of redundancies in waged employment during this time, this is not surprising. Self-financing based on agricultural earnings, on the other hand, declined in importance. Women's starting capital was usually borrowed from a family member. A noticeable number of traders in both periods had traded fruit and vegetables prior to moving into grain. Unlike many other agricultural crops, fruit and vegetables have never been subjected to government marketing controls.

Contrary to expectations, only 20 per cent of the traders cited aspects of the economic crisis as the direct reason for starting to trade. The majority of traders gave economic incentive as the instigating force, which cannot be divorced from the general lack of alternative economic opportunities during the crisis. Although no specific questions were asked about the traders' educational backgrounds, it was apparent from the interviews that most of them had not progressed beyond primary school. Since 1976, the Tanzanian government has provided universal primary education without expanding places in secondary schools. As a result, most young people have some eduation, but only a very small percentage of the school age population finish secondary school.[1] Most of the traders hailed from the large pool of Standard 7 (or less) school leavers, whose formal wage employment prospects are mostly limited to menial jobs. However, as real formal wages have declined, the attractiveness of informal sector employment has risen. Thus, becoming a trader was generally viewed in a positive light against other options.

1.2 Demographic Characteristics

Of the 196 traders interviewed, 75 per cent were male. The sexual composition varied from 100 per cent male in Dar es Salaam to 33 per cent in Mbeya (Table VI.2). With the exception of Mbeya, women were only occasionally found amongst the ranks of the mobile produce-supplying intermediaries or wholesalers. Women traders generally dealt in the main grain commodity produced in their town's hinterland and traded smaller quantities than the men. They tended to be slightly older than the male traders, with an average age of 36.1 years as opposed to the men's 32.9 years.

1.   Hazlewood, A., *Education, Work and Pay in East Africa* (Oxford, Clarendon Press, 1989), 221.

The traders came from a wide assortment of ethnic affiliations, with only the Chagga numbering over 10 per cent of the total sample. Dar es Salaam, the most cosmopolitan town, contained the largest number of tribes, with a preponderance of Eastern coastal tribes (Table VI.3). Interestingly the tribe indigenous to Dar es Salaam, the Zaramo, was outnumbered by the Luguru from the hilly areas of Morogoro, who have been very active in supplying Dar es Salaam with fruit and vegetables for several decades. Staple food traders in the four up-country towns were usually born within the region, but outside the town. Mwanza was the only place in which the town's local tribe dominated trade. The pattern for the other three towns was for a tribe in a nearby agriculturally-constrained area to be most numerous. Thus, in Arusha, the Chagga of land-scarce Kilimanjaro[2] outnumbered the Waarusha. Similarly, in Mbeya the Nyakyusa from densely populated rural Rungwe outnumbered the Safwa of Mbeya and, in Songea, the Yao of arid, agriculturally infertile Tunduru far outnumbered the local Ngoni of Songea.

Whatever their birthplace, traders invariably resided in the town in which they traded. Only in Mbeya was there a hint of the commuter trader who lived in a nearby rural area and traded in the town.

1.3 Occupational Characteristics

Contrary to the notion that staple food trading was a seasonal secondary occupation, over 90 per cent of the interviewed traders indicated that it was their primary occupation to which they devoted almost 90 per cent of their work time. Only in Arusha and Songea were 13 and 26 per cent of the traders respectively pursuing staple food trading as a secondary occupation. In all the other towns they regarded it as their primary occupation. Everywhere, farming was the most common secondary occupation mentioned, ranging from only 9 per cent of Dar es Salaam and Mwanza traders, to 33 per cent in Arusha and Mbeya and a very large 54 per cent in Songea, the most rural of the towns.

Likewise, the population of the town and hence size of the food market mirrored the time traders spent trading. Dar es Salaam and Mwanza traders were almost fully occupied with it, spending approximately 98 per cent of their time trading. Arusha and Mbeya traders struck an intermediary position by trading for 82 per cent of their work time, while the Songea ones were the least committed in devoting 69 per cent of their work time to trade.

Although most of the traders had started trading relatively recently, trading experience did differ from town to town, but not in accordance with the above association between population size and trading intensity.

2.   Kilimanjaro and Arusha are separate regions administratively, but Kilimanjaro is very proximate to Arusha town.

The Dar es Salaam sample contained several seasoned traders, which raised the average number of years trading to seven. Arusha and Mbeya followed closely behind with an average of six years. Surprisingly, the Mwanza traders were comparatively inexperienced with 3.7 years. Given the fairly long-established parallel grain market in Mwanza, it is apparent that either traders were reluctant to admit that they had been trading prior to the implementation of the government's market liberalization policies, or the economic sabotage campaign in Mwanza had eliminated many of the early traders in this market and other less experienced traders had taken their place, or the sample was systematically biased.

All the traders interviewed were trading on their own account. About one-third were involved in partnerships, usually with only one other person. Generally the partner was a family member, most frequently a sibling of the same generation.

1.4 Changing Face of Urban Traders

It is revealing to compare the results of the 1988 trader survey with that of the 1971 NUMEIST[3] random sample survey of non-waged, informal sector workers carried out in Dar es Salaam, Mwanza, Arusha, Mbeya and three other towns.[4] Street traders selling food comprised a sub-sample of this survey. Relative to the other categories of non-waged workers[5] street traders were relatively young, with 31 per cent aged 14–24 years, 54 per cent 25–49 years and 15 per cent 50 or over. In comparison, only 17 per cent of the traders surveyed in 1988 were under 24 years, 72 per cent were in their prime economically active years between 25 and 49 years and 11 per cent were 50 or over.

Whereas the NUMEIST survey revealed that Tanzania's urban self-employed could not generally be readily categorized as part of an easy entry and exit 'informal sector', street trading stood out as the occupational category most closely resembling a marginal economic activity, i.e. it was composed of young, poorly educated people with low earnings who had been engaged in the activity for a relatively short time and were looking for another job.[6] Very few had had previous involvement with wage employment. Occupational flexibility was inferred in that 28 per cent worked short hours while 40 per cent worked long hours. In Dar es Salaam the local Zaramo dominated such trading activities.

The 1971 and 1988 surveys are not strictly comparable. In the 1971

3. National Urban Mobility, Employment and Income Survey of Tanzania (NUMEIST).
4. Tanga, Dodoma and Tabora.
5. Namely crafts/manufacture, contracting, shopkeeping, hotel/barkeeping, house rental, farming and other.
6. Bienefeld, M.A., 'The Self-Employed of Urban Tanzania', Economic Research Bureau Paper 75.11, University of Dar es Salaam (June 1975), pp. 56–58.

survey 'street trading', obviously a generic term for informal sector traders, embraced trade in non-food items as well. None the less, the degree of functional overlap between the two surveys should be great enough to afford some rough comparison. By 1988, the average age of traders had risen. There was more occupational commitment in terms of the time they devoted to trading, in their sense of identity as traders and in their willingness to continue trading in preference to other economic activities. The more diverse ethnic composition in Dar es Salaam, shown by the declining representation of indigenous Zaramo, suggests that trading was becoming more specialized and competitive, relying more on the trader's work commitment than any advantage derived from being native born and having extensive local contacts. Furthermore, there was a much higher incidence of family members working together in 1988. Thus, although occupationally food traders were a relatively 'infant group' in 1988, their willingness to invest more time and effort to trade than their 1971 predecessors suggests that they were not intending to be casual, informal sector workers.

2. Traders' Commodity Marketing

According to the 1976 Household Budget Survey, the 'preferred cereals', namely maize, rice and wheat, account for 76 per cent of urban staple food consumption by value (Table I.1). Maize and rice vie for first place at 31 and 27 per cent respectively. The percentage of surveyed traders dealing in each staple food commodity was roughly proportional to the ordering of urban staple food preference: 55 per cent paddy/rice, 51 per cent maize, 11 per cent wheat, 7 per cent millet, 6 per cent bananas, 4 per cent cassava and 4 per cent potatoes (Table VI.4).

This section will focus on maize and rice as the two most widely traded staple foodstuffs in urban Tanzania. The physical infrastructure and functional organization of the open market will be reviewed before examining the specific pattern of trade for each commodity.

2.1 Market Infrastructure

Chapters III and IV dwelt on the organizational problems that faced previous marketing regimes. These regimes were underpinned by centrally directed state agencies or the cohesiveness of an Asian trading/transport network. How have the more decentralized and ethnically heterogeneous private African traders managed to surmount the logistical problems inherent in Tanzania's staple food commodity marketing?

What is striking about the 1988 open market is the low degree of trader capitalization. Less than 2 per cent of the surveyed market traders own any form of motorised transport. Human porterage for short distances and transport hire over longer distances is the norm. Between the rural central collection point and the town, small loads are generally transported directly by producers or traders using buses or 'by-the-way' transport. Usually there is a charge for the produce transported in this manner, often pocketed by the bus conductor and/or driver. Larger loads are most frequently collected by hired pick-up. Often a group of town-based traders will pool together to hire transport to go to a rural district market or, alternatively, to a village having first sent a reconnaissance agent to purchase the load in readiness for transportation. In towns, a variety of forms of transport are hired to get bags of produce from wholesale to retail points, including hired porters, ox carts, hand-pulled carts or pick-ups. In the case of the latter, Dar es Salaam retail traders frequently mentioned pooling together to hire a seven-ton pick-up to carry their produce from urban point of purchase to its sale location.

For decades, large lorries have primarily been owned by Arabs, Somalis and Asians. Their fleets operate on Tanzania's major trunk routes. Private African transporters usually own smaller vehicles which can be driven on the feeder roads. Hire rates of private transporters are based on commercial viability and are considered expensive by most users. There are also parastatal Regional Transport Corporations (RETCOs) in some of the regions where adequate numbers of private transporters have not materialized. KAURU in Ruvuma is an example of this. RETCOs are more likely to charge rates in accordance with government-set price controls on intra-regional transport, but to operate at a loss. As a result vehicles tend to be more poorly maintained and less reliable. Some village governments operate lorries as well, which are usually purchased at subsidized prices. They serve village transport needs in addition to being hired out periodically on a commercial basis to outside parties.

Transport prices are subject to negotiation and vary a great deal depending on who the trader is negotiating with. Arab and Asian transport owners providing long-distance large-haul services have predictable commercial rates. Rates charged by drivers of private and state vehicles are more variable. Their costs are determined more by availability of space, risk of detection and calculations of how much the trader is willing to pay. Drivers of state vehicles are said to offer the lowest rates, but to carry the highest risk of police harassment and thus place the accompanying trader in a compromised position.

The lack of transport ownership on the part of traders can be explained by the extreme scarcity of vehicles and their exhorbitant purchase price and maintenance costs.[7] The expense is beyond the means

7. Only three traders in the sample owned their own transport. They were: (1) an Asian with 40 years trading experience, dealing in legumes, who owned a VW Combi; (2) a Lindi-based farmer-trader of maize and finger millet operating for the past six years with two Scania trucks; and (3) a Chagga trading in rice, maize and bananas, travelling between DSM, Morogoro, Iringa and Mbeya with an Isuzu pick-up.

of the vast majority of staple food traders.[8] There is little evidence that the well-established commercial transporters are willing to diversify into staple food trading, which is a less lucrative and possibly more risky area of commerce than that to which they are accustomed. As a result staple food trading and transport remain largely separate enterprises, though evidence suggests this is less true for Ruvuma, Lindi and Mtwara. During the suspension of the Ruvuma Cooperative Union's operations, African traders were of the opinion that in Songea large Asian transporters were the town's most important grain traders.[9] The transporters, however, were taking steps to relinquish their trading role by nurturing a few local African shopkeepers who had previously been uninvolved in maize trading. These shopkeepers were given favourable lorry hire terms with demand for payment withheld until the maize was sold and the lorry returned to Songea.

Similarly, African trader ownership of storage space was limited. Only 17 per cent reported having their own storage facilities; most often this was a room set aside for the purpose in their own house. The highest incidence of owned storage was in Mbeya and Songea, where surplus staple foodstocks would mount while awaiting shipment out of the region. In Mbeya, traders sometimes rented special transit sheds at roadside markets in which to store their especially perishable foods like bananas and potatoes for a few days while awaiting available lorry transport to Dar es Salaam. Elsewhere, most traders relied on keeping their unsold stocks in shaded or even unshaded parts of the market, which they were entitled to do when they were paying market fees. Maximum volumes stored by traders were influenced by the size of the town's market and the functional role of the trader (Table VI.5). The amounts that Dar es Salaam wholesalers and retailers had been known to store dwarfed those of traders in other towns. Given the severe storage constraints, in general the strategy of both retailers and wholesalers was to achieve a rapid turnover, thereby minimizing storage time rather than holding stocks speculatively (Table VI.5). Fumigation of stocks was rare. Packaging materials were primarily limited to sisal or hemp bags.

Besides transport, storage and packaging costs, some traders paid loading charges and wages of hired labour, especially in Dar es Salaam (11 per cent). Frequently a group of traders with stalls close to each other shared the costs of hiring a night watchman. Those selling maize flour

8. Van Donge's study of Luguru fruit/vegetable traders reveals that even the successful large-scale traders could not manage the purchase and maintenance of a vehicle on their own and feared going into joint ventures with other traders due to the proven difficulties of maintaining a viable working partnership with kin or non-kin for any length of time (van Donge, J., 'Waluguru Traders in Dar es Salaam: An Analysis of Social Construction of Economic Life', Paper presented at the Biennial Conference, African Studies Association (UK), Birmingham (September 1990).

9. None of the Asian transporters were available for interview.

were subject to milling costs, as were a few traders in Mbeya purchasing paddy and selling rice. Complaints about recent increases in milling charges were voiced. Usually the increase was immediately passed on to the consumer. The only other major expenses the traders incurred were licensing fees and market levies. Bribes to officials at road-blocks and municipal council licensing authorities were primarily mentioned by Dar es Salaam and Songea traders.

Table VI.6 provides a breakdown of costs incurred per kg. by one Dar es Salaam wholesaler. It is interesting to note that the charges for transporting and loading rice were substantially higher than they were for maize. Rice afforded higher margins, of which transporters and porters managed to get a share through their negotiations with traders.

Transactions between consumers and retailers and between retailers and wholesalers were overwhelmingly conducted in cash. Wholesalers also paid cash for their large bulk purchases from produce intermediaries and producer/traders, but they tended not to pay the full negotiated amount on delivery. The sellers would often let the wholesaler take the consignment away with little more than a partial payment to cover transport charges and accomodation expenses for the seller's stay in the town. The wholesaler then set about 'auctioning' the consignment, i.e. finding buyers. After securing buyers for the consignment, the wholesaler would then pay the up-country selling agent. This process could take up to a week. It was a point of honour for the wholesaler eventually to pay the selling agent as agreed, rather than to return the goods unsold. For obvious reasons, the selling agent generally felt more comfortable selling to a wholesaler with whom he had previously traded or with one who had a reputation for reliability. The lack of money credit can be attributed to the embryonic nature of the trading network, rapid inflation undermining the value of loans, inadequate legal or social enforcement of debt repayment and the security risks involved in handling large amounts of money. Preference for credit to be given in kind reverses the flow of credit in such a way that large traders get credit from small traders who, in turn, are known in some cases to get credit from farmers; for example, some Arusha farmers leave their produce with retailers receiving payment only after the retailer has succeeded in selling it.

2.2 Market Organizational Structure

While it can be said that Tanzanian traders are, in general, extremely under-capitalized and have very little infrastructure at their disposal with which to facilitate efficient commodity exchange, this has not prevented the emergence of a division of labour amongst traders associated with different levels of market organization in the towns under study.

A typology of urban staple food markets is depicted in Figure VI.1.

The major classifying factor is the surplus/deficit status of the food market. With respect to maize and rice, the five surveyed towns represent four major types: first, a two-commodity surplus market (Mbeya); second, a two-commodity deficit market (Dar es Salaam); third, a maize surplus/rice deficit market (Arusha and Songea); and, fourth, a maize deficit/rice surplus market (Mwanza). The second classifying factor is whether or not the town market dominates the regional open food market. This relates to the size of town demand. In deficit town markets, notably Dar es Salaam and, to a lesser extent, Mwanza, the town market dominates the region whereas, in surplus markets, much of the regional grain supply is destined for other regions and towns. In these cases, the town market will be a gravitational force in the regional open market if one or more favourable circumstances prevail, namely liberal open market policies on the part of the municipal council, the lack of an established network of rural farmer markets, and/or the availability of transport and costs that give the town an advantage over other regional locations as a bulking point for transhipment. Mbeya and especially Songea are examples of town-based, outward-directed surplus markets, whereas the staple food market structure of Arusha town is not, having been superseded in importance by a network of rural-based surplus markets supplying other regions (Figure VI.1). Mwanza is difficult to classify since its status as a deficit market lends it a town-based character in maize whereas in rice this is less true.

The traders' functional division of labour in each town naturally reflects differences in market types. Three major trading types are identifiable in the Tanzanian staple food open market – the mobile intermediaries who collect produce from supply areas and are engaged in its onward sale to demand areas, the stationary wholesalers who bulk produce in specific localities for onward sale to retailers, and the retailers who distribute produce to final consumers. The extent to which these three types are clearly distinguished and identified with individual traders in the five surveyed towns is determined by supply and demand variables. On the supply side, generally, the more locationally proximate the supply, the less likely there will be a clear division of roles in trade. Similarly, on the demand side, functionally delineated trader activities will not be able to emerge under conditions of small and sporadic demand.

Table VI.7 categorizes traders into these three functional roles on the basis of the type of onward sale, the location of purchase and the volume of sales. Considering each role in turn, the most prevalent trading role in all the towns was that of the retailer. In both surplus and deficit markets retailers were the common denominator. All the towns exerted enough demand to warrant the presence of retailers, although there was a hint of their relative unimportance in Mbeya, where direct non-market food supplies were plentiful.

In surplus markets, retailers tend to take on many of the functions of intermediaries and wholesalers because there is easy access to plentiful supplies, but market demand can be quite weak, thereby limiting the survival and growth potential of the retailer. In deficit markets, on the other hand, there is a clearer division of labour between functional tiers. Retailers are less constrained by lack of demand and turnover is faster, but, due to the development of entrenched supply arrangements between mobile intermediaries and wholesalers, there is a tendency for upward mobility of retailers to be severely limited.

Subject to varying municipal council regulations and fees, the emergence of retailers has depended on sufficient demand and a starting capital of only a bag or two of grain, which can be obtained through the retailer's agricultural efforts or very modest capital accumulation.

Not all towns generated a significant number of mobile intermediaries who were distinguishable from retailers. In some cases, the supply areas were so close to the town that retailers could easily purchase directly from villages and farmers' markets. For example, the presence of intermediaries in Arusha's town market is constrained by the well-developed network of rural markets and lower costs and market fees involved in purchasing in these markets and transporting goods directly to the main sources of demand, i.e. Mwanza and Dar es Salaam.[10] Likewise, relatively good rural transport services make it possible for Arusha retailers to purchase directly from producers in rural localities rather than having to depend on specialized intermediaries. If and when large-scale intermediaries enter Arusha town they usually prefer to conduct their business from a hotel or guest house rather than the marketplace.

There were other combinations of 'unspecialized' mobile intermediaries. In Mwanza, wholesale traders also served as mobile intermediaries, thus making it very difficult to categorize them. Alternatively, producers themselves acted as intermediaries, either bringing small amounts by bus and selling at the bus-stop, or bringing larger amounts by hired transport to the town. The former tended to sell soon after the harvest and usually came from a not-too-distant point in a limited radius around the town. The latter were large farmers or farmer/traders who bulked their own and other farmers' crops and were willing to come from distant localities and hold off selling until a sufficient amount of time had elapsed after the harvest for prices to rise. This type of mobile intermediary was most evident in the Dar es Salaam market.

Traders who confined their role to that of a mobile intermediary were prominent in the surplus markets of Mbeya and Songea. In these two localities supply so exceeded town requirements and distances from supply to ultimate centres of demand were so large that the intermediary role could clearly emerge. Arusha mobile intermediaries, on the other hand,

10. Gordon found this to be the case in the Iringa surplus market as well (Gordon, 'Open Markets for Maize and Rice', pp. 11-14).

were obviously prevalent in the town's surplus-producing hinterland, but did not actively pursue trading activities in the town in order to keep costs down and avoid taxation.

Those conducting long-distance trading activities from a town used a variety of transport modes to visit rural areas to buy produce, i.e. bus, 'by-the-way' transport arranged with the driver of the vehicle, or, more formally, they hired transport from the vehicle owner. Town-based intermediaries sought to minimize transport costs and often separated their buying activities into two stages: commodity search and transportation of the load. They travelled to the rural supply area by passenger transport, ascertained that there was produce to buy and then, and only then, hired transport either from a town-based transport firm or from a rural source, for example a village in which there was a collectively-owned lorry for hire.

Market entry into town-based specialized mobile intermediary trading was more stringent than it was for a retailer. Intermediaries had to have the capital to buy produce in bulk loads of anywhere between about 0.5 and 30 tons or more and to transport it. Furthermore, they had to have a good network of contacts in order to gain sufficient market information to know where to go to buy and sell. Numbers of intermediaries in surplus areas depended to a large extent on the relative availability and cheapness of transport. This was seen in the proliferation of mobile intermediaries in Mbeya associated with the town's extremely advantageous location on the TANZAM highway and TAZARA railway. In comparison, the concentration of intermediaries in more remote Songea was smaller, a reflection of the more demanding starting capital requirements arising from high transport costs.

The rigours of crop transport are many. Mobile intermediaries have to face the possibility of having to bribe guards at road-blocks and engage in hard bargaining with transporters who can capitalize on the fact that the crop is perishable. Lack of security and the real danger of theft *en route* mean that the more junior mobile intermediaries have to keep a 24-hour vigil on the consignment to the point of delivery.

Mobile intermediaries occupy a high-risk position unless they restrict themselves to collecting produce from their original home locality or an area with which they have an affinity, and limit sale to a location where they have well-established contacts or are assured of customers through rapid market turnover. Mbeya rural women rice intermediaries are a prime example of this lower-risk intermediary trading approach. Theoretically, rural-based mobile intermediaries with their fingers on the pulse of local supply should emerge. There is, however, little evidence of this sort of trader in the survey, perhaps because a rural-based trader is severely hampered by lack of transport and market information regarding town prices and demand.

Moving on to the third category, that of the wholesaler, only deficit markets were capable of generating the necessary conditions for specialized wholesaling (Table VI.7). Wholesaling functions undoubtedly exist in all the surveyed towns, but only in Dar es Salaam and, to a lesser extent, in Mwanza were there markets big enough to support clearly distinguishable wholesalers.

Given the specificities of the Tanzanian open staple food market (poor transport, storage and credit infrastructure and a lack of readily available market information) some of the functions one normally assumes are fulfilled by wholesalers are not evident in Tanzania. The Dar es Salaam and Mwanza wholesalers did not have any better storage facilities than retailers or intermediaries. Nor were they found to be offering substantial amounts of credit to suppliers or client retailers. Quite the contrary, suppliers usually offered wholesalers credit by advancing their commodities while the wholesaler looked for a purchaser. The wholesaler merely paid the supplier enough of an advance to pay off the transporter and finance the suppliers' stay in the city for the few days necessary to find a purchaser/s. The wholesaler's primary function was to bulk commodities and act as a 'buyer of first resort' for large deliveries at a fixed location throughout the year. In a highly uncertain market infrastructure, in which suppliers and retail distributors had to cope with marked fluctuations in supply and demand, the wholesaler's main service was merely 'to be there' for buying and selling.

It seems paradoxical that, while wholesalers appeared to have the easiest role to fulfil with the least risks, the position of wholesaler was the hardest to achieve and was envied by other traders. Gordon and Scarborough mention the wholesaler's need for large amounts of starting capital.[11] According to one highly successful Dar es Salaam wholesaler, however, access to large amounts of capital is not vital; rather the main prerequisite is 'being known'. Several traders confirmed the importance of being popular. A wholesaler has to have 'akili'[12] and a reputation for having many clients, being well-liked, respected and trustworthy. An outgoing personality, shrewdness and an aura of invincibility as 'Mr Fix-it' combine to form the mystique of the successful wholesaler. Not all aspiring retailers and mobile intermediaries can expect to make the grade, nor can they assume that this elevated position is permanent.

2.3 Maize Marketing

The maize open market represents a vast decentralized trading network catering to a large dispersed clientele in Dar es Salaam and Tanzania's

11. They estimate wholesalers' starting capital is roughly TSh. 100,000, five to ten times greater than that of retailers (Scarborough, 'Current Status of Food Marketing', 39; and Gordon, 'Open Markets for Maize and Rice', 27).
12. Translated 'intelligence' or 'nous'.

other urban settlements. Many of its clientele were, until recently, served by the highly centralized NMC single channel marketing system. How have the traders managed to offer an alternative distribution network with such widespread distribution in such a short period of time? The survey data, which constitute a small sample of visible traders in the network, can only begin to provide some of the answers.

Over the years, regional sources of maize supply to the national market have varied depending on local weather and harvest conditions. However, Ruvuma, Iringa, Rukwa, Mbeya and Arusha regions have consistently generated the largest maize harvests, according to Ministry of Agriculture production estimates. Tabora and Shinyanga have been large and fairly consistent producers as well (Table VI.8). The 'Big Four' regions, i.e. Ruvuma, Rukwa, Iringa and Mbeya, provided the bulk of official supply during the 1980s, but it is evident that they have also been able to supply the open market (Table IV.1). Map VI.1 shows the Marketing Development Bureau's estimation of the origin and destinations of open market maize flows. It will be observed that the major centres of demand are Tanzania's largest city and towns – Dar es Salaam, Mwanza, and Tanga, respectively, with Dodoma, Morogoro, Kigoma and Bukoba serving as secondary centres of demand.

Turning to the survey data, the procurement volumes of Dar es Salaam traders supersede those of Mwanza, Songea, Arusha and Mbeya (Table VI.9). A breakdown of maize traders by type shows that, on average, the volumes procured by Dar es Salaam and Mwanza mobile intermediaries were larger than elsewhere (Table VI.10A), with Dar es Salaam volumes being twice those of Mwanza. Dar es Salaam retail volumes superseded those of all the other towns by a very wide margin. Possibly because of the conflation of produce buying, wholesaling and retailing in Arusha, retail volumes there were more than twice those of Mwanza. Not surprisingly, Songea's retailers dealt in miniscule amounts, reflecting a low demand from town residents (Table VI.10C).

Comparing volumes handled between types of traders within the same town reveals that the bulking function of wholesalers relative to retailers was similar in Dar es Salaam and Mwanza. In both places the annual amounts handled by wholesalers were between five and six times greater than those of retailers in 1988/89. Each year Dar es Salaam wholesalers were dealing in amounts six times greater than those of the mobile intermediaries, whereas in Mwanza the intermediaries handled slightly more than the wholesalers. The small size of the sample, however, does not warrant drawing any inferences from this observation.

Comparing the differences between mobile intermediaries and retailers in Songea shows that the mobile intermediaries dealing in maize, primarily between Dar es Salaam and Songea, work on a vastly larger scale than the stationary retail traders of Songea town.

Arusha and Mbeya do not afford any intra-town trader comparisons since all the Arusha traders were retailers who also provided intermediary and wholesaling services on a moderate scale to Arusha town consumers, whereas all the Mbeya maize traders were mobile intermediaries supplying maize to the lucrative Lupa goldfields market at Chunya. There is virtually no market for maize amongst Mbeya town residents because of easy non-market access and a local preference for other staple foodstuffs over maize.

Maize traders overwhelmingly accounted for consumer price variation in terms of supply fluctuation. Most Songea maize is a high yielding variety that has been recently introduced and is considered by consumers to be of inferior quality to the harder flint varieties from other parts of the country, hence its lower price. Detailed maize price data showing ranges are included in Table VI.10.

Table VI.11 provides an overview of average purchase and sale prices by trader type and town, revealing the margins at each level of the marketing chain. Purchase prices by mobile intermediaries ranged from a low of only TSh. 7/kg. in Songea to a high of TSh. 13.25/kg. in Mwanza, roughly in accordance with regional differences in maize availability. Mwanza's high maize prices have also been attributed to the recent increase of Bukoba traders, who had come from across the lake in search of supplies to make up for a food deficit in their area brought about by banana weevil infestation which has undermined the traditional food economy. The mobile intermediaries' margins superseded those of other types of traders, thus reflecting the fact that they have to cover transport costs between areas of supply and demand. As expected, Songea's mobile intermediaries' margins topped the league, for they covered the Songea–Dar es Salaam transport charges. The Dar es Salaam intermediary margin is surprisingly low and should not be taken as representative in that it is based on the reply of only one respondent from a relatively close supply area. Dar es Salaam intermediary margins vary widely because of the large number of areas supplying Dar es Salaam.

Registering slightly over TSh. 2/kg, wholesale margins were roughly at parity in Dar es Salaam and Mwanza. Contrary to expectations the wholesale margins are not markedly smaller than the retail margins. In fact, in Mwanza the wholesale margin supersedes the retail margin by over 30 per cent. This is consistent with Scarborough's Mwanza data. She observed the same phenomenon on an even more pronounced scale when she calculated gross profits for wholesalers and retailers taking account of traders' costs.[13]

Retail margins are greatest in Dar es Salaam and lowest in Songea, which is in line with gradations of demand. Both Arusha and Songea are

13. Scarborough, 'Current Status of Food Marketing', 37.

surplus markets, but Arusha's retail margin is considerably higher and might relate to the combination of roles that Arusha retailers fulfil. Arusha retailers are more prone to make purchases at rural markets, whereas Songea retailers buy primarily from producers who deliver to Songea's central market.

The reported sale and purchase prices between the various levels of traders do not match in Table VI.11. For example, in Mwanza there is a gap of roughly TSh. 2.50 between the stated average sale price of mobile intermediaries and the purchase price of wholesalers and another gap of about TSh. 2.00 between the sale price of wholesalers and the purchase price of retailers. Under the assumption that traders will be more candid about their purchase price than their selling price, Table VI.12 has been constructed on the basis of stated purchase prices for each level of trader and the final retail sale price has been compared with the Marketing Development Bureau's monthly consumer price data for November 1988. The margins that result look more realistic, with wholesale margins becoming less than retail margins in Mwanza and Dar es Salaam. Intermediary margins, however, look too small in view of the transport costs they embody.

It is useful to consider whether or not specific characteristics of the traders might influence margins. Differences in age and experience between mobile intermediaries and wholesalers does not reveal any clear patterns (Table VI.10A and B). On average, mobile intermediaries are in their thirties, ranging from 30 in Mwanza to 39 in Mbeya. While wholesalers are roughly the same age as mobile intermediaries in Dar es Salaam, they are on average four years younger in Mwanza. When comparing the accumulated trading experience of intermediaries and wholesalers in Mwanza it is apparent that wholesalers have only a very slight edge, with five years of trading compared to the intermediaries' four. In Dar es Salaam, wholesalers do lay claim to seniority, with nine years of experience compared to the intermediaries' five.

Ethnically, only a quarter of the mobile intermediaries and wholesalers in Mwanza are not members of the local tribe, the Sukuma. Interestingly, the salient minority are Ha from Kigoma. In comparison, Mwanza retailers are much more ethnically mixed, with the Sukuma constituting only 46 per cent of their numbers and the Ha 4 per cent. In Dar es Salaam, the local tribe, the Zaramo, accounts for only 13 per cent of all surveyed wholesalers and intermediaries, the Luguru from Morogoro are the most numerous (representing 38 per cent) and the rest hail from far-flung parts of western and southern Tanzania. In Mbeya, 60 per cent of all intermediaries are from the local Safwa tribe of experienced maize growers and 40 per cent are from the nearby Nyakyusa. In Songea all the intermediaries were members of nearby tribes, i.e. Yao, Ndendeuli and Matengo. Overall, wholesalers and intermediaries do tend to come from the indigenous ethnic groups of the town or the ethnic groups of major supply areas. It is likely that tribal affiliations are a stronger qualifying factor than experience in the non-retailing spheres of the maize trade in up-country towns. If tribal consolidation exists, it could help to explain the larger than expected wholesale margins.

The maize wholesale and intermediary trade is almost exclusively the preserve of men. Women surfaced as 20 per cent of the Songea inter-mediaries' sample and 25 per cent of the Mwanza wholesalers' sample. Women were predominantly retailers and overwhelmingly so in Songea and in Arusha.

It is strange to note that, while the surveyed Dar es Salaam retailers were about four years younger than the intermediaries and wholesalers, in Mwanza and Songea they are on average between two and ten years older than intermediaries and wholesalers. Mwanza's retailers have chalked up virtually the same number of years' experience as the intermediaries and wholesalers, whereas Songea intermediaries are a couple of years ahead of their retailing counterparts. Van Donge's life histories of Luguru traders provide clues as to why there is no clear progression of age associated with different levels of trade. The numerous risks in trade result in frequent bankruptcy at all levels. Mobile intermediary and wholesale traders can easily plummet to being retailers, even just street hawkers. So too, humble retailers with attractive personalities can, under favourable circumstances, become large-scale traders within a relatively short time. This volatility leads traders to hold the view that their careers are propelled by luck rather than hard work or skill.[14]

In terms of commodity specialization, while Mbeya and Songea mobile intermediaries restrict themselves primarily to maize trading, all Dar es Salaam and Mwanza mobile intermediaries deal in more than one commodity. Wholesalers in the latter two towns are roughly divided between those who sell only maize and those who have branched out. Retailers in Dar es Salaam, Mwanza and Arusha follow a similar split. Songea maize retailers, on the other hand, are rarely found dealing in a second commodity. It is apparent that the single-mindedness of Songea traders towards maize relates to the ease of obtaining maize and the lack of availability of other staple food crops. In Mbeya, maize intermediary traders have developed a highly specialized market niche by selling to consumers in food-scarce Lupa. The distance between Lupa and Mbeya is not great; they enjoy a well-padded margin and obviously feel no need to branch into other crops. The general mixed pattern elsewhere reflects a flexible approach in which attempts to maximize returns depend on fluctuations in supply and demand.

14. van Donge, 'Waluguru Traders', 21.

2.4 Rice Marketing

Rice, which in value terms rivals maize in urban consumption, is none the less very different from maize. According to the 1976 Household Budget Survey, rice consumption in urban areas, measured by weight, was more than 50 per cent below that of maize. It is a much more expensive commodity. During the survey, consumers were paying between 2.5 and 10 times more for rice than maize. Though rice is not restricted to the wealthier classes, it is none the less considered a luxury staple food and not central to national food security. This may explain why the government has been more tolerant of its marketing by private traders since the mid-1970s compared with maize.

The volume of rice produced in Tanzania is generally only about 20–25 per cent that of maize. A higher percentage of this rice does, however enter commercial channels – an estimated 50 per cent compared with 30 per cent of the maize. Small amounts of upland rice are grown in every region. Major commercial rice production is restricted to Shinyanga, Mwanza, Morogoro and Mbeya, with smaller amounts produced for the market in Rufiji (Coast Region), Tabora, Ruvuma, Lindi and Mtwara. Transport has proven less of an impediment to the marketing of rice than of maize because rice is a higher value crop and its major production areas are more accessible. Historically, rice from Mwanza and Shinyanga has been railed to Dar es Salaam, whereas Morogoro's proximity to Dar es Salaam has given its rice a ready market. The extremely good road and rail connections Mbeya enjoys has helped bolster rice production in the frontier Usangu plains of the region.

Survey data on average rice procurement volumes per rice/paddy trader by town (Table VI.13) again suggest that Dar es Salaam traders generally operate on a far larger scale than elsewhere. Broken down by type of trader, the same pattern pertains to mobile intermediaries and retailers (Table VI.14A–C).

The survey was able to identify and interview wholesalers only in Dar es Salaam. It is likely that stationary rice wholesalers in Mwanza are largely redundant because of the nearby supply. Hence Mwanza retailers can get their supplies directly from producers or from mobile intermediaries.

Dar es Salaam wholesalers handled nineteen times more rice than the retailers and five times more than the mobile intermediaries. This difference between the wholesalers' and retailers' volumes suggests that rice wholesalers do far more bulking than maize wholesalers. The volumes handled by mobile intermediaries and retailers in Mwanza and Mbeya were from five to eight times lower than in the other towns. Unfortunately, no mobile intermediaries or wholesalers were identified in Arusha, but they undoubtedly exist because there are no large rice production areas close by.[15] In Songea, purchasing by retailers takes place either at the producer's farm (23 per cent), from the Songea National Milling Corporation branch (8 per cent), from mobile intermediaries at the central market (8 per cent) or, in the majority of cases, from mobile intermediaries at spontaneous meetings anywhere in the town (57 per cent). A major complaint by Songea retailers was that it was difficult to find supplies. Mobile intermediaries preferred to sell their scarce supplies of rice from guest houses and private homes in the town, thereby evading the scrutiny of town officials. Retailers constantly had to be on the alert for gossip concerning possible sale locations.

In Mwanza and Arusha the surveyed rice retailers handled volumes that were about half those of maize retailers, whereas in Songea rice retailers handled about 25 per cent more than the average maize retailer (Table VI.14C).

The rice traders' explanations of the causes of the fluctuations in the rice price were far more varied than those proffered for maize. In addition to the factors related to supply variation, external costs, product differentiation, government intervention and even inter-personal influences were mentioned. Mbeya rice was considered to be of a much higher quality than that from other places and was thus more expensive. But food prices were highly inflated in Mbeya generally, with high local transport charges as well.[16] It was observed that the retail price in the Songea market rose in a step-wise fashion with all traders raising their prices in unison.

Ranges in rice prices tended to be slightly greater than in maize prices (Tables VI.14A–C and VI.10A–C) and reported margins were substantially larger (Tables VI.15 and VI.11). The mobile intermediaries' margins in Mbeya stood out as extremely high. There were two types of mobile intermediary in Mbeya – women traders who purchased paddy from farms, transported and milled it and then sold the rice; and male traders who purchased rice in Mbeya town and sold it at the goldmines of Chunya. The latter's margin stood out as exorbitant.[17]

Reported retail margins for rice were greatest in Songea and least in Dar es Salaam, the reverse of what prevailed for maize. Differences in the balance of supply and demand in the two locations accounted for the interesting contrast.

15. Magugu in Babati district and parts of Arumeru district do supply some rice to Arusha market.
16. Rice transport between the Usangu supply area of Igurusi and Mbeya town, a distance of 80 km., cost TSh. 300/bag compared with TSh. 900/bag between Mbeya and DSM, approximately 800 km. in distance.
17. As mentioned in Chapter I, high food prices at Chunya during the 1930s were blamed on traders' excessive margins. Fifty years have elapsed and Chunya remains relatively remote and subject to high food prices. It should be noted that prices of consumer goods are generally high at mining sites throughout Tanzania.

Rice mobile intermediaries and wholesalers are more likely than their maize-trading counterparts to be dealing in only one commodity, whereas the opposite is the case for the retailing category in Arusha, Mwanza and Dar es Salaam.

Table VI.16 is another attempt to smooth out the inconsistencies in reported prices between types of traders by using only purchase price data at intermediary and wholesale trader levels. Comparing Table VI.16 with Table VI.12 reveals that rice margins were consistently greater than maize margins at all levels in all five locations, especially for retailers and Dar es Salaam wholesalers. One might rationalize the difference in retail margins in terms of the smaller amounts of rice sold. For example, a Mwanza rice trader sold only 40 per cent of the volume of his counterpart maize trader but received approximately 275 per cent greater margin for rice, which roughly evens out returns. Arusha rice traders selling 54 per cent of the volume of maize traders obtained a generous margin of 575 per cent more. Songea retailers benefited the most with a 25 per cent larger volume than maize traders and a 1690 per cent larger margin. It appears that the greater difficulty experienced in procuring scarce rice was worth the effort. However, the biggest returns accrued to Dar es Salaam rice wholesalers selling three times the volume of surveyed maize wholesalers and receiving a 525 per cent greater margin.

Age and accumulated experience were not always associated with high margins. Many young traders had chalked up more trading experience than their older colleagues. Mobile intermediaries in Dar es Salaam were only in their mid-to-late twenties and had relatively low margins. As expected, Mbeya–Chunya intermediaries were experienced, having traded on average for nine years; their boastful self-confidence and enormous margins were unique in the survey. Female intermediaries in Mbeya were slightly younger (37 years) with only six years experience and more modest margins. Likewise, Dar es Salaam and Arusha rice retailers in their early thirties had been trading for an average of seven to eight years, with low and moderate margins respectively. Mwanza's and Songea's slightly younger traders, who had only traded for approximately four years, had moderate and very high margins respectively. Mbeya rice retailers aged 37 on average were older but had a comparatively late start with only four years trading experience. All of them were women. Women in general seemed to be found in low profit niches of the market hierarchy.

There was more ethnic concentration amongst rice traders than maize traders. Most striking was the dominance of the Luguru as mobile intermediaries and wholesalers in Dar es Salaam, the Sukuma as intermediaries in Mwanza, the Chagga as retailers in Arusha and the Nyakyusa as retailers in Mbeya. With the exception of the Nyakyusa female retailers in Mbeya, all these trading groups were getting comparatively high margins (Table VI.16).

3. Traders' Attitudes and Perceptions

Staple food trading in Tanzania, characterized by extremely low overheads, is none the less a risky business, rife with difficulties. How do traders view staple food markets? What constraints do they find most irksome?

When asked traders were very forthcoming about the problems they faced. In Dar es Salaam, the most frequently cited problem was government intervention, namely price control, police harassment and road-blocks. Difficulties associated with fluctuation of demand and supply, especially seasonal commodity shortages, belied the deficit status of Dar es Salaam's markets. The shortage and unreliability of transport were also high on the list of complaints, followed by dissatisfaction with trading infrastructure, especially marketplaces and the availability of gunny bags. Others felt that there was too much competition and they had difficulty coping with price fluctuations and low profits. Security and the ethical environment of trade posed a worry as well. Theft, cheating on weighing, unreliable business deals and the need to bribe were listed as additional problems.

In Mwanza, traders were concerned about demand and supply constraints. Seasonal commodity shortages were frequently mentioned. Conversely, slow commodity movement and lack of customers worried others. Government intervention, mainly in the form of excessive taxation, was viewed as a great nuisance. Price fluctuations posed a problem for many. Unreliable and expensive transport, as well as an erratic electricity supply for milling, were part of a difficult work environment.

Arusha traders were most preoccupied with the ups and downs of demand and supply. Slow commodity movement loomed as a major obstacle. Government intervention in the form of excessive fees and taxes was viewed in a dim light. In contrast to the other towns, unreliable transport was not mentioned very often. The poor storage facilities were considered more problematic.

In stark contrast, Mbeya traders were obsessed with unreliable and expensive transport, which seems ironic in view of Mbeya's excellent railway and road connections compared with those of other localities. This seeming anomaly, however, relates to the large percentage of mobile intermediaries in the Mbeya sample, many of whom were dependent on 'by-the-way' lorry transport whose availability was difficult to predict. With prices subject to negotiation between driver and trader, traders were in a poor bargaining position if and when they had inadequate storage and/or their commodity was perishable. Lack of secure storage, not surprisingly, figured high on their list of complaints. A substantial number of Mbeya traders were of the opinion that competition was too stiff. No one complained about government intervention.

Traders in Songea felt that the demand and supply factors were the most perplexing. Lack of demand in the form of slow commodity movement and the absence of customers was a major constraint. Conversely, seasonal supply shortages and the time spent searching for supplies in a town where rice sales, in particular, were often conducted away from the central marketplace, also posed obstacles. Government taxation was deeply resented and there was annoyance with police harassment and road-blocks. Poor transport was mentioned frequently in addition to dissatisfaction with the adequacy of the marketplace.

The improvements traders desired reflected their assessment of the problems. In Dar es Salaam, Mwanza, Arusha and Songea, the strongest appeal was for less government intervention, the removal of government controls and the easing of taxation. Somewhat contradictorily, traders in Mwanza, Mbeya and Songea voiced a hope for government action to guarantee commodity supply (Songea), provide storage space (Mbeya), fix transport rates (Mbeya), restrict big traders to inter-regional trade and prohibit trading without a licence (Mwanza). Enforcing trading licence restrictions was an issue in Arusha as well, where licensed traders resented having to compete with the unlicensed ones who had evaded paying any fees. The need for a new or better marketplace was strongly felt in Dar es Salaam, Arusha and Songea, whereas in Mwanza an improvement in the electricity supply was the most important infrastructural concern. In Mbeya, an improvement in the credit constraint was what was most wanted, which belied the Mbeya traders' more ambitious trading objectives. The sophistication of Mbeya traders was further demonstrated in their desire for infrastructural changes, which included transport improvements, better storage facilities, market information and more coordination between themselves and long-distance external buyers.

The traders' future plans were influenced by their perception of the trade outlook for their region. Arusha and Songea traders were pessimistic, with a high proportion of them not planning for the future. It should be noted that both places were maize surplus regions which had been subjected to near glut conditions by good harvests. In Dar es Salaam and, to a lesser extent, Mwanza and Mbeya, traders were keen to expand their trading activity. In Mbeya this took the form of wanting to trade in other regions, while in Mwanza and Dar es Salaam the desire was to move into other types of trading, specifically wholesaling, having a shop or export. Mbeya traders again distinguished themselves by primarily hoping to improve their assets and trading performances through acquiring a vehicle, ox cart or store house and thus enlarging their volume of trade and working capital.

When asked in which commodities they would like to expand their business, despite their acknowledged competitiveness, rice and maize were predominant. Beans ranked third. The lack of urban purchasing power makes food trading in non-staple food commodities an arena for limited numbers of traders. In all the towns the majority of traders were of the opinion that the number of grain traders had increased, most markedly in Dar es Salaam, Mwanza and Mbeya.

The traders' view of their scale of trade and position in the trading network relative to others reveals a number of facets. On the whole, stationary wholesalers in Dar es Salaam saw themselves as large-scale operators, whereas Mwanza wholesalers were more modest. Mobile intermediaries slotted themselves in the small to large range, weighted towards being 'average'. Retailers tended to see their operations as small to average.

There was a strong tendency for traders not to feel they held any advantages in the trading position they occupied, especially in Arusha and Songea. For those who could cite some advantage there was a wide range of answers. The most frequently mentioned advantage was with respect to income, with 14 per cent stating that trading provided them with a daily income for their purchased needs. Another 5 per cent felt that trading gave them reasonable and sometimes high profits. The advantages of their position with respect to other traders or customers was also seen to be important – 8 per cent felt fortunate that they had become well known and had built up 'goodwill'.

Traders were far more forthcoming about the disadvantages of their trading position. Again income considerations topped the list, with 23 per cent complaining of low profit. Troubled relations with other traders, customers and the authorities were common and encompassed an array of specific concerns. Over 5 per cent felt there was too much competition. In Mwanza this took the form of big traders monopolizing supplies during shortages. In Mbeya there was an acute sense that some had made it as successful traders, while others lacked popularity and were unable to attract customers. Many of the perceived disadvantages related to high operating costs, an inability to expand trade and restrictions on volume and turnover.

4. Trade Differentiation and Organizational Dynamics

The main goal of most of the surveyed traders was to earn an income from their trading activities – profit-maximization *per se* was secondary. Generally traders believed that the bigger their scale of operations, the less vulnerable they were and the more likely they were to improve their income.

Many traders expressed an interest not just in expanding the amount or range of commodities in which they dealt, but in moving into another level of trade. Retailers looked on wholesalers with envy. Retail trade in rice and especially maize affords easy entry. Competition can become quite intense, particularly in places like Arusha and Songea, where maize supply is abundant relative to consumer demand. It is precisely in these markets that the leap from retailer to wholesaler is most improbable. Wholesalers are largely redundant.

How does a trader achieve the status of a wholesaler? In Dar es Salaam, the survey evidence showed that wholesalers had an early entry advantage. Tribal affiliation also seemed instrumental. Informal interviewing which revealed aspects of the wholesaler's biographical profile indicated that a stationary wholesaling role is usually assumed after serving time as a mobile intermediary. Being a mobile intermediary not only gives one an acquaintance with various levels of the marketing chain, but it also puts the trader in contact with a wide circle of producers and traders, which is useful for any prospective wholesaler. Some Dar es Salaam wholesalers had trading experience in neighbouring countries or even further afield on the African continent.[18]

For a retailer, entry into the ranks of the mobile intermediaries is not too financially taxing if and when bus and 'by-the-way' transport to rural locations is available, but it requires time, considerable mobility and a high level of risk-taking, of which not many retailers are capable. The uncertainty surrounding transport arrangements, availability of supplies and destination markets and the need to cultivate good relations with suppliers and other traders for the purpose of gathering market and transport information make a resilient and gregarious individual most suitable for the role. Another hidden hazard of the job is the possibly greater exposure to the AIDS virus, particularly in the Lake zone around Mwanza and in Dar es Salaam.[19] Retailers who wish to break into the arena of mobile intermediaries often seek to incorporate one (or more) family member, so that one member can continue to sell in an on-site market stall while the other travels. This strategy ensures an outlet for the intermediaries' procurement while offsetting the risk of venturing into a new field of trade.

As mentioned previously, the suspension of the Ruvuma Cooperative Union's purchasing activities in Songea created the conditions for the emergence of a group of new large-scale intermediary traders. These

18. Van Donge's year-long study of Luguru traders revealed that the large-scale fruit and vegetable wholesalers were rumoured to be involved in lucrative smuggling activities in contraband ivory, gold, etc. (van Donge, 'Waluguru Traders', 6). The 1988 survey interviews with rice and maize traders did not uncover this dimension. None the less, a couple of the more candid traders who were interviewed mentioned that they had spent time in gaol during the Anti-Economic Sabotage Campaign.

19. The higher risk of contacting AIDS is associated with mobile intermediaries' travelling and the outwardly-directed social lifestyle many pursue in which drinking *pombe* (local beer) with male acquaintances and having contact with prostitutes often occur.

traders were not from the ranks of the town's petty maize traders. They were shopkeepers dealing in non-food items, who saw the business potential of getting involved in the long-distance grain trade. It was estimated that their starting capital was at least TSh. 200,000, a far larger sum than elsewhere due to the high cost of transport and the large bulk loads that are taken by lorry from Songea to Dar es Salaam.[20]

Trader differentiation, as embryonic as it is, has caused feelings of envy and resentment on the part of retailers. Mwanza retailers voiced this most strongly, charging that large-scale traders engaged in monopoly practices during commodity shortages. A sense of competition and 'survival of the fittest' prevails between different types of traders, whereas the evidence suggests that, within each functional level of trade, cooperation and mutual support are widespread, with the exception of the antagonism that exists between licence-paying and tax-evading unlicensed retailers. Amongst retail traders occupying the same marketplace, various forms of cooperation take place. Retailers will mind each other's stalls when a colleague has to absent himself/herself for short periods of time. They will pool their funds to hire commodity transport. Mobile intermediaries are objectively in a very competitive situation with one another, yet they must depend on each other for market information and joint transport arrangements. Retail and mobile intermediary cooperation tends to be informal and *ad hoc*, but very important in overcoming occupational constraints.

There is evidence that Dar es Salaam wholesalers have achieved a more binding sense of cooperation through forming syndicates characterized by a shared group identity among popular, large-scale wholesalers. At the time of the survey there were two major syndicates in maize wholesaling and another two in rice. The syndicates consist of between five and eight traders who are known corporatively as 'Trader X's' group. The syndicate leader hand picks the members on the basis of his estimation of their skill as traders and trustworthiness as individuals. It is thereafter understood that the group members will cooperate with each other and look after each other's stocks when a trader has to absent himself from the marketplace. More importantly, a member is obliged to give a fellow member the 'first option' to buy when he is approached by a supplier but is not in a position to manage the deal on his own. Pooling of capital and income did not appear to take place. Even loans between members were not a normal function of the group. The syndicates were, in essence, loose mutual support groups based on trust and the need to extend one's network of supply and range of clients when handling large

20. Gordon estimates traders' starting capital in DSM ranged between TSh. 20,000 and 100,000 while Scarborough cites a figure of between TSh. 5000 and 100,000 in Arusha, Moshi and Mwanza (Gordon, 'Open Markets for Maize and Rice', 27; and Scarborough, 'Current Status of Food Marketing', 39).

consignments. Whether they would develop into more closely knit groups with market control objectives is a speculative question.

Van Donge's insightful study of Luguru fruit and vegetable traders in Dar es Salaam provides an extremely good source of information on trader differentiation and business dynamics. He points out that, as early trade entrants, the Luguru view Tanzania's market liberalization policies as bad for trade. They face much more competition than before. Their peculiar circumstances in their home area, namely land shortage and matrilineal inheritance, have precluded a farming fallback if and when they are hit by the vicissitudes of a trading career. Matrilineage and few prospects of obtaining land in their home areas are associated with an avoidance of partnership with kin and attempts at distancing themselves from extended family appeals to share access to cash. Luguru traders have to balance their trepidation about family incursions into their businesses with the need for assistance, especially in stall-minding. Most family alliances for business purposes are shortlived and restricted to hierarchical apprenticeships, or cooperation between equals on a venture basis, with no intention of making a permanent partnership. For fear that a partner will walk off with the cash or goods and squander the proceeds on drink, partnerships are usually avoided. The only enduring ones have been between husbands and wives; usually the wife is based in the rural supply area while the husband lives in Dar es Salaam. Avoidance of partnerships restricts the scale and diversification of trade. The volatility of trade propels the trader to seek a fallback, either through land acquisition in his home area, through his wife, or through capital accumulation, i.e. investing in a rentable or resaleable house or property in Dar es Salaam or on the perimeter of the city.[21] More research has to be done to establish how much of this investment pattern is specific to Luguru traders as opposed to Tanzanian traders in general.

Turning to the traders' political activities and identity, there was no indication that they thought of themselves as a corporate interest group. General disgruntlement over taxation, fees and the govenment's ambiguity over trading policy prevailed, but resignation rather than protest was the most common reaction. Marketplaces were often subject to party influence. Tandale wholesale market in Dar es Salaam had a party office on site. The detailed cost breakdown of one large wholesaler revealed periodic contributions to support party activities and gala visits by party dignitaries. At the time of the survey, district party officials were organizing public protests against the IMF's stipulations on the Tanzanian government. The Tandale party chairman, representing the Tandale traders, appeared to see no contradiction between the interests of traders and those of the government vis-à-vis the IMF. The issue was not couched in terms of capitalist enterprise versus socialist state control. Nationalism was the theme – Tanzania versus the imposition of an unfair international economic order.

21. Van Donge, 'Waluguru Traders'.

Ironically, Songea retail traders, most of whom were relatively new to trade, had lodged a protest against the imposition of licence fees in 1987. They went on strike, refusing to sell in the marketplace until the municipal council agreed to lower the licence fee and waive the licence requirement for the extremely small-scale women retailers. However, their protest was more an expression of economic need than the manifestation of an organized political platform.

On the whole, the political climate and public wariness about traders was not conducive to traders forming political pressure groups. It was apparent that their interests *vis-à-vis* the government and party were better served by individual action that combined keeping a low political profile with a willingness to bribe if officials demanded additional payments at road-blocks or for trade licensing.

Did politically powerful individuals in the government or party use their position to gain economically powerful positions in the market, what Cowen and Kinyananjui have termed 'straddling' in the Kenyan context?[22] Were astute state agents taking advantage of economic opportunities in the staple food markets? In Mwanza, an ex-regional party official had become one of the town's biggest wholesalers, supplying schools and government institutions. Rumours within Mwanza suggest the possibility of officials' disguised involvement in staple food trading and associated efforts to control the market for their own profit. Thus the town's high taxation on private traders and the unrealistic stipulations that traders refrain from up-country procurement could act as a deterrent to the ordinary citizens' engagement in trade while benefiting an official with staple food trading ambitions. Mwanza, as a cross-roads for international trade with Kenya, Uganda, Ruanda and Burundi is fertile ground for trading investments. Survey enquiries in the other towns did not yield such insinuations. Background information on the surveyed grain traders suggests that in general they were not, nor had been, party activists or government officials. It is likely that the easy-entry and labour-intensive nature of staple food trading does not make it a preferred sector for investment by higher income state and party bureaucrats.

5. Interaction between the Open and Official Grain Markets

Having examined aspects of the operation of the open market and private traders' organization, it remains to consider whether, as market liberalization proceeds, the relationship between the open and official grain markets

22. Cowen, M. and K. Kinyananjui, 'Some Problems of Capital and Class in Kenya', University of Sussex, IDS (1977).

is simply a zero-sum game. Is the open market continually gaining at the expense of the official market, or is it more complicated?

Evidence has already been presented to show that official NMC/cooperative produce buying and consumer sales have declined (Tables IV.1, IV.2 and V.5). One might logically assume that the open market has expanded to fill the void. The belief on the part of the traders themselves that their numbers have increased considerably between 1985 and 1988 lends credence to this view.

However, since comprehensive data on quantities handled by the open market are not available, there is no way of accurately knowing the volume of commodities traded. But on the basis of Ministry of Agriculture crop production estimates and of assumptions about what proportion of their harvests farmers market on average, it is possible to make some estimates.[23] Tables VI.17–24 give estimates of marketed tonnage for maize and rice between 1983 and 1988. Using the marketed surplus estimates from these tables and the cooperative purchase figures (Table VI.25), one can arrive at rough approximations about how much of the produce market the open market captured between 1986 and 1988. With regard to maize, cooperative marketing got off to an extremely good start in Ruvuma and Arusha in 1985/86, with cooperative purchases considerably exceeding estimated regional market surpluses. As cooperative finance and resources declined, however, the off-take decreased to around 40 per cent in these two regions. Mwanza and Mbeya, on the other hand, were not notable for maize cooperative marketing.

Mwanza and Mbeya paddy crops both figure in cooperative marketing initially. The Mbeya cooperative's percentage steadily increased. In the bumper harvest year of 1987/88, both Mbeya and, to a lesser extent, Mwanza paddy was being channelled through the cooperatives in significant amounts, because of the decline in the producer price differential between the official and open market.

These volume estimates are, however, extremely notional. Time series price data are perhaps a better indicator of changes in the open market. An examination of 1985–88 spatial price integration, updating the 1982–85 spatial price correlation analysis of Table V.3, might provide some insights.

Table VI.26 shows the results of monthly inter-market price correlations for maize between January 1986 and January 1989. First quartile correlation scores have not improved from the 0.25–0.29 reading set in 1983–85, whereas the second quartile score has risen slightly to 0.15–0.19.

23. Accepting MDB estimates of maize and rice marketed surplus at 25% and 50% of total production respectively, it was none the less necessary to revise this crude figure for individual regions. Maize marketed surplus in Mwanza is assumed to be only 10% of a normal harvest and 40% in Arusha, Mbeya and Songea where maize is a major cash crop.

A comparison of the price correlations in Map V.1 with Map VI.2 infers a more extensive, virtually nationwide network in the latter period. The 1986–89 pattern suggests that the 'Big Four' regions, Rukwa (Sumbawanga), Mbeya, Iringa (Njombe) and Ruvuma (Songea), continued to be important maize suppliers but that the direction of their supply had a more northeasterly bias. The Lake deficit area is more apparent but less tightly integrated into the more central and southern parts of the country. This might relate to the comparatively good harvests experienced in supply areas closer to Mwanza, notably Shinyanga and Tabora. Inexplicably, very remote Lindi features on the map. Some of the strongest correlations between 1983 and 1985 were between deficit and supply points, whereas in the latter period the higher correlations tend to be between supply areas, for example Songea and Arusha, or between deficit areas like Lindi and Mpwapwa. This could reflect the exercise of 'just price' criteria on consumer prices in deficit areas and/or the convergence of official and unofficial maize prices. However, one needs to be cautious. Correlations of 0.40–0.60 are too low for drawing conclusions.

Moving to a consideration of the national open rice market, the first quartile correlation scores for the 23 paired rice markets during 1986–88 improved from 0.25– 0.29 to 0.30–0.34 with a slightly more concentrated set of values as indicated by improvement in the second quartile as well (Table VI.26). This evidence suggests that the open rice market was becoming more integrated over time and was more coherent than the open maize market. Looking at Map VI.3, one is struck with what appears to be the opposite tendency in the open maize market. The maize market extended areally while the rice market seems to have become more centralized, with extremely strong integration between the Lake supply area and Singida and Dodoma as central transit points. Curiously Mbeya rice supply dropped out of the picture, while the size of the Dar es Salaam market does not figure, despite its status as the major centre of rice demand. No doubt, this can be explained by Dar es Salaam's diverse sources of supply which would create a unique amalgamated rice price formation.

Overall, the maize and rice price correlations do not provide evidence that the open market became more integrated under the government's market liberalization policies. After 1985, traders were legally freer to trade; there were probably more consumers relying on the open market because of the cutback in NMC supplies; and many constraints on transport were being eased with improved availability of petrol and vehicle spare parts, which facilitated the movement of staple food commodities. The state's tight constrictions on the parallel market in both maize and rice had hesitantly 'opened', making market coherence more likely. However, an open market could not be equated with the ubiquity of market forces in national grain distribution. There were still two distinct market distribution systems and a number of non-market forms of distribution in operation. The net result was a welter of complex distributional forms blending and clashing with one another. Price analysis alone cannot adequately encapsulate the complexity.

Blending was most apparent with respect to gradual price convergence in the two market systems between 1985 and 1988. Tables VI.27 and VI.28 show how the gap between official and open market consumer prices for both maize and rice narrowed. Under IMF pressure NMC staple food consumer prices were allowed to rise. By 1988, the open market price for maize was actually less than the official price in four out of the five surveyed towns and, in the case of rice, in three out of the five towns. This narrowing of the gap and the continuing, albeit declining, recourse that urban consumers had to NMC supplies no doubt caused some disturbance in open market price integration. The NMC official price could have helped to even out seasonal and spatial differences in open market prices in towns where NMC supplies were more plentiful as opposed to towns lacking NMC supply.[24]

While consumer prices in the official and open market converged, producer prices offered by the two systems and overall margins continued to differ. Tables VI.12 and VI.16 contrast the two sets of margins. In general, the open market gave producers a higher percentage of the consumer sale price, ranging between 63 per cent (Mwanza) and 93 per cent (Songea) compared with 53 per cent under the official system. Similarly, the open rice market was from 53 per cent (Mbeya paddy/rice) to 67 per cent (Dar es Salaam), as opposed to 29 per cent for the official market.

Focusing on structural differences in the official and open markets points to several complementarities between the two. The centralized nature of the official system, formerly controlled from Dar es Salaam, then given a more regional basis through the operation of the cooperative unions, had the edge on the open market with regard to national market information. The Ministry of Agriculture's Crop Monitoring and Early Warning Programme put out regular harvested crop estimates. Cooperative societies reported on local purchases and stocks. Cooperative unions conveyed this information and reports on stocks bulked at the headquarters to the NMC. The cooperatives' and NMC's storage facilities consisted of go-downs dotted throughout the country which were not adequate in good harvest years, but were none the less vastly superior in quantity and quality to the makeshift arrangements of private traders.

The open market's decentralized structure, on the other hand, had, by virtue of its extreme lack of physical infrastructure, much lower capital

24. Gordon, H., 'Maize Marketing, Seasonal Prices and Government Policy in Tanzania', mimeo, DSM (1989).

overheads. Notwithstanding the deficiencies in national market information, private traders were probably as aware of the availability of supply at farm and local market level in their regions as cooperative officials. Given their reliance on buses, hired commercial pick-ups and 'by-the-way' lorry transport they were more responsive to the need for timely produce buying from peasants than cooperatives, whose bureaucratic procedures slowed down transport arrangements. Furthermore, the ultimatums served on debtor cooperative unions by the banks during the 1987/88 and 1988/89 buying seasons held up or even precluded cooperative purchasing. When this happened, the buying services of private traders were actively sought, not only by peasants but sometimes by the regional authorities.

Structural complementarity and force of circumstance caused a great deal of interaction between the official and open markets. Due to lack of detailed information regarding long-distance sources of supply, open market mobile intermediaries' reliance on regional cooperative unions for supply was not uncommon.[25] As the NMC cut back on its purchases from the cooperative unions, sales to private traders became a vital lifeline to many cooperative unions, particularly in the more remote areas like Ruvuma.

Cooperative unions, facing a shortage of bank credit with which to buy crops, tended to start purchasing from peasants late in the harvest season and often had to close down buying services early. Some cooperatives were known to operate for only a month. The traders' produce buying was of longer duration and more spatially dispersed.

The Rukwa Cooperative Union could not muster the requisite funds and transport to mount timely produce buying as the harvest piled up in 1988/89. The Mbeya Cooperative Union stepped in, offering to buy Rukwa peasants' produce at the official price plus transport costs. Private traders quickly responded and brought the maize to the cooperative union go-downs in Mbeya town, where they were paid at the union's specified into-store price. The cooperative later alleged that the private traders, posing as farmers, had made super profits.

It was apparent in some cases that the cooperative union was a major source of illicit supply of gunny bags for traders; for example, it was alleged that Mwanza traders acquired bags from the Nyanza Cooperative Union through a circuitous route. In this and other instances, some cooperative unions were subsidizing the private traders' requirements, often with cooperative personnel or other intermediaries undoubtedly enjoying personal financial gain.

The most dramatic case of cooperative/private trader interaction took

25. Personal communication from Ruvuma Cooperative Union official to author, September 1988; Scarborough, 'Current Status of Food Marketing', 17, and Gordon, 'Open Markets for Maize and Rice', 10.

place at the time of the survey in Songea town. The cooperative union's closure by the government pending investigation into corrupt practices halted cooperative buying. The willingness, if not eagerness, of private traders to fill the void was instrumental to the government, for it prevented peasant producers becoming demoralized through not having buyers for their maize crop.

Thus, the ambiguity in the government's market liberalization amidst attempts at resuscitating the cooperative marketing system actually served to encourage *ad hoc* cooperation between the two systems in several areas. However, the functional exchange that arose between the two underlined the fact that private traders were reaching out in order to expand their trading capabilities and scope, whereas the cooperative system was seeking interaction to try to maintain its purchasing levels and economic viability. No amount of interaction with the private market could compensate for the effects of the official system's tapering bank credit. The interaction between the cooperatives and private traders seemed to be part and parcel of the cooperatives' attempt to prolong life in the face of a terminal illness.

6. Summary

The government's trade liberalization policies prompted substantial numbers of economically active working class people in towns to become staple food traders. While the majority of staple food traders were men, women traders were especially prevalent in retailing and in areas where female produce trading was important traditionally. In the 1988 Trader Survey, the traders' demographic characteristics did not vary markedly between towns.

In contrast, the organization of trade in the five towns surveyed differed widely depending on the nature of supply and demand in the town and each area's history of regional market development. Figures VI.2 and VI.3 present a schematic picture of the marketing chain for each town for maize and rice respectively. While all the towns had *in situ* retailers, the distinctive role of the mobile intermediary bringing staple food commodities from the rural areas to the town was more developed in some localities than others.

In Songea, farmers were apt to sell their maize directly to retailers in the Central Market, whereas in Arusha the town retailer often went to rural markets and bought directly from the farmer. In these two places 'long-distance' mobile intermediaries who transferred maize from the rural supply area to a market outside the region, notably Dar es Salaam and Mwanza, were more important than 'short-distance' intermediaries bringing maize to Songea or Arusha town. Short-distance intermediaries, operating intra-regionally or between neighbouring regions, appeared to be more prominent in the Mbeya and Mwanza cases. Mwanza, however, had long-distance traders who bought from markets in the Arusha and Singida regions. The presence of specialized wholesalers was closely related to the size of the market and was therefore restricted to Dar es Salaam and Mwanza.

Rice trading operated on similar principles. Mbeya and Mwanza were rice supply areas in which direct sales often took place between farmers and retailers, thereby reducing the significance of the short-distance intermediary trader, but long-distance intermediaries were the key to the movement of rice from these areas to Dar es Salaam. Evidence suggests that rice wholesaling was only very well-entrenched in Dar es Salaam. Luguru traders dominated rice wholesaling.

Economic differentiation between traders was muted. Wholesalers and mobile intermediaries appeared to be getting higher margins than retailers, yet accumulation had not taken place sufficiently for them to invest in their own motor transport. Competition between traders was tempered by the need for cooperation to overcome the constraints of a seriously inadequate physical infrastructure for trade in terms of lack of transport, storage and market information.

Interestingly, an examination of the open market and official systems also revealed many areas of complementarity, sometimes even cooperation, rather than merely zero-sum rivalry. None the less, the growing economic strength of the open market presented a large threat to cooperatives in the longer run. In any case, private traders were operating on lower margins.

This chapter has dealt primarily with traders' activities and attitudes. It is time to turn to the perspective of the urban staple food consumer.

VII
Satisfying
Urban Consumers

Since the 1940s national food policy has been heavily influenced by the needs of the expanding urban population. Some authors have gone so far as to argue that 'urban bias' in government staple food pricing and marketing organization during the 1970s and 1980s undermined peasant producer incentives.[1] Considering the multiple objectives of food policy and the anti-urban stance of Tanzanian development policy generally this outlook is over-simplified.[2] But reconciling urban consumer needs and peasant producer incentives has involved constant trade-offs with sub-optimal outcomes for both objectives.

The 'basic needs' orientation of national policy-making made urban food security a prominent policy issue in the 1970s. As argued in Chapter I, food security has historically been bound up with state responsibility to its citizenry. Market liberalization of the staple food trade in urban areas has called into question the state's historically accepted role in this area. Not unlike the state marketing system, open market traders in staple foodstuffs have concentrated their efforts on supplying the urban market, so the issue is not 'urban bias', but agency. Who is supplying the towns with staple foods and how successfully are they doing so? Urban residents are in the best position to answer these questions.

This chapter reviews available data on the growth of Tanzania's urban population and the nature of urban food demand before introducing the objectives and methodology of my own 1988 Urban Household Survey of five towns. Characteristics of the households, their food consumption patterns and the attitudes of informants towards open market traders and national food policy will be examined in successive sections.

---

1 See Bates, R.H., *Markets and States in Tropical Africa* (Berkeley, University of California Press, 1981) and Lofchie, M.F., *Agricultural Performance in Kenya and Tanzania* (London, Lynne Rienner, 1989).
2 Bryceson, 'Urban Bias Revisited: Staple Food Pricing in Tanzania', in Hewitt de Alcántara (ed.) *Real Markets* (1992).

1. Urban Growth

Precise estimation of the total urban population and growth rates is difficult because of the changing definition of what constitutes an 'urban' population. Historically, Tanzania's townships were local administrative capitals. If one takes a minimum population of 20,000 as the cut-off point for defining an urban area, there is still confusion. Since 1978 'urban' districts have included designated 'rural' and 'mixed' wards. Furthermore in the most recent 1988 census many 'rural' wards in rural districts have exceeded 20,000 people. Table V.4 provides a conservative estimate of urban growth rates, using the *urban* ward populations of *urban* districts with over 20,000 people in 1978 as the basis for calculation. With these delimitations, 10.9 per cent of the population lived in urban areas in 1988. When all urban, rural and mixed wards in rural and urban districts that exceed 20,000 in population are listed, this count results in an estimated 28 per cent of the Tanzanian population living in settlements exceeding 20,000 people. Probably the best way of estimating how many Tanzanians have an urban life-style is to use the count of the population of urban, rural and mixed wards of the regional capital cities. By this definition, 15 per cent of the Tanzanian population lived in urban areas in 1988.

For the first half of this century the African population of towns was very limited in size. The Second World War was a turning point. The dislocations and opportunities of the wartime economy brought significant numbers of young men to Dar es Salaam. After the war, the emergence of the nationalist movement gave further impetus to the drift towards towns with the rural exodus reaching its highest rate of growth during the 1957–67 inter-censal period (Table V.4).

Both colonial and post-colonial government policy was antagonistic to rapid expansion of Dar es Salaam and the other major secondary cities. Uncontrollable urban growth, which outstripped the development of formal sector employment, was considered a drain on the economy. Informal sector employment was viewed as an unproductive waste of manpower that should be redirected to rural agriculture. The *ujamaa* and villagization programmes were, in part, efforts to deter urban migration.

But clearly, during the 1960s and 1970s, the government's attempt to keep young school leavers 'down on the farm' was not succeeding. The urban influx posed an economic threat *vis-à-vis* the provisioning of urban infrastructure and social services. The establishment of parastatal food marketing and the maize subsidy were largely the outcome of the government's felt duty to guarantee an adequate staple food supply at affordable prices for the urban working class. Urban food shortages, particularly in the capital city, were seen as a potential threat to political stability.[3]

3. In a nation-wide speech in 1979 Nyerere admitted that 'Sugar and *sembe* [shortages]

Whatever methodology is employed for defining urban populations, the urban population growth rate between 1978 and 1988 was more than halved relative to the preceding decade. Tanzania's economic recession beginning in 1979 transformed urban areas from economic panaceas to deserts for prospective migrants. The contraction of job opportunities, the downward spiral of real wages and deteriorating urban infrastructure combined with the basic insecurity of staple food supply difficulties to deter high rates of urban growth.

Significantly, Dar es Salaam and the large urban towns, namely Mwanza and Mbeya, experienced the greatest declines in urban growth between 1978 and 1988 (Table V.4). The greatest increase in urban settlement took place in the small concentrations of population numbering 20,000 to 30,000.

There is a possible association between town population growth and the difficulties of urban food supply during this period. Correlating the 1978–88 population growth rates of the 20 regional towns with their average maize prices yields a negative r^2 which was low, but significant at the 0.05 confidence level.[4]

2. Urban Food Consumption Patterns

What constitutes an adequate staple food supply for an average urban household? Have its content and form changed over time? Colonial and post-colonial household budget surveys (HBS) provide some of the answers to these questions. In the most recent HBS (1976) urban maize consumption by weight was at parity with rural consumption, amounting to roughly 40 per cent of total staple food consumption. Divergence between rural and urban diets is seen with respect to rice and wheat. For example, 17 per cent of the staple food consumption of urban households was rice and 11 per cent wheat, whereas only 6 per cent of rural household staple food consumption consisted of rice or wheat. Rural households were more apt to be eating millet/sorghum, bananas and root crops such as sweet potatoes and yams (Table I.1).

Comparing the food consumption patterns of income groups within urban areas, maize consumption stays relatively constant between 30 and 40 per cent of staple food consumption by weight, except in the highest two income groups where it drops into the 20–30 per cent range and is superseded by rice. The consumption of wheat products is influenced by income. Low-income urban households consume virtually no wheat and

(cont.) bothered him most especially in DSM which was very different from places like Musoma. The shortage of the two items in DSM caused quite a stir' (*Daily News*: 'Mwalimu on food situation: no need to panic', 16/12/79).

4.   Bryceson, 'Urban Bias Revisited'.

very little rice. Their diet approximates that of rural dwellers with a heavier concentration of millet, sorghum, cassava and sweet potato.

Measured by expenditure, the 1976/77 figures show maize and rice each accounting for roughly 30 per cent of total staple food expenditure on average. However, the lowest income group spent only 9 per cent of its staple food budget on rice as opposed to the richest spending 34 per cent, with fairly steady increments in between.

An examination of past HBS findings reveals that urban dietary differences between income groups has remained roughly the same since the early 1950s. Changes through time, such as the decline in expenditure on rice in 1976/77 compared with 1969, involved all income groups.[5] Furthermore, staple food expenditure as a percentage of total food expenditure has stayed constant at 40–45 per cent.

However, there has been a gradual rise in Dar es Salaam residents' expenditure on food generally. In the 1940s low income earners were spending approximately 50 per cent of their income on food, increasing to 65 per cent in the 1950s, declining to 56 per cent in 1965 and reaching roughly 80 per cent according to the 1976/77 HBS and another Dar es Salaam food budget survey.[6] The high income earners' food bill crept from 30 per cent in the 1960s to about 55 per cent in the 1980s.

The 1950s was a decade of rising wage levels. Leslie refers to the hungry period of every month when money to buy food ran out before the next wage payment, but this pertained to the period preceding the establishment of the minimum wage and his description of 'hunger' referred to bachelors not families.[7] Urban food prices were very stable during the 1960s and their rise only began to supersede that of non-food commodity prices in the early 1970s, becoming a notable feature of the mid-1970s, declining during the good harvest of 1977 then escalating thereafter (Table VII.1) After 1978, the minimum wage level did not keep pace with non-food and especially food price increases. Only very large government-announced increases in the minimum wage gave households some relief. The most notable improvement came after the 50 per cent increase in the minimum wage in July 1987, which eased a period of rampant price inflation (Table VII.1).

Dar es Salaam had higher food prices than other towns in the early 1950s.[8] The tendency over time appears to have been for food costs to rise

---

5. See a compilation of DSM household food expenditure 1950–69 in Bryceson, D.F., 'A Century of Food Supply in Dar es Salaam', in Guyer, J. (ed.), *Feeding African Cities* (London, Manchester University Press, 1987), 196–7.

6. Bryceson, 'Century of Food Supply', 174–5.

7. Leslie, J.A.K., *A Survey of Dar es Salaam* (London, Oxford University Press, 1963), 113–116.

8. Tanganyika, Labour Department Annual Report 1952, 46.

faster in the secondary towns than in Dar es Salaam.[9] However, the 1969 HBS did not reveal any clear price advantage for consumers of staple grains in secondary cities as opposed to consumers in Dar es Salaam.[10]

Any consideration of monetary expenditure on food does not give a full picture of the economics of urban household food supply. Non-monetary sources of supply have varied in their significance over time. In a 1950 survey of African labourers in Dar es Salaam, 14 per cent of those interviewed had farms within the perimeter of the town, the majority of which were devoted to subsistence crops, mainly rice.[11] Some 18 years later, in the wake of minimum wage legislation and stable food prices, a survey of the Kinondoni area of Dar es Salaam did not find any of the interviewed residents engaged in farming.[12]

Seemingly conflicting evidence arises from the 1967 population census, which included a question on the incidence of urban farming.[13] Of the Dar es Salaam households that answered the question, 19 per cent were engaged in farming. However, this was a relatively small proportion in comparison with the secondary towns, which averaged 35 per cent, ranging between 10 and 58 per cent.[14] Cities with proportionally larger female populations had a higher incidence of urban farming by household. Since the 1967 census did not enumerate which household members were involved in agricultural production, it is impossible to say whether women were the main producers, but it is likely that they were and, if so, it indicates that their traditional identification with food cropping was being transferred to an urban context. The incidence of urban farming was also inversely correlated with city size, although not at a significant level.[15]

The 1976/77 HBS provides evidence of the widespread incidence of non-monetary sources of urban household food supply (Table VII.2). Urban households in the lowest expenditure group derived as much of

9. Kriesel, H.C. *et al.*, *Agricultural Marketing in Tanzania: Background Research and Policy Proposals* (East Lansing, Michigan State University, 1970), 37.

10. With Dar es Salaam prices set at 100, the staple food price index for nine towns, namely Arusha, Bukoba, Dodoma, Iringa, Lindi, Morogoro, Moshi, Mwanza and Tanga was: maize flour, *dona*, 112; maize flour, *sembe*, 98; wheat flour, 96; rice, 100; white bread, 101 (Tanzania, Bureau of Statistics, *1969 Household Budget Survey, III* (DSM, 1972), 11).

11. Tanganyika, 'Report of the Committee on Rising Costs', DSM, Government Printer (1951), 63.

12. Hoad, P., 'Report on a Socio-Economic Survey of Kinondoni', Institute of Public Administration, Physical Training Course, University College, DSM (1968).

13. Tanzania, Bureau of Statistics, *1967 Population Census*, Vol. II, 178–180.

14. Similarly, in Heijnen's survey of Mwanza town, 35% of all families and almost a quarter of all unmarried town residents cultivated a farm (Heijnen, J.D., *Development and Education in the Mwanza District (Tanzania): A Case Study of Migration and Peasant Farming* (Rotterdam, Bronder-Offset, 1968).

15. The Spearman's Rank Correlation Coefficient was −0.55 for inter-town incidence of farming and urban sex ratios, which is significant at the 0.005 level. The correlation between urban population size and urban farming was −0.40, which was not significant.

their cereal supplies from non-monetary sources as an average rural household. As household expenditure increases the proportion of food from non-monetary sources declines, ranging from 87 per cent to 3 per cent with an average of 31 per cent overall, compared with rural households' 85 per cent.

While past HBS data are useful for tracing changes up to the 1980s, they cannot be used to infer the situation during the 1980s. The intensity of the economic crisis in Tanzania, its impact on urban households and government policies to mitigate urban food supply constraints, as well as the removal of the *sembe* subsidy and NMC supply shortages, generated new responses and patterns of urban household food provisioning and consumption. It was necessary to conduct a household survey to assess the situation prevailing in the late 1980s.

3. 1988 Urban Household Survey Methodology

In conjunction with the five-town trader survey, a household survey was conducted encompassing 188 households, of which 64 were in Dar es Salaam and the rest apportioned roughly equally between Mwanza, Arusha, Mbeya and Songea. The objective of the survey was to identify differences in staple food consumer behaviour between towns and, to a lesser extent, between households within towns, following the food supply difficulties of the 1980s, the new market liberalization policies of the government and the development of private food trading networks.

Administered by the same enumerators who carried out the trader survey, the household survey consisted of a small, selective cross-section sample, which might best be termed a 'spectrum approach'. Enumerators were asked to interview households from all the major neighbourhoods in their towns to obtain wide coverage of the income and ethnic groups residing in the town. Permission to approach households for questioning was sought from the municipal government and party officials. In neighbourhoods where the enumerator did not have contacts to facilitate household introductions and casual encounters were not feasible as a basis for widening the selection field, party authorities were often instrumental in putting the enumerators in contact with households from which to select. The enumerators were, however, careful to avoid being identified with officialdom. In addition to interviewing households from a spectrum of different income and ethnic groups, the enumerators ensured that different household sizes were represented and households of female headship were included in the sample. It cannot be claimed that the spectrum sampling approach adopted produced a statistically unbiased sample of the town's household composition. The enumerators, as long-time residents of the town, applied their in-depth knowledge of the town's population to the selection of households. The result has been a small household sample with sufficient socio-economic variation to distinguish tentatively different household patterns. More importantly, at the inter-town level, the findings of the household survey can be juxtaposed to the trader survey, revealing relationships between the food trading patterns and urban household food provisioning strategies.

The household questionnaire centred on the composition of the staple food consumption of household members, their market and non-market sources of staple food supply, the proportion of household income spent on food, coping strategies through periods of food crisis, and attitudes towards traders. These were all considered to be non-controversial topics. Direct questions on household income were avoided out of respect for the sensitivities of the respondents, but answers to the questions on the portion of household income spent on staple foods made it possible to get a rough estimate of household income for the purposes of household income categorization. The enumerators were asked to make careful observations about the household's ownership of consumer durables and amenities, as well as to ask casual questions about income sources not revealed through ascertaining the occupations of household members. Some households, especially in Mwanza, displayed a strong reluctance to give any information about their ancillary sources of income. After each household interview the enumerator gave the household a rating on a seven-point socio-economic scale ranging from 'very poor' to 'very wealthy' (Table VII.3). The mean average of the household socio-economic score in all five towns turned out to be 'lower middle income', a useful control in assessing inter-town differences.

The household interviews were conducted with male heads of households, female heads of households, or senior females in the household. Given the proliferation of income-earners within urban households resulting from economic crisis conditions, interviews with any one household member could not yield a fully informed, comprehensive picture of the household's earnings and expenditure. It is apparent that, while pooled income for household staple food consumption is the norm, discrete income streams of individual household members can and do affect intra-household consumption patterns. None the less, this is truer for non-staple foodstuffs than for staple foods, which are generally cooked within the household and eaten by all household members. Previous food consumption studies have indicated that men as well as women are active in purchasing household foodstuffs.[16] Thus, it was considered possible to conduct interviews on the topic of household food budgeting with either men or women. It should be noted, however, that the women interviewed

16. Mgaza, O. and H. Bantje, H., *Infant Feeding in Dar es Salaam*, Tanzania Food and Nutrition Centre and BRALUP (DSM, 1980).

tended to be more candid than the men regarding sources of food supply and income.

4. Household Characteristics by Town

Before considering the food consumption patterns and attitudes of the surveyed households, it is helpful to describe some of their main demographic and socio-economic characteristics.

The interviewees were on average aged in their mid-thirties to early forties. As is common in Tanzania's urban areas, most were migrants to their respective towns. Overall, only 14 per cent had been born in the town, a further 28 per cent gave their birth location as within the region, whereas 42 per cent had come from a distant region. In Dar es Salaam, over 85 per cent of those interviewed fell into the latter category. Mwanza's, Mbeya's and Songea's interviewees, on the other hand, tended to be predominantly from rural locations that were not too far from the town. Arusha was an intermediate case. Table VII.4, showing the region of birth of interviewees, reflects the extremely heterogeneous population in Dar es Salaam in comparison with the other towns. Most migrants arrived in the town after independence. However, over 50 per cent of the Mwanza and Mbeya interviewees were very recent migrants who came during the 1980s.

The average household size was 5.5 persons, not too dissimilar from the average household size of 5.0 recorded in the 1976/77 HBS. Mbeya households were the smallest on average at 4.3 and Songea's the largest at 6.9 members (Table VII.5). Of the households interviewed, 16 per cent were female-headed. The ratio of adults to children was high, with almost 75 per cent of the households registering an adult membership of 50 per cent or more of total members. Most households had between 30 and 50 per cent of their membership earning an income. In Songea the number of household earners in relation to non-earners was even higher.

Occupationally, household heads were engaged in a wide array of employment activities. Roughly a third of household heads in Dar es Salaam, Mwanza and Arusha had 'high level' formal employment of a professional nature compared with Mbeya and Songea, where these occupations accounted for less than 20 per cent of the total. Junior level formal employment was pronounced in Songea and, in all five towns, constituted 17 per cent of the sample on average. Service employees were most prevalent in the Dar es Salaam and Arusha samples and were found in very small numbers in Mbeya and Songea. The vast majority of Mbeya household heads were self-employed. Songea also registered very high numbers of self-employed. Elsewhere roughly a quarter to a third of the town samples consisted of self-employed household heads (Table VII.6).

In examining the household head's occupation and the other household members' economic activities to see how many are engaged in activities that may be instrumental in improving the household's access to direct market or non-market sources of food, interesting patterns emerge. A very large percentage of households have at least one member engaged in trading activities. This is as high as 77 per cent in Mbeya and Songea, 70 per cent in Mwanza and 59 and 52 per cent in Dar es Salaam and Arusha respectively. The household members' trading activities could be directly instrumental in obtaining food supplies or, indirectly, in facilitating food purchase by keeping household earnings abreast of inflation, thereby offsetting the incessant deflationary spiral in formal sector earnings.

A direct non-market supply of food from the household members' farming is apparent. Almost 75 per cent of Songea households have at least one member engaged in farming, with three or four members being the norm. This agrarian pattern is unique to Songea and undoubtedly reflects the small size of the town and its only recent urban growth. In Dar es Salaam and Mwanza, only 15 per cent of the households have one or more members engaged in agriculture. The intermediary cases are Arusha and Mbeya, where over 25 per cent of the households have one or more members thus engaged (Table VII.7).

Since the party has been instrumental in food rationing and has influence over local food policy-making, it is relevant to note how many households reported party officials amongst their membership. Overall only 2.7 per cent of the households fitted into this category, the largest proportions being in Arusha (6.7 per cent) and Songea (5.7 per cent). The figure for Dar es Salaam was 1.6 per cent and none in Mwanza and Mbeya.

It is apparent that, in all but the highly agrarian Songea case, household purchasing power is critical to ensuring food adequacy. Per capita household monthly income was estimated indirectly through questions on total amounts spent on food and percentage of household income spent on food. The resulting figures are extremely notional, but for inter-town comparison are sufficient. Not unexpectedly, the Dar es Salaam household's average per capita monthly income of approximately TSh. 6000 topped the league, followed by Mwanza (TSh. 3400), Mbeya (TSh. 3100), Songea (TSh. 2000) and Arusha (TSh. 1500). Arusha's figures seem exceptionally low and are possibly influenced by a lower average age of the informants and the preponderance of women informants, who tend to earn less than men and who may have limited information on the earnings of male household members.

5. Household Food Supply

The following sub-sections will examine the survey findings of each town in turn.

5.1 Dar es Salaam

Maize was the main staple consumed in three-quarters of all Dar es Salaam households, most of the rest consumed rice and less than 5 per cent were dependent on other staples, e.g. bananas (Table VII.8). The consumption pattern of secondary staple foodstuffs was reversed, with rice being the most popular (71 per cent) followed by maize.

Only 20 per cent of the households cultivated some of their food supply (Table VII.9). In half these cases, the cultivated foodstuffs amounted to 10 per cent or less of total household supply. Bananas were the most frequently grown, followed by maize, cassava, rice and sweet potatoes. But Dar es Salaam households were as likely to be cultivating non-staple foods. Fruit (usually mango, pawpaw and citrus) and coconut trees, typical coastal crops, were the most common.

Generally only one member of the household was involved in cultivation (Table VII.10), usually the male head of household. One-third of all cultivators were, in fact, employed workers rather than household members (Table VII.11). The influence of the market pervades Dar es Salaam household cultivation with respect to land as well as labour. Almost one-fifth of the farming households have large holdings of over 10 acres (Table VII.12), which suggests that these farms not only supply household needs but are run for commercial purposes. While Dar es Salaam had proportionately fewer farming households than the rest of the towns, per capita acreages of the farming households were two to six times larger than elsewhere (Table VII.13). Even if the exceptionally large farm of 100 acres is removed, the per capita hectarage of farm-holding households in Dar es Salaam is still higher than in the other towns. Almost half of those with farms were households that had been categorized as 'moderately wealthy'. None of the 'poor ' or 'moderately poor' reported having farms. Less than 20 per cent of the middle income groups had farms, whereas over 85 per cent of the 'moderately wealthy' did. In most cases the farms had been purchased and were located within the town perimeter, rather than being adjacent to the residence or forming part of the family's holdings up-country (Table VII.14).

Over a third of the households received staple foodstuffs from extra-household sources, but usually supply was reported to be occasional and the percentage of household staple foodstuffs covered by such supply was generally below 10 per cent of total consumption (Table VII.15). Receipt of non-purchased staple foodstuffs did not seem closely associated with household income. Households classified as 'very poor' as well as the 'upper middle' group received above average amounts of non-purchased staple foodstuffs. In three-quarters of the cases the source of supply was the extended family; it thus tended to come from the regional birthplace of the interviewee. However, Mbeya, Iringa, Ruvuma and Tanga stand out as disproportionately large regional suppliers. Maize was by far the most frequently mentioned non-purchased food item received, followed by rice and bananas (Table VII.16).

Dar es Salaam households were more reliant than others on market purchases of staple foodstuffs, which on average accounted for 89 per cent of the total household supply (Table VII.17). Maize purchases in the preceding week amounted to 2.1 kg. per capita. Most households were purchasing roughly a *debe* a week of maize grain from retailers; a *debe* is a standard volume measure in East Africa sold in large tins amounting to approximately 17 kg. Most households bought some portion of their maize supply in the official market. However, two-thirds of all maize-purchasing households relied on the open market for over 90 per cent of their supply (Table VII.18). In the week preceding the interview all the households conducted their purchases in the open market. Comparing the replies to the question of what the 'usual' price for maize was on the open market with what open market retailers reported revealed a discrepancy of a couple shillings. Consumers reported paying 13 per cent more on average.

Weekly average per capita rice purchases were almost on a par with maize purchases at 1.8 kg. However, this average was boosted by a few households making large bulk purchases. Generally, reliance on the open market was even more pronounced for rice than for maize. None the less, during the week preceding the interview 15 per cent of rice-purchasing households had managed to obtain supplies from the official market. They were the only households in the entire national survey to have done so. The usual prices that consuming households reported paying on the open market were just 4 per cent more than the retailers' reported selling prices.

Dar es Salaam household staple food purchases were restricted primarily to rice, maize grain and maize flour. The only other staple food that a significant number of households bought was bananas. The interviewees' rough approximations of monthly per capita expenditure on staple foodstuffs were highest in Dar es Salaam at TSh. 837 (roughly £4) (Table VII.19). None the less, with higher average incomes in Dar es Salaam (Table VII.20), the proportion of household income spent on staple foods was estimated at 37 per cent, not as high as in Mwanza and Arusha (Table VII.21). Total food expenditure as a percentage of income was almost double that figure at 65 per cent.

Most households reported a fairly stable pattern and level of expenditure on staple foodstuffs. Some food substitution due to price variation and availability of income was noted. The presence of house guests also made an impact on purchase levels. Economical bulk purchasing was more common for maize than rice. The maize was usually obtained at Dar es Salaam's Tandale wholesale market and transported by bus or, in the case of more affluent households, by office transport or hired pick-up (Table VII.22).

The food supply situation was deemed to be adequate at the time of the survey in 1988. Looking back, the most difficult period for food availability began in 1982 and culminated in 1984 (Table VII.23). Deficiencies in market supply were cited most frequently as the cause of food supply difficulties (Table VII.24). Rice shortages were seen to be especially problematic. The Dar es Salaam informants were far more likely to view the inadequacies of market supply as the root cause of their households' food supply difficulties than elsewhere. The households' reactions to the difficulties were highly variable. Food substitution was common, followed by resorting to purchase in the parallel market (Table VII.25). Reliance on the official market was very heavy until 1982–84 when shortages began to force households to switch to purchasing more expensively priced maize on the open market. Compared with Mwanza, Mbeya and Songea, far fewer households in Dar es Salaam took up farming.

When asked what could be done to improve the food supply situation, the most common response was more market liberalization (Table VII.26). A number of measures to improve agricultural production were cited as well as the need for transport infrastructural improvements. A minority were of the opinion that more government intervention was needed. When asked specifically what remedial measures the government should pursue, the main response was that it should allow the market to operate unimpeded, remove road barriers and encourage private traders with the provision of improved market premises and reduced taxation on traders (Table VII.27). Many interviewees, acknowledging the continuing operation of the official market, suggested various improvements to it, notably increased producer prices.

The informants' recommendations regarding the activities of traders largely supported their existence and consisted of suggestions about how to expand and 'reform' their activities to serve the consumer better (Table VII.28). Notable was the view that the marketing chain should be streamlined to reduce the number of middlemen, preferably with the Dar es Salaam trader buying direct from the producer. A number of informants had reservations about the traders' integrity and felt they should be more honest in their dealings.

5.2 Mwanza

Maize is even more popular as the primary staple food in Mwanza than in Dar es Salaam. Rice is the secondary staple to the exclusion of all others, except one household consuming cassava (Table VII.8).

The proportion of Mwanza households farming was close to the national survey average at 41 per cent (Table VII.9). Of these over half farmed less than 20 per cent of the household's staple food requirements. Compared with Dar es Salaam, the cropping pattern of these households was geared more to the production of staple foods, especially the two main staples, rice and maize, with cassava of lesser importance. The Mwanza households' farming efforts involved more family members; 50 per cent of those farming had two or more members cultivating (Table VII.10). The cultivating role of resident relations outside the immediate nuclear family surfaced. Employed workers constituted a smaller proportion of the total, but were none the less prominent (Table VII.11).

While proportionately more households had acreages than in Dar es Salaam, Mwanza acreages were substantially smaller than those of any of the other towns (Tables VII.12 and VII.13). Two-thirds of these plots were family holdings and one-third were either purchased or rented (Table VII.14). Locationally, one-third were within the town perimeter, another third in a nearby home area and the others equally divided between those within the town, those in a distant home area and those in a distant non-home area. Thus, most household plots were relatively near the town. There was no clear association between the incidence of household farming and income. Roughly half the moderately poor and middle income groups had plots. The vast majority of the upper middle and very wealthy groups were farming households, but the moderately wealthy were not involved in farming. The income group samples, however, are too small to come to any firm conclusions.

The receipt of non-purchased staple foodstuffs from extra-household sources was not an important feature in Mwanza. Only 31 per cent received any foodstuffs and usually only a modicum (Table VII.15). These food parcels of rice and maize, sometimes cassava or potatoes, were invariably from family members, usually gifts, primarily from parents living in rural areas of Mwanza region (Table VII.16).

With 79 per cent of their total staple foodstuffs being purchased, Mwanza households were slightly less dependent on the market purchase of staple foodstuffs than Dar es Salaam ones (Table VII.17). Maize purchases over the preceding week were close to the survey's national average at 1.7 kg. per capita. Nearly 90 per cent of the households were relying almost solely on open market supply (Table VII.18) and were paying on average the highest open market prices in the survey. Prices reported by consumers and by traders differed only slightly.

Rice purchases during the preceding week were less frequent and considerably smaller in quantity than those of maize, even though Mwanza enjoyed the lowest open market rice prices. The proximity of rice production, and the households' ability to get rice through family and friends, served to depress the level of rice purchase. What purchases were made always took place in the open market and were apt to occur early in the season when prices were lower. The Mwanza households' purchases of other staple foodstuffs in the preceding week were negligible, indicating the pre-eminence of rice and maize in the diet.

Despite complaints about high food costs, the interviewees' estimates of monthly staple food costs per capita were moderate, lower than in all the towns except Songea (Table VII.19). This might relate to the Mwanza households' relatively low expenditure on rice, which is the most desirable but costly staple food in Tanzania, as well as to their larger than average family size, which could offer economies of scale in food purchase. This finding, together with Mwanza's second highest estimated monthly income per capita (Table VII.20), conflicts with a reported high percentage of income spent on staple foods and food generally (Table VII.21). The data have to be considered unreliable because of the extremely small number of households willing to answer questions on income and food expenditure.

Mwanza households reported less variation in household staple food purchase than elsewhere. The main reason given for an increase in food expenditure was the expansion of household requirements arising from visitors. Linking this to the importance of extended family members from nearby rural areas in the provisioning of household foodstuffs might suggest that urban–rural ties are strong in Mwanza. Bulk purchases of maize and rice were not frequent and when they did occur they were usually made at the town market or a local rural market (Table VII.22).

It is interesting to note that, whilst 1984 stood out as a difficult year for food availability in Mwanza town, the preceding years were not perceived as being as acute as they were by the Dar es Salaam interviewees (Table VII.23). Overwhelmingly, food supply difficulties were seen in terms of high food prices (Table VII.24). Household reactions to a food crisis were wide-ranging. Measures that seemed relatively important in Mwanza, compared with the other towns, included efforts to withstand high food prices by increasing household income through trade or other money-making ventures, reducing consumption, resorting to patron–client relations for supply, and initiating or increasing household farming (Table VII.25).

In contrast to Dar es Salaam, the Mwanza interviewees seemed considerably less enamoured with the open market. A large proportion of them wanted the government to step in and stabilize consumer prices. Otherwise, opinion leaned towards the view that the problem had to be solved at its root by increasing agricultural production and producer prices. Improving farmer input supply was considered useful and many were of the opinion that everyone should farm. This belief was extended to a call for government to give plots to civil servants and other urban dwellers (Tables VII.26 and VII.27).

The Mwanza informants took a dim view of the role of traders, with only a handful considering them 'useful'. The vast majority felt that their activities should be curbed. In other words, they should be made to adhere to price control, their prices should be lowered to a 'reasonable' level, and they should reduce their profit-seeking (Table VII.28).

5.3 Arusha

Arusha respondents revealed a dependence on three staple foods, namely, bananas, maize and rice (Table VII.8). Many of the households in the sample with a preference for bananas were Chagga from nearby Kilimanjaro.

Arusha households were situated halfway between Mwanza's higher and Dar es Salaam's lower incidence of farming their own food (Table VII.9). But the Arusha farming households were more likely to contribute substantially to household supplies, i.e. over a third of total supply, compared with the other two towns. The relatively low incidence of farming undoubtedly relates to the shortage of land not taken up by coffee plantations in the vicinity of Arusha. However, because the land in the area is generally quite fertile, those who have access to it can get good returns from their labour input. The staple food crops grown are primarily maize and bananas. Even more popular is the cultivation of beans and onions, Arusha being especially suited to these crops, which fetch good prices in the open market.

Cultivation of household plots primarily involved household labour, with employed workers making very little input. Unlike Dar es Salaam and Mwanza, the role of wives in household cultivation was striking; male heads of household were far less important (Table VII.11). This might relate to the fact that a much bigger portion of Arusha household plots were in the town, adjacent to the house and thus making it easier for housewives to combine their agricultural activities with other domestic chores (Table VII.14).

The average size of household acreages was larger than in Mwanza and on a par with Mbeya and Songea. Small acreages of one acre or less were the norm, acreages of 1–6 acres were not uncommon and a couple of households maintained large farms of 10–20 acres. These large farms owned by upper middle and moderately wealthy households serve to raise the town's average per capita acreage figure (Table VII.13). Removing them from the sample places per capita acreages on the same level as those of Mwanza. Half the plots were family holdings and only 10 per cent of them were purchased (Table VII.14). Arusha household plots were distinctive in being overwhelmingly within the town or the town perimeter. Only a few were in nearby home areas and none were in distant home or non-home areas. This pattern is associated with the presence of European settler and large state farms in the environs of Arusha, which precludes widespread access to land. Furthermore, the

population born in a distant region, which constituted a large percentage
of the sample, would have had difficulties procuring land. Many of the
residents of Arusha are Chagga who migrated to Arusha and other towns
in response to lack of land in their home area of Kilimanjaro.

Arusha households, more than elsewhere, rely on non-purchased staple
foodstuffs, primarily from family and friends (Table VII.15). In over half
the cases the amount of food is 5 per cent or less of total household
requirements. Most of the others receive between 6 and 25 per cent.
Recipients of food parcels tend to be households at the lower end of the
income scale. Most food gifts consist of maize or bananas and, less
frequently, rice and beans (Table VII.16).

The Arusha and Mwanza households share the same level of
dependence on purchased foodstuffs. Roughly 80 per cent of total
household supply is obtained from a market (Table VII.17). In the week
before the survey, 40 per cent of the households purchased maize These
purchases calculated on a per capita basis were on average larger than
elsewhere. Since maize prices on the open market were at their lowest in
Arusha at the time of the survey, it made sense to buy in greater quantity.
Almost two-thirds of Arusha households had at some time over the year
purchased maize in bulk, mostly from the town market or bus stand, using
a hired pick-up or handcart to transport it home (Table VII.22). Virtually
all maize purchases were made in the open market (Table VII.18). There
was a discrepancy of 24 per cent between what consumers reported
paying and what traders purported to charge. This difference can partly
be explained by variations in the location of the transaction. Prices at the
bus stand and other unofficial market locations were lower than in the
town market.

Twice as many households bought rice during the preceding week than
maize, but the quantity of rice purchased was small. All rice was obtained
in the open market and again prices reported by consumers exceeded
those reported by traders. Bananas and maize flour were purchased
during the preceding week as well.

Per capita expenditure on staple foodstuffs was roughly at the same
level as in Mwanza (Table VII.19) and, according to the informants'
estimates, amounted to a high 46 per cent of total income, while total food
costs were approximately 82 per cent (Table VII.21). The large component of household income going to staple foodstuffs in Arusha seems
anomalous considering the relatively moderate level of food prices,
particularly for maize. However, according to Table VII.20, there were
far more low income households in Arusha than elsewhere, with a
monthly per capita income of less than TSh. 1000. Slight to moderate
variations in monthly staple food purchases were reported, generated
primarily by food substitution in response to price fluctuation.

People spoke of favourable food supply conditions in 1988. During the preceding decade, 1984 was the only year that posed severe food supply difficulties for the surveyed households (Table VII.23). A difficult year was described as a year of high prices and shortages of rice, beans and bananas (Table VII.24). Households responded to the shortages by substituting starchy roots (where permitted by NMC supplies and government ration shops), purchasing direct from rural markets, and initiating family businesses to help ride the crest of inflationary food prices (Table VII.25). Informants largely shared the opinion of their Mwanza counterparts that the food shortages had to be addressed through increased production assisted by government measures to make market distribution more efficient (Table VII.26). Less than 15 per cent of responses cast market liberalization as the solution (Table VII.27), whereas almost 40 per cent wanted the government to regulate consumer prices, eliminate middlemen or improve the official market system and producer prices. The remainder were suggestions for the government to improve the transport or producer infrastructure. The Arusha respondents' views about the traders' activities were dismissive or disparaging, with 85 per cent saying that traders should adhere to price controls or have their numbers reduced through more direct buying from producers (Table VII.28). Only 5 per cent of the replies were positive about traders.

5.4 Mbeya

Despite the proximity of the Usangu paddy fields, maize is the main staple for the vast majority of Mbeya residents, while rice is the most popular secondary staple foodstuff (Table VII.8). Mbeya households enjoy a much wider variety of secondary staple foods compared with the other towns. These include wheat, Irish potatoes and bananas.

Household food farming in Mbeya is quite common, with 57 per cent of all those interviewed reporting some portion of household staple food consumption derived from their own farm production (Table VII.9). Generally self-provisioning over 30 per cent of their requirements, these households were farming more substantial amounts than the Dar es Salaam, Mwanza and Arusha ones. Maize was the most popular crop, followed by beans and Irish potatoes. Heads of household tended to dominate field cultivation (Table VII.11). Employed workers were rare.

Usually households had only one plot or, at the most, two (Table VII.10). The average acreage size was similar to that of Arusha but with less polarization of large and small holdings (Table VII.12). Per capita acreage size was relatively high at four-fifths of an acre (Table VII.13). The distribution of acreage between income groups was fairly egalitarian. Half to three-quarters of moderately poor, lower middle, middle and upper middle households had acreages. The very poor and the moderately wealthy did not have any land. Almost 60 per cent of the acreages were family holdings, another 18 per cent were purchased and the remainder were 'borrowed' (Table VII.14). This latter category suggests that the market for agricultural land around Mbeya is not highly developed and access to land is easier than in the three towns already reviewed. Borrowing land usually entails negotiated exchanges of a non-monetary nature between friendly households. As long as land borrowing remains an option, there is the likelihood that agricultural land distribution between households will not be too skewed in favour of the high-income households.

As in Arusha, more than half the Mbeya households received non-purchased household staple foods, consisting usually of less than 15 per cent of total consumption (Table VII.15). Interestingly, there was a tendency for the incidence of staple food gifts to rise with income. As in the other up-country towns, the food originated primarily from parents and other family members in the immediate or neighbouring regions. An extremely wide range of foodstuffs was received, with bananas from neighbouring Tukuyu heading the list (Table VII.16).

Because of the relatively high incidence of own-farm production and food parcels from extended family, the purchased component of household staple food consumption amounted to only 62 per cent on average (Table VII.17). About a third of the households were heavily dependent on food purchase, a quarter had little recourse to food purchase and the rest purchased between 35 and 75 per cent of their staple foods.

The incidence of maize purchases in the week before the interview was low. Open market purchases predominated. A comparison of the MDB reported open market price for maize with the interviewees' stated average price reveals a tendency for the interviewees to inflate the price, perhaps an indication of their distrust of traders.

A large percentage of households had purchased rice in the preceding week and virtually all these purchases were made in the open market. The average price households reported paying was 9 per cent over that reported by the traders themselves and 39 per cent over the MDB reported open market price. The discrepancy with the latter relates to the fact that many households purchase rice in very small amounts[17] from neighbourhood retailers, which raises the overall price they pay.

Mbeya households were in the habit of frequently buying other staple foodstuffs, notably bananas, Irish potatoes and maize flour. Per capita food expenditure was extremely high, second only to that of Dar es Salaam, which is surprising in view of the Mbeya households' greater reliance on their own farm production and non-purchased supplies.

17. Purchases were made on the basis of a small bowl volume measurement called an *ndonya*, which amounts to approximately 0.5 kg.

According to consumers, despite the proximity of an ample supply, Mbeya food prices are highly inflationary because the food traders are geared to the prices and market of Dar es Salaam. On the other hand, a large number of those interviewed were themselves traders or self-employed people whose incomes kept up with the rate of inflation. Thus, the percentage of income spent on staple food and food generally was below the survey average (Table VII.21).

Household staple food purchase did vary from month to month. This related primarily to the consumers' food substitution according to the availability and price levels of different commodities. However, it appeared that most households were not in the habit of buying maize or rice in bulk at any time of year (Table VII.22).

Replies to the question on food supply difficulties revealed a very different pattern to that of the other surveyed towns. Since 1979 there had not been a single year that household respondents generally identified as difficult (Table VII.23). The years 1982 and 1983 were considered more difficult than the others, but only marginally so. Inflated food pricing was seen as the biggest problem, followed by inadequate market supply. Non-cultivating households complained that it was difficult to manage without a farm (Table VII.24).

Household reactions to these difficulties focused on the rural area or their own farm supply (Table VII.25). In periods of inadequate town supply, many households sought alternative rural market sources of supply or relied on rural relations. Suggestions for improving the town's food supply centred on agricultural production. Some simply expressed the belief that agricultural production must be increased, others, more specifically, felt this could be accomplished by practising 'scientific' agriculture. A substantial number opined that everyone should farm regardless of urban residence (Table VII.26).

The views of Mbeya respondents regarding government action revealed an eagerness for more state control over the market, particularly in the form of price regulation (Table VII.27). Elimination of middlemen, giving the cooperatives a grain market monopoly and the opening of NMC retail shops were favoured courses of action. Only a small percentage of people thought that the traders' activities should be expanded (8 per cent), the same number held traders in low regard, while two-thirds of the respondents felt that their activities had to be reformed, notably by a reduction in profit-seeking and by refraining from underweighing, hoarding and hawking. Practical suggestions for traders included buying directly from producers and setting up permanent stalls rather than hawking. Some felt that traders should themselves farm, perhaps as a form of 're-education'.

5.5 Songea

Songea householders had the most simple staple food diet of the survey; they were overwhelmingly dependent on maize as a mainstay and rice secondarily (Table VII.8). Their diet is undoubtedly influenced by their approach to food procurement. Songea residents cultivate maize to provide the bulk of their staple food requirements. Only 17 per cent of the households did not farm any staple foods (Table VII.9). Most households were producing 60 per cent or more of their staple food requirements. Cassava, a drought-resistant crop eaten when the maize crop fails, followed maize in importance in the list of crops grown. The cropping pattern of the Songea households bore a stronger resemblance to their rural counterparts than to the other urban dwellers in the survey. The majority of households grew three or more crops and engaged three or more cultivators (Table VII.10), involving far more family members than elsewhere (Table VII.11). Husbands and wives were almost equally active, with offspring and other relations providing additional labour. Wage labour accounted for only 1 per cent of the total labour input.

The households' average acreage was high and not skewed by big commercial landholdings (Table VII.12). Per capita acreages, however, were slightly below average, depressed by the larger than average size of the Songea households (Table VII.13). As in Mbeya, the incidence of farm ownership was not influenced by income level. Virtually all those without farms were not native to the region. Over a third of all the farms were family holdings, but the majority were 'borrowed' (Table VII.14). Less than 10 per cent were purchased. The even larger proportion of borrowed land compared with Mbeya testifies to the relative abundance of land around Songea town. As many as 90 per cent of the plots farmed by the households were within the town perimeter or in a nearby home area. The proximity of the plots facilitated the involvement of whole families in the cultivation effort.

With the high percentage of Songea households involved in agriculture themselves, it is not surprising to find that there is a relatively low incidence of staple food being received from extended family or friends. Only 20 per cent of the households received any foodstuffs, and the amounts were negligible (Table VII.15). Of the food received, rice was the most important, representing a luxury that could not be grown in any quantity around Songea. Households with family or friends living in the Lusewa area, where paddy flourished, could enjoy the occasional rice food parcel.

The percentage of staple food purchased by Songea was extremely low, at only 36 per cent of total staple foodstuffs (Table VII.17). A mere 11 per cent of the households purchased maize in the week preceding the interview and their purchases were, by weight, way below the survey average. Not unlike the other towns, the vast majority of maize purchases were made in the open market (Table VII.18). It is worth noting that the average price of open market maize reported by the consumer was actually below the price reported by the traders.

Rice purchases were far more prevalent with 60 per cent of the households buying it sometime during the preceding week. Unlike anywhere else, average per capita rice purchases were slightly higher than per capita maize purchases. Less than 3 per cent of the households were dependent on the official market for their rice supply. Again the average open market price for rice quoted by consumers was actually below that stated by traders.

Maize flour was the only other cereal staple the respondents reported buying. Despite the town's small per capita average income, staple food costs per capita were extremely low relative to the other towns as a result of the high degree of self-provisioning pursued by Songea households (Tables VII.19 and VII.20). The percentage of income spent on staple foods is lowest in Songea, at 27 per cent on average (Table VII.21). Monthly variation in food purchases was slight, influenced primarily by increased purchases required to cater to visitors' needs. Bulk purchases of maize and rice were rare (Table VII.22).

Household food supply difficulties were remarkably infrequent over the decade. The only year widely considered to be problematic was 1984 (Table VII.23). Most telling is the fact that the difficulties were seen from the perspective of a producer rather than a consumer in the majority of cases. Poor farm harvests on their own farms, shortages of food during the pre-harvest period and over-selling harvested production were seen as the main causes of household food insufficiency (Table VII.24). The usual complaints made about shortfalls of market supply and high commodity prices were voiced less frequently.

The major coping strategies the households used during this period were resorting to market purchase, more careful usage of harvested production, and substituting cassava for maize consumption (Table VII.25). Songea respondents gave extremely varied responses to the question on what the government should do to improve the town's food supplies. Less than 2 per cent opted for more market liberalization *per se* (Table VII.26). Various measures were mentioned, with roughly equal frequency, under the headings of mixed marketing, increasing government market control and improving the official marketing system. As producers themselves, many respondents desired government efforts to improve farmer input supply and crop storage (Table VII.27).

The Songea respondents had by far the most positive attitude towards traders. Over a fifth of those answering expressed favourable opinions about them and a handful even called them 'saviours'. Roughly 30 per cent wanted to see the traders' activities expanded, whereas another third made various suggestions for their reform (Table VII.28). It appears that the Songea residents' high estimation of traders was directly influenced by the prevailing predicament of the suspended Ruvuma Cooperative Union. More from the perspective of producers than consumers, the traders' activities were seen as highly beneficial to the region's economy, affording an outlet for surplus maize production which helped to avert disaster when cooperative buying stopped.

6. Household Perspectives on Food Traders: Practicalities and Prejudices

Having reviewed the survey findings for each town in detail, it is now possible to draw some conclusions about consumer attitudes towards staple food traders. According to NMC figures and consumer statements, a reliance on private traders for supply of household staple foodstuffs has grown very rapidly over the preceding decade. Have changes in public attitudes kept up with this practical reality? Has the traditional wariness about the traders' profit-seeking activities softened? In this sub-section I look at how differences in food availability, food costs and local cooperative performance affect attitude formation before going on to analyse the roots of the people's prejudices towards traders.

6.1 Reckoning Food Availability

The indispensability of staple foodstuffs to people's lives makes changes in food availability the most forceful influence on attitudes towards food traders and causes people to feel strongly about food marketing policies generally. Decisive factors in attitude formation were the lack of NMC-supplied staples in some towns as opposed to others and the degree of gradualness in the removal of NMC town supply. Not surprisingly, Dar es Salaam and Mwanza, the two largest towns with a heavy reliance on market-supplied food, had the greatest number of respondents stating the need for market liberalization (Tables VII.26 and VII.27). However, pro-market liberalization views outnumbered pro-government intervention views only in Dar es Salaam. In 1985/86 Dar es Salaam had experienced drastic cutbacks of NMC staple food supplies (Table V.5). Since the traders had provided the major supply fallback during this period of acute food shortage, the city's residents understandably felt threatened by any possible restrictions on private traders. The need for a fallback option overshadowed the fact that NMC-supplied maize was more prevalent in Dar es Salaam households than elsewhere (Table VII.18). Interestingly, the Mbeya respondents, who received the smallest NMC supply relative to their requirements, were the most eager to see an increase in government market control (Table VII.27). Thus the allure of 'something different' prevailed in the minds of dissatisfied consumers.

Attitudes towards traders were conditioned by the availability of alternative supply possibilities. For first generation urban dwellers, farming is a knee-jerk reaction to food shortages. However, its feasibility varies from town to town and from household to household. It is unfortunate that the previous household budget surveys do not offer disaggregation of data for up-country towns, enabling a comparison of former levels of household self-provisioning. The 1967 census, however, did include a question regarding the incidence of farming activity of urban household members. The proportion of households with cultivating members was 22 per cent in Mbeya, 19 per cent in Dar es Salaam, 18 per cent in Arusha and 10 per cent in Mwanza.[18] Songea was not included. In contrast, the 1988 Urban Household Survey found the incidence of agricultural households as follows: 74 per cent in Songea, 27 per cent in Mbeya and Arusha, 16 per cent in Dar es Salaam and 14 per cent in Mwanza (Table VII.7). The 1967 and 1988 figures are not strictly comparable, but, taking the 1988 findings at face value, suggest that there could have been an increase of cultivating households in Mwanza, Mbeya and especially Arusha and a decrease in Dar es Salaam. Dar es Salaam's sheer size as a city gave its residents less opportunity to cultivate than elsewhere. And those Dar es Salaamites wishing to cultivate in their up-country home areas had much further to travel during a period when petrol and vehicle shortages in the country made travel difficult. It appears that urban dwellers in general tried to alleviate the market shortage of staple foods during the 1980s with self-provisioning, but those in up-country towns were in a better position to do so.

According to the 1976 HBS figures, the low-income households were the ones that tended to depend on non-monetary sources of foodstuffs (Table VII.2). The 1988 survey evidence strongly suggests that this pattern has changed. In Dar es Salaam, Mwanza and, to a lesser extent, Arusha, households with farms have above average incomes. Dar es Salaam and Arusha households had statistically significant positive correlations between the percentage of food they farmed and their income level. In all the towns, the per capita acreage of land the household farmed was inversely related to the number of years one lived in the urban locality. In the case of Dar es Salaam, Mbeya and Arusha, the correlations were significant. The survey results suggest that the market for farm land is already well-established in Dar es Salaam, Mwanza and Arusha. In Mbeya and Songea, on the other hand, 'land borrowing' is still found. However, only

18. Cited in Bryceson, D.F., 'Urbanization and Agrarian Development in Tanzania with Special Reference to Secondary Cities', Report for the International Institute for Environment and Development, London (February 1984), 56.

Songea offers a relative abundance of nearby farm land and easy access for the newcomer.

Getting food parcels from relations or friends is a feature of all the towns and there are no clear associations between its incidence and the socio-economic features of the household. Only Mbeya displayed a significant positive association between the receipt of food parcels and the year of arrival in the town. Those who had arrived most recently, usually from nearby Rungwe, tended to receive more food. Dar es Salaam households are not disadvantaged relative to households in other towns. Non-purchased food transfers average between 5 and 10 per cent of total household consumption in Dar es Salaam, Mwanza, Arusha and Mbeya, with a wide variation between households within towns. Some households receive substantial amounts, whereas most receive nothing. In Songea, on the other hand, food transfers are negligible. The highly agrarian nature of Songea households makes food parcels from rural relations unnecessary.

Survey evidence clearly indicates that dissatisfaction regarding food availability is far more marked in Dar es Salaam. Taking the average annual percentage of households experiencing food supply difficulties by year as a measure of public discontent, Dar es Salaam's average was three times that of Arusha, Mbeya and Songea and 65 per cent greater than Mwanza's (Table VII.23). When asked to specify their grievances, Dar es Salaam informants mentioned supply shortages most frequently, whereas complaints about food prices were more prevalent in the other towns (Table VII.24). When market supplies fail them, Dar es Salaam households are in a weaker position. Self-provisioning of food was more difficult for them, and particularly for the lower-income households. The purchased component of Dar es Salaam household supply superseded that of the other towns (Table VII.17). The more favourable attitude towards traders voiced by Dar es Salaam householders during the survey reflects the stark realism that they do not trust the official marketing system to supply them adequately with staple foods and their own capability to self-provision is weak.

A less extreme but similar situation prevails in Mwanza. The town's food supply is irregular. Households have not had recourse to sufficient supplies from the NMC for many years. Traders are accepted as a fact of life, but reform of their activities is placed high on the agenda (Table VII.28).

Songea presents a fascinating contrast. With its small population and land abundance, the town's residents are largely self-provisioning. Urban food availability has only been a problem in 1984, a year noted for its extremely bad harvest. The popularity of traders in Songea stems not from their role as suppliers of food, but as purchasers of food (Table VII.28). Songea urban residents found traders a vital fallback when the cooperatives failed to purchase their harvested surplus.

In Arusha and Mbeya, both located in grain surplus areas that are well-integrated into the national market, traders are viewed with cynicism. This cynicism is exercised from the safety of Arusha's relatively favoured NMC supply (compared with other up-country towns) and the Mbeya residents' substantial self-provisioning of their staple food requirements. Mbeya residents, in particular, identified traders with profiteering and felt that their activities should be curbed (Table VII.28). Traders' pricing practices were most at issue.

6.2 Pricing Food

So much of the writing on Tanzanian food supply dwells on the impact of pricing. Given that price data are more available than other information, this is understandable. However, food prices are not as revealing as some commentators assume. The level of self-provisioning and elusive sources of household income cloud our interpretations of food price data. None the less, any examination of household food economies is incomplete without the pricing dimension.

From the perspective of the consuming household, relative food prices are the most significant. Food costs are weighed against income. Estimated per capita household income was highest in Dar es Salaam, followed by Mwanza, Mbeya, Songea and Arusha. Staple food expenditure as a percentage of income from highest to lowest was: Arusha, Mwanza, Dar es Salaam, Mbeya and Songea (Table VII.21). The large amount of self-provisioning by the Mbeya and Songea residents lowered the proportion of income that had to be spent on staple foods. Removing these two towns from the list, one finds the expected inverse relationship between income level and proportion of staple food expenditure. Dar es Salaam's comparatively affluent residents were least concerned about food prices, while complaints about pricing were strongest amongst the Mwanza and Arusha informants (Table VII.24).

If and when the NMC provided sufficient staple foodstuffs at government-controlled prices, urban dwellers escaped the annual and seasonal fluctuation of staple food availability and prices. As consumers fell under the sway of the open market, however, they had to acclimatize themselves to the food price variations arising from the natural rhythm of the harvest. Nominal maize prices were most drastic in the lean months before the harvest in February to April, stabilizing and sometimes even dropping from May through November.[19] Nominal rice prices followed a similar seasonal pattern. The coefficient of variation for monthly maize

19. Gordon made a similar observation for Songea, Mwanza and Arusha (Gordon, H., 'Maize Marketing, Seasonal Prices and Government Policy in Tanzania', mimeo, DSM (1989).

prices was greatest in Arusha, followed by Mwanza, Songea, Mbeya and Dar es Salaam. Rice prices presented a different picture, with the descending order of coefficients of variation as follows: Mbeya, Mwanza, Dar es Salaam, Songea and Arusha (Tables VI.27 and VI.28). Thus, there is a tendency for towns in major production areas to experience greater price fluctuation. Despite the seasonal variation of prices, very few of the survey households reported making bulk purchases during the post-harvest price dip. Many households lacked storage space and/or the purchasing power to buy large amounts of grain at any one time. Only the Asian households, interviewed in Mbeya, followed a calculated bulk purchase strategy.

Using Ministry of Agriculture annual crop estimates and open market price data, it is possible to trace the effects of annual harvest fluctuations on year-to-year maize and rice prices. Assuming that nationally 75 per cent of maize production is retained on the farm (60 per cent in maize surplus areas and 90 per cent in maize deficit areas), Tables VI.17–21 compare real price and marketed surplus indices for each town in turn with respect to maize. Figure VII.1 shows that, as expected, real prices are inversely related to market availability of maize and rice. For all areas 1983/84 was a bad harvest year. Real prices have fairly steadily decreased since then everywhere except Mwanza. Between 1983 and 1988, Mwanza's annual marketed maize output on average declined (Table VII.29). None the less, the decline in prices was greater than the decline in marketed output, representing an overall improvement for consumers. Both Arusha and Mbeya experienced substantial increases in surplus with proportionately even greater declines in price. In Dar es Salaam maize prices were less responsive and did not drop in proportion to the national rise in marketed output (Figure VII.1 and Table VII.29).

Tables VI.22–24 present an identical analysis for Dar es Salaam and the major rice-producing areas of Mbeya and Mwanza. From an extremely large paddy surplus in 1983/84, output has on average declined in Mbeya and prices have behaved similarly to those of Mwanza maize (Figure VII.1 and Table VII.30). The Dar es Salaam consumer has benefited from increasing national surpluses and an over-compensating reduction in price. Mwanza, on the other hand, has experienced the greatest increases in marketed output but the rate of price reductions has lagged behind. From this limited data base, it would appear that consumer rice prices are more 'sticky' than maize prices.

Any charge of extortionate pricing on the part of traders contradicts the fact that food prices have risen more slowly than the general cost of living everywhere except in Mwanza and Mbeya (Tables VI.17–24). Rice price increases in Mbeya, however, have to be seen in the light of the declining marketed output of that region. The same argument can be made for maize in Mwanza. Thus, evidence of 'over-pricing' is only available for the Mwanza rice. The public belief that traders are rampantly profiteering in Mwanza and Mbeya largely ignores the market supply conditions of those regions. Objectively, the consumers' perception of traders as extortionate is conditioned more by the general erosion of the purchasing power of their salaries than by staple food traders managing to charge higher prices in real terms.

6.3 Continuing Allegiances

Reality and the consumers' perception of reality have to be distinguished with respect to elements as tangible as food availability and price levels. Such a distinction becomes even more necessary in relation to the role of cooperatives in food marketing. Cooperatives have historically occupied a pivotal position in the politics as well as the economy of the nation. In each of Tanzania's 20 regions, however, the importance of the cooperatives has varied. It is worth considering the consumers' attitudes towards the role of the cooperatives. Did the reinstatement of the cooperatives rekindle old allegiances to the cooperatives? Did consumers perceive a conflict of interest between traders and the cooperatives? Were traders believed to be usurping the role of cooperatives? Or were cooperatives seen to be acting as an undesired brake on the traders' activities?

There were no divided loyalties on the part of Dar es Salaam consumers. For decades Dar es Salaam has been strictly an urban area with virtually no cooperative agricultural marketing activity. Whatever sentiments consumers had regarding cooperatives would have been formed in their home areas. The occasional call for cooperative reform (Table VII.27) was outweighed by a desire for more market liberalization.

One would expect Mwanza, the birthplace of the cooperative movement, to be a different story. Informants' responses, however, did not reveal any strong feelings for or against the cooperatives, with the exception of one person who felt that the NMC should be displaced by the cooperative. Consumers were much more preoccupied with the reform of trader behaviour *per se*. It appears that private traders are accepted as a fact of everyday life by Mwanza consumers. One does not have to delve too far below the surface of Mwanza's cooperative history to discover that the founders of the cooperative movement in the early 1950s were a small group of African traders from Mwanza town who were frustrated by the Asian merchants' trading monopoly in cotton.[20] The expansion of the

---

20. See Maguire, G.A., *Toward 'Uhuru' in Tanzania* (Cambridge, Cambridge University Press, 1969) and Saul, J.S., 'Marketing Co-operatives in a Developing Country: The Tanzanian Case' in Cliffe, L. and J.S. Saul (eds), *Socialism in Tanzania* (DSM, East African Publishing House, 1973).

movement and its association with the embryonic nationalist struggle rested on the involvement of the region's producers, but the central role of town-based patrons hints at a fundamental aspect of the Tanzanian cooperative movement, namely the producers' collective trading interests did not exclude, and indeed were often congruent with, individual profit realization.[21] It is likely that Mwanza consumers have long grown accustomed to a gap between rhetoric and reality in the sphere of marketing.

Cooperative marketing activity in Arusha region has never had a high political profile. Emerging in the mid-1950s, somewhat late in view of Arusha's large cash crop production, the Arusha Region Cooperative Union's (ARCU) influence was impeded by a lack of cohesion arising from its diverse tribal membership and competition from the Tanganyika Farmers' Association, a primarily European settler organization. Throughout the 1960s and early 1970s, ARCU suffered from mismanagement and defalcations.[22] The strong comeback of the union since its reinstatement in 1983 is remarkable. Available evidence suggests that cooperative purchases made huge inroads into the open market in 1985/86.[23] By 1988, ARCU had split into two – the Arusha Cooperative Union and the Rift Valley Cooperative Union.[24] The cooperatives' portion of the maize produce had tapered, but the cooperatives were none the less a notable feature of maize marketing in Arusha. The consumers' responses reflected this in their practical concern about the cooperatives' timely purchase of crops (Table VII.27).

With a relatively underdeveloped export cash-cropping base during the colonial period, cooperatives were not a strong force in Mbeya's regional history. After the reinstatement of cooperatives Mbeya region was the first to have two within its boundaries, the MBECU and KYERECU. The split was largely due to a sense of rivalry between the Nyakyusa

21. Migot-Adholla, S.E., 'The Politics of a Growers' Cooperative Organisation', in Cliffe, L. *et al.* (eds), *Rural Cooperation in Tanzania* (DSM, Tanzania Publishing House, 1975).

22. Mwase, N.R.L., 'Cooperatives and Ujamaa: A Case Study of the Arusha Region Cooperative Union Limited (ARCU)' in Hyden, G., *Cooperatives in Tanzania: Problems of Organisation* (DSM, Tanzania Publishing House, 1976).

23. The extremely large percentage of the product market that the cooperatives captured in 1985/86 relates to the narrowing gap between the open market and cooperative produce prices and possibly the effect of liberalization measures. Liberalization of imports brought a flood of consumer goods. Previously such goods had trickled in from Kenya and it was believed that many young men from Arusha facilitated the trade, taking Tanzanian maize and coffee to Kenya and exchanging it for small manufactured consumer items like soap and toothpaste. Liberalization measures would have made a dent on their trade and might have caused many to relinquish their activities.

24. The Arusha Cooperative Union geographically covers Arumeru, Arusha, Monduli and Kiteto districts whereas the Rift Valley Cooperative Union operates in Babati, Hanang and Mbulu.

migrants to Mbeya town and the indigenous Safwa, who resented the Nyakyusa's more entrepreneurial approach to agriculture. The MBECU is generally considered to be efficient and, as paddy harvests improved between 1985/86 and 1987/88, it succeeded in capturing an increasing share of the local paddy market (Table VI.25). This performance has won the approval of a large segment of the consuming public who feel more government market control is needed. Some were of the opinion that the cooperatives should be given a monopoly in the grain market (Table VII.27).

Feelings about the cooperatives were, undoubtedly, strongest in Songea. As cooperative performance floundered, town residents, whose views were formed more from the perspective of the producer than the consumer, became more and more pro-market. At the same time, however, the long history of cooperatives in Ruvuma – their establishment in the 1930s for the input provisioning and marketing of tobacco – precluded their complete dismissal as a marketing option. Calls for cooperative reform were genuine and were not seen to contradict the desire for open market expansion. A mixed marketing solution that maximized options was preferred (Tables VII.27 and VII.28).

6.4 Staple Food and Public Schizophrenia

The consuming public's views on traders range from condemnation to praise. In the main, pragmatism has won the day. Where official market staple food supplies and household self-provisioning capability have fallen short of household requirements, traders have been hesitantly accepted, if not wholeheartedly approved. Prejudice against 'parasitic' traders has partially given way to a conditional acknowledgement that they are providing a needed service. As long as real prices remain stable or decline, this approval is likely to prevail. None the less, in the event of a poor harvest and a rise in open market prices, the consuming public's tolerance of traders will be put to the test. Any rise in consumer prices will be weighed against the notion of a 'just price', i.e. reasonably affordable food prices for low-income earners. Adverse price changes due to harvest fluctuations are easily interpreted as the traders' capitalizing on misfortune rather than responding to a fluctuating market.

At the time of the survey, it was clear that consumer pragmatism had granted traders social legitimacy. It was also clear that this acceptance was not deeply rooted. The inevitability of a harvest downturn sometime in the future seemed likely to bring the consumers' normative views to the fore. At that point, the staple food traders could easily be relabelled public enemies. Yet many urban food consumers were now themselves traders trying to keep one step ahead of inflation and price fluctuations, well aware of commodity market dynamics. Staple food, however, had not escaped its status as a commodity above market principles, in other words, a commodity subject to the the society's sense of moral justice.

7. Summary

From an extremely small base, urban areas grew very rapidly from the 1940s to the late 1970s. Despite a slower rate of growth during the 1980s, by 1988 roughly 15 per cent of the national population lived in Dar es Salaam and the administrative capitals of Tanzania's other 19 regions.

Urban staple food consumption was dominated by maize followed by rice in the households of all five towns surveyed. Historically, staple food expenditure constituted approximately 40–45 per cent of total food expenditure in urban areas. The 1988 survey data suggest this figure has crept up to almost 55 per cent (Table VII.21).

Previous household budget surveys indicate that household dependence on non-market supplied food rose as income declined. Survey data did not confirm this pattern. In Dar es Salaam, Mwanza and Arusha, higher income households were more likely to be farming a portion of their own food. Receipt of food gifts, however, was not related to income level.

Wealthier households in Dar es Salaam, Mwanza and Arusha are better able to gain access to scarce land and transport to pursue self-provisioning of food. In Mbeya and Songea, land is less of a constraint, giving more people the option to farm. None the less, only the Songea residents were found to produce more household food than they purchased (Tables VII.9 and VII.17).

The majority of maize and rice purchases took place in the open market in all five towns (Table VII.18). Although complaints about traders' prices were frequently voiced, open market prices were, in fact, quite favourable to consumers. Seasonal price fluctuations were greatest in the maize and rice surplus regions, where many people depended on a degree of non-market supply . Annual price fluctuations examined for the years between 1983/84 and 1988/89 revealed that real prices generally declined as market supplies improved following good harvests. Only in Mwanza did rice prices not fall as harvest conditions improved. In those areas where crop harvests had been poor, notably Mbeya rice and Mwanza maize, prices remained relatively high.

The consumers' attitudes towards traders were not uniform. Dar es Salaam urban consumers and Songea 'urban' producers were most enthusiastic about their activities. In Mwanza, Arusha and Mbeya, traders were often regarded with wariness and distrust. However, Mwanza consumer supply was based on open market trading. Arusha residents, to some extent, could remain relatively indifferent to traders since they could short-circuit the trading chain and buy from producers at local markets.

Furthermore, Arusha cooperative performance was relatively creditable. In Mbeya, the greater degree of household food self-provisioning gave town dwellers a strong sense of self-righteousness *vis-à-vis* 'unproductive' traders.

The household survey demonstrated that attitudinal change regarding market liberalization is underway, but at varying degrees and from different perspectives in each town. To win legitimacy and popularity, Tanzanian party officials and government policy-makers were obliged to keep abreast of public opinion. But the lack of uniformity between towns, as well as the gap between the consumers' pragmatic actions and normative views, made the formulation of food marketing policies anything but straightforward.

VIII

Trade-Offs on Trade: Food Market Liberalization

This chapter summarizes the findings of the previous chapters and offers concluding remarks about the nature of food marketing policies, the policy formulation process and the role of staple food traders in Tanzania's political economy.

Chapters III and IV described the different phases of market policy since the Second World War. The juggling of market and state bias in policy sequentially unfolded with the operation of a free market during the inter-war period, the increasing imposition of state control during and after the war, the reassertion of the free market for a short interlude prior to independence, followed by growing state control in the form of the cooperatives and later the parastatals and, finally, market liberalization measures beginning in 1984/85. Some semblance of a pattern can be discerned; the state imposes control during times of poor harvests and duress, while a free market is more likely to prevail during good harvest years.

As argued in Chapter I, Tanzania's policy tradition is highly interventionist. Pre-colonial and colonial legacies lent legitimacy to the prominence of the state in food distribution matters and resulted in deepening state control during the 1970s. By the early 1980s, parastatal management and price control at virtually every level and every facet of food marketing presented a formidable official edifice. To its critics, the National Milling Corporation was an over-centralized, under-performing and loss-generating scandal. To state policy makers, the NMC, no matter how inefficient, was none the less the embodiment of the government's concern for the basic food needs of the non-agricultural population, testifying to the priority that the state gave to national food security. From their perspective, to have ignored this welfare concern would have been synonymous with neglect and inept government during a period when national food output was falling short of national requirements.

In Chapter II, the post-colonial national economic and political context within which food marketing policies were formulated is documented. Rapid urbanization generated increasing market demand for staple foods. The urban food problem was an issue upon which both party and parastatal control expanded. However, the severity of the economic crisis during the 1980s, which forced the Tanzanian state to seek external finance, notably from the International Monetary Fund, led to the introduction of a counteracting pressure on food policy formulation. IMF conditionality encompassed demands for the lessening of state control over staple food marketing. Meanwhile, the expansion of parallel grain marketing, chronicled in Chapter V, was intimately associated with the deepening of the economic crisis and the over-valuation of the Tanzanian shilling. The growing prevalence of the parallel market, which was itself a factor in the undermining of NMC performance, placed further pressure on the Tanzanian state to relent and liberalize staple food marketing. But official sanctioning of the open market was not accompanied by any state disavowal of its role in guaranteeing national food security. The state had an array of aims in food policy formulation to satisfy the multifarious, sometimes conflicting, demands of the Tanzanian population and international donors. Thus market liberalization was added to a policy menu rich in diversity and nuance.

1. Disentangling the Strands of Food Marketing Policy

In 1988, the accretion of different, sometimes overlapping and conflicting, food policies led to a state of confusion in the minds of the consuming public and traders. Government officials, depending on their regional location and ideological orientation, slanted implementation of food policies towards greater or lesser degrees of control and taxation on the open market. Policies made at national level were not always in congruence with those at regional level. Implementation of national policies was often selectively undertaken at the local level.

While traders were naturally keen to minimize their tax burden and maximize their freedom of operation, they were wary of appearing to be in non-adherence of official policies. Consumers were less concerned and merely purchased supplies where they could, at the lowest possible prices.

The following sub-sections attempt to provide a summary of the different policy strands. Consideration will be given to the source of the policy initiative, the status of the policy at the time of the study (1988), the constituency that the policy was intended to serve and the actual performance of the policy in terms of its own stated objectives and of ensuring an adequate urban food supply and reasonable prices. For the sake of demonstrating overlap the policies are dealt with in reverse order to the actual sequence in which they appeared.

1.1 Policy towards Food Traders

As Chapter V elaborated, private traders in staple foodstuffs operated long before they were officially sanctioned. From 1979, it is apparent that they were increasing in number. Some up-country towns, notably Mbeya, which were cut off from adequate NMC supplies, had local policies that were not antagonistic to private traders. Others, like Mwanza, did not officially condone private traders. Nevertheless, traders managed to conduct their businesses subject to informal rules about when, where, how and for how much. Everywhere, the possibility of an anti-trader/loiterer campaign was one of the many hazards threatening the traders' enterprises.

From 1984 onwards, official controls began to be eased, albeit very gradually. President Mwinyi's intervention in 1986, answering a general popular appeal by consumers and traders for a wholesale market area in Dar es Salaam, accelerated the process. The birth of Tandale market was a watershed economically and politically. The market immediately became the hub of an emerging nationwide staple food market. In addition, its establishment signalled to municipal officials throughout the country that an open market in staple foods was in fact a 'popular' solution. This entailed switching the emphasis on the policy's effects from that of facilitating the traders' profits to serving the needs of urban consumers. Furthermore, it was just at this time that municipalities were eager to find new sources of revenue. The revived Local Government Act had greatly decreased central government contributions, while increasing local government revenue requirements with the expansion of municipal jurisdiction for infrastructure provisioning. Meanwhile, structural adjustment policies were biting hard financially, leaving municipalities with fewer means for manoeuvre. Thus, the licensing of traders and the development of a panoply of taxes on open market trading was seized upon by many municipal governments. Some were less sensitive than others to the disincentive effects of setting trader taxation too high.

Whether or not it was politically calculated, the progressive lifting of sanctions on the open market was quite shrewd. At a national level, it had the potential of endearing the recently installed president to those sections of the electorate anxious about their next bowl of *ugali* [1] (particularly in Dar es Salaam) and, at the same time, it pleased the IMF. On the other hand, it risked displeasing the party, which had long been suspicious of traders, whom it regarded as budding capitalists capable of undermining Tanzania's socialist goals.

---

1. Stiff maize porridge made from *sembe*, which is the most common dish served in Tanzania, generally accompanied by a much smaller portion of cooked beans or meat.

Given party sensibilities, it is not surprising that high-level government officials in the capital[2] tended to cast market liberalization policies as short-term, stop-gap or experimental measures. After all, so many of the market liberalization measures were based on municipal by-laws or a directive from the president, which could be altered quite readily. This tentative, 'we'll wait-and-see' perspective was rationalized with the argument that in the past Tanzanian policy had sometimes been subjected to hasty 'overnight' upheavals. Seeking to avoid this approach, the liberalization measures would be tested first and other policies would not be scrapped until the superiority of the new measures was proven.

Other officials, more technocratic in disposition and training, especially economists and those in the agricultural sector, tended to have fewer reservations about market liberalization. Many held the view that the policy changes of 1984–86 represented a true turning point. They argued that the improvements in food supply and the national economy from that date had arisen from the more 'realistic' policy footing Tanzania was on.

Urban consumers at large did not experience the same cathartic feeling towards market liberalization. For them, the market liberalization policies merely officially confirmed what they already knew, i.e. that fulfilment of their daily household food requirements depended, to a greater or lesser degree, on the existence of an open market.

Between 1984 and 1988, indications were that the staple food sector was highly competitive, operating with lower margins than those of the cooperative with few suggestions of inflated prices relative to marketing costs. It must be quickly added that this good performance took place under favourable harvest conditions. As in the past, market liberalization was a natural course to follow under these circumstances. Conversely, there was a general expectation on the part of consumers and officialdom that the traders' performance would suffer in times of production shortfalls.

An additional aspect of the policy, which was never cited but was of obvious benefit to a depressed economy, was that market liberalization encouraged job creation. Market trading, involving the transport of crops and their security, was highly labour-absorbing.

1.2 Policy towards Cooperatives

Market liberalization was introduced on top of an already comprehensive national food marketing strategy, that of regional cooperative produce buying and NMC distribution. The party-led reinstatement of the cooperatives in 1982 and the gradual relaunch of regional cooperative union and society operations between 1983 and 1985 was accomplished under ambiguous legislation and diverging views about the role of cooperatives in Tanzania's political economy. Party activists, who had

2. Notably those in the Prime Minister's Office and other non-technical ministries.

been involved in the 1970s villagization initiative, saw the cooperatives as a way of continuing socialist mobilization of the countryside. For them, the cooperative societies were to serve as the lowest level in a party-politicized chain of command. Cooperative old-timers, on the other hand, remembering the original objectives of the cooperative movement in the 1950s, emphasized economic viability of the cooperative society and the society's need for a large degree of self-determination and democracy. These differences were not publicly debated.

To all intents and purposes, the party and government committed itself to cooperative reconstruction in 1982 and did not sway from that position despite the concurrent promulgation of market liberalization. The comparatively trouble-free expansion of the private traders' operations contrasted with the numerous problems encountered in the reintroduction and performance of cooperative marketing, which were amply reported in the national media. None the less, officially there was no competition between the two marketing systems. In fact, in some government documents, the reintroduction of cooperatives is classified as a market liberalization measure.[3] Cooperatives were, in the eyes of its proponents, a nationalist solution to the country's marketing needs, protected by legislation. The open market did not enjoy such a worthy status. However, at regional and society levels, cooperative officials were well aware of the fragility of the situation. The threat of the bank withholding its large cash advances for crop purchase until payment of a previous debt and government investigations into cooperative mismanagement, pilfery and fraud in some regions made it very clear to them that they were on trial.

Support for the reinstatement of cooperatives was not restricted to party activists. The cooperative unions in some areas gave peasant producers a better opportunity to obtain productive inputs and consumer goods. The distribution of productive inputs to peasant farmers had been seriously impaired by the decline of crop parastatals during the 1980s. The outbreak and the spread of crop disease, for example the 'Scania' maize borer[4] first sited in Tabora region, the banana weevil in Kagera[5] and the cassava mealy bug in Lindi, reached alarming proportions in several areas and were exacerbated by the economic recession and by the crop parastatals' reduced input distribution capacity.

At the time of the study, cooperative economic performance, albeit highly variable between regions, was on the whole not encouraging. Co-operative debt was mounting rapidly. Some unions were again resorting

3. Tanzania, *Emergency Social Action Programme, July 1989–June 1992: Preliminary Draft for Discussion* (DSM, April 1989), 67.

4. See Golob, P. and R. Hodges, 'Study of an Outbreak of *Prostephanus truncatus* (Horn) in Tanzania', Tropical Products Institute, G164 (London, 1982).

5. See Kajumolo-Tibaijuka, A., 'An Economic Analysis of Smallholder Banana–Coffee Farms in Kagera Region, Tanzania', Report 240, University of Agricultural Sciences, Uppsala, Sweden (1984).

to the unpopular promissory note in lieu of a cash payment to the peasant producer. Transport and storage problems caused changes in the topography of surplus grain areas, i.e. maize and rice 'mountains' were appearing at some of the major bulking points. The National Milling Corporation no longer guaranteed purchase of all cooperative-procured grain, giving rise to a new problem, that of finding a buyer. In 1989 it was announced that marketing boards would relinquish their ownership claim to cooperative purchases and serve merely as marketing agents to the cooperatives. In effect, this would divest central government of financial responsibility for produce marketing and make cooperatives 'free', autonomous agencies minus official underwriting.[6] Meanwhile, there were rumblings that the structure of cooperatives was undemocratic. Peasant farmers desired more autonomy to make decisions in their societies. In April 1991 new cooperative legislation was passed by Parliament, which took power away from the Registrar and gave more scope for decision-making to the societies.[7]

1.3 Policy towards the National Milling Corporation

From1982 onwards, the NMC's functions were gradually curtailed. By 1988, it had been reduced to serving as the 'buyer of last resort' and custodian of the Strategic Grain Reserve (SGR), with significant pruning of staff and fixed assets scheduled to take place. In view of its 1973 mandate under single channel marketing and pan-territorial pricing, the fall in power was drastic. The days of the NMC grain empire were gone. None the less, being custodian of the SGR retained the NMC's role as guarantor of national food security. This was no small task in the context of the Tanzanian state's unswerving commitment to food security as a national welfare priority.

The NMC shrank in size and stature, but the government was intent on keeping it as a viable working structure on call in case of food emergencies. But what was a food emergency? In the government's draft 'Emergency Social Action Programme for July 1989 to June 1992', it is interesting to note that both Dar es Salaam's and Mwanza's food supply problems for the 1988/89 marketing year were identified as being caused by rice shortages and high prices.

[O]ne effective way of keeping food prices down and more stable is to improve the flow of food grains from the surplus areas to the major urban centres especially Dar es Salaam which is the largest food deficit

6. *Tanzanian Economic Trends*, 2(2), July 1989, 41.
7. A report on parliamentary matters in the *Bulletin of Tanzanian Affairs*, 39 (May/June 1991) notes that: 'a four-tier structure was applauded by several Members of the Assembly but the Government was warned ... [by the Minister of Agriculture, Anna Abdullah] ... that the law alone could not help to solve all the problems facing the movement'.

area in Tanzania and consequently has the highest prices for grain. This objective qualifies as a component of the Emergency Social Action Programme because the erosion of real incomes in urban centres due to the artificial scarcity of food grains[8] is currently very severe and must be alleviated...

The movement of surplus grain from the surplus rural areas to Dar es Salaam should, in view of the above, become an overriding priority and concerted efforts must be put into achieving the desired results. NMC therefore should concentrate on this function and also be encouraged to adopt *a systematic price stablization policy* [sic] by releasing its stocks to traders at times of relatively high prices. Cooperative Unions also need to be assisted on an emergency basis to move uncollected food from buying centres to NMC depots and where possible to DSM.[9]

Contradicting all the government's recently implemented market liberalization policies, the NMC received TSh. 2000 million from the government to buy piled up crops in the regions in November 1989.[10]

Thus, the converse of the government's hazy position on the status of traders in Tanzanian policy is a certain impreciseness and room for manoeuvre over the role of the NMC. The above quotation suggests that the NMC has a very important role to play in holding buffer stocks for food price stabilization. It is not difficult to imagine that very active price intervention on the part of the NMC could necessitate more operational capacity at some future date.

The NMC, unlike the other crop parastatals, was not transferred to the Ministry of Local Government. Thus the NMC, SGR and MDB all report to the Ministry of Agriculture. This special arrangement helps to keep the government nerve centre for food monitoring and distribution bureaucratically centralized. It should not go unnoticed that both the MDB and the SGR have received heavy inputs from the United Nations Food and Agriculture Organization (FAO). It is likely that such bureaucratic centralization facilitates relations, not only with the FAO, but also, in the event of a national food crisis, with bilateral and multi-lateral donors of food aid. One could argue that the international community's need for efficient action on the part of the Tanzanian government during a food crisis protects the NMC from the full brunt of the IMF's cost-cutting. Given the country's history of food shortages, only

8. From the text, this appears to refer to the scarcity created by extremely poor grain haulage facilities between producing areas and deficit towns rather than artificial shortages created by traders' profiteering.

9. Tanzania, *Emergency Social Action Programme*, 69–70.

10. The regions involved were Arusha, Iringa, Dodoma, Ruvuma, Rukwa, Singida and Mbeya (*Tanzanian Economic Trends*, 2(3 and 4), January 1990, 97).

the most vociferous critics of Tanzanian food policy could suggest the NMC's complete annihilation.

By keeping the NMC intact, many NMC employees' jobs are saved, the long-term food security interests of urban dwellers, at least in Dar es Salaam, are appeased and the work of the Tanzanian technocrats in the Ministry of Agriculture and their foreign colleagues who provide back-up support is facilitated. In the case of Tanzania, Bienen's argument that the compromised solutions of African governments for meeting external pressures to liberalize are propelled by the governing élite's urban bias and aggrandizement of power and parastatal employment opportunities is over-simplified to the point of being misleading.[11] Tracing the logic of the reform that has taken place suggests that it is food security *per se* rather than government power that the Tanzanian state finds most difficult to relinquish. Furthermore, international agencies are themselves in partnership with the Tanzanian government in this position.

Whatever the scale of the NMC's operations, it is evident that it will continue as a parastatal, primarily serving the government's welfare concerns rather than fulfilling its parastatal role as a profit-generating enterprise. For over a decade, the NMC shouldered the government's famine relief and its *sembe* and transport subsidy programmes. It did so in the face of the urban consumers' growing reliance on the open market for food supply. During this period, NMC sales plummeted and debts soared. Under market liberalization, the NMC's new status largely precluded the possibility of financial recovery. Future debts will undoubtedly be smaller as a result of NMC's reduced scale of operation. However, under its new mandate, the issue of cost recovery can no longer be fudged. It is abundantly clear that the Tanzanian taxpayer rather than the consumer will have to cover the costs of the NMC's welfare role as the St Bernard of public food security.

2. Haphazard or Harmonic Ambiguity: Food Policy Formulation

When examining the complex layering of contradictory food policies during the 1980s, one is struck with how non-conflictual the interaction of marketing agents, with distinct if not opposing interests, has been. The highly tolerant and non-litigious character of the Tanzanian public has assisted this outcome, but one is none the less left wondering if there was some grand scheme in policy formulation which produced a finely tuned integration of divergent marketing policies capable of 'keeping the lid' on

11. Bienen, H., 'The Politics of Trade Liberalization in Africa', *Economic Development and Cultural Change* 38(4) (July 1990).

a potentially explosive issue. After all, neighbouring Zambia experienced vehement public protest and food riots following food marketing 'adjustments', specifically the removal of its maize meal subsidy[12] Tanzania, in a similar position *vis-à-vis* IMF conditionality, none the less remained relatively tranquil. Somehow consumers' needs were sufficiently fulfilled and differences between food distributors, i.e. parastatal personnel, cooperative staff and traders, were reconciled so that political manifestations of the public's displeasure were absent.

How was this political success in introducing radically new food policies achieved? This sub-section explores aspects of the policy formulation process followed by a discussion of how the non-congruence of policies was rationalized and maintained.

2.1 Technocrat's Design versus Party Activist's Vision

It is no secret that there is a tension between influential government policy-makers who are 'pragmatic' and view market liberalization favourably versus influential Tanzanians, often connected to the party, who see such policies as an unwanted encroachment on the hard-won gains of Tanzania's socialist path. Even though this split does not often surface in the national media, it is the staple item of political gossip in Tanzanian homes and offices. The international press has been eager to dramatize the significance of this split.

The divergence of approach, however, is nothing new. Since the independence struggle there have been impatient party cadres calling for rapid, broad-based radical reform and more cautious pragmatists guided by parameters of economic realism. From the outset of the Tanzania–IMF confrontation in 1979, these two lines were in evidence. The party's NEC and Nyerere, who were defensive about the IMF's demands for social service cuts in the budget, clashed with the then Minister of Finance, Edwin Mtei. The minister quietly resigned over the matter. A brief *rapprochement* between Tanzania and the IMF took place in 1980, followed by five years when, for all intents and purposes, the IMF was at loggerheads with 'Nyerere's Tanzania'. During that period, Tanzanian economists became polarized, with numbers increasingly gathering on the pro-IMF reform side. But it is important to emphasize that, even though they fell short of the levels dictated by the IMF, during this period IMF-like reforms were taking place, notably budget cutbacks and currency devaluations. Thus there was a gradualism leading to the 1984 budget and economic liberalization measures associated with Mwinyi's presidency.

The divide between pragmatists and activists has remained relatively muted. Although it is difficult to dissect the divide because it consists of

12. See London *Guardian*: 'Price rise fuels Zambian riots', 27/6/90, and London *Independent*: 'Kaunda under pressure as riots spread', 28/6/90.

notional delineations of vast numbers of individual views, the five year
hiatus between the IMF and Tanzania brought about the slow conversion
of pragmatists to another outlook, but left the activists' position relatively
unchanged. The pragmatists, mainly professionally trained civil servants
and policy advisers, had originally vested their development plans and
programmes in the hands of parastatals. Gradually, many of them fell in
line with IMF thinking, and rejected heavy reliance on the parastatal
sector. It appears that they did so on the basis of evidence of the massive
inefficiency of that sector, notably the performance of the NMC,
skyrocketing debt and the implosion of inter-parastatal debt, which made
the sector untenable. It is more than likely that the pragmatists' greater
awareness of international developmental trends, i.e. the expanding
influence of Thatcherite and Reaganite economic thinking, was also a
factor in their change of heart. In 1988, the collapse of socialism in
Eastern Europe was still far from anyone's crystal ball forecasts.
Tanzanian party activitists could therefore stand firm in their conviction
that the socialist path to development was correct.

Thus one of the two institutional planks of Tanzanian socialist nation-
building, i.e. the parastatals, received a vote of no confidence from the
very people who had created and masterminded the development of that
sector. The other plank, however, the party, remained institutionally intact
and ideologically unperturbed. The party had preceded the appearance of
parastatals and did not have to feel threatened by the parastatals' fall from
grace.

While the possibility that pragmatists' and activists' views would diverge
to the point of an unbridgeable gulf could never be ruled out, extreme
polarization, however, did not occur. A deep-seated nationalist identity
held the two groups together. The pragmatists, many of whom were well-
educated, often foreign-trained professionals, worked side-by-side with
expatriates with a similar training, but earning far higher salaries.
Tanzanian professionals were understandably aggrieved. Having hitherto
relied primarily on their salaried income, their standard of living was very
vulnerable to the deepening economic crisis. Most of Tanzania's many
expatriates were part and parcel of foreign aid programmes. In a sense, this
added insult to injury because the expatriates were purportedly in Tanzania 'to help'. Yet they largely escaped the deprivations of the economic
crisis. Aid agencies hedged around the pay issue, rarely clarifying the basis
upon which they remunerated different employee categories.

The fundamental material divide between Tanzanian and non-
Tanzanian was a powerful force in perpetuating a strong sense of
nationalism amongst professionals and white-collar employees. Ultimately,
they felt more affinity with their less educated compatriots than with their
wazungu.[13] colleagues and associates. As a result, only a handful of high-

13. Translated 'Europeans' and more widely 'foreigners'.

powered Tanzanian economists and advisers with prospects of jobs abroad could, or would, risk appearing pro-IMF and being considered anti-Tanzanian.

Besides the strong nationalist sentiments that bound technocrats and party activists, there were possibilities of beneficial exchanges between the two groups. Tanzanian politics belie a symbiosis between political populism and economic rationalism. In some cases, phases of politically populist policies alternate with more economistic policies. For example, it is probably not accidental that policies along IMF lines were so quickly and easily introduced after the Anti-Economic Sabotage campaign. The original popularity of the campaign, which gave way to excess and engendered the public's sense of disillusionment, facilitated the introduction of previously unpalatable policies. In contrast, the IMF-imposed successive devaluations brought about public demoralization. The party organized public denunciations of IMF conditionality, which allowed people to vent their anger.

More often, political populism and economic rationalism are accommodated concurrently. Thus, the reinstatement of the cooperatives proceeded apace with two interpretations of the objectives of the policy. Both pragmatists and village development visionaries were given room for manoeuvre.

This seemingly happy coexistence is premised on an implicit division of labour between government pragmatists and party activists. While the party identifies broad policy directions, government technocrats are engaged in the formulation of implementable policies. The party's vaguely defined policy formulation role needs further examination, particularly with respect to IMF conditionality. The party constitutes a curious combination of capabilities. Its extensive neighbourhood organizational network makes it ideal for the communication and implementation of policies at the grassroots level. At the other end of the hierarchy, there is a distinct lack of party machinery for formulating policies in any form other than what could best be described as 'broad brush' policies. The NEC meets only biannually, in a large conference forum where the perceptions and enthusiasm of a crowd momentarily gathered can overcome considerations of long-term practicality. The lack of policy formulation machinery at intervening levels between the neighbourhood cells and the national level, which could adapt national policies to local conditions, affords no buffers against the tidal wave effect of party policies on the population. 'Broad brush' party policies have a recurrent philosophical theme, i.e. the preservation of an egalitarian order. The party sees itself as the common man's guardian against exploiters, be they domestic or foreign. The IMF is one such enemy of the common man. Party-organized protests against the IMF in districts of Dar es Salaam during 1988 represented the party's active vigilance against such threats.

Party interventions such as these have to be placed in perspective. During the market liberalization reforms of the late 1980s, the supremacy of the party and what it stood for was not openly challenged, but its policies were subjected to constant reinterpretation in daily life without the benefit of party spokesmen or, indeed, enforcement officers to correct deviations from the original enunciated policy. The party continued to exert itself, creating national images for popular consumption, and to win political popularity. It would, however, be a mistake to deduce that the forceful but sporadic statements that emanated from the party represented an unswerving Tanzanian national position in which policy formulation and implementation were irrevocably embedded.

Both external and internal party policy was malleable. The most glaring evidence that the combination of economic crisis and market liberalization was having an impact on the party came in the form of the party's Zanzibar Declaration of February 1991. This revoked the restraints of the Leadership Code. Thus, party members were permitted to earn more than one salary/income, rent houses, buy shares and take up directorships in private companies. The rationale for this drastic about-face was the need to reduce corruption on the part of government and parastatal-employed party members, whose official salaries were acknowledged to be insufficient to cover basic living costs.

While stressing the interactive effects of government pragmatists and party visionaries on the formulation and implementation of a complex web of food policies, it must not be forgotten that ambiguous government policies regarding market liberalization could most easily be reconciled by semantics. With adept wording and 'conceptual adjustment' of the tenets of structural adjustment, Tanzanian food policy took on a chameleon character that, depending on the context, could pacify the party's commited socialists or IMF adherents. With respect to the latter, the reinstatement of the cooperatives did not constitute a policy in opposition or in place of market liberalization, it was instead part and parcel of market liberalization. By giving market liberalization a very wide meaning, any and all measures that put a check on the NMC's market monopoly became synonymous with market liberalization. In this way, overlapping and ambiguous policies became the norm, open to different interpretations. For government, this approach had the added advantage of giving nationally determined policies flexibility at regional and local levels. Policy implementers at these levels were afforded a range of valid interpretations depending on their preferences. In the event of an individual administrator unfairly implementating a policy or manipulating it for his or her own personal benefit, he or she could be labelled unjust, whereas the policy itself was still intact and the notion of just government remained.

2.2 The Hidden Hand: Signals from the Presidential Executive

In the tussle between 'market pragmatists' and 'state activists' what political mechanism determined the balance of forces? How did the Tanzanian state manage to chart a course which appeased both the IMF, party activists and the urban consuming public, thereby averting civil unrest?

Chapter II cited the importance of presidential initiative in party policy formulation. The president, as head of party and government, was Tanzania's most powerful political personage. Several political scientists have identified the relatively minor role played by Parliament. In comparison, the president's wide powers of government appointment and dismissal, as well as his own lack of formal accountability, added up to decisive control over national policy formulation.[14] Under these circumstances, the political objectives and personality of the individual president require special consideration.

There is no doubt that Nyerere, as president and party chairman, was the pace-setter for national policy until 1985. His views as an African socialist with Fabian leanings and his leadership role as father of the nation, charismatic politician and articulate statesman are well known. During his long sojourn as president, state intervention increased amidst distrust and containment of market development.

Did Nyerere relinquish his commanding control over national policy formulation when he left the presidency in 1985? This is a question that international journalists frequently asked. After all, contrary to previous practice, Ali Hassan Mwinyi, his successor as president, did not assume the party chairmanship, which was retained by Nyerere. It was not until 1990 that the two positions were recombined and vested in Mwinyi. Furthermore, Nyerere's political skill and continued high esteem made it highly likely that he could be an effective cue prompter in national policy formulation.

It is impossible to get a definitive answer to this question since so much of Tanzanian political decision-making is resolved informally. Subsequent to his departure from the presidency, between 1985 and 1988 it was rumoured that Nyerere was critical of the rate and extent of market liberalization, but publicly he generally adopted a conciliatory tone.[15] It

14. Mlimuka, A.K.L.J. and P.J.A.M. Kabudi, 'The State and the Party', in Shivji, I.G. (ed.), *The State and the Working People in Tanzania* (London, Codesria, 1986), 65–67, and Msekwa, P., *Towards Party Supremacy* (Arusha, Eastern African Publications,1976), 62. Hartmann argues that there is a tripartite system in which the president, government and party formulate policy through an unstructured process of issuing public policy statements which interactively reinforce or cancel preceding elements of the unfolding policy (Hartmann, J., 'The Arusha Declaration Revisited', *African Review* 12(1) (1985)).

15. For example, when asked about the significance of Tanzania's growing private sector, he stated that 'the private sector was only pronounced in preferential areas of Tanzania's economy' and 'does not constitute a real or potential threat to the building of socialism in Tanzania' (*Daily News:* 'Private sector no threat – Nyerere', 12/9/87).

should, however, not be forgotten that he himself sanctioned a process of gradual market liberalization during the early 1980s, particularly in 1984. In any case, as party chairman, Nyerere's role in defining Tanzanian policy *vis-à-vis* market liberalization was circumscribed because he was no longer involved in detailed negotiations with the IMF. His efforts as party chairman were concentrated on updating and strengthening political features of national development. Furthermore, he retained his role as an international statesman, serving as chairman of the South–South Commission, which necessitated his frequent absence from the country. Thus, evidence is weighted in favour of Nyerere's limited part in the formulation of Tanzania's market liberalization policies after 1985. Following from this, *ceteris paribus*, Ali Hassan Mwinyi, exercising presidential initiative, was pivotal to the determination of Tanzania's market liberalization path.

With the spotlight on Mwinyi, it is necessary to ask who he was and what he stood for. He was, in many ways, Nyerere's opposite. He did not have an international reputation nor was he a well-known national figure. Well-qualified, he had none the less travelled a circuitous route to the presidency.[16] Most noteworthy was the fact that he was not a mainlander. He was a Zanzibari who had succeeded in gaining prominence at the national level and, most importantly, had achieved acceptance in the fraught arena of Tanganyika mainland and Zanzibar union politics.

Like Nyerere, Mwinyi was champion of the common man, but he used a different approach to communicate this position. While Nyerere, the statesman, adopted an egalitarian philosophical stance and sought sweeping institutional changes aimed at benefiting the masses of agricultural producers, Mwinyi eschewed public pronouncements and ambitious development schemes. Making it known that he was ready to listen to anyone's problems and complaints, he became the 'approachable president'. On an *ad hoc*, one-to-one basis, he was willing to use his office

16. Mwinyi had wide political experience including serving as a national cabinet minister during the 1970s. At that time he won the reputation of being a principled politician with his resignation as Minister of Home Affairs following national media coverage of police brutality in an up-country murder case over which he had had no control or awareness at the time of the incident. He went on to be Tanzania's High Commissioner to Egypt and later the appointed Interim President of Zanzibar Island. He was thus in a good position at the time of the 1985 national election for selection as the nation's presidential candidate when the then prime minister, Salim Ahmed Salim, another Zanzibari, seeking candidature for the presidency, was refused support by the Zanzibar wing of the CCM party. According to the *Daily News* Nyerere's endorsement of Mwinyi on election day was as follows: 'Mwalimu [Nyerere] described Ndugu Mwinyi as a polite, humble and a trustworthy person of firm principles, who stood for what he believed in. He is also a consistent and stable supporter of the policy of Socialism and Self-Reliance as well as the unity of all Tanzanians ... [A]part from being a democrat, Ndugu Mwinyi's record showed that he was responsive to the wishes and interests of the people' (*Daily News:* 'Ali Hassan Mwinyi: Man of the people', 27/10/85).

to seek justice for the petitioner. Some labelled it 'kitchen politics'. Rather than the pursuit of broad, idealistic goals, this approach lent itself to concern with matters of daily survival. It was in tune with most people's preoccupation with devising coping strategies in the context of a national economic crisis. Mwinyi's personal answerability as a leader had its roots in the traditional *risala*[17] and *malalamishi*[18] forums that chiefs had held in the past. Despite the low profile Mwinyi adopted as a public figure, as long as he enjoyed the reputation of being a leader who fought for justice and the daily survival needs of the population, he retained public respect and legitimacy in the one-party state system.

Seen in this light, Mwinyi's consent to the IMF structural adjustment, soon after he assumed the presidency, could be viewed positively, i.e. as the only way of securing a better livelihood for the Tanzanian population and respite for their beleaguered economy. Mwinyi, positing himself as the custodian of the Nyerere legacy, avoided charges of capitulation to foreign dictates and selling out the ideals of Tanzanian socialism. Tanzania, it was argued, had no choice.[19] Many of Tanzania's professional economists were the first to support this position.

What is perhaps most noteworthy in Mwinyi's relationship with the IMF is not the early agreement after protracted and bitter disagreement during negotiations between the Tanzanian state and the IMF under Nyerere, but rather the absence of any sharp break with past policies subsequent to the agreement. As has already been discussed, previous marketing policies remained in force. Market liberalization was added to the policy mix, leaving policy makers and consumers to pick and choose. In so doing, many potential conflicts between political factions capable of destabilizing the government and party and ultimately civil order were avoided. By refraining from trying to reconcile conflicting aspects of these policies, or from defining a hierarchy between the triple layering of policies with respect to the NMC, the cooperatives and the open market, there was no felt need for compromise on the part of vested interests.

This *laissez-faire* way of introducing new policies contrasted with past practice. Previously a new policy had been announced with a fanfare and projected as a new and superior way of proceeding. Naturally, this entailed completely abolishing the old policy and its associated organizational structures. A prime example of this approach was the introduction

17. Translated 'petitioning'.
18. Translated 'complaints'.
19. Mwinyi defended the original agreement saying that 'since the signing of the first IMF agreement in 1986, things had begun to move in the right directions' (*Daily News*: 'Mwinyi outlines economic situation, stresses', 16/11/88). After accepting still harsher IMF terms and a further 21% devaluation in November 1988, Mwinyi was reported to have said that agreeing to the Fund's conditionality did not mean that the government was unaware of the harsh outcome, adding 'we had to choose the lesser evil' (*Daily News*: 'Mwinyi pledge to ease load on people', 5/11/88).

of single channel marketing of the NMC and the abolition of cooperatives in 1976.

When asked during the study why seemingly conflicting policies were allowed to coexist, one high-ranking official in the Prime Minister's Office explained it in terms of an acknowledgement on the part of the Tanzanian government that policy changes in the past had been too sudden and too sweeping. This attitude undoubtedly reflects the outlook of many policy makers who experienced the euphoria of independence and African socialism and now, more soberly, value subtlety in national policy formulation.

However, it is worth commenting that policy-making by accretion also accords well with the objective circumstances of Mwinyi's presidency. In addition to being new to the position and contending with being the successor to Nyerere, who could be described as 'a hard act to follow', Mwinyi is not a mainlander. His Zanzibari origins and consequently his lack of a well-entrenched following on the mainland undoubtedly made it wise for him to try to avoid stepping on the interests of existing factions associated with previous policies, notably the cooperatives and the NMC.

On close examination, Mwinyi's presidency represents pluralism with regard to market *and* state development. While Nyerere, as father of the nation, was largely the creator of Tanzania's public institutions, President Mwinyi was largely created by Tanzania's institutions. As a Zanzibari, he has acted as a non-partisan president. During his term of office, the Local Government Act was introduced (conferring more power on regional governments relative to central government), the pros and cons of multi-partyism were publicly debated and the party itself instituted internal reform, recasting the duties of party members in a more liberal vein. Mwinyi was rarely identified as the instigator of these moves. He was a liberal executive who gave green light signals for change without specifying the precise direction.

2.3 Balancing Act: Status of Market Liberalization Policies

In essence, the formulation of food market liberalization policy between 1985 and 1988 consisted of making offerings and avoiding offence. During negotiations, amongst other concessions, Mwinyi offered the IMF the gradual lifting of bans on private food trading in return for the financial support Tanzania had hitherto been denied. So too, in an extremely popular move soon after becoming president, Mwinyi sanctioned the creation of a Tandale wholesale market (in the face of municipal restrictions) and this measure set in train a more liberal approach to urban marketing throughout Tanzania. This was an offering to the urban consumer, who, in return, soldiered on under the economic duress of IMF structural adjustment measures. Thus, in contrast to the situation in some neighbouring countries, civil protest and food riots were avoided.

At the same time, due to the layering of food marketing policies, the cooperatives were given space and the party was allowed to save face. Whether this course of action was masterminded or occurred by default, it amounted to political tightrope-walking, which proved successful in terms of keeping the IMF and the Tanzanian public just happy enough to get by.

The status of market liberalization policies hung in balance, satisfying domestic consumer demand and international donor demand to a point. Several donors, not least the IMF, would have preferred to have the debt-ridden cooperative market structure disbanded. Consumers, on the other hand, according to survey results, had a wide range of views on how staple food marketing could be improved. Some wanted less state control, whereas many others wanted the state to act as a price 'watchdog', or even distributor.

The layering of food market policies (i.e. market liberalization, co-operative and parastatal marketing policy) was ill-defined and experi-mental. All three layers were on trial. Any of them could be put out of business by decree or legislation. While the superimposition of market liberalization on existing food marketing policy could be viewed as the government policy-makers' conditional acceptance of the private food trader, emphasis must be placed on the word conditional. To go further would have been incompatible with the nationalist legacy of post-colonial independence. However, this conditional acceptance gave traders the opportunity to pursue a livelihood and gain economic experience

3. Vulnerability and Resilience: Food Traders in National Politics and the Economy

There is no such thing as an average staple food trader. Depending on his or her regional location of supply and urban location of demand, food traders' activities are subject to wide variation in the commodities traded, scale of operations, extent of a trading hierarchy and economic returns. Thus, it is difficult to make general observations about food traders. Instead, this section attempts to situate the phenomenon of the private food trader *vis-à-vis* Tanzanian policy formulation, politics and economics.

3.1 Against the Odds: Traders' Appearance and Proliferation

No evidence exists to suggest that the process of trader legitimization between 1984 and 1988 was due to political pressure from traders themselves. As active agents, staple food traders were invisible in policy formulation. Rather they were an expedient to Tanzanian policy-makers. The official sanctioning of their activities helped the central government meet the IMF's demands and provided local governments with much needed revenue.

The noticeable appearance of staple food traders in the late 1970s arose from the convergence of declining employment opportunities in urban areas, declining returns from cash cropping and the shortcomings of the official marketing system. The proliferation of their numbers during the first half of the 1980s was met with party and government hostility. Yet, in various parts of the country where conducive supply and demand conditions prevailed, they began to become an economic force to be reckoned with.

Between 1985 and 1988, under the government's market liberalization policies, there was a rush of both men and women into staple food trading. The policy changes represented the removal of some, but not all, of the restrictions on staple food trading which had deterred those with an inclination to trade. It is apparent that women traders felt more 'liberated' by the policies than men. Presumably this was because women had been more intimidated by the previous restrictions on trade. Business entry was easier in some towns as opposed to others, given the level of municipal taxation, the size of market demand and the extent of functional differentiation between traders.

Open market staple food traders of this era were venturing into relatively new and uncharted economic terrain. For many it was a comparatively easy entry. A bag of grain and a bus journey often sufficed. The Luguru traders, who had already carved a niche for themselves as open market rice traders, observed the market expansion with dread.[20] Tanzanian staple food markets were becoming increasingly competitive. The motivation for entry into staple food trading almost invariably was to secure a livelihood. The preponderant majority of traders interviewed received a modest income for their efforts. High profits were exceptional.

A trading hierarchy of wholesalers, mobile intermediaries and retailers was most fully developed in Dar es Salaam. As described in Chapter VI, functional differentiation of traders was less pronounced in Mwanza, Arusha, Mbeya and Songea. The survey yielded inconclusive evidence of a pattern of wealth differentiation between types of traders. While wholesalers were universally envied, it was not always apparent that they were enjoying substantially larger financial returns. The risks of mobile intermediaries seemed inordinately high, but they were vital to gaining the experience and contacts needed to become a wholesaler. Retailers in most towns faced extremely competitive margins.

20. 'It is odd to hear regularly that trade liberalization has been bad for business as it has allowed many more entrants into the market' (van Donge, 'Waluguru Traders', 15).

The period between 1985 and 1988 represented very early days in the evolution of Tanzania's open staple food market. The open market's critics, who feared the traders' wealth accumulation and profiteering at the expense of the consumer, so far had few grounds for complaint based on the survey findings. The combination of easy entry into staple food trading, the ability of traders to operate with extremely low fixed overheads, and the non-convergence of trading and transport enterprise made it unlikely that excess profits would accrue to traders. However, these conditions, by no means represented a steady state.

Ironically, the government itself did not seem to appreciate the advantages of the traders' low operating costs associated with minimal overheads. The 1989 draft of the government's Emergency Social Action Programme argues that high food prices are due to lack of transport and poor storage facilities for staple foodstuffs in the urban areas. It is proposed that government set up 'Grain Centre' godowns in towns for wholesaling. Space in these centres would be rented out to cooperatives and 'business entities or people with adequate financial and managerial capability'. These wholesalers would be expected to use 'special train wagons for grain transportation'.[21] Such schemes involving sizeable financial outlays are contrary to the highly flexible, low overhead strategy of private traders at all levels of the trading hierarchy and would be more likely to raise rather than lower food prices.

In 1988, the close proximity of traders to farm produce through continued ties with their rural homesteads guaranteed easy entry into staple food trade. The absence of both formal and informal credit perpetuated low investment in trading infrastructure. Finally, the dominance of experienced Asians and Arabs in long-distance road transport limits the possibility of African traders branching into transport, whereas non-African transporters, given the experience of post-independence food marketing policy, were reluctant to invest in staple food trading.

As a consequence, African staple food trading was extremely competitive because virtually all traders pursued a low-investment strategy. This was in consonance with the uncertainty of their future status *vis-à-vis* government marketing policy.

3.2 Keeping a Low Profile

It can be stated with some conviction that between 1985 and 1988 African traders experienced the most favourable business conditions that this century had to offer. A combination of factors produced this effect, namely good harvest years ensuring supply, food demand from 'hungry'

21. Tanzania, *Emergency Social Action Programme*, 73.

urban areas, the absence of Asian competition and, most importantly, comparatively tolerant government marketing policies. Market liberalization policies gave existing traders respite from the government's 'irritating' trade restrictions, whereas it gave new traders the impetus to try their luck at trade.

Despite the fact that they had 'never had it so good', traders, be they highly experienced or new traders, saw room for improvement in the government's policies and their implementation. The surveyed traders' views can be broken down into five main categories. First, there were those, particularly in Dar es Salaam and Songea, who desired more comprehensive or consistent market liberalization, specifically the removal of road-blocks and other controls still obstructing the free flow of staple food commodities. Second, there were complaints, primarily from Arusha and Mwanza traders, about the patchy enforcement of market policy, notably the municipal government's failure to stop unlicensed traders from operating and thereby undercutting licensed traders. Third, there were bitter outcries, especially in Mwanza, Arusha and Songea, about being over-taxed by the municipal authorities. Fourth, there were pleas for government to improve the market infrastructure. This took the form of a call for government to improve the transport and credit in Mbeya and to build proper marketplaces in Dar es Salaam, Arusha and Songea. Finally, there was the Songea traders' 'call from the wilderness', in effect a pro-government intervention position advocating that the government guarantee the supply of scarce commodities like rice.

While traders were never short of suggested government marketing policy measures, there was, however, a noticeable lack of political organization amongst traders to agitate for change. In Dar es Salaam, trading syndicates were coalescing, but these were founded on the need for cooperation between traders and for the convenience of trading operations internal to the marketing process. The traders' overt political expressions were limited to protest against unbearable taxation. Individual and/or collective attempts to put pressure on the government to implement further market reforms did not appear to be on the trading community's agenda.

While this lack of assertive collective will might, in the case of mobile intermediaries, have resulted from their highly mobile circumstances, the same cannot be said of the primarily stationary retailers and wholesalers. The reasons for their low profile most probably relate to the relative newness of staple food traders as a legitimate occupational category, the Tanzanian government's dislike of spontaneous, non-party-initiated political organization and the precariousness of the traders' material existence.

Economically, the low margins for the vast majority of traders made each day a struggle for survival. Furthermore, in the up-country towns surveyed, large seasonal fluctuations of supply and demand called into question staple food trading as a viable form of livelihood. The economic insecurities of trading combined with political vulnerability. Traders were well aware of their tenuous status in the nation's political economy. Their popularity with the consuming public was based on cheaper prices relative to government controlled prices. But traders' lower prices depended on good harvests. Equally tenuous, traders' legitimacy *vis-à-vis* the national government was premised on economic exigency, namely the IMF's pressure on the government. These fortuitous circumstances were not enduring. Public and official opinion about them was bound to change.

4. Trader or Traitor?

Ultimately, both Tanzanian traders and policy-makers are answerable to the consuming public. A study of the interaction between traders and officials would be incomplete without considering the mediating effect of the public's attitudes towards the country's staple food economy and its facilitating agents. This final section reviews past and present attitudes towards traders and analyses their underlying rationale.

4.1 Public Suspicion

As argued in Chapter VII, while there is an extremely wide range of public opinions about traders, the 1980s witnessed growing acceptance of the role of the private trader in urban staple food supply. While acknowledging their usefulness, most consumers interviewed during the survey still harboured reservations about the traders' long-term role in provisioning sufficient, reasonably priced supplies. These suspicions rested on notions of exploitation by traders that can be traced back to the period when Asian merchants dominated staple food trading. Asian merchants were 'outsiders' to the local community in terms of having no kin ties and being part of a non-agrarian, foreign culture. African peasant producers and migrant workers had recourse to them if and when their own farming efforts did not yield sufficient food supplies for the household.[22] Cultural differences in perceiving this objective situation created the original basis for the anti-trader views held by most African consumers.

From the perspective of the African peasant producer, who virtually always sought to be self-sufficient in food production, a poor harvest and shortfall of necessary household supplies were a misfortune. Traditionally, in such circumstances, it was the chief, as custodian of communal stores, who ensured distribution of supply to the needy. This community-based food security system gave way to a colonial order in which peasants were

22. For further discussion of this see Bryceson, *Food Insecurity*, 44–51, 102–112.

expected to buy food, if necessary by selling livestock and other assets. Colonial famine relief was only administered when the harvest shortfall was severe, community-wide and its victims too impoverished to have recourse to a market solution.[23]   For the peasant producer, purchasing food supplies from Asian merchants was galling in several respects. First, a farmer having experienced a misfortune would have been accorded sympathetic material help under patronage of a chief, but he was now expected to fend for himself. Second, the supplier of food was an outsider who had not used his own labour to produce the food. As a merchant, he was essentially 'unproductive' and got a livelihood from the agricultural sweat of others. Third, the price paid for the food, however large or small, was inevitably compared with the 'free food' from the producer's own *shamba*.[24]

In contrast, the sale of staple food items to peasant producers was entirely market-motivated on the part of the Asian trader. Simply, there was a demand that the trader was willing to fulfil. He knew that this demand was subject to 'just price' criteria with both the peasant producer and British colonial officers remaining vigilant consumer watchdogs. However, low margins on staple foodstuffs were compensated by higher margins on other goods in his panoply of sales merchandise.

The moral economy of subsistence food producers was founded on the limited scale of the local rural economy, its restricted volume of production as well as the restricted volume of demand. Significantly, its morality pertained to a strictly delimited location and population, an ethnically defined community with a simple division of labour based primarily on age and sex rather than class. Consequently, it was a community with strong egalitarian impulses. The restricted numbers within the community made its leadership directly accountable to the populace, usually on a face-to-face basis. This limited political distance between leaders and followers made consensus more feasible and was particularly useful in distress situations when community members, well aware of each other's problems, could seek sympathetic redress.

One could argue that today's urban resident, largely deriving his livelihood from non-farming activities, would have little grounds for continuing to view food traders with the disgust of his agrarian forefathers. The moral economy and dynamics of the small-scale rural society after all are a far cry from the circumstances of Tanzanian urban dwellers of the late 1980s. The scale of urban settlement and food needs are comparatively enormous. Furthermore, the division of labour has proliferated.

23. See Bryceson, D.F., 'Colonial Famine Responses', *Food Policy* (May 1981) and 'Changes in Peasant Food Production and Food Supply in relation to the Historical Development of Commodity Production in Pre-colonial and Colonial Tanganyika', *Journal of Peasant Studies* 7(3), 281–311 (1980).
24 Translated 'farm'.

However, it would be a mistake to overlook the persistence of a deeply-entrenched moral economy of public food security in urban areas which bears some similarity to the past.

Fundamentally, the deterioration in the standard of living of urban residents during an economic crisis has made most people still very close to basic subsistence requirements and reliant on agrarian and kin-based survival strategies. Thus, the imperative for a moral economy of food supply remains, even though the material and locational scale of public food supply logistics has multiplied ten thousand-fold in the involved population's transition from rural community to urban town residence.

As outlined in Chapter I, state legitimacy was traditionally bound up in the issue of public food security. The degree of food insecurity in Tanzania's urban areas with respect to both availability and price has militated for the state's continued role as guarantor of staple foodstuffs. However financially untenable the role of the state has been in this regard, it remains realistic in terms of 'responsible government'. The alternative is the very real possibility of political instability and the dissolution of civil order.

None the less, this 'pure' concern on the part of the state for public food security has been amalgamated with several other state objectives and agendas. State institutional creations such as the cooperatives and the parastatals have been made synonymous with the urban food security strategy of the state. The state's historical role in dismantling the Asian national produce buying network and subsequent anti-trader campaigns reflect its deep suspicion of the profit motive as a legitimate foundation for national staple food distribution. These state suspicions rest on public suspicions and the two mutually reinforce each other.

4.2 Circumstantial Evidence

Staple food traders are rarely judged in the light of an awareness, let alone an appreciation, of year-to-year and season-to-season domestic grain production, or the operating costs of trading. The public, as well as the government, evaluate them on the basis of their output alone, i.e. the availability and price of their commodities at any given time.

As the survey findings revealed, the public's estimation of traders varies from one town to another depending on local production conditions and supply alternatives. In areas where there is a great deal of household self-provisioning, urban householders adopt a position similar to that of the peasant producer, who is disdainful of the trader who 'overcharges' for food items and discounts the costs of his own household's time and effort in production. At the opposite end of the spectrum, households in places where self-provisioning is difficult through lack of land or poor climatic conditions and which therefore have no fallback option are, not surprisingly, more willing to accept the trader's usefulness to the local and national economy. Between these two extremes are a whole range of consumer attitudes which are critical of traders in some respects and affirmative in others.

The Songea residents' attitudes were formed from a different perspective entirely. From the viewpoint of producers rather than consumers and with the failure of their local cooperative union to purchase their production surpluses, Songea's residents, who are largely self-provisioning and often commercial producers themselves, had extremely favourable opinions of traders.

The survey took place amidst a spate of good harvests. It is more than likely that positive attitudes towards traders would start to erode during a bad harvest year as food prices rose and the possibility of shortages occurred. Even during the 1985–88 period, the traders did not succeed in shedding their public image as 'unproductive middlemen'. Many consumers expressed the view that there were too many traders and that marketing should be streamlined to 'cut out the middlemen'. While it was possible in a few towns for consumers to buy directly from producers, for example in Arusha, where there were nearby district markets and producers could visit town frequently because of the relatively good transport and numerous established market locations, there was no appreciation that the conditions making this possible were not prevalent everywhere.

No one seemed prepared to acknowledge that traders and the functional division of labour between traders in the marketing chain represented a positive, cost-cutting specialization. The public overlooked the labour time and transport savings embedded in the trader's specialization.[25] Given the complexity of commodities sold and the transport distances, the consumer's preference for eye-to-eye contact with the producer at the time of purchase was unlikely to produce the desired effect, i.e. lower prices. Whatever the length of the marketing chain, the margins of each trader in the chain were subjected to competition.

Inescapably, the traders faced a consumer belief that they were profiteering. Chapter VII's analysis of annual regional production patterns and food price changes largely dispelled the verity of this view for the five towns surveyed. Mwanza rice prices were the notable exception. There was a period of rapid inflation between 1985 and 1988. Food price inflation was generally less marked than that of non-food items. None the

---

25. To cite just one example, in Mbeya region small local farmer/traders habitually use very low-cost transport to get their commodities to Mbeya town. For them to proceed to DSM would require a far greater outlay of time and money whereas a trader specialized in getting goods onto the TANZAM Highway lorries cheaply is much better placed to take the produce to DSM. He, however, is not in a good position to spend days and days in DSM retailing his consignment.

less, because urban household consumption was so heavily weighted towards food, the fact that food cost increases were outstripping income was sufficient grounds for the consumer charge that traders were profiteering.

The government, with its array of data collecting agencies within the Ministry of Agriculture and Central Statistical Bureau, occupied a better vantage point for evaluating the traders' performance. However, recourse to these figures and careful market analysis was not always evident in its documents and statements by officials. The 1989 draft Emergency Social Action Programme exemplifies this.[26] It is asserted that food prices are too high and these prices are attributed to lack of transport and storage resulting in regional crop pile-ups and commodity scarcity in centres of urban demand. However, the analysis of market performance and prices fails to distinguish the activities of cooperatives and private traders. The lack of transport and regional crop pile-ups are primarily the problem of the cooperatives. Private traders, using a multitude of different kinds of transport arrangements, were managing to get their commodities to market. Were food prices too high? Undoubtedly, too high in terms of consumers' pocketbooks following a large devaluation, but were they too high relative to traders' marketing costs? This question was never posed.

The complexity of the government's layered marketing policy makes it possible for any general discussion of staple food marketing to be highly misleading. The outcome of deficiencies on the part of the cooperatives can be attributed to the traders or vice versa. Given the institutional orientation of the government, it is more likely that the former would take place. Facts can easily become irrelevant in the highly politicized arena of national food security.

4.3 Verdict Pending

There is little prospect of any Saatchi and Saatchi[27] transforming the public image of traders from villains to angels of mercy. The status of traders in Tanzanian society hangs in the balance. The avoidance of an anti-trader backlash – as national harvests inevitably fluctuate along with the public's acceptance of traders more generally – depends on acknowledging their role in an increasingly complex society. Complete acceptance of them is conditional on some fundamental changes in attitude on the part of the consuming public. The notion of a food trader as an unproductive appendage to the economy must be the first to go.

Expectations regarding food prices would also have to be revised. The notion of a 'just price' would have to be abandoned in recognition of the

26. Tanzania, *Emergency Social Action Programme*, 64–75.
27. Public relations firm in the United Kingdom which has transformed the image of several news-making personalities including the former prime minister, Mrs Thatcher.

fact that, in times of poor harvests and scarcity, prices go up due to lack of supply, not just due to profiteering. Finally, and perhaps hardest to swallow, because it calls into question the future welfare of large segments of the population, would be the abandonment of the state's role as guarantor of staple food supplies. As long as the government shoulders this onerous task, it is bound to fail on occasion and it is going to be very tempting to blame the ensuing distress on traders.

Attitudinal changes on the part of the public and the relinquishing of state responsibility for guaranteeing food supply can only come naturally, and without incurring heavy suffering and disillusionment, when the material conditions are right in Tanzania. As long as Tanzania experiences shortfalls of domestic production, thereby jeopardizing the food supply of its non-farming population in urban areas, the state guarantee and associated public attitudes are vital to national survival. Respectively, they represent the commitment to and a belief in the integrity of the nation-state to prevent life-threatening starvation. The bottom line is drawn. Government policy in this regard is better classified as defence rather than economic policy.

Until these changes take place, traders will be politically vulnerable. Depending on national food availability, their fate will fluctuate between acceptance as part of a national division of labour, collectively forming a service network, and revulsion as a gang of racketeers, traitors to the basic material welfare of the nation.

Bibliography

Books, Articles, Research Papers, Theses and Official Publications

Afro-Aid and BUMACO, 'Co-operative Policy and Development on Mainland Tanzania: Results of a Survey of Primary Society Members and Union Management on the Present Organisation and Future Needs of the Co-operative Movement' (DSM, June 1988)

Airey, T., D.F. Bryceson and J. Howe, 'Interim Evaluation of the Songea–Makambako Road', Report submitted to the Ministry of Communications and Works under assignment by the Overseas Development Administration, London (July 1989)

Alpers, E.A., 'The Coast and the Development of the Caravan Trade', in Kimambo, I.N. and A.J. Temu (eds), *A History of Tanzania* (Nairobi, East African Publishing House, 1969)

Anderson, B., *Imagined Communities* (London, Verso Editions and New Books, 1985)

Anderson, D. and D. Throup, 'Africans and Agricultural Production in Colonial Kenya: The Myth of the War as a Watershed', *Journal of African History*, 26(4) (1985)

Arens, W., 'Change and Development in a Tanzanian Community', in Skar, H. (ed.), *Anthropological Contributions to Planned Change and Development* (Gothenberg, Acta Universitatis Gothoburgensis, 1985)

Bates, R.H., *Markets and States in Tropical Africa* (Berkeley, University of California Press, 1981).

Bevan, D., A. Bigsten, P. Collier, and J.W. Gunning, *East African Lessons on Economic Liberalization* (Hampshire, U.K., Gower, 1978)

Bharati, A., 'A Social Survey', in Ghai, D.P. and Y.P. (eds.), *Portrait of a Minority, Asians in East Africa* (Nairobi, Oxford University Press, 1970)

Bienefeld, M.A., 'The Self-Employed of Urban Tanzania', Economic

Research Bureau Paper 75.11, University of Dar es Salaam (June 1975)

Bienen, H., *Tanzania: Party Transformation and Economic Development* (Princeton, Princeton University Press, 1970)

—'The Politics of Trade Liberalization in Africa', *Economic Development and Cultural Change* 38 (4) (July 1990)

Bryceson, D.F., 'Changes in Peasant Food Production and Food Supply in relation to the Historical Development of Commodity Production in Pre-colonial and Colonial Tanganyika', *Journal of Peasant Studies* 7(3) (1980)

—'Colonial Famine Responses', *Food Policy* (May 1981)

—'Second Thoughts on Marketing Cooperatives in Tanzania', Plunkett Development Series 5 (1983)

—'Urbanization and Agrarian Development in Tanzania with Special Reference to Secondary Cities', Report for the International Institute for Environment and Development, London (February 1984)

—'Food and Urban Purchasing Power: The Case of Dar es Salaam, Tanzania', *African Affairs*, 84(337) (1985)

—'A Century of Food Supply in Dar es Salaam: From Sumptuous Suppers for a Sultan to Maize Meal for a Million', in Guyer, J. (ed.), *Feeding African Cities* (London, Manchester University Press, 1987)

—'Household, Hoe and Nation: Development Policies of the Nyerere Era', in Hodd, M. (ed.), *Tanzania after Nyerere* (London, Pinter Publishers, 1988)

—*Food Insecurity and the Social Division of Labour in Tanzania, 1919–85* (London, Macmillan, 1990)

—'Urban Bias Revisited: Staple Food Pricing in Tanzania', in Hewitt de Alcántara, C. (ed.), *Real Markets: Essays on the Political Economy of Food Pricing and Marketing Reforms,* special issue of the *European Journal of Development Research* (December 1992)

Bryceson, D.N.M.,'Price, Production and Marketing Policies for Maize', Paper No. 60 of 1968, submitted by the Minister for Agriculture and Cooperatives, MDPC/A.50/26/4, n.d.

Bulletin of Tanzanian Affair, (various issues)

Campbell, H., 'The Politics of Demobilization in Tanzania: Beyond Nationalism', in *Taamuli* I (1 and 2) (1990), 64.

Canadian International Development Agency (CIDA), *Report of the Wheat Sector Study Team Tanzania 1977,* Manitoba Pool Elevators (1977)

Carvalho, V.N., 'The Control of Managing Agents in Tanzanian Parastatal Organizations with Special Reference to the National Development Corporation', *Eastern Africa Law Review* 5(1) (1977)

Chama cha Mapinduzi, *CCM Constitution* (DSM, Tanganyika Standard Ltd., n.d.)

Coopers and Lybrand Assoc. Ltd, *Grain Storage and Milling Project,* DSM (1977)

Coulson, A., *Tanzania: A Political Economy* (Oxford, Clarendon Press, 1982)

Cowen, M. and K. Kinyananjui, 'Some Problems of Capital and Class in Kenya', Institute of Development Studies, University of Sussex (1977)

Desai, R.H., 'Afro-Asian Relationships in Small Towns', in East African Institute of Social and Cultural Affairs (ed.), *Racial and Communal Tensions in East Africa* (Nairobi, East African Publishing House, 1966)

Due, J.M., *Costs, Returns and Repayment Experience of Ujamaa Villages in Tanzania, 1973–1976* (Washington, DC, University Press of America, Inc., 1980)

Dumont, R., *Tanzanian Agriculture after the Arusha Declaration* (DSM, Ministry of Economic Affairs and Development Planning, 1969)

East African Statistical Department, 'African Population of Tanganyika Territory: Geographical and Tribal Studies', *East African Population Census*, 1948 (Nairobi, 1950)

—*East African Trade Reports*, Nairobi (1949–76)

Economist Intelligence Unit, *A Survey of Wholesale and Retail Trade in Tanganyika* (London, 1962)

Ellis, F., 'Agricultural Marketing and Peasant–State Transfers in Tanzania', *Journal of Peasant Studies*, 10(4) (1983)

El-Namaki, M.S. *Problems of Management in a Developing Environment: The Case of Tanzania (State Enterprise between 1967 and 1975)* (Amsterdam, N. Holland Publishing Company, 1979)

FAO/Kilimo, *Food Security Bulletins* (Dar es Salaam, various issues)

—Crop Monitoring and Early Warning System Project, 'Consolidated Assessment of the National Food Supply Situation' (DSM, June 1988)

Fortmann, L., 'An Evaluation of the Progress of the National Maize Project at the End of One Cropping Season in Morogoro and Arusha Regions', USAID/Tanzania (1976)

Friis-Hansen, E., 'An Assessment of Changes in Land Tenure and Land Use since Villagisation and the Impact of the Development of Peasant Agricultural Production in Tanzania', Centre for Development Research Report, Copenhagen (May 1986)

Ghai, D.P. and Y.P. (eds), *Portrait of a Minority, Asians in East Africa* (Nairobi, Oxford University Press, 1970)

Golob, P. and R. Hodges, 'Study of an Outbreak of Prostephanus truncatus (Horn) in Tanzania', Tropical Products Institute, G164 (London, 1982)

Gordon, H. 'Open Markets for Maize and Rice in Urban Tanzania: Current Issues and Evidence', mimeo, DSM (November 1988)

—'Maize Marketing, Seasonal Prices and Government Policy in Tanzania', mimeo, DSM (1989)

Goulbourne, H., 'The Role of the Political Party in Tanzania since the Arusha Declaration', in H. Goulbourne (ed.), *Politics and State in the Third World* (London, Macmillan Press Ltd., 1979)

Great Britain, Colonial Office, *East Africa Royal Commission 1953–1955 Report* (London, HMSO, 1955)

Gulliver, P.H., 'The Evolution of Arusha Trade', in Bohannan, P. and G. Dalton (eds), *Markets in Africa* (Chicago, Northwestern University Press, 1962)

Hansard, Proceedings of the Tanzanian Legislative Assembly, various sessions

Hartmann, J., 'The Arusha Declaration Revisited', *African Review*, 12(1) (1985)

Hawkins, H.D.G., *Wholesale and Retail Trade in Tanganyika: A Study of Distribution in East Africa* (New York, Frederick A. Praeger Publisher, 1965)

Hazlewood, A., *Education, Work and Pay in East Africa* (Oxford, Clarendon Press, 1989)

Heijnen, J.D., *Development and Education in the Mwanza District (Tanzania): A Case Study of Migration and Peasant Farming* (Rotterdam, Bronder-Offset, 1968)

Helleiner, G.K., 'Agricultural Marketing in Tanzania – Policies and Problems', Economics Research Bureau Paper 68.14, University of Dar es Salaam (1968)

Hoad, P., 'Report on a Socio-Economic Survey of Kinondoni', Institute of Public Administration, Physical Training Course, University College, DSM (1968)

Hofmeier, R., *Transport and Economic Development in Tanzania* (Munich, Weltforum Verlag, 1973)

Honey, M.S., 'An Economic History of Asians in Tanzania and Zanzibar c. 1840–1940,' Ph.D. thesis, University of Dar es Salaam (1982)

Hyden, G., *Beyond Ujamaa in Tanzania* (London, Heinemann, 1980)

Iliffe, J., *A Modern History of Tanganyika* (Cambridge, Cambridge University Press, 1979)

International Bank for Reconstruction and Development, *The Economic Development of Tanganyika* (Baltimore, Johns Hopkins Press, 1961)

International Labour Office, *Distributional Aspects of Stabilisation Programmes in the United Republic of Tanzania 1979–84* (Geneva, ILO, 1988)

Jackson, D., 'The Disappearance of Strikes in Tanzania', *Journal of Modern African Studies* 17(2) (1979)

Jamal, V., 'The Political Economy of Devaluation in Tanzania', mimeo, International Labour Office, Addis Ababa (1984)

Jones, W.O., *Staple Food Crops in Tropical Africa* (New York, Cornell University, 1972)

Journal of the Tanganyika European Civil Servants Association, 37 (January 1944) and (March 1946)

Kaberuka, D., 'Evaluating the Performance of Food Marketing Parastatals', *Development Policy Review* 2 (1984)

Kajumulo-Tibaijuka, A., 'An Economic Analysis of Smallholder Banana–Coffee Farms in Kagera Region, Tanzania', Report 240, University of Agricultural Sciences, Uppsala, Sweden (1984)

Keeler, A., 'A Preliminary Report on the Parallel Market for Grains in Tanzania', Marketing Development Bureau, DSM (March 1983)

Keeler A. *et al.*, *The Consumption Effects of Agricultural Policies in Tanzania*, Sigma One Corporation, USAID (1982)

Kim, K., 'Enterprise Performance in the Public and Private Sectors: Tanzanian Experience', *Journal of Developing Areas* 15(3) (1981)

Kiondo, A., 'The Nature of Economic Reforms in Tanzania', in *Taamuli* I (1 and 2) (1990)

Kjaerby, F., 'Agricultural Productivity and Surplus Production in Tanzania: Implications of Villagization, Fertilizers and Mixed Farming', Discussion Paper, University of Dar es Salaam (1979)

—*Peasants ahead of the State? – Agricultural Intensification and Peasant Production under Crisis Conditions in Northern Tanzania*, Centre for Development Research, Copenhagen (January 1984)

—'Scratching the Surface: The Tanzanian Tractor Fiasco, the Undiscovered Oxenization Boom and the Drag of Mixed Farming', Draft, Centre for Development Research, Copenhagen (November 1984)

—'Villagization and the Forms of Agricultural Production in Hanang', Centre for Development Research, Copenhagen (1985)

Knight, J.B. and R.H. Sabot, 'Public Sector Pay and Employment Policy and the Rate of Return to Education', Revised Draft (February 1985)

Koponen, J., *People and Production in Late Precolonial Tanzania: History and Structures* (Finland, Monograph of the Finnish Society for Development Studies No. 2, 1988)

Kriesel, H.C. *et al.*, *Agricultural Marketing in Tanzania: Background Research and Policy Proposals* (East Lansing, Michigan State University, 1970)

Kydd, J. and V. Scarborough, 'Liberalisation and Privatisation in Sub-Saharan African Food Marketing: A Survey of the Issues', Overseas Development Natural Resources Institute, mimeo (December 1988)

Leibenow, J.G., *Colonial Rule and Political Development in Tanzania* (Nairobi, East African Publishing House, 1971)

Leslie, J.A.K., *A Survey of Dar es Salaam* (London, Oxford University Press, 1963)

Livingstone, I., 'Production, Price and Marketing Policy for Staple Foodstuffs in Tanzania', Economics Research Bureau Paper 71.16, University of Dar es Salaam (1971)

Lofchie, M.F., *Agricultural Performance in Kenya and Tanzania* (London, Lynne Rienner, 1989)

Loft, M. and J. Oldevelt, 'Developments in Peasant Agriculture in Kigoma Region during the Post-Villagisation Years', Economics Research Bureau, University of Dar es Salaam (1981)

Mackintosh, M., 'Abstract Markets and Real Needs', in Bernstein, H., B. Crow, M. Mackintosh and C. Martin (eds), *The Food Question* (London, Earthscan Publications Ltd, 1990)

Maguire, G.A., *Toward 'Uhuru' in Tanzania* (Cambridge, Cambridge University Press, 1969)

Maliyamkono, T.L. and M.S.D. Bagachwa, *The Second Economy in Tanzania* (London, James Currey Ltd, ESAURP – Heinemann Kenya, 1990).

Mangat, J.S., *A History of the Asians in East Africa c. 1886–1945* (Oxford, Oxford University Press, 1969)

Mbilinyi, M., 'Co-operative Organisation in Isange Village', in Koda, B. *et al.*, *Women's Initiatives in the United Republic of Tanzania* (Geneva, International Labour Office, 1987)

McCall, M. and M. Skutsch, 'Strategies and Contradictions in Tanzania's Rural Development: Which Path for the Peasants?', in Lea, D.A. and D. Chaudhri (eds), *Rural Development and the State* (London, Methuen, 1983)

McCarthy, D.M.P., *Colonial Bureaucracy and Creating Underdevelopment: Tanganyika, 1919–1940* (Iowa, Iowa State University, 1982)

Mgaza, O. and H. Bantje, *Infant Feeding in Dar es Salaam*, Tanzania Food and Nutrition Centre and BRALUP (DSM, 1980)

Mgeni, B.C., 'Diffusion of an Agricultural Innovation: Hybrid Maize in Njombe District', M.A. Thesis, University of Dar es Salaam (1978)

Migot-Adholla, S.E., 'The Politics of a Growers' Cooperative Organisation', in Cliffe, L. *et al.* (eds), *Rural Cooperation in Tanzania* (DSM, Tanzania Publishing House, 1975)

Mihyo, P.B., *Industrial Conflict and Change in Tanzania* (DSM, Tanzania Publishing House, 1983)

Mlimuka, A.K.L.J. and P.J.A.M. Kabudi, 'The State and the Party', in Shivji, I.G. (ed.), *The State and the Working People in Tanzania* (London, Codesria, 1986)

Mohele, A.T., 'The Ismani Maize Credit Programme', Economics Research Bureau Paper 75.2, University of Dar es Salaam (1975)

Moore, M.P. and P. Stutley, 'Smallholder Food Production in Tanzania', DSM, Report to SIDA and the Government of Tanzania (1981)

Moshi, H.P.B., 'Adequacy of Control in Tanzania's Public Enterprises', *Public Enterprises*, 5(1) (1984)

Msambichaka, L.A., S.M.H. Rugumisa, and J.J. Semboja, *The Role of the Public Sector in Development – Tanzania*, Economics Research Bureau, University of Dar es Salaam (June 1985)

Msekwa, P., *Towards Party Supremacy* (Arusha, Eastern African Publications, 1976)

Mwansasu, B.U., 'The Changing Role of the Tanganyika African National Union', in Mwansasu, B.U. and C. Pratt (eds), *Towards Socialism in Tanzania* (DSM, Tanzania Publishing House, 1979)

Mwapachu, J.V., *Management of Public Enterprises in Developing Countries: The Tanzania Experience* (New Delhi, Oxford & IBH Publishing Co., 1983)

Mwase, N.R.L., 'Cooperatives and Ujamaa: A Case Study of the Arusha Region Cooperative Union Limited (ARCU)' in Hyden, G. (ed.), *Co-*

operatives in Tanzania: Problems of Organisation, (DSM, Tanzania Publishing House, 1976)

Ndulu, B., 'The Impact of Inter-regional Transport Subsidy Policy on Commercial Supply of Food Grains in Tanzania: The Case of Paddy and Maize', Economics Research Bureau Seminar Paper, University of Dar es Salaam (November 1979)

Ngware, S.S.A., 'Emerging Trends after Villagisation', Paper prepared for ILO/JASPA, DSM (1981).

Nyerere, J.K., *Socialism and Rural Development* (DSM, Government Printer, 1967)

— *The Arusha Declaration Ten Years After* (DSM, Government Printer, 1977)

Odegaard, K., 'A Study of Agricultural Producer Prices, their Inter-relationships and Impact on Agricultural Marketing in Tanzania, 1962–1972', mimeo (DSM, Office of the Prime Minister and Second Vice-President, April 1974)

— 'An Analysis of the Food Market in a Dual Market Structure: The Case of Maize in Tanzania', Arne Ryde Symposium, University of Lund, Sweden (August 1983)

Pratt, C., *The Critical Phase in Tanzania 1945–68* (Nairobi, Oxford University Press, 1978)

Raikes, P., 'The Development of Mechanized Commercial Wheat Production in North Iraqw, Tanzania' Ph.D. thesis, Stanford University (1975)

Rasmussen, T., 'The Green Revolution in the Southern Highlands of Tanzania', Centre for Development Research Project Paper A85.7, Copenhagen (1985).

— 'The Private Market for Maize in Tanzania – A Preliminary Analysis', Centre for Development Research Paper D.85.13, Copenhagen (1985)

— 'Commercialised Maize Production among Smallholders in the Southern Highland, Tanzania', Centre for Development Research Project Paper 86.3, Copenhagen (February 1986)

Saul, J.S., 'Marketing Co-operatives in a Developing Country: The Tanzanian Case', in Cliffe, L. and J.S. Saul (eds), *Socialism in Tanzania* (DSM, East African Publishing House, 1973)

Scarborough, V. 'The Current Status of Food Marketing in Tanzania', mimeo, Wye College, United Kingdom (March 1989).

Schneider-Barthold, W., 'Farmers' Reactions to the Present Economic Situation in Tanzania with Respect to Production and Marketing', German Development Institute, Berlin (June 1983)

Semboja, J., 'The Parastatal Study: Analysis of the Qualitative and SCOPO Data', University of Dar es Salaam (July 1987)

Sen, A.K., *Poverty and Famines* (Oxford, Clarendon Press, 1980)

Shaidi, L.P., 'Trade Liberalization and the Law', in *Taamuli* I (1 and 2) (1990).

Shivji, I., *Class Struggles in Tanzania* (DSM, Tanzanian Publishing House, 1975)

Smith, A., 'The Wealth of Nations', in Abbott, L.D. (ed.), *Masterworks of Economics* (New York, Doubleday & Company, 1946)

Southworth, V. Roy, W.O. Jones and S.R. Pearson, 'Food Crop Marketing in Atebubu District, Ghana', *Food Research Institute Studies* 17(2) (1979)

Srivastava, B.P., 'The Constitution of the United Republic of Tanzania 1977: Some Salient Features – Some Riddles', University of Dar es Salaam, Professorial Inaugural Lecture Series, No. 34, Dar es Salaam University Press (1983)

Sym, J., *Food Security and Policy Interventions*, Tinbergen Institute/Centre for Development Planning, Erasmus University, Rotterdam (November 1990)

Tanganyika, *African Census Report 1957* (DSM, Government Printer, 1963)

— *Annual Report on Cooperative Development* (DSM, various years)

— *Blue Books*, DSM (1920–48)

— Department of Agriculture Annual Reports (DSM, various years)

— Department of Commerce and Industry Annual Reports (DSM, various years)

— Grain Storage Department Annual Report July 1956–July 1957 (DSM, Government Printer, 1957)

— Labour Department Annual Reports (DSM, various years)

— 'Report of the Committee on Rising Costs', DSM, Government Printer (1951)

— *Report on the Census of the Non-Native Population Population taken on the Night of 25 February, 1948* (DSM, Government Printer, 1953)

— *Report on the Census of the Non-African Population taken on the Night of 20/21st February, 1957* (DSM, Government Printer, 1958)

— *Tanganyika Trade Reports*, DSM (1946–48)

— *Transport Licensing Authority 1956–1957 Annual Report* (DSM)

Tanganyika African Nationalist Union, *TANU Guidelines 1971* (DSM, Government Printer, 1971)

Tanzania, *Economic Recovery Programme* (DSM, May 1986).

— *Emergency Social Action Programme, July 1989–June 1992: Preliminary Draft for Discussion* (DSM, April 1989)

— *Hali ya Uchumi wa Taifa katika Mwaka* (DSM, Government Printer, various years)

— 'Tanzanian Trade Reports' (DSM, 1977–84)

— *The Economic Survey* (DSM, Government Printer, various years)

Tanzania, Bank of Tanzania, *Economic and Operations Report* (DSM, 1975–84)

Tanzania, Bureau of Statistics, *Analysis of Accounts of Parastatals* (DSM, Government Printer, various years)

— *1967 Population Census*, Vols. I-VI (DSM, 1970–73)

— *1969 Household Budget Survey*, III (DSM, 1972)

— 1976/77 Household Budget Survey, computer printouts (n.d.)

— *1978 Population Census,* Vols. II, IV, VI and VIII (DSM, 1983)
— *1988 Population Census: Preliminary Report* (DSM, 1989)
Tanzania, EWCMP, 'The Situation of Grains and Cassava Marketed through Official Channels in Tanzania' (DSM, June 1979)
— 'The Availability of Food in Tanzania in 1981/82', FAO/Kilimo, Annex II (DSM, July 1981)
— 'Final Crop Condition Assessment and Production Estimate' (DSM, July 1983)
Tanzania, Food and Nutrition Centre, *Data Report on the Food and Nutrition Situation in Tanzania* (DSM, 1978 and 1982)
Tanzania, MDB, 'A Review of the Production and Marketing Arrangements for Maize, Paddy and Wheat with Particular Reference to the Milling Sector', II, DSM (1972)
— 'A Strategic Grain Reserve Programme for Tanzania', II, DSM (November 1974)
— 'Review of Crop Buying Arrangements 1976/77', DSM (February 1977)
— 'The Inter-regional Transport of Major Agricultural Commodities in Tanzania', R5/79, DSM (1979)
— 'Report on Investigation into the Financial and Operating Position of Kilimo Crop Authorities: NMC', DSM (1979)
— 'An Analysis of Regional and Seasonal Price Options for Maize in Tanzania', DSM (November 1980)
— 'Proposals for Staple Food Prices under the Structural Adjustment Programme', DSM (1983)
—'Aspects of the Open Market for Food Commodities in Mainland Tanzania', DSM (June 1986)
— 'Annual Review of Agricultural Marketing', DSM (1987 and 1988)
— 'Annual Review of Maize, Rice and Wheat', DSM (1987)
— 'Monthly Marketing Bulletin' (DSM, December 1982–December 1988)
— 'Agricultural Price Policy Reviews' (DSM, various years)
Tanzania, Ministry of Agriculture, 'Tanzania: National Food Strategy', Second draft (June 1982)
Tanzania, Ministry of Agriculture and Livestock Development, 'Food Distribution System in Tanzania with Special Reference to Institutional Functions, Inter-regional Trade, Pricing and Cost Reductions' (DSM, June 1987)
Tanzanian Economic Trends, various issues
Temu, P., 'The Employment of Foreign Consultants in Tanzania: Its Value and Limitations', *African Review* 3(1) (1973)
— 'Marketing Board Pricing and Storage Policy with Particular Reference to Maize in Tanzania', Ph.D. thesis, Stanford University (1975)
Tibaijuka, A., 'An Economic Survey of Village Projects in Iringa, Mbeya and Ruvuma Regions, 1979', Economics Research Bureau Paper 81.3, University of Dar es Salaam (1981)

— 'Grappling with Urban Food Insecurity in the Midst of Plenty: Government Launches "Operation Okoa Mazao"', *Tanzanian Economic Trends* 2(3 & 4) (October 1989/January 1990)

Tibenderana, H.K., 'The Factors affecting Tanzania's National Milling Corporation's Performance (1968–1981)', M.A. thesis, University of Dar es Salaam (1982)

Tripp, A.M., *Defending the Right to Subsist: the State vs. the Urban Informal Economy in Tanzania* (World Institute for Development Economics Research of the United Nations University, Working Paper 59, August 1989)

UNCTAD, *Handbook of International Trade and Development Statistics* (1987)

Urasa, 'National Maize Project Report', mimeo (DSM, December 1983)

USAID, 'Tanzania: Food Needs Assessment 1990/91' (DSM, October 1990)

van Cranenburgh, O., *The Widening Gyre: The Tanzanian One-Party State and Policy towards Rural Cooperatives* (Delft, Holland, Eburon, 1990)

van Donge, J., 'Waluguru Traders in Dar es Salaam: An Analysis of Social Construction of Economic Life', Paper presented at the Biennial Conference, African Studies Association (UK), Birmingham (September 1990)

von Clemm, M., 'People of the White Mountain: The Interdependence of Political and Economic Activity amongst the Chagga in Tanganyika with Special Reference to Recent Changes' D.Phil. thesis, Oxford University (1962)

Williams, D.V., 'Authoritarian Legal Systems and the Process of Capitalist Accumulation in Africa', Paper presented at the Southern African Universities Social Science Conference, Dar es Salaam (1979)

World Bank, Tanzania Programme for Transport Sector Recovery: The Transport Sector Donors' Conference: Technical Working Papers', Arusha (December 1987)

— *Parastatals in Tanzania Towards a Reform Program* (Washington DC, 1988)

Wright, F.C., *African Consumers in Nyasaland and Tanganyika* (London, Her Majesty's Stationary Office, 1955)

Wright, M., *Lords and People in South Rukwa* (forthcoming)

Archival Sources

Rhodes House, Oxford

Leslie, J.A.K., Rhodes House Mss. Afr. s. 1516, 16 (1950–54)

Malcolm, D.W., Diary 29/11/35, Rhodes House Mss. Afr. s. 1445

McCleery, H.H., 'Extent and Conditions under which Natives are occupying Land in the Outskirts of Dar es Salaam', Rhodes House Mss. Afr. s. 870

Pearson, N., 'Trade Unionist on Safari, 1949', Rhodes House Mss. Afr. s.
    394
Sillery, A., Rhodes House Mss. Afr. s. 1749
Tanganyika National Farmers' Union Correspondence, Rhodes House
    Mss. Afr. s. 1222

Public Records Office, London

Public Records Office 852/428/17600/Part II

Tanzania National Archives

TNA Acc. 61	Dar es Salaam district files
TNA SMP 10138	'System of Marketing Produce', 1927–45
TNA SMP 13044	'Native Agriculture General', 1933–48
TNA SMP 19533	'Maize Industry', 1930–41
TNA SMP 28259/8	'Agricultural Produce: Maize', 1939–50
TNA SMP 30157	'Crop Production, Guaranteed Prices and Marketing', 1941–42
TNA SMP 30626	'Crop Production', 1942–5
TNA SMP 31301/III	'Crop Production, Guaranteed Prices and Marketing', 1943–44
TNA SMP 31555/1	'Allocation of Controlled Foodstuffs and Rationing Scheme for Africa', 1942–46
TNA SMP 31886	'Increased Production of Crops', 1944–1954
TNA SMP 34927	'Black Marketing', 1946
TNA SMP 35085	'Food Subsidy Fund', 1946–47
TNA SMP 35181	'Cereal Storage', 1947–51
TNA SMP 38804	'Maize Prices in Relation to those for Export Group and the Stimulation of Agricultural Production Generally', 1948–53
TNA SMP 39114	'Retail Prices and Subsidization of Grain', 1949

Newspapers

Daily News (Dar es Salaam)
Guardian (London)
Independent (London)
Sunday News (Dar es Salaam)
Tanganyika Standard (Dar es Salaam)

Tables

Table I.1: Percentage Composition of Household Staple Food Consumption by Value and Weight in Rural and Urban Areas, 1976/77

Staple Foodstuffs	BY VALUE			BY WEIGHT		
	National	Rural	Urban	National	Rural	Urban
As % of Total Expenditure	34.4	38.5	20.1			
As % of Total Food Expenditure/Weight	52.0	54.6	39.3	73.2	75.8	61.2
As % of Staple Foodstuffs:						
Maize	43.5	45.3	31.0	40.2	40.3	38.3
Rice/Paddy	13.7	11.8	26.9	6.3	5.3	16.9
Wheat/Bread/Cake	3.6	1.5	18.0	1.4	0.5	10.5
Millet/Sorghum	10.1	10.9	4.2	8.8	9.2	5.5
Barley/Other Cereals	2.1	2.2	1.6	2.8	3.0	1.2
Cassava	5.9	6.1	4.5	8.6	8.6	8.3
Sweet potatoes/Yams	5.0	5.1	4.3	7.9	8.2	5.9
Potatoes	2.1	2.1	2.3	2.2	2.2	2.2
Bananas/Plantains	7.6	8.0	4.7	11.9	12.3	6.8
Other Starches	6.4	7.0	2.5	9.9	10.4	4.5
Total	100.0	100.0	100.0	100.0	100.0	100.1

Source: 1976/77 Household Budget Survey, Tanzania, Bureau of Statistics

Table II.1: Value of Net Import/Export, 1939–88 (TSh '000,000)

Year	Imports	Exports	Balance	Year	Imports	Exports	Balance
1939	60.8	38.3	−22.5	1963	808.4	1271.1	462.7
1940	60.0	79.4	19.4	1964	879.5	1402.2	522.7
1941	73.1	89.6	16.4	1965	1000.9	1255.6	254.7
1942	73.8	121.6	47.8	1966	1285.0	1582.1	297.1
1943	92.5	108.1	15.6	1967	1300.5	1553.6	253.1
1944	112.8	139.4	26.6	1968	1531.7	1585.4	53.7
1945	134.9	154.5	19.6	1969	1418.8	1666.8	248.0
1946	162.5	169.2	6.7	1970	1939.2	1688.7	−250.5
1947	274.5	214.7	−59.8	1971	2414.4	1735.4	−679.0
1948	451.5	314.6	−136.9	1972	2597.6	2027.2	−570.4
1949	551.5	384.7	−166.8	1973	3139.5	2238.3	−901.2
1950	480.0	475.4	−4.6	1974	5429.7	2537.4	−2892.3
1951	562.4	786.9	224.5	1975	5288.1	2548.6	−2739.5
1952				1976	4751.8	3815.0	−936.8
1953	568.5	690.9	122.4	1977	6161.3	4393.8	−1767.5
1954	639.2	725.0	85.8	1978	8797.7	3631.7	−5166.0
1955	870.6	723.8	−146.8	1979	8941.0	4313.2	−4627.8
1956	717.7	896.1	178.4	1980	10210.5	4700.0	−9740.5
1957	785.5	789.5	40.0	1981	9739.5	4705.8	−5033.7
1958	671.4	834.1	162.7	1982	10529.7	4143.9	−6385.8
1959	689.1	905.7	216.6	1983	8876.5	4138.6	−4737.9
1960	756.3	1096.5	340.2	1984	14282.7	6347.1	−7935.6
1961	793.7	973.0	179.3	1985	17199.7	4916.2	−12283.5
1962	796.3	1024.8	228.5	1986	39966.9	13263.4	−26703.5
				1987	78949.0	23841.9	−55107.1
				1988	122587.8	38486.4	−84101.4

Sources: 1939–48: Tanganyika Blue Books
1949–76: East African Annual Trade Reports
1977–83: Tanzania Annual Trade Reports
1984–88: *Tanzanian Economic Trends* 3(2), July 1990

Table II.2: Gross Domestic Product by Kind of Economic Activity at 1976 Prices (TSh '000,000)

Year	1964	1965	1966	1967	1968	1969	1970	1971	1972	1973	1974	1975
GDP at Factor Costs	12085	12416	14018	14678	15429	15782	16730	17208	18365	18926	19399	20545

Year	1976	1977	1978	1979	1980	1981	1982	1983	1984	1985	1986	1987	1988
GDP at Factor Costs	21653	21739	22202	22849	23419	23301	23439	22882	23656	24278	25070	26049	27885
Imputed bank service charge	−424	−462	−485	−501	−531	−549	−667	−716	−755	−797	−886	−862	−920
Total Economic Activity	22077	22201	22687	23350	23950	23850	24106	23538	24411	25075	25956	26911	28005

Sources: Bureau of Statistics, Tanzania, The Economic Survey 1971–72 (Dar es Salaam, Government Printer, 1972), 7; Tanzania, The Economic Survey 1977–78 (Dar es Salaam, Government Printer, 1979);

Tanzanian Economic Trends 3(2), July 1990

Table II.3: Terms of Trade Indices, 1970–86 (1980 = 100)

	EXPORTS			IMPORTS			Barter Terms of Trade	Income Terms of Trade
Year	Value	Unit Value	Quantum	Value	Unit Value	Quantum		
1970	51	26	198	26	27	95	94	187
1973	72	40	182	41	39	103	101	184
1974	79	66	120	60	54	111	122	146
1975	73	58	126	63	58	109	100	126
1976	96	63	152	53	59	90	108	165
1977	107	82	130	61	64	95	129	167
1978	94	77	121	93	72	130	108	131
1979	101	83	122	88	85	103	97	118
1980	100	100	100	100	100	100	100	100
1981	121	89	136	99	98	101	91	123
1982	90	85	105	92	95	97	89	94
1983	72	82	88	67	91	73	90	79
1984	74	83	89	73	90	81	93	83
1985	56	79	70	84	90	94	89	62
1986	68	89	77	64	88	72	101	77

Source: UNCTAD, *Handbook of International Trade and Development Statistics* (1987), 545

Table 11.4: Central Government Budget, 1976/77–1988/89 (TSh. Million)

		% *Distribution:*						Para-	Other
			Import*/					statal	Non-
	Total	Customs	Export+	Sales	Income	Other	Total	Divi-	tax
Year	Revenue	Duty	Tax	Tax	Tax	Tax	Tax	dends	Revenue
1976/77	6129.0	13.2	–	41.9	26.8	18.0	84.9	1.6	13.5
1977/78	6082.1	23.9	–	34.6	31.2	10.3	87.7	1.9	10.4
1978/79	6812.0	18.5	–	44.6	28.0	8.0	82.6	2.9	14.4
1979/80	7757.3	11.9	6.9+	42.8	35.5	3.6	87.5	2.7	9.8
1980/81	8872.0	8.1	2.6+	53.3	33.5	2.5	91.7	1.6	6.7
1981/82	9783.0	7.2	0.5+	56.0	33.6	2.4	93.5	2.0	4.4
1982/83	12445.6	6.7	0.2+	56.8	32.3	4.1	89.2	2.8	8.1
1983/84	14193.8	6.8	–	55.4	27.9	5.4	95.6	–	4.4
1984/85	17957.6	8.5	7.1*	49.4	26.1	5.0	96.1	–	3.9
1985/86	20831.9	7.0	6.5*	44.6	29.6	6.6	94.4	–	5.6
1986/87	31386.9	13.0	11.7*	39.6	23.4	6.4	94.1	–	5.9
1987/88	46954.3	11.7	11.3*	37.1	24.2	7.2	91.7	–	8.3
1988/89*	70212.0	14.3	12.5*	38.7	22.3	6.4	94.2	–	5.8

EXPENDITURE			Recurrent			Deficit as
	Total	% Recurrent	Surplus or	% Development	Total	% of
	Expenditure	Expenditure	Deficit	Expenditure	Deficit	GDP
1976/77	7956.8	59.2	1426.5	40.8	–1817.8	8.8
1977/78	8894.1	62.6	518.8	37.4	–2812.0	10.6
1978/79	13044.9	63.6	–1483.0	36.4	–6232.9	21.1
1979/80	14413.0	64.0	–1471.7	36.0	–6655.7	20.4
1980/81	14895.0	68.0	–1264.0	32.0	–6023.0	16.6
1981/82	17387.0	74.1	–3120.0	25.9	–7604.0	18.9
1982/83	19215.0	76.7	–2290.4	23.3	–7215.0	16.8
1983/84	23918.0	76.0	–3988.2	24.0	–9724.0	
1984/85	26727.6	79.8	–3378.9	20.2	–8770.0	
1985/86	33219.3	82.5	–6570.4	17.5	–12387.4	
1986/87	55481.1	72.8	–9003.3	27.2	–24094.2	
1987/88	76856.0	80.4	–14837.9	19.6	–29901.7	
1988/89*	118672.0	76.1	–20097.3	23.9	–48460.0	

FINANCING	Bank	Non–bank		External Loans
	Borrowing	Borrowing	Others	and Grants
1976/77	–	308.6	107.2	1402.0
1977/78	232.3	563.3	644.6	1368.8
1978/79	3056.7	454.4	285.6	2427.2
1979/80	2804.0	671.0	860.7	2320.0
1980/81	2916.0	751.0	484.0	1872.0
1981/82	3278.0	803.0	1685.0	1838.0
1982/83	4295.0	900.0	–	2020.0
1983/84	4699.0	675.0	719.0	1134.0
1984/85	4837.4	1437.0	726.0	3015.0
1985/86	4925.0	1308.0	–	2911.1
1986/87	1656.0	2857.5	–	8567.3
1987/88*	913.6	2500.0	–	19864.1
1988/89*	600.0	2500.0	–	45360.0

Sources: Ministry of Finance, Economic Affairs and Planning, *Economic Survey, 1982* (Dar es Salaam, Government Printer); *Tanzanian Economic Trends* 3(2); Bureau of Statistics , *National Accounts of Tanzania, 1972–82*, as quoted in ILO, *Distributional Aspects of Stabilisation Programmes in the United Republic of Tanzania, 1979–84* (Geneva, ILO, 1988), 80
* Estimates

Table II.5: Central Government Expenditure by Sector, 1975/78–1987/88

Year	% DISTRIBUTION: General Public Services	Defence	Education	Health	Other Social Services	Water Supply	Agri-culture	Other Economic Services	Public Debt	Other
1975/76	15.8	12.2	14.1	7.1	4.6	8.6	14.2	14.1	7.3	2.0
1976/77	17.4	12.3	13.6	7.1	3.7	5.4	11.6	21.0	5.9	2.0
1977/78	15.0	15.1	14.3	7.3	3.2	4.9	9.2	22.3	7.4	1.3
1978/79	14.4	24.4	11.6	5.4	2.8	4.3	7.0	20.8	8.4	0.9
1979/80	17.1	8.9	13.0	5.7	3.8	5.2	10.6	26.1	8.7	0.9
1980/81	18.6	11.2	12.1	5.5	2.8	4.1	10.1	23.1	11.7	0.8
1981/82	16.6	12.2	12.8	5.2	3.0	5.4	7.4	19.3	17.4	0.7
1982/83	16.9	8.2	13.3	5.4	3.3	4.6	7.7	15.8	23.9	0.9
1983/84	22.0	12.8	11.7	5.5	3.3	3.3	7.4	15.2	18.0	0.7
1984/85	29.2	13.3	6.5	4.8	3.5	2.5	6.0	15.1	18.3	1.3
1985/86	37.0	12.4	5.8	6.2	3.1	2.2	5.0	10.1	17.2	0.9
1986/87*	24.0	12.5	7.9	4.2	2.9	2.7	8.2	12.5	24.7	0.6
1987/88†	21.9	9.4	5.4	4.0	2.0	3.4	7.4	12.3	33.2	0.6

Sources: 1975/76–1982/83: Ministry of Planning and Economic Affairs, *Economic Survey*, various issues
1983/84–1987/88: Ministry of Planning and Economic Affairs, *Hali ya Uchumi wa Taifa katika Mwaka 1987* (Dar es Salaam, Government Printer)
* Provisional actual
† Planned

Table II.6: Index of Real Wages by Salary Level, 1965–85 (1969 = 100)

Year	Sectors	Minimum Wage	Average Wage	Middle Salary	Top Salary
1968	All	90	97	95	102
1969		100	100	100	100
1970		96	103	103	93
1971		93	103	105	88
1972		119	99	106	75
1973		109	102	96	67
1974		135	133	91	56
1975		103	108	68	44
1976		83	104	64	39
1977		71	98	58	33
1978		61	86	51	30
1979		58	77	45	26
1980		63	65	37	21
1981	Parastatal	60	56	24	18
1982	Only	49	47	24	14
1983		40	39	17	12
1984		46	31	16	11
1985		31	NA	NA	9

Source: World Bank, *Parastatals in Tanzania Towards a Reform Program* (Washington D.C., 1988), 15

Table II.7: Minimum Wage Levels, Nominal and Real Indices, 1966–88 (1970 = 100)

Year	General Monthly Minimum Wage	Civil Servants' Monthly Minimum Wage	Nominal Minimum Wage Index	Real Minimum Wage Index*
1966	150		88	
1967	150		88	
1968	150		88	
1969	170		100	
1970	170		100	100
1971	170		100	96
1972	240		141	125
1973	240		141	113
1974	340		200	135
1975	380		224	119
1976	380		224	112
1977	380		224	100
1978	380		224	90
1979	380		224	79
1980	480		282	76
1981	480		282	61
1982	600		353	59
1983	600		353	46
1984	810		476	46
1985	810		476	35
1986	810		476	26
1987	810	1055	476	20
1988	1260	1370	741	24

Sources: Jackson, D., 'The Disappearance of Strikes in Tanzania: Incomes Policy and Industrial Democracy', *Journal of Modern African Studies* 17(2) (1979), 248
Jamal, V., 'The Political Economy of Devaluation in Tanzania', ILO, Addis Ababa (1984), 32
Daily News 15/6/84
Tanzanian Economic Trends 1(1).
* Deflated by the National Consumer Price Index (see TABLE VII.1).

Table II.8: Cost of Living Indices, 1963–87 (1970 = 100)

Year	Retail Price Index – Wage Earners Dar es Salaam				Cost of Living Index – Middle Grade Civil Servants			
	General	% Change	Food	% Change	General	% Change	Food	% Change
1963	78	–	85	–	77	–	78	–
1964	80	3	85	0	82	6	80	3
1965	85	6	92	8	86	5	88	10
1966	89	5	95	3	90	5	90	2
1967	91	4	95	0	95	6	93	3
1968	95	4	97	2	97	2	97	4
1969	97	2	96	-1	99	2	97	0
1970	100	3	100	4	100	1	100	3
1971	103	3	104	4	101	1	104	4
1972	114	11	115	11	104	3	108	4
1973	124	9	122	6	119	14	120	11
1974	163	31	166	36	149	25	156	30
1975	243	49	229	38	199	34	229	47
1976	294	21	305	33	221	11	250	9
1977	345	17	361	18	247	12	276	10
1978	403	17	432	20	295	19	325	18
1979	426	6	448	4	348	18	377	16
1980	503	18	537	20	413	19	459	22
1981	647	28	675	26	544	32	613	34
1982	797	23	848	26	684	26	819	34
1983	983	23	1009	19	851	24	1003	22
1984	1155	17	1104	9	1082	27	1128	12
1985	1693	47	1610	46	1547	43	1669	48
1986	2383	41	2406	49	2132	38	2328	39
1987	3018	27	3025	26	2795	31	3101	33

Sources: Bank of Tanzania, *Economic and Operations Report* (June 1975 and 1984)
Tanzania, *Hali ya Uchumi wa Taifa katika Mwaka 1987*, Ministry of Finance and Economic Planning (DSM, Government Printer, 1988)

Table II.9: Peasant Income Index, 1956–87 (1963 = 100)

Year	Estimated Real Income of Commercial Maize Producer*	Year	Estimated Real Income of Commercial Maize Producer*
1956	93	1972	65
1957	84	1973	62
1958	86	1974	64
1959	80	1975	59
1960	69	1976	72
1961	96	1977	68
1962	99	1978	68
1963	100	1979	65
1964	83	1980	66
1965	92	1981	59
1966	79	1982	64
1967	80	1983	60
1968	76	1984	57
1969	66	1985	60
1970	70	1986	63
1971	68	1987	61

Sources: Bank of Tanzania, *Economic and Operations Report* (1975 and 1984); Ministry of Finance and Economic Planning, *Hali ya Uchumi wa Taifa katika Mwaka 1987*; Kriesel, H.C. *et al.*, *Agricultural Marketing in Tanzania: Background Research and Policy Proposals* (East Lansing, Michigan State University, 1970), 38; Odegaard, K., 'A Study of Agricultural Producer Prices', Office of the Prime Minister (1974), Annex Table I.4; Marketing Development Bureau, *Annual Review of Agricultural Marketing, 1988*
* Figures are for maize producers in Iringa region. It is assumed that 40% of income derives from subsistence production and is not subject to price changes, whereas the rest derives from sale of maize. Maize prices are deflated by the Non-Food Retail Price Index for Dar es Salaam (1963=100).

Table II.10: Parastatal Enterprise Growth, 1966–87

Year	Parastatals	Total Wage Employment	% of National Wage Employment	Contribution to Monetary GDP	% of Total National Monetary Capital Formation
1966	43	18,601	5		11
1967	64	26,292	8		23
1968	73	34,690	10		23
1969	78	49,925	14		14
1970	85	54,613	15		35
1971	99	67,880	17		43
1972	111	68,429	17	10	53
1973	121	70,492	15	11	46
1974	144	80,057	17	10	34
1975	147	82,374	17	10	30
1976	150	92,269	19	10	30
1977	160	105,875	22	10	34
1978	163	128,929	24	13	31
1979	176	150,261	25	12	25
1980	190	153,623	25	14	26
1981	168*	144,387			22
1982	171*	165,132	24		29
1983	180*	168,320	25	13	21
1984	167*	175,953	28	12	19
1985	NA*	171,751	26	11	23
1986	NA	171,031	25	9	26
1987					15

Sources: Tanzania, Bureau of Statistics, *Analysis of Accounts of Parastatals* (1976), 2–4: (1983), 2–9,13; Tanzania, Ministry of Finance and Economic Planning, *Hali ya Uchumi was Taifa katika Mwaka 1986*, and *1987* (Dar es Salaam, Government Printer, 1987 and 1988)
* Data for these years derive from the second reference cited. The drop in number of parastatals probably reflects a change in number of parastatals reporting.

Table II.11: Exchange Rates, 1977–88 (TSh. = US$)*

Year/Month		TSh.	Year/Month		TSh.
1978:	March	7.8601	1984:	March	12.3681
	June	7.8463		June	**17.1742**
	September	7.5783		September	17.7304
	December	7.4520		December	18.1057
1979:	March	8.3100	1985:	March	17.7881
	June	8.2779		June	**17.7333**
	September	8.2715		September	16.8336
	December	8.2627		December	16.4993
1980:	March	8.2769	1986:	March	16.0409
	June	8.2294		June	**40.3429**
	September	8.2231		September	44.5212
	December	8.2230		December	51.7189
1981:	March	8.2598	1987:	March	57.1756
	June	8.3500		June	63.4835
	September	8.3697		September	70.2288
	December	8.3268		December	83.7174
1982:	March	**9.4069**	1988:	March	93.4945
	June	9.4981		June	97.1871
	September	9.6338		September	98.1166
	December	9.5156		December	**125.0000**
1983:	March	9.8175			
	June	**12.2414**			
	September	12.3396			
	December	12.4567			

Sources: Bank of Tanzania, *Economic and Operations Report* (June 1983)
  Tanzania Economic Trends 3(2), July 1990
* Bold figures denote announced devaluations

Table III.1: Grain Storage Department Purchases and Sales of Maize/Mtama by Province, 1949/50–1956/57 (tons)

Province	1949/50	1950/51	1951/52	1952/53	1953/54	1954/55	1955/56	1956/57
Territory:								
Purchases	15,831	54,840	61,838	39,995	22,386	71,611	116,963	2,977
Sales	111,050	43,424	36,809	74,280	61,219	47,035	7,061	1,614
Net Amount	-95,219	11,416	29,029	-34,285	-38,833	24,576	109,902	1,363
Northern								
% of Terr. Purch.	37	48	41	40	43	25	30	11
Purchases	5,785	26,220	25,430	15,840	9,734	17,604	35,665	320
Sales	10,527	4,575	3,630	2,916	7,022	4,207	1,246	4
Net Amount	-4,742	21,645	21,800	12,564	2,712	13,397	34,419	316
S. Highlands								
% of Terr. Purch.	0	6	12	30	6	18	22	0
Purchases	–	3,230	7,598	11,821	1,407	12,743	25,589	–
Sales	1,403	–	317	298	976	3,747	739	–
Net Amount	-1,403	3,230	7,281	11,523	431	8,996	24,850	–
Central								
% of Terr. Purch.	3	0	7	1	0	0	3	12
Purchases	429	166	4,432	255	57	–	3,399	359
Sales	12,843	418	139	2,549	15,110	6,396	17	–
Net Amount.	-12,414	-252	4,293	-2,294	-15,053	-6,396	3,382	359
Southern								
% of Terr. Purch.	44	9	4	0	19	21	3	0
Purchases	6,942	4,952	2,563	198	4,214	15,167	2,937	–
Sales	6,240	7,177	4,937	7,818	3,799	2,579	1,517	–
Net Amount	702	-2,225	-2,374	-7,620	415	12,588	1,420	–
Eastern								
% of Terr. Purch.	14	17	16	15	8	12	18	66
Purchases	2,190	9,211	10,105	5,836	1,865	8,329	20,577	1,965
Sales	28,787	15,823	12,531	29,692	16,403	12,610	1,276	1,293
Net Amount	-26,597	-6,612	-2,426	-23,816	-14,538	-4,281	19,301	672
Tanga								
% of Terr. Purch.	0	11	5	0	5	0	8	11
Purchases	38	6,070	3,362	8	1,093	294	9,303	324
Sales	24,513	9,872	12,200	21,123	7,840	14,270	1,363	308
Net Amount	-24,475	-3,802	-8,838	-21,115	-6,747	-13,976	7,940	16
Lake								
% of Terr. Purch.	0	3	3	11	0	6	3	0
Purchases	–	1,913	2,026	4,401	1	3,981	3,073	–
Sales	20,177	3,127	2,238	8,317	8,958	2,992	842	–
Net Amount	-20,177	-1,214	-212	-3,916	-8,957	989	2,231	–
Western								
% of Terr. Purch.	3	6	10	5	18	19	14	0
Purchases	447	3,078	6,322	1,996	4,015	13,493	16,420	9
Sales	6,560	2,432	817	1,607	1,111	234	61	–
Net Amount	-6,113	646	5,505	389	2,904	13,259	16,359	9

Source: Compiled from Tanganyika, Grain Storage Department, Annual Report of the Grain Storage Department, July 1956–July 1957 (DSM, Government Printer, 1957), 14.

Table III.2: NAPB/NMC Maize Purchases by Region, 1963/64–1972/73 (Tons)

Region	1963/64	1964/65	1965/66	1966/67	1967/68	1968/69	1969/70	1970/71	1971/72	1972/73
National Total										
Purchases	108,890	30,430	69,550	107,820	105,125	130,181	47,000	186,400	43,000	106,400
Sales		83,800	89,500	74,800	93,100	104,500	123,400	116,600	160,000	154,000
Balance		−3,370	−19,950	33,020	12,025	25,681	−76,400	69,800	−117,000	−47,600
Arusha	16,630	18,340	3,263	16,840	24,400	18,821	12,800	45,100	7,600	17,100
% of total	15	23	5	16	23	14	27	24	18	16
Kilimanjaro	12,670	1,870	391	15,980	14,880	13,397	13,900	16,000	2,900	11,800
% of total	12	2	1	15	14	10	30	9	7	11
Northern Area %	27	25	5	30	37	25	57	33	24	27
Mbeya	1,740	3,120	1,381	3,180	730	1,213	300	2,500	200	100
% of total	2	4	2	3	1	1	1	1	0	0
Iringa	32,880	32,500	29,654	25,440	25,800	28,154	3,200	36,500	7,700	8,200
% of total	30	40	43	24	25	22	7	20	18	8
S.Highlands Area %	32	44	45	27	25	23	7	21	18	8
Dodoma	21,870	12,450	20,794	26,570	18,200	43,940	400	58,600	15,600	54,100
% of total	20	15	30	25	17	34	1	31	36	51
Singida	−	850	809	4,770	2,530	1,162	0	5,400	1,000	700
% of total	0	1	1	4	2	1	0	3	2	1
Central Area %	20	17	31	29	20	35	1	34	39	52
Ruvuma	2,040	30	2,776	2,850	1,545	665	1,000	1,700	0	500
% of total	2	0	4	3	1	1	2	1	0	0
Lindi	−	−	−	−	−	−	−	−	−	−
% of total										
Mtwara	1,380	0	250	0	245	−	400	0	0	0
% of total	1	0	0	0	0	0	1	0	0	0
Southern Area %	3	0	4	3	2	1	3	1	0	0
Morogoro	11,600	5,530	7,826	5,140	4,570	6,700	3,800	6,700	3,900	9,600
% of total	11	7	11	5	4	5	8	4	9	9
Coast	50	30	0	330	0	0	0	0	0	0
% of total	0	0	0	0	0	0	0	0	0	0
Eastern Area %	11	7	11	5	4	5	8	4	9	9
Tanga	2,850	890	352	2,830	2,705	2,483	900	900	100	0
% of total	3	1	1	3	3	2	2	0	0	0
Tanga Area %	3	1	1	3	3	2	2	0	0	0
Shinyanga	0	710	0	0	1,110	3,093	0	200	1,400	0
% of total	0	1	0	0	1	2	0	0	3	0
Kagera	250	120	0	80	0	0	0	0	0	0
% of total	0	0	0	0	0	0	0	0	0	0
Mwanza	0	0	0	190	20	489	600	1,300	100	200
% of total	0	0	0	0	0	0	1	1	0	0
Mara	2,010	1,830	447	2,700	5,830	7,777	8,400	10,000	1,600	3,600
% of total	2	2	1	3	6	6	18	5	4	3
Lake Area %	2	3	1	3	7	9	19	6	7	3
Kigoma	370	320	398	190	130	37	0	200	0	0
% of total	0	0	1	0	0	0	0	0	0	0
Tabora	2,550	1,840	1,201	730	2,430	2,250	1,300	1,300	900	500
% of total	2	2	2	1	2	2	3	1	2	0
Rukwa	−	−	−	−	−	−	−	−	−	−
% of total										
Western Area %	3	3	2	1	2	2	3	1	2	0

Sources: NAPB figures quoted in
1. Kriesel *et al.*, *Agricultural Marketing*, 21
2. Coopers and Lybrand Assoc. Ltd., *Grain Storage and Milling Project*, Vol. II, DSM (1977), Tables A1.17 and A1.36
3. Tanzania, MDB, 'Price Policy Recommendations', Vol. I: Maize, Rice and Wheat (DSM, 1981), Appendix 2.1

Table III.3: NAPB/NMC Rice and Paddy Purchases by Region, 1963/64–1972/73 (Rice Equivalent* Tons)

Region	1963/64	1964/65	1965/66	1966/67	1967/68	1968/69	1969/70	1970/71	1971/72	1972/73
National Total										
Purchases		−24,516	12,880	24,310	19,630	29,705	38,870	60,800	44,600	47,500
Sales		−22,153	23,600	31,700	34,400	35,200	41,800	52,100	75,800	88,000
Balance		−2,363	−10,720	−7,390	−14,770	−5,495	−2,930	8,700	−31,200	−40,500
Arusha				0	0	0	0	0	0	0
% of total										
Kilimanjaro				845	130	715	2,145	2,210	2,340	5,135
% of total				3	1	2	7	4	5	11
Northern Area %				3	1	2	7	4	5	11
Mbeya				8,320	7,995	4,550	10,335	12,480	14,365	11,830
% of total				34	41	15	35	21	32	25
Iringa				0	585	455	585	1,300	780	455
% of total				0	3	2	2	2	2	1
S. Highlands Area %				34	44	17	37	23	34	26
Dodoma				0	0	0	0	0	0	520
% of total										1
Singida				0	0	0	0	0	0	325
% of total										1
Central Area %				0	0	0	0	0	0	2
Ruvuoa				65	65	0	0	0	195	65
% of total				0	0	0	0	0	0	0
Mtwara				65	195	0	260	0	325	130
% of total				0	1	0	1	0	1	0
Lindi				–	–	–	–	–	–	–
% of total										
Southern Area %				0	1	0	1	0	1	0
Morogoro				1,560	3,380	1,170	1,430	3,185	6,630	6,435
% of total				6	17	5	5	5	15	14
Coast/DSM				2,990	2,145	0	65	0	3,055	2,600
% of total				12	11	0	0	0	7	5
Eastern Area %				19	28	5	5	5	22	19
Tanga				520	0	65	520	0	260	1,755
% of total				2	0	0	2	0	1	4
Tanga Area %				2	0	0	2	0	1	4
Shinyanga				910	2,340	3,250	1,300	4,095	1,950	9,360
% of total				4	12	11	4	7	4	20
Kagera				0	0	0	0	0	0	0
% of total										
Mwanza				910	585	2,535	6,175	12,675	1,820	1,560
% of total				4	3	9	21	21	4	3
Mara				455	845	1,820	2,665	5,590	2,470	1,235
% of total				2	4	6	9	9	6	3
Lake Area %				9	19	26	35	37	14	26
Kigoma				195	195	195	0	910	455	65
% of total				1	1	1	0	1	1	0
Tabora				7,345	845	14,950	3,900	17,420	9,945	6,110
% of total				30	4	50	13	29	22	13
Rukwa				–		–	–	–	–	–
% of total										
Western Area %				31	5	51	13	30	23	13

Sources: NAPB figures quoted in
1. Livingstone, I., 'Production, Price and Marketing Policy for Staple Foodstuffs in Tanzania', *ERB* Paper 71.16, 32
2. Coopers and Lybrand Assoc. Ltd., *Grain Storage and Milling Project*, Vol. II, DSM (1977), Tables A1.17 and A1.36
3. Tanzania, MDB, 'Price Policy Recommendations', Vol. I: Maize, Rice and Wheat (DSM, 1981), Appendix 2.1

* Note: 1 ton paddy = 0.65 ton rice

Table III.4: Nominal and Real Peasant Producer Prices for Maize, 1956–1987 (1963 = 100)

Year	Nominal Price (TSh/Kg)	Nominal Price Index	Real Price Index*
1956	0.29	84	
1957	0.25	72	
1958	0.27	78	
1959	0.23	67	
1960	0.17	49	
1961	0.33	96	
1962	0.35	101	
1963	0.35	100	100
1964	0.28	80	72
1965	0.34	98	86
1966	0.27	78	63
1967	0.30	87	66
1968	0.30	87	60
1969	0.25	72	44
1970	0.28	81	50
1971	0.26	75	46
1972	0.26	75	41
1973	0.27	78	37
1974	0.35	101	40
1975	0.50	145	32
1976	0.80	232	53
1977	0.80	232	47
1978	0.85	246	46
1979	0.85	246	41
1980	1.00	290	43
1981	1.00	290	31
1982	1.50	435	40
1983	1.75	507	34
1984	2.20	638	28
1985	4.00	1159	34
1986	5.25	1522	39
1987	6.30	1826	35
1988	8.20	2377	n.a.
1989	9.00	2609	n.a.

Sources: Bank of Tanzania, *Economic and Operations Report* (1975 and 1984)
Ministry of Finance and Economic Planning, *Hali ya Uchumi wa Taifa katika Mwaka 1987*
Kriesel, H.C. *et al.*, *Agricultural Marketing in Tanzania: Background Research and Policy Proposals*, (East Lansing, Michigan State University, 1970), 38
Odegaard, K., 'A Study of Agricultural Producer Prices', Office of the Prime Minister (1974), Annex Table I.4
Tanzania, MDB, *Annual Review of Agricultural Marketing, 1988*

* Deflated by the Non-Food Retail Price Index.

Table IV.1: NMC Maize and Sembe Purchases and Sales, 1973/74–1988/89 ('000 Tons, Maize Equivalent)*

Region	1973/74	1974/75	1975/76	1976/77	1977/78	1978/79	1979/80	1980/81	1981/82	1982/83	1983/84
NATIONAL											
Purchases	73.8	23.9	91.1	127.5	213.2	220.4	161.1	104.6	89.4	68.7	71.0
Sales	209.7	202.7	137.8	125.8	103.3	156.0	223.0	295.0	287.0	208.3	244.3
Balance	−135.9	−178.8	−46.7	1.7	109.9	64.4	−61.9	−190.4	−197.6	−139.6	−173.3
ARUSHA											
% of Nat. Purchase	9	12	11	12	28	32	29	17	4	1	9
Purchase	7.0	2.9	10.1	14.8	60.3	69.5	47.4	17.4	3.2	1.0	6.3
Sales		21.6	9.6	8.1	3.2	4.0	16.0	17.0	10.0	7.9	8.7
Balance		−18.7	0.5	6.7	57.1	65.5	31.4	−0.4	−6.8	−6.9	−2.4
KILIMANJARO											
% of Nat. Purchase	8	20	5	5	11	6	4	0	0	1	0
Purchase	6.0	4.8	4.8	6.1	22.9	13.6	5.9	0.1	0.0	0.0	0.1
Sales		0.5	2.1	3.6	2.1	2.0	8.0	10.0	6.0	2.0	7.0
Balance		4.3	2.7	2.5	20.8	11.6	−2.1	−9.9	−6.0	−2.0	−6.9
MBEYA											
% of Nat. Purchase	2	3	2	4	5	3	4	5	8	12	11
Purchase	1.4	0.7	2.2	5.5	11.7	7.2	6.4	5.4	7.2	8.0	7.7
Sales		0.0	1.1	0.2	0.2	2.0	2.0	3.0	1.0	3.3	3.2
Balance		0.7	1.1	5.3	11.5	5.2	4.4	2.4	6.2	4.7	4.5
IRINGA											
% of Nat. Purchase	15	17	12	12	10	12	16	21	37	29	35
Purchase	11.2	4.1	10.5	14.7	20.9	27.2	26.3	21.8	33.1	20.0	25.1
Sales		6.5	2.6	1.7	3.2	4.0	7.0	6.0	6.0	5.2	8.6
Balance		−2.4	7.9	13.0	17.7	23.2	19.3	15.8	27.1	14.8	16.5
DODOMA											
% of Nat. Purchase	47	0	7	9	8	17	17	23	5	1	7
Purchase	34.5	0	6.0	11.5	17.8	37.0	27.1	23.7	4.4	1.0	5.3
Sales		13.6	13.3	11.1	7.4	5.0	15.0	16.0	30.0	21.6	17.6
Balance		−13.6	−7.3	0.4	10.4	32.0	12.1	7.7	−25.6	−20.6	−12.3
SINGIDA											
% of Nat. Purchase	2	0	1	1	0	2	0	0	0	0	0
Purchase	1.6	0	0.5	1.1	1.0	3.6	0.7	0.4	0.2	0.0	0.1
Sales		9.1	1.4	5.1	1.1	2.0	7.0	2.0	2.0	0.7	2.5
Balance		−9.1	−0.9	−4.0	0.1	1.6	−6.3	−1.6	−1.8	−0.7	−2.4
RUVUMA											
% of Nat. Purchase	0	18	14	8	8	10	11	13	24	26	18
Purchase	0.1	4.2	12.7	10.0	16.1	22.7	17.8	14.0	21.1	18.0	12.9
Sales		0.7	0.6	0.5	0.3	0.3	0.3	1.0	1.0	0.6	1.1
Balance		3.5	12.1	9.5	15.8	22.4	16.8	13.0	20.1	17.4	11.8
LINDI											
% of Nat. Purchase	0	0	1	2	1	1	0	0	0	0	0
Purchase	0	0	1.2	2.7	3.0	2.0	0.0	0.2	0.4	0.2	0.0
Sales		n.a.	n.a.	n.a.	n.a.	3.0	5.0	6.0	3.0	2.4	1.3
Balance						−1.0	−5.0	−5.8	−2.6	−2.2	−1.3
MTWARA											
% of Nat. Purchase	0	0	3	3	1	0	0	0	0	0	0
Purchase	0	0	2.7	4.4	1.8	1.0	0.0	0.2	0.0	0.0	0.0
Sales		n.a.	n.a.	n.a.	n.a.	4.0	4.0	7.0	6.0	3.5	2.1
Balance						−3.0	−4.0	−6.8	−6.0	−3.5	−2.1
MOROGORO											
% of Nat. Purchase	7	4	12	7	7	2	1	1	0	0	0
Purchase	5.4	1.0	10.5	9.2	14.5	5.0	1.1	0.7	0.4	0.3	0.1
Sales		16.5	1.1	6.5	0.6	3.0	8.0	8.0	9.0	4.8	5.9
Balance		−15.5	9.4	2.7	13.9	2.0	−6.9	−7.3	−8.6	−4.5	−5.8

Table IV.1 cont.: NMC Maize and Sembe Purchases and Sales, 1973/74–1988/89 ('000 Tons, Maize Equivalent)*

Region	1973/74	1974/75	1975/76	1976/77	1977/78	1978/79	1979/80	1980/81	1981/82	1982/83	1983/84
COAST/DAR ES SALAAM											
% of Nat. Purchase	0	0	2	2	1	0	0	0	0	0	0
Purchase	0	0	1.5	2.4	2.1	0.7	0.0	0.0	0.0	0.0	0.1
Sales		67.1	58.3	50.7	52.3	88.0	107.0	133.0	137.0	127.8	138.7
Balance		−67.1	−56.8	−48.3	−50.2	−87.3	−107.0	−133.0	−137.0	−127.8	−138.6
TANGA											
% of Nat. Purchase	0	13	22	16	3	3	0	0	1	1	1
Purchase	0	3.8	20.2	20.8	7.2	7.3	0.4	0.1	1.3	0.6	1.0
Sales		17.5	10.8	16.9	12.6	15.0	26.0	31.0	13.0	3.7	6.2
Balance		−13.7	9.4	3.9	−5.4	−7.7	−25.6	−30.9	−11.7	−3.1	−5.2
SHINYANGA											
% of Nat. Purchase	0	0	1	0	1	1.	1	0	0	0	0
Purchase	0	0	0.7	0.0	2.5	2.4	1.1	0.2	0.2	0.2	0.1
Sales		2.9	5.9	2.5	0.5	1.0	2.0	12.0	14.0	6.0	10.5
Balance		−2.9	−5.2	−2.5	2.0	1.4	−0.9	−11.8	−13.8	−5.8	−10.4
KAGERA											
% of Nat. Purchase	0	0	0	1	1	0	0	0	0	0	1
Purchase	0	0	0.2	1.1	1.3	0.8	0.7	0.0	0.0	0.0	0.4
Sales		0.7	2.4	2.9	3.2	13.0	2.0	7.0	4.0	2.8	4.3
Balance		−0.7	−2.2	−1.8	−1.9	−12.2	−1.3	−7.0	−4.0	−2.8	−3.9
MWANZA											
% of Nat. Purchase	1	0	3	1	1	2	1	0	0	0	0
Purchase	0.4	0	2.9	1.3	2.4	4.2	2.0	0.0	0.0	0.0	0.0
Sales		11.8	9.2	11.8	3.2	6.0	5.0	15.0	19.0	5.6	6.9
Balance		−11.8	−6.3	−10.5	−0.8	−1.8	−3.0	−15.0	−19.0	−5.6	−6.9
MARA											
% of Nat. Purchase	8	7	1	5	3	2	2	0	0	0	2
Purchase	6.2	1.7	1.1	5.9	5.5	4.2	3.0	0.0	0.3	0.2	1.1
Sales		8.6	3.3	3.3	2.0	2.0	3.0	11.0	11.0	6.1	4.2
Balance		−6.9	−2.2	2.6	3.5	2.2	0.0	−11.0	−10.7	−6.9	−3.1
KIGOMA											
% of Nat. Purchase	0	0	0	1	0	0	0	0	0	0	0
Purchase	0	0	0.2	0.7	0.9	1.0	0.4	0.2	0.4	0.2	0.3
Sales		0.4	0.4	0.4	0.6	0.4	1.0	1.0	2.0	1.4	3.0
Balance		−0.4	−0.2	0.3	0.3	0.6	−0.6	−0.8	−1.6	−1.2	−2.7
TABORA											
% of Nat. Purchase	0	0	0	3	5	3	3	2	1	1	0
Purchase	0	0	0.1	3.5	10.0	5.8	4.9	2.4	1.2	1.0	0.3
Sales		n.a.	7.6	2.0	0.5	1.0	2.0	5.0	9.0	2.4	8.5
Balance			−7.5	1.5	9.5	4.8	2.9	−2.6	−7.8	−1.4	−8.2
RUKWA											
% of Nat. Purchase	0	3	3	9	4	2	10	17	18	26	14
Purchase	−	0.7	3.0	11.8	8.5	5.2	15.9	17.8	16.0	18.0	10.1
Sales		n.a.	0.0	0.0	0.4	1.0	2.0	4.0	4.0	0.5	4.2
Balance						4.2	13.9	13.8	12.0	17.5	5.9

Table IV.1 cont.: NMC Maize and Sembe Purchases and Sales, 1973/74–1988/89 ('000 Tons, Maize Equivalent)*

Region	1984/85	1985/86	1986/87	1987/88	1988/89
NATIONAL PURCHASES					
Cooperative[†]	–	195.6	202.0	263.0	n.a.
NMC	85.0	174.8	172.8	229.4	123.9
REGIONAL PURCHASES					
Arusha	3.0	36.1	46.4	n.a.	n.a.
Kilimanjaro	0.0	0.7	0.0	n.a.	n.a.
Mbeya	7.3	16.0	11.8	n.a.	n.a.
Iringa	23.0	38.0	36.4	n.a.	n.a.
Dodoma	1.1	12.0	7.1	n.a.	n.a.
Singida	0.1	5.1	4.8	n.a.	n.a.
Ruvuma	33.6	29.1	22.3	n.a.	n.a.
Lindi	0.1	0.6	0.2	n.a.	n.a.
Mtwara	0.0	0.6	0.2	n.a.	n.a.
Morogoro	0.6	0.7	0.6	n.a.	n.a.
Coast/DSM	0.0	0.0	0.0	n.a.	n.a.
Tanga	3.0	0.6	3.6	n.a.	n.a.
Shinyanga	0.2	2.7	4.1	n.a.	n.a.
Kagera	0.0	0.2	1.0	n.a.	n.a.
Mwanza	0.0	5.0	2.0	n.a.	n.a.
Mara	0.1	0.0	0.4	n.a.	n.a.
Kigoma	0.2	0.1	0.9	n.a.	n.a.
Tabora	0.4	1.4	2.2	n.a.	n.a.
Rukwa	16.6	29.3	28.2	n.a.	n.a.

Sources: Compiled from:
1. Tanzania, MDB, 'Price Policy Recommendations', Vol. I: Maize, Rice and Wheat (DSM, 1981: Appendices 2.1 and 2.3; 1983: 46 and 1984: 52–53)
2. Coopers and Lybrand Assoc. Ltd, *Grain Storage and Milling Project*, Vol. II, DSM (1977), A1.36
3. TFNC, *Data Report on the Food and Nutrition Situation in Tanzania* (DSM 1982 and 1978)
4. Marketing Development Bureau, 'Annual Review of Agricultural Marketing 1988' (DSM, 1988, 18–19)
5. Marketing Development Bureau, 'Annual Review of Maize, Rice and Wheat 1987' (DSM, 1987, 62)
6. FAO/Kilimo, 'Food Security Bulletin for June 1988'

* Note: *Sembe* maize flour included in maize sales total. When MDB has not specified a maize equivalent, I have calculated *sembe* at a 95% extraction rate: 1 ton maize = 0.95 *sembe*.
† Note: Not all cooperative purchases were passed on to the NMC.

Table IV.2: NMC Paddy and Rice Purchases and Sales, 1973/74–1988/89 ('000 Tons, Rice Equivalent*)

Region	Year 73/74	74/75	75/76	76/77	77/78	78/79	79/80	80/81	81/82	82/83	83/84
National											
Purchase	38.7	14.8	11.9	15.1	35.1	33.0	29.0	13.0	15.0	20.9	22.0
Sales	82.3	42.9	34.7	52.3	74.6	70.1	61.3	77.6	77.8	71.9	79.1
Balance	−43.6	−28.1	−22.8	−37.2	−39.5	−37.1	−32.3	−64.6	−62.8	−51.0	−57.1
Arusha											
% of Nat. Purchase	0	0	0	0	1	0	0	0	0	0	0
Purchase	0.0	0.0	0.0	0.0	0.2	0.0	0.0	0.0	0.0	0.0	0.0
Sales		1.9	1.9	2.5	5.0	6.2	2.6	4.1	3.4	1.8	1.6
Balance		−1.9	−1.9	−2.5	−4.8	−6.2	−2.6	−4.1	−3.4	−1.8	−1.6
Kilimanjaro											
% of Nat. Purchase	2	6	1	2	4	3	0	0	1	0	1
Purchase	0.8	0.9	0.1	0.3	1.5	1.0	0.0	0.0	0.1	0.1	0.2
Sales		1.9	2.2	3.2	4.0	2.5	1.7	3.5	1.7	2.9	1.3
Balance		−1.0	−2.1	−2.9	−2.5	−1.5	−1.7	−3.5	−1.6	−2.8	−1.1
Mbeya											
% of Nat. Purchase	19	45	63	62	53	45	41	85	93	74	75
Purchase	7.5	6.6	7.5	9.4	18.6	15.0	12.0	11.0	14.0	15.4	16.4
Sales		0.1	0.4	0.4	2.0	1.7	0.8	0.7	1.7	1.8	3.9
Balance		6.5	7.1	9.0	16.6	13.3	11.2	10.3	12.3	13.6	12.5
Iringa											
% of Nat. Purchase	0	3	3	0	0	0	0	0	0	0	0
Purchase	0.1	0.0	0.0	0.0	0.0	0.0	0.0	0.0	0.0	0.0	0.0
Sales		0.9	0.6	1.3	1.0	1.6	1.2	1.5	1.6	1.1	1.4
Balance		−0.4	−0.3	−1.3	−1.0	−1.6	−1.2	−1.5	−1.6	−1.1	−1.4
Dodoma											
% of Nat. Purchase	0	0	0	0	0	0	0	0	0	0	0
Purchase	0.1	0.5	0.3	0.0	0.0	0.0	0.0	0.0	0.0	0.0	0.0
Sales		1.0	1.8	1.6	3.0	2.3	1.4	3.2	2.8	2.7	1.6
Balance		−1.0	−1.8	−1.6	−3.0	−2.3	−1.4	−3.2	−2.8	−2.7	−1.6
Singida											
% of Nat. Purchase	0	0	0	0	0	0	0	0	0	0	0
Purchase	0.0	0.0	0.0	0.0	0.0	0.0	0.0	0.0	0.0	0.0	0.0
Sales		1.1	0.6	1.3	0.7	0.8	0.4	0.2	0.3	0.2	0.5
Balance		−1.1	−0.6	−1.3	−0.7	−0.8	−0.4	−0.2	−0.3	−0.2	−0.5
Ruvuma											
% of Nat. Purchase	0	0	0	2	1	0	0	0	0	0	0
Purchase	0.0	0.0	0.0	0.3	0.2	0.0	0.0	0.0	0.0	0.0	0.1
Sales		0.2	0.4	0.4	1.0	0.9	1.2	0.7	0.3	0.7	0.6
Balance		−0.2	−0.4	−0.1	−0.8	−0.9	−1.2	−0.7	−0.3	−0.7	−0.5
Lindi											
% of Nat. Purchase	0	0	0	2	1	0	0	0	0	0	0
Purchase	0.0	0.0	0.0	0.3	0.1	0.0	0.0	0.0	0.0	0.0	0.0
Sales		n.a.	n.a.	n.a.	n.a.	1.6	1.3	1.6	1.3	0.7	1.0
Balance						−1.6	−1.3	−1.6	−1.3	−0.7	−1.0
Mtwara											
% of Nat. Purchase	0	0	0	2	0	0	0	0	0	0	0
Purchase	0.0	0.0	0.0	0.3	0.0	0.0	0.0	0.0	0.0	0.0	0.0
Sales		n.a.	n.a.	n.a.	n.a.	1.7	1.2	2.4	1.4	0.8	0.7
Balance						−1.7	−1.2	−2.4	−1.4	−0.8	−0.7
Morogoro											
% of Nat. Purchase	4	5	13	7	8	6	0	0	1	15	13
Purchase	1.4	0.7	1.5	1.1	2.8	2.0	0.0	0.0	0.2	3.2	2.8
Sales						1.7	1.3	2.2	1.3	2.4	3.0
Balance						0.3	−1.3	−2.2	−1.1	−0.8	−0.2

Table IV.2 cont.: NMC Paddy and Rice Purchases and Sales, 1973/74–1988/89 ('000 Tons, Rice Equivalent*)

Region	Year 73/74	74/75	75/76	76/77	77/78	78/79	79/80	80/81	81/82	82/83	83/84
Coast/Dar es Salaam											
% of Nat. Purchase	0	0	0	5	3	6	0	0	0	0	0
Purchase	0.0	0.0	0.0	0.7	0.9	2.0	0.0	0.0	0.0	0.0	0.0
Sales		22.6	9.0	24.4	36.8	30.9	37.6	43.1	52.4	49.6	55.8
Balance		−22.6	−9.0	−23.7	−35.9	−30.9	−37.6	−43.1	−52.4	−49.6	−55.8
Tanga											
% of Nat. Purchase	0	0	0	0	0	0	0	0	0	0	0
Purchase	0.0	0.0	0.0	0.0	0.0	0.0	0.0	0.0	0.0	0.0	0.0
Sales		2.5	3.6	2.4	6.0	4.3	2.7	8.0	3.8	1.6	2.5
Balance		−2.5	−3.6	−2.4	−6.0	−4.3	−2.7	−8.0	−3.8	−1.6	−2.5
Shinyanga											
% of Nat. Purchase	26	16	5	1	10	18	28	8	1	3	7
Purchase	9.9	2.3	0.6	0.1	3.6	6.0	8.0	1.0	0.1	0.6	1.6
Sales		0.5	1.0	3.1	1.0	1.2	2.3	0.9	1.0	1.1	1.2
Balance		1.8	−0.4	−3.0	2.6	4.8	5.7	−0.1	−0.9	−0.5	−0.4
Kagera											
% of Nat. Purchase	0	0	0	0	0	0	0	0	0	0	0
Purchase	0.0	0.0	0.0	0.0	0.0	0.0	0.0	0.0	0.0	0.0	0.0
Sales		2.1	1.6	1.1	1.0	3.9	0.7	0.6	0.7	0.7	0.6
Balance		−2.1	−1.6	−1.1	−1.0	−3.9	−0.7	−0.6	−0.7	−0.7	−0.6
Mwanza											
% of Nat. Purchase	7	7	6	6	3	9	14	0	0	1	1
Purchase	2.6	1.0	0.7	0.9	1.0	3.0	4.0	0.0	0.0	0.2	0.3
Sales		1.7	1.5	0.6	2.0	3.1	1.4	1.3	0.8	1.3	0.8
Balance		−0.7	−0.8	0.3	−1.0	−0.1	−2.6	−1.3	−0.8	−1.1	−0.5
Mara											
% of Nat. Purchase	1	1	0	0	0	0	0	0	1	0	0
Purchase	0.3	0.1	0.0	0.0	0.0	0.0	0.0	0.0	0.1	0.1	0.0
Sales		1.0	1.0	1.5	1.0	1.7	0.8	1.0	1.2	0.6	0.6
Balance		−0.9	−1.0	−1.5	−1.0	−1.7	−0.8	−1.0	−1.1	−0.5	−0.6
Kigorma											
% of Nat. Purchase	1	2	3	4	2	0	0	0	1	0	1
Purchase	0.5	0.3	0.3	0.6	0.7	0.0	0.0	0.0	0.2	0.1	0.2
Sales		0.5	1.4	0.7	1.0	0.7	0.4	0.6	0.5	0.6	1.0
Balance		−0.2	−1.1	−0.1	−0.3	−0.7	−0.4	−0.6	−0.3	−0.5	−0.8
Tabora											
% of Nat. Purchase	38	16	3	3	13	12	17	0	1	6	1
Purchase	14.8	2.3	0.3	0.5	3.9	4.0	5.0	0.0	0.1	1.2	0.2
Sales		n.a.	n.a.	n.a.	n.a.	2.5	1.5	1.4	0.9	1.0	0.6
Balance						1.5	3.5	−1.4	−0.8	0.2	−0.4
Rukwa											
% of Nat. Purchase	0	0	0	5	1	0	0	0	1	0	0
Purchase	0.0	0.0	0.0	0.7	0.5	0.0	0.0	0.0	0.0	0.0	0.1
Sales		n.a.	n.a.	n.a.	n.a.	0.8	0.8	0.6	0.7	0.5	0.5
Balance						−0.8	−0.8	−0.6	−0.7	−0.5	−0.4

Table IV.2 cont.: NMC Maize and Sembe Purchases and Sales, 1973/74–1988/89 ('000 Tons, Maize Equivalent) *

Region	1984/85	1985/86	1986/87	1987/88	1988/89
NATIONAL PURCHASES					
Cooperative†	–	8.4	9.9	47.6	57.4
NMC	12.0	16.0	11.4	43.2	48.3
REGIONAL PURCHASES					
Arusha	0.0	0.0	0.0	n.a.	n.a.
Kilimanjaro	0.0	0.0	0.1	n.a.	n.a.
Mbeya	10.6	11.6	5.0	n.a.	n.a.
Iringa	0.0	0.0	0.0	n.a.	n.a.
Dodoma	0.0	0.0	0.0	n.a.	n.a.
Singida	0.0	0.0	0.0	n.a.	n.a.
Ruvuma	0.1	0.0	0.0	n.a.	n.a.
Lindi	0.0	0.0	0.4	n.a.	n.a.
Mtwara	0.0	0.0	0.5	n.a.	n.a.
Morogoro	0.8	0.3	1.5	n.a.	n.a.
Coast/DSM	0.0	0.1	0.0	n.a.	n.a.
Tanga	0.1	0.0	0.0	n.a.	n.a.
Shinyanga	0.1	2.6	2.1	n.a.	n.a.
Kagera	0.0	0.0	0.0	n.a.	n.a.
Mwanza	0.1	0.7	0.8	n.a.	n.a.
Mara	0.0	0.0	0.0	n.a.	n.a.
Kigoma	0.1	0.0	0.2	n.a.	n.a.
Tabora	0.1	0.3	0.4	n.a.	n.a.
Rukwa	0.2	0.2	0.4	n.a.	n.a

Sources: Compiled from:
1. Tanzania, MDB, 'Price Policy Recommendations', Vol. I: Maize, Rice and Wheat (DSM, 1981: Appendices 3.1–3.2; 1983: 47 and 1984: 52–54)
2. Coopers and Lybrand Asoc. Ltd, *Grain Storage and Milling Project*, Vol. II, DSM (1977), A1.37
3. TFNC, *Data Report on the Food and Nutrition Situation in Tanzania* (DSM 1982 and 1978)
4. Marketing Development Bureau, 'Annual Review of Agricultural Marketing, 1988', DSM, 1988, 18–19
5. Marketing Development Bureau, 'Annual Review of Maize, Rice and Wheat 1987', DSM, 1988, 62
6. FAO/Kilimo, 'Food Security Bulletin for June 1988'

* Note: 1 ton paddy = 0.65 ton rice.
† Note: Not all cooperative purchases were passed on to the NMC.

Table IV.3: Net Imports/Exports of Maize, Rice, and Wheat by Year, 1970–87 ('000 Tons)

Year	Maize	Rice	Wheat	Total Grain
1970	19.0	−6.8	−31.9	−19.7
1971	0.5	−5.8	−24.0	−29.4
1972	−143.8	−0.4	−41.8	−186.1
1973	−24.4	−0.7	−8.4	−170.7
1974	−48.2	−71.2	−102.7	−222.1
1975	−240.5	−64.0	−135.1	−439.6
1976	−74.6	−8.8	−15.0	−98.3
1977	−27.2	−52.1	−58.1	−137.3
1978	36.3	−47.2	−75.2	−86.1
1979	15.9	−25.3	−32.9	−42.2
1980	−251.4	−102.7	−44.1	−398.1
1981	−155.3	−45.1	−59.7	−260.0
1982	−133.1	−103.3	−68.7	−305.1
1983	−121.0	−63.8	−11.1	−195.9
1984	−106.8	−25.8	−46.3	−178.9
1985	−278.0	−53.4	−48.4	−379.9
1986	−35.0	−106.1	−41.4	−182.5
1987	13.3	−20.2	−96.9	−103.8

Sources: East African Trade Reports 1970–1976
Tanzanian Trade Reports 1977–1987

Table IV.4: Official Producer Prices for Grain, 1973/4-1988/9 (TSh./Kg)

Year	Maize	Paddy	Wheat
1973/74	0.33	0.57	0.57
1974/75	0.50	0.65	0.77
1975/76	0.80	1.00	1.00
1976/77	0.80	1.00	1.20
1977/78	0.80	1.20	1.25
1978/79	0.85	1.20	1.25
1979/80	1.00	1.50	1.35
1980/81	1.00	1.75	1.65
1981/82	1.50	2.30	2.20
1982/83	1.75	3.00	2.50
1983/84	2.20	4.00	3.00
1984/85	4.00	6.00	4.50
1985/86	5.25	8.00	6.00
1986/87	6.30	9.60	7.20
1987/88	8.20	14.40	9.00
1988/89	9.00	17.30	10.35

Sources: Marketing Development Bureau, 'Price Policy
Review for the 1984 Agricultural Price Review:
Summary', Appendix IV
Marketing Development Bureau, 'Annual Review
of Agricultural Marketing 1988', Appendix III

Table IV.5: Official Consumer Prices for Grain, 1973–1988 (TSh./Kg)

Year	Sembe	Maize	Rice	Wheat Flour
1973	0.80		1.65	1.65
1974	1.25		2.00	2.40
1975	1.25		4.00	3.75
1976	1.75		4.00	3.75
1977	1.75		3.50	3.75
1978	1.75		3.50	3.75
1979	1.75		3.50	3.75
1980	1.25		5.35	5.65
1981	2.50		5.35	5.65
1982	2.50	3.35	5.35	5.65
1983	2.50	4.39	7.20	8.00
1984	8.00	5.40	13.40	14.50
1985	13.75	7.60	14.50	17.20
1986	dc*	12.20	19.00	25.15
1987	dc	12.20	32.00	35.00
1988	dc	17.00	59.70	55.85

Sources: Marketing Development Bureau, 'Price Policy
Review for the 1984 Agricultural Price Review:
Summary', Dar es Salaam (1984), Appendix IV
Marketing Development Bureau, 'Annual Review
of Maize, Rice and Wheat', Dar es Salaam (1987),
30
Tanzanian Economic Trends 3(2), July 1990
* Decontrolled price.

Table IV.6: Official Grain Mark-Ups,* 1973–84

Year	Sembe	Rice	Wheat
1973	142	190	190
1974	150	208	212
1975	56	300	275
1976	119	300	213
1977	119	192	200
1978	106	192	200
1979	75	133	178
1980	25	206	242
1981	67	133	157
1982	43	78	126
1983	14	80	167
1984	100	123	222
Average			
1973–84	85	178	199
1964–72**	309	244	212

* The difference between the producer and consumer
prices divided by the producer price.
** Calculated from cooperative union producer price
series for maize (Iringa Farmers CU/Iringa), paddy
(Nyanza CU/Ukerewe), wheat (Arusha Region CU/
Mbulu) and Dar es Salaam retail prices recorded by the
Bureau of Statistics (listed in Odegaard, K., 'A Study of
Agricultural Producer Prices, their Interrelationships and
Impact on Agricultural Marketing in Tanzania, 1962–
1972', Office of the Prime Minister and Second Vice
President (April 1974), Annex Tables III.1–3 and
Schedule No. 12).
Sources: Coopers and Lybrand Assoc. Ltd., *Grain Storage
and Milling Project,* Vol. II, DSM (1977), Table A1.38; Tan-
zania, Ministry of Agriculture, 'The Availability of Food in
Tanzania in 1981/82', EWCMP, FAO/ KILIMO, DSM
(July 1981), Annex II; Tanzania, Marketing Development
Bureau, *Price Policy Recommendations,* various years.

Table V.1: Maize Parallel Market Prices by Town, 1982/83–1985/86 (TSh/Debe)[1]

	1982/83 (Nov–June)			1983/84 (July–June)			1984/85 (July–June)			1985/86 (July–June)		
	Mean	C.V.	Months Maize not Available	Mean	C.V.	Months Maize not Available	Mean	C.V.	Months Maize not Available	Mean	C.V.	Months Maize not Available
Arusha	66.00	.069	0	216.36	.670	0	278.13	.161	0	181.6	.235	0
Bukoba	108.75	.178	0	159.63	.247	0	308.75	.365	6	242.4	.164	0
DSM	116.67	.247	0	—	—	12	104.76	.084	3	233.8	.175	4
Dodoma	104.00	.053	0	198.00	.579	0	209.63	.154	0	184.1	.257	0
Gonja	111.67	.212	5	208.64	.345	0	223.33	.282	0	189.00	.166	0
Iringa	74.69	.012	2	146.88	.514	0	157.71	.065	0	170.31	.284	0
Kigoma	103.13	.165	0	137.27	.323	0	195.00	.308	0	208.13	.330	0
Lindi	81.00	.025	0	113.12	.244	5	153.90	.173	0	170.96	.336	0
Lushoto	96.25	.099	1	198.13	.431	0	228.96	.163	0	210.54	.149	0
Maswa	75.00	.141	0	207.22	.491	1	300.00	.240	0	152.50	.273	0
Mbeya	75.00	.077	0	203.33	.403	0	117.25	.161	0	145.56	.210	0
Mbulu	85.83	.119	0	126.67	.526	0	126.04	.263	0	95.21	.073	0
Morogoro	159.29	.729	1	208.00	.628	0	183.13	.154	0	200.98	.286	0
Moshi	66.75	.134	0	198.88	.608	0	228.54	.250	0	181.46	.165	0
Mpwapwa	93.57	.168	1	158.41	.741	1	149.38	.215	0	165.00	.312	0
Mtwara	85.00	.059	0	125.10	.112	2	193.13	.167	1	247.50	.161	1
Musoma	115.00	.061	1	178.33	.249	2	319.38	.313	0	200.63	.122	0
Mwanza	112.50	.061	0	200.91	.428	0	285.42	.311	0	196.82	.207	0
Njombe	45.00	.000	0	86.79	.616	0	111.25	.164	0	115.00	.183	0
Sengerema	85.60	.399	0	135.92	.403	0	181.44	.448	0	177.13	.369	0
Shinyanga	116.88	.123	0	240.06	.413	0	267.08	.313	0	171.04	.237	0
Singida	83.29	.081	0	201.82	.485	0	194.17	.214	0	140.00	.147	0
Songea	49.64	.196	0	64.83	.456	0	77.08	.097	0	90.53	.210	0
Sumbawanga	50.63	.164	0	124.79	.596	0	115.00	.111	0	109.17	.207	0
Tabora	66.00	.109	1	141.67	.369	5	138.75	.238	1	154.38	.237	0
Tanga	87.50	.121	4	190.83	.614	4	185.34	.177	0	228.54	.228	0
Tarime	70.00	.062	0	127.50	.194	0	270.91	.326	0	239.25	.206	0
Tunduru	55.00	.257	0	90.15	.139	5	122.50	.268	2	124.29	.168	0
Urambo	55.00	.049	0	168.33	.560	0	127.50	.437	0	120.71	.417	0
MEAN	86.02	.144	.55	162.77	.442	1.3	191.50	.228	.24	174.04	.225	.17
Std. Dev.	25.89	.141		45.16	.166		68.98	.098		44.26	.78	
C.V.	.301	.979		.277	.376		.360	.431		.254	.346	

1 'Debe' – local volume measure of approximately 17 kg.

Source: Compiled from Tanzania, MDB, Monthly Market Bulletin, March 1983–September 1986

Table V.2: Rice Parallel Market Prices by Town, 1982/83–1985/86 (TSh./Kg.)

Town	1982/83 (Nov–June)			1983/84 (July–June)			1984/85 (July–June)			1985/86 (July–June)		
	Mean	C.V.	Months Rice not Available	Mean	C.V.	Months Rice not Available	Mean	C.V.	Months Rice not Available	Mean	C.V.	Months Rice not Available
Arusha	23.21	.168	1	33.45	.316	2	47.31	.143	0	45.63	.215	0
Bukoba	26.25	.067	2	25.83	.100	5	52.75	.225	1	40.64	.099	0
DSM	15.27	.384	3	—	—	12	37.92	.040	3	48.33	.224	3
Dodoma	10.38	.554	4	17.75	1.211	4	36.63	.090	0	38.52	.175	0
Iringa	18.63	.203	0	27.67	.364	0	28.79	.212	0	34.98	.301	0
Kigoma	22.50	.198	4	29.63	.247	4	41.88	.136	0	37.71	.197	0
Lindi	16.50	.000	4	—	—	11	28.69	.168	0	39.07	.420	0
Lushoto	13.42	.083	2	23.86	.324	1	36.38	176	0	35.31	.256	0
Mbeya	13.33	.194	1	27.07	.418	0	41.20	.360	1	37.50	.306	0
Mbulu	16.17	.170	0	21.04	.379	6	25.00	.141	10	48.43	.290	1
Morogoro	14.50	.093	1	28.54	.426	0	30.88	.173	0	44.29	.346	0
Moshi	17.22	.137	0	29.52	.475	0	42.47	.102	0	47.14	.251	0
Mpwapwa	16.17	.407	2	24.36	.092	4	38.64	.053	1	42.57	.179	1
Mtwara	6.09	.166	1	25.42	.097	1	28.85	.179	0	45.36	.311	0
Musoma	17.50	.000	4	—	—	8	50.00	.080	5	35.88	.202	0
Mwanza	14.10	.096	1	—	—	11	39.56	.223	4	30.20	.270	0
Njombe	16.92	.159	1	22.95	.142	1	29.51	.211	0	32.18	.104	0
Shinyanga	13.06	.103	0	26.96	.521	0	32.54	.220	0	26.73	.251	0
Singida	16.80	.200	2	26.25	.212	1	35.83	.069	0	32.75	.226	0
Songea	16.42	.071	1	20.60	.133	7	28.81	.211	0	35.91	.233	0
Tabora	12.00	.250	2	22.43	.486	2	33.57	.160	1	32.35	.216	0
Tanga	14.17	.201	3	—	—	11	37.05	.112	1	29.73	.309	0
Urambo	14.75	.101	0	28.54	.461	0	32.08	.235	0	28.46	.186	0
MEAN	15.89	.174	1.57	25.66	.356	3.87	36.36	.162	1.17	38.25	.242	1.0
Std. Dev.	4.22	.129		3.82	.259		7.26	.073		6.32	.074	
C.V.	.265	.742		.149	.729		.200	.454		.165	.305	

Source: Compiled from Tanzania, MDB, *Monthly Market Bulletin*, March 1983–September 1986

Table V.3: Comparative Results of Grain Price Correlations Among Pairs of Markets, Dec. 1982–Dec. 1985

Correlation Coefficient*	DISTRIBUTION OF COEFFICIENTS (%) Maize: 1982–85	Rice: 1982–5
0.65–0.69		.004
0.60–0.64		.008
0.55–0.59	.003	.012
0.50–0.54	.027	.016
0.45–0.49	.034	.028
0.40–0.44	.027	.036
0.35–0.39	.057	.051
0.30–0.34	.054	.091
0.25–0.29	.091	.067
0.20–0.24	.086	.115
0.15–0.19	.101	.146
0.10–0.14	.106	.079
0.05–0.09	.094	.119
0.00–0.04	.081	.067
−0.04–0.00	.076	.055
−0.09–0.05	.049	.063
−0.14–0.10	.044	.016
−0.19–0.15	.037	.024
−0.24–0.20	.022	.004
−0.29–0.25	.003	
−0.34–0.30	.005	
−0.39–0.35	.003	
Total	.999	1.001
No. of markets	29	23
No. of pairs	406	253
1st quartile	.25–.29	.25–.29
2nd quartile	.10–.14	.15–.19

Source: Compiled from Tanzania, MDB, *Monthly Market Bulletin*, Dec.1982–Jan.1989

* Statistically significant: CRITICAL VALUE (1 – TAIL, .05) = + or −.27881, N = 36

Data Handling Procedure
The MDB's monthly parallel market prices are the average of open retail prices reported by on-site incognito Ministry of Agriculture personnel for the 1st and 15th of each month. I calculated price changes by subtracting each monthly observation from the one preceding it to obtain first differences. Months when the commodity was not available were calculated with a dummy price of TSh. 1000 to indicate its scarcity value. Missing data (31% of the total) were estimated on the basis of a smooth progressive increase or decrease during the intervening months between available data. Each market was represented by a data set of 36 monthly first difference values. Spearman's Rank Correlation Coefficients for each pair of markets were then calculated.

Table V.4: Tanzanian Urban Ward Census Totals[†]

	Urban Settlement <20,000	% of National Pop. in Urban Settlement >20,000	Dar es Salaam	Mwanza	Mbeya	Arusha	Songea
1988 Population	2,464,273	10.9	1,117,334	156,908	116,069	77,092	46,955
pgr*	4.1		3.8	3.6	4.2	3.4	10.1
1978 Population	1,655,167	9.7	769,445	110,553	76,601	55,223	17,955
pgr	10.4		9.9	11.2	18.1	5.1	11.5
1967 Population	557,750	4.7	272,515	34,396	12,325	32,012	5,430
pgr	12.8		7.8	5.7	5.9	12.3	14.5
1957 Population	166,795	1.9	128,742	19,877	6,932	10,038	1,401

Source: National population censuses 1957, 1967, 1978 and 1988
† Includes only urban wards of the urban districts. It should be noted that the urban totals are subject to future revision due to reclassification of rural and urban boundaries. Any revision of the classification of urban and rural wards in urban districts is likely to give higher urban totals, but it is not anticipated that the increase would exceed an overall growth rate of 5.5%.
* population growth rate.

Table V.5: NMC Maize, Rice and Wheat Supplies to DSM and Regional Towns: Volume and % Requirement Fulfilment ('000 Tons)

Year	DAR ES SALAAM				MWANZA				ARUSHA			
	Populat.	Food Req'mt*	NMC Supply	% Fulfilment	Populat.	Food Req'mt*	NMC Supply	% Fulfilment	Populat.	Food Req'mt*	NMC Supply*	% Fulfilment
1988/89	1360947	175.9	86.5	49	223013	28.8	3.7	13	134708	17.4	5.0	29
1987/88	1297312	167.7	100.4	60	216981	28.1	3.5	12	128914	16.7	4.1	25
1986/87	1236652	159.9	88.0	55	211112	27.3	2.9	11	123369	15.9	3.4	21
1985/86	1178830	152.4	97.7	64	205401	26.6	6.4	24	118062	15.3	5.1	33
1984/85	1123710	145.3	184.6	127	199845	25.8	8.4	33	112984	14.6	6.7	46
1983/84	1071168	138.5	168.3	122	194440	25.1	7.0	28	108124	14.0	9.1	65
1982/83	1021083	132.0	164.6	125	189180	24.5	5.8	24	103474	13.4	9.1	68
1981/82	973339	125.8	182.8	145	184063	23.8	16.2	68	99023	12.8	11.6	91
1980/81	927828	119.9	167.2	139	179084	23.2	13.4	58	94764	12.3	17.0	138
1979/80	884445	114.3	147.4	129	174240	22.5	5.5	25	90688	11.7	15.4	132
1978/79	843090	109.0	143.4	132	169527	21.9	9.3	42	86787	11.2	8.8	79
1977/78	760902	98.4	109.5	111	146823	19.0	5.8	30	79363	10.3	7.2	70
1976/77	686726	88.8	85.4	96	127159	16.4	14.1	86	72574	9.4	8.8	94
1975/76	619782	80.1	72.5	90	110129	14.2	13.2	93	66366	8.6	9.9	115
1974/75	559363	72.3	97.0	134	95380	12.3	13.0	106	60688	7.8	19.9	254

Year	MBEYA				SONGEA			
	Populat.	Food Req'mt*	NMC Supply	% Fulfilment	Populat.	Food Req'mt*	NMC Supply	% Fulfilment
1988/89	152844	19.8	1.7	9	86880	11.2	1.5	13
1987/88	142920	18.5	0.5	3	82094	10.6	2.9	27
1986/87	133640	17.3	0.7	4	77571	10.0	1.4	14
1985/86	124962	16.2	3.8	23	73298	9.5	2.3	24
1984/85	116848	15.1	3.6	24	69260	9.0	1.8	20
1983/84	109261	14.1	5.9	42	65444	8.5	1.4	17
1982/83	102167	13.2	4.3	33	61839	8.0	1.4	17

Table V.5 cont.: NMC Maize, Rice and Wheat Supplies to DSM and Regional Towns: Volume and % Requirement Fulfilment ('000 Tons)

Year	MBEYA Populat.	Food Req'mt*	NMC Supply	% Fulfilment	SONGEA Populat.	Food Req'mt*	NMC Supply	% Fulfilment
1981/82	95533	12.4	2.6	21	58432	7.6	1.3	17
1980/81	89330	11.5	3.2	28	55213	7.1	1.4	20
1979/80	83530	10.8	2.6	24	52171	6.7	2.1	31
1978/79	78106	10.1	4.2	41	49297	6.4	1.7	26
1977/78	66111	8.5	1.9	23	40339	5.2	1.8	34
1976/77	55958	7.2	1.2	17	33009	4.3	1.3	30
1975/76	47365	6.1	1.9	31	27011	3.5	1.8	50
1974/75	40091	5.2	0.1	2	22103	2.9	1.1	39

1) Town population totals include all urban, rural and mixed wards of the urban district.
2) The food supply requirements are calculated under the following assumptions:
   a) 40.4% of the population are under 15 years of age (1978 census);
   b) under 15s consume 90 kg of cereals per year and adults consume 180 kg per year;
   c) 10% of the cereals consumed by adults and children are grains other than maize, wheat and rice (1976/77 HBS);
3) The following assumptions are made regarding NMC supply of maize, rice and wheat to the town:
   a) Flour to grain conversions are: 0.95 ton maize flour = 1.0 ton maize; 0.75 ton wheat flour = 1.0 ton wheat.
   b) Paddy to rice conversion: 1 ton paddy = 0.65 rice.
   c) 80% of NMC regional distribution goes to the regional town and the immediate district area.

* NMC Arusha wheat sales are very high and appear to result from the Arusha depot being a regional supply centre instead of DSM. Therefore it is assumed that only 10% of Arusha NMC sales are purchased by the Arusha town population. The same procedure was applied to Arusha maize in 1987/88 and 1988/89 for the same reason.

Sources:
1) 1988, 1978 and 1967 Tanzanian national censuses.
2) Tanzania, MDB, Agricultural Price Reviews 1981, 1983, 1984 and 1986.
3) Tanzania, Bureau of Statistics, Provisional Data of the 1976/77 Household Budget Survey.
4) Sales data from the NMC.

Table VI.1: Origin of Trading Capital by Town and Period Trading Started

Sex/Origin	DSM Pre-1984	DSM 1984-1988	DSM Total	MWANZA Pre-1984	MWANZA 1984-1988	MWANZA Total	ARUSHA Pre-1984	ARUSHA 1984-1988	ARUSHA Total	MBEYA Pre-1984	MBEYA 1984-1988	MBEYA Total	SONGEA Pre-1984	SONGEA 1984-1988	SONGEA Total
MALES No.	26	43	69	9	18	27	9	10	19	9	1	10	3	18	21
% of Sample	37.7	62.3	100.0	28.1	56.3	84.4	31.0	34.5	65.5	30.0	3.3	33.3	8.6	51.4	60.0
Origin of Trading Capital No. Answered	25	39	64	9	18	27	9	10	19	9	1	10	5	18	23
SELF-FINANCED EMPLOYMENT	20.0	25.6	23.5	22.2	16.7	18.5	22.2	20.0	21.1				20.0		4.3
casual labour	4.0	5.1		22.2			11.1						20.0		
salaried lab.	16.0	20.5		22.2	16.7		11.1	20.0							
SELF-FINANCED BUSINESS	36.0	33.3	34.4	22.2	5.6	11.1	11.1	50.0	31.6					50.0	39.1
veg/fruit		5.1		22.2		11.1	50.0							22.2	
tradesman		2.6													
petty trade	[36.0]	25.6			5.6									27.8	
SELF-FINANCED AGRICULTURE	20.0	7.7	12.5	11.1	5.6	7.4	22.2		10.5				60.0	33.3	39.1
SELF-FINANCED UNSPECIFIED					5.6	3.7									
BORROWED from:			20.3			48.1			36.8			30.0			
family member	4.0	30.7		44.4	50.0		44.4	30.0		22.2	100.0	66.6	20.0	11.1	13.0
friend	4.0	25.6		33.3	27.8		44.4	30.0		66.6			20.0	11.1	13.0
unspecified		5.1		11.1	11.1					33.3					
FAMILY CONNECTION	16.0	2.6	7.8		16.7	11.1						10.0			
inheritance	8.0		3.1							11.1				5.6	
family business	8.0	2.6	4.7		16.7	11.1				11.1					5.6
BANK LOAN	4.0		1.6											5.6	4.3
TOTAL	100	99.9	100.1	99.9	100.2	99.9	99.9	100.0	100.0	99.9	100.0	100.0	100.0	100.0	99.8

Table VI.1 Cont.: Origin of Trading Capital by Town and Period Trading Started

Sex/Origin	DSM			MWANZA			ARUSHA			MBEYA			SONGEA		
Period Started Trading:	Pre-1984	1984–1988	Total	Pre-1984	1984–1988	Total	Pre-1984	1984–1988	Total	Pre-1984	1984–1988	Total	Pre-1984	1984–1988	Total
FEMALES No.										10.0	10.0				
% of Sample										33.3	33.3				
Origin of Trading Capital															
No. Answered				1	3	4	3	7	10	10	10	20	0	10	10
SELF-FINANCED EMPLOYMENT									10.0			5.0			
casual labour								14.3			10.0				
salaried labour								14.3							
SELF-FINANCED BUSINESS									30.0						20.0
veg/fruit							33.3	28.6						20.0	
tradeswoman							33.3	14.3							
petty trade								14.3							
SELF-FINANCED AGRICULTURE														10.0	10.0
BORROWED from:				100.0	66.6	75.0	66.6	57.2	60.0	90.0	90.0	90.0		70.0	70.0
family member				100.0	66.6		33.3	42.9		60.0	80.0			70.0	
friend							33.3			20.0	10.0				
unspecified								14.3		10.0					
FAMILY CONNECTION					33.3	25.0						5.0			
inheritance										10.0					
family business					33.3										
TOTAL				100.0	99.9	100.0	99.9	100.1	100.0	100.0	100.0	100.0		100.0	100.0

Source: 1988 Trader Survey

Table VI.2: Traders by Town, Sex and Age (%)

Sex/Age	DSM	Mwanza	Arusha	Mbeya	Songea	TOTAL
Total	69	32	30	30	35	196
Mean Age	33.3	30	33.4	37	33.7	33.4
Male Total	69	27	20	10	21	147
% Male	100	84.4	66.7	33.3	60.0	75.0
Age (%)						
15–19	2.9	3.8	10.0	0.0	0.0	3.4
20–24	18.8	26.9	10.0	0.0	4.8	15.8
25–29	24.6	30.8	35.0	20.0	28.6	27.4
30–34	15.9	7.7	15.0	10.0	38.1	17.0
35–39	11.6	11.5	10.0	20.0	19.0	13.0
40–44	7.2	7.7	5.0	40.0	4.8	8.9
45–49	5.8	3.8	10.0	0.0	0.0	4.8
50–54	4.3	3.8	5.0	10.0	4.8	4.8
55–59	5.8	0.0	0.0	0.0	0.0	2.7
60–64	1.4	0.0	0.0	0.0	0.0	0.7
65–69	1.4	3.8	0.0	0.0	0.0	1.4
Male mean age	33.3	30.9	30.8	38.0	31.1	32.9
Female Total	0.0	5.0	10.0	20.0	14.0	49.0
% Female	0.0	15.6	33.3	66.7	40.0	25.0
Age (%)						
10–14		20.0	0.0	0.0	0.0	2.0
15–19		0.0	0.0	0.0	0.0	0.0
20–24		20.0	0.0	5.0	14.3	8.2
25–29		20.0	30.0	15.0	14.3	18.4
30–34		20.0	10.0	15.0	14.3	14.3
35–39		20.0	10.0	40.0	14.3	24.5
40–44		0.0	20.0	10.0	7.1	10.2
45–49		0.0	10.0	0.0	14.3	6.1
50–54		0.0	10.0	15.0	7.1	10.2
55–59		0.0	10.0	0.0	7.1	4.1
60–64		0.0	0.0	0.0	0.0	0.0
65–69		0.0	0.0	0.0	7.1	2.0
Female mean age		25.4	38.5	36.5	37.6	36.1

Source: 1988 Trader Survey

Table VI.3: Traders by Town and Ethnic Group (%)

Ethnic Group	DSM	Mwanza	Arusha	Mbeya	Songea	TOTAL
Sample Size	69	32	30	30	35	196
Percentage Distribution:						
WESTERN	5.9	78.2	3.5	3.3	0.0	15.9
Ha	2.9	9.4	3.5	0.0	0.0	3.1
Manyema	0.0	3.1	0.0	3.3	0.0	1
Mjita	0.0	6.3	0.0	0.0	0.0	1
Nyamwezi	1.5	6.3	0.0	0.0	0.0	1.6
Sukuma	1.5	53.1	0.0	0.0	0.0	9.2
NORTHWESTERN	8.7	9.4	3.5	0.0	0.0	5.1
Hangaza	0.0	6.3	0.0	0.0	0.0	1
Haya	8.7	0.0	3.5	0.0	0.0	3.6
Nyarwonde	0.0	3.1	0.0	0.0	0.0	0.5
NORTHERN	8.7	3.1	86.3	3.3	0.0	17.3
Arusha	0.0	0.0	17.3	0.0	0.0	2.6
Chagga	8.7	3.1	48.3	3.3	0.0	11.5
Meru	0.0	0.0	6.9	0.0	0.0	1.1
Pare	0.0	0.0	13.8	0.0	0.0	2.1
NORTHEASTERN	15.9	0.0	3.5	0.0	0.0	6.1
Bondei	0.0	0.0	3.5	0.0	0.0	0.5
Digo	10.1	0.0	0.0	0.0	0.0	3.6
Pemba	2.9	0.0	0.0	0.0	0.0	1
Sambaa	2.9	0.0	0.0	0.0	0.0	1
EASTERN	40.6	0.0	0.0	0.0	0.0	14.3
Kwere	1.5	0.0	0.0	0.0	0.0	0.5
Luguru	27.5	0.0	0.0	0.0	0.0	9.7
Zaramo	10.1	0.0	0.0	0.0	0.0	3.6
Zigua	1.5	0.0	0.0	0.0	0.0	0.5
CENTRAL	4.4	9.3	3.5	0.0	0.0	3.6
Gogo	1.5	0.0	0.0	0.0	0.0	0.5
Irangi	2.9	3.1	3.5	0.0	0.0	2.1
Kondoa	0.0	0.0	0.0	0.0	0.0	0
Nunguru	0.0	3.1	0.0	0.0	0.0	0.5
Nyaturu	0.0	3.1	0.0	0.0	0.0	0.5
SOUTHERN	10.3	0.0	0.0	0.0	94.3	20.5
Makonde	4.4	0.0	0.0	0.0	5.7	2.6
Makua	1.5	0.0	0.0	0.0	0.0	0.5
Matengo	0.0	0.0	0.0	0.0	2.9	0.5
Mwera	2.9	0.0	0.0	0.0	0.0	1
Ndendeule	0.0	0.0	0.0	0.0	17.1	3.1
Ngindo	1.5	0.0	0.0	0.0	0.0	0.5
Ngoni	0.0	0.0	0.0	0.0	14.3	2.6
Yao	0.0	0.0	0.0	0.0	54.3	9.7
SOUTHWESTERN	3.0	0.0	0.0	93.3	5.7	16.4
Fipa	1.5	0.0	0.0	0.0	0.0	0.5
Kinga	0.0	0.0	0.0	10.0	0.0	1.5
Nyakyusa	1.5	0.0	0.0	56.7	0.0	9.2
Nyasa	0.0	0.0	0.0	3.3	5.7	1.5
Nyiha	0.0	0.0	0.0	3.3	0.0	0.5
Safwa	0.0	0.0	0.0	20.0	0.0	3.1
NON-AFRICAN	3.0	0.0	0.0	0.0	0.0	1.1
Arab	1.5	0.0	0.0	0.0	0.0	0.5
Ismailia	1.5	0.0	0.0	0.0	0.0	0.5
TOWN TOTAL	100.5	100.0	100.3	99.9	100	100.2
% Local Tribe	10.1	53.1	24.2	20.0	14.3	21.5
% Reg'l Tribes	40.6	87.6	89.8	93.3	94.3	73.5

Source: 1988 Trader Survey

Table IV.4: Traders by Town and Type of Commodity Sold (%)

Commodity Sold	DSM	Mwanza	Arusha	Mbeya	Songea	TOTAL
Maize	47.8	68.8	70.0	16.7	54.3	51.0
Grain	39.1	46.9	36.7	16.7	34.3	
Flour	2.9	12.5	26.7			
Both	5.8	3.1				
Grain–Flour		6.3	6.7		20.0	
Paddy/Rice	63.8	65.6	50.0	46.7	37.1	54.6
Rice	63.8	62.5	50.0	36.7	37.1	
Paddy						
Both						
Paddy–Rice		3.1		10.0		
Wheat	4.4	15.6	43.3	0.0	0.0	10.7
Grain	4.4		20.0			
Flour		15.6	23.3			
Bananas	7.3	0.0	0.0	23.3	0.0	6.1
Millet	13.0	12.5	0.0	0.0	0.0	6.6
Potatoes	2.9	0.0	3.3	13.3	0.0	3.6
Cassava	0.0	18.8	0.0	0.0	2.9	3.6
Root		15.6				
Flour		3.2				
Cassava–Flour					2.9	

Source: 1988 Trader Survey

Table VI.5: Average Storage Time, Maximum Amounts Stored and Reasons for Storage by Town (%)

	DSM	Mwanza	Arusha	Mbeya	Songea
Average Storage Time (Weeks)					
MAIZE					
All Traders	3.3	3.2	5.0	12.3	2.4
Mobile Intermediaries	9.0	2.5	12.5	2.7	
Wholesalers	0.7	9.5			
Retailers	3.5	1.9	5.0	12.0	2.3
RICE					
All Traders	2.1	6.0	5.1	5.5	5.8
Mobile Intermediaries	0.2	1.3		4.4	–
Wholesalers	0.9	24.0			
Retailers	2.6	5.7	5.1	6.4	5.8
Maximum Stored Amount (Tons)					
ALL	41.5	0.6	0.6	1.8	5.5
MOBILE INTERMEDIARY:					
average	33.5	1.5		3.2	16.8
high	100.0	3.0		10.0	20.0
low	0.0	0.0		0.8	10.0
WHOLESALER:					
average	161.8	0.9			
high	1520.0	3.0			
low	0.2	0.0			
RETAILER:					
average	9.6	0.4	0.6	0.7	1.3
high	215.0	1.5	4.0	3.0	3.0
low	0.0	0.0	0.1	0.1	0.2
Why Stored					
No. Replied	59	24	30	28	34
STOCK MOVEMENT	81.4	91.7	26.7	60.7	79.3
1) keep stocks/ avoid closure			3.3		
6) regulate supply	5.1	4.2	16.7	10.7	2.9
7) slow trade		87.5	6.7	10.7	
8) awaiting sale	72.9			17.9	67.6
9) awaiting transp.				14.3	8.8
10) awaiting milling				7.1	
12) large deliveries	3.4				.
ECONOMY MEASURE	11.9	0.0	26.7	0.0	0.0
2) economy of scale	6.8		20.0		
5) minimize transp. cost	5.1		6.7		
ENTREPRENEURIAL MOVE	6.8	4.2	43.3	39.3	20.6
3) price speculation	6.8	4.2	43.3	39.3	20.6
PERSONAL NEED	0.0	4.2	3.3	0.0	0.0
4) avoid excessive liquidity			3.3		
11) personal consumption		4.2			
TOTAL	100.1	100.1	100.0	100.0	99.9

Source: 1988 Trader Survey

Table VI.6: Dar es Salaam Traders' Cost Breakdown for Maize and Rice (TSh./Kg)

Trading Cost	Maize*	Rice**
Village Levy	0.11	0.10
Transport Cost to DSM from:		
Mbeya	5.56	9.00
Songea	5.56	9.00
Shinyanga		8.50
Arusha	4.44	
Dodoma	2.22	
Tanga	2.22	
Loading Charges at:		
Mbeya		1.50
DSM	0.44	0.70
Bags***	0.01	0.01
Watchman/night	0.10	0.11

Source: 1988 Trader Survey
* Calculated on basis of standard weight 90 kg maize bag.
** Calculated on basis of standard weight 100 kg rice bag.
*** Each bag costs approximately TSh. 60 and is used for 3–4 months.

Table VI.7: Types of Traders by Town (%)

Type	DSM	Mwanza	Arusha*	Mbeya	Songea	TOTAL
No. Replied	69	32	29	30	35	195
RETAILER procures from:	76.8	71.9	100.0	36.7	85.8	74.9
–own produce					5.7	1.0
–producer in rural area	5.8	0.0		0.0	8.6	3.6
–village wholesaler			3.5	3.3		1.0
–district trade centre			37.9			5.6
–producer/agents in town	10.1	21.9	34.5	33.4	68.6	29.7
–produce buyer/town wholesaler	60.9	50.0	24.1	0.0		33.3
–NMC/cooperative unions					2.9	0.5
MOBILE INTERMEDIARIES	5.9	15.6	0.0	63.3	14.3	17.0
Sells to Distant Wholesaler/ Retailer procures from:						
–producer in rural area	4.4	12.5		13.3	14.3	8.2
–village wholesaler		3.1		10.0		2.0
–produce buyer/town wholesaler				6.7		1.0
Large Farmer/Trader sells own Produce–Transports Long Distance	1.5					0.5
Sells to Long-Distance Transporter, procures from Producer in Village				16.7		2.6
Sells to Long-Distance Transporter, procures from Producer/Agents in Town				3.3		0.5
Sells to Town, procures from Rural Producer, Transports & Mills				13.3		2.0
STATIONARY WHOLESALERS	17.4	12.5	0.0	0.0	0.0	8.2
Sells to Retailers or Large Consumers, procures from Producer/Agents in Town	14.5	12.5				7.2
Tenderer	2.9					1.0
TOTAL	100.1	100.0	100.0	100.1	100.1	100.1

Source: 1988 Trader Survey
* 1 trader in Arusha did not give enough information to allow classification.

Table VI.8: FAO/KILIMO Production Estimates of Maize and Paddy Crops by Region, 1983/84–1986/87 ('000 Metric Tons)

Region	MAIZE						PADDY					
	87/88	86/87	85/86	84/85	83/84	82/83	87/88	86/87	85/86	84/85	83/84	82/83
Arusha	242	266	198	129	97	87	9	5	3	3	1	
Ccast/DSM	12	3	12	12	15	23	33	39	28	32	48	61
Dodoma	45	56	17	24	19	42	0	2	0	2	4	
Iringa	436	388	282	372	430	250	1	4	2	3	1	
Kagera	51	62	37	68	66	72	5	6	1	11	2	2
Kigoma	47	51	62	73	55	81	1	1	1	3	3	
Kilimanjaro	61	41	63	60	37	68	12	16	5	13	7	11
Lindi	5	12	26	22	16	9	3	24	20	21	9	14
Mara	28	30	27	31	23	39	2	1	3	1	2	
Mbeya	336	262	232	240	287	143	45	59	37	48	55	96
Morogoro	97	97	114	119	95	69	80	122	149	80	80	73
Mtwara	25	44	24	22	16	34	29	21	26	26	24	21
Mwanza	106	118	107	78	47	102	181	107	86	38	24	36
Rukwa	129	196	136	160	138	117	13	9	13	12	6	
Ruvuma	241	296	206	144	194	115	36	42	33	21	20	9
Shinyanga	226	103	297	287	183	79	103	131	81	61	38	24
Singida	64	41	34	23	26	21	1	2	4	2	1	
Tabora	155	232	213	166	101	92	56	40	38	45	29	17
Tanga	38	60	124	63	94	106	5	14	17	5	2	15
TOTAL	2339	2359	2210	2093	1939	1549	615	664	547	427	356	379

Source: FAO/KILIMO Crop Monitoring and Early Warning System Project, 'Consolidated Assessment of the National Food Supply Situation' (DSM, June 1988); Tanzania, EWCMP, 'Final Crop Condition Assessment and Production Estimate' (July 1983)

Table VI.9: Maize Traders' Volume of Operations by Town (Kg)

Volume of Maize Traded	DSM	Mwanza	Arusha	Mbeya	Songea	TOTAL
ALL TRADERS						
Last year:						
No. of traders	69	32	30	30	35	196
Average procurement (kg)	75854	10938	7590	2833	5476	31062.7
Range: Low	0	0	0	0	0	0
High	2190000	140000	48000	39000	80000	2190000
This year:						
No. of traders	69	32	30	30	35	196
Average procurement (kg)	73207	11672	9353	3367	6330	30754.8
Range: Low	0	0	0	0	0	0
High	2190000	140000	50000	40000	70000	2190000
Last week's average						
procurement	2464	590	192	33	347	1060.2
MAIZE TRADERS* ONLY						
Last year:						
No. of Traders: TOTAL	24	16	18	5	11	74
GRAIN TRADERS	22	13	9	5**	8**	57
FLOUR TRADERS	2	3	9	0	3	17
Average procurement (kg)	189636	19825	12650	17000	16427	72457.6
Range: Low	2500	1000	1300	5000	300	300
High	2190000	140000	48000	39000	80000	2190000
Tonnage handled: TOTAL	4551260	317200	227700	85000	180700	5361860
GRAIN	4329660	312300	111800	85000	178900	5017660
FLOUR	221600	4900	115900	0	1800	344200
Traders' assessment of year[†]	0.5	1.1	2.7	1	2	1.4
This year:						
No. of Traders: TOTAL	30	18	19	5	17	89
GRAIN TRADERS	28	14	9	5	14	70
FLOUR TRADERS	2	4	10	0	3	19
Average procurement (kg)	161055	18806	14768	20200	12288	64726.4
Range: Low	5000	500	1500	5000	400	400
High	2190000	140000	50000	40000	70000	2190000
Last week's average						
procurement	6350	1041	442	1000	1146	2720.4
Tonnage handled: TOTAL	4831650	338508	280600	101000	208900	5760658
GRAIN	4606650	332008	128300	101000	207000	5374958
FLOUR	225000	6500	152300	0	1900	385700

Source: 1988 Trader Survey

* Includes maize and maize flour traders.

** Mbeya's sample had 5 long-distance maize traders operating between Mbeya and Chunya.
  Songea's sample included 4 long-distance maize traders operating between Songea and DSM.

† Scale: 1 = good, 2 = average, 3 = bad, 4 = very bad.

Table VI.10: Profile of Maize Traders by Type of Trader and Town

A. MOBILE INTERMEDIARIES

	DSM	Mwanza	Arusha	Mbeya	Songea
Number	2	3	0	5	5
Sex ratio	2:0	3:0		5:0	4:1
Average age	36	30		39	33
Years trading	5	4		8	5
% selling other food					
commodities	100%	100%		20%	0%
Procurement: (Tons)					
Last year					
High	120.0	140.0		39.0	80.0
Low	50.0	0.0		3.0	0.0
Average	85.0	46.7		17.0	34.0
This year					
High	140.0	140.0		40.0	70.0
Low	30.0	0.0		5.0	20.0
Average	85.0	46.7		20.2	38.4
Last week					
High	47.3	2.0		1.0	5.0
Low	0.0	0.0		0.0	0.0
Average	23.6	0.8		0.2	2.2
Assessment of Previous					
Year's Trade*	1.0	1.0		1.0	1.8
1988 Purchase Price/Kg:					
High	16.00	18.00		13.13	8.25
Low	8.00	10.00		9.75	6.25
Average	11.50	13.25		11.00	7.00
1988 Sale Price/Kg:					
High	16.50	23.50		23.88	20.50
Low	13.00	20.30		16.63	15.00
Average	15.00	21.05		19.23	17.75
Average Margin	3.50	7.80		8.23	10.75

B. STATIONARY AFRICAN† TOWN WHOLESALERS

	DSM	Mwanza	Arusha	Mbeya	Songea
Number	6	4	0	0	0
Sex ratio	6:0	3:1			
Average age	37	26††			
Years trading	9	5††			
% selling other					
food commodities	67%	50%			
Procurement: (Tons)					
Last year					
High	2190.0	7.0			
Low	70.0	10.0			
Average	469.9	28.8			
This year					
High	2190.0	50.0			
Low	70.0	25.0			
Average	490.0	33.8			
Last week					
High	42.0	3.0			
Low	0.0	2.0			
Average	15.3	2.9			
Assessment of Previous					
Year's Trade*	1.3	1.3			

Table VI.10 Cont.: Profile of Maize Traders by Type of Trader and Town

	DSM	Mwanza	Arusha	Mbeya	Songea
1988 Purchase Price/Kg:					
High	15.25	20.00			
Low	11.92	12.50			
Average	13.38	16.38			
1988 Sale Price/Kg:					
High	18.08	20.30			
Low	13.75	16.80			
Average	15.63	18.58			
Average Margin/Kg:	2.25	2.20			

† Note one of the maize wholesalers surveyed was Asian and therefore is omitted from this table.
†† Excludes a 14-year-old girl who was functioning as a wholesaler on behalf of her mother.

C. TOWN RETAILERS**

	DSM	Mwanza	Arusha	Mbeya	Songea
Number	22	9	9	0	11
Sex ratio	22:0	7:2	4:5		1:10
Average age	32	36	32		35
Years trading	6	4	5		2
% selling other food commodities	41%	67%	44%		9%
Procurement:					
Last year					
High	324.0	20.0	25.0		3.5
Low	2.5	0.0	2.1		0.0
Average	95.7	6.5	12.4		0.9
This year					
High	400.0	18.0	30.0		4.0
Low	5.0	1.0	2.0		0.5
Average	86.3	6.3	14.3		1.6
Last week					
High	4.6	0.7	2.8		0.1
Low	0.0	0.0	0.0		0.0
Average	1.2	0.3	0.4		0.03
Assessment of Previous Year's Trade*	1.4	1.6	2.3		2.2
Purchase Price:					
High	17.10	20.00	13.31		7.10
Low	12.86	17.00	8.88		5.70
Average	14.71	18.44	10.20		6.45
Sale Price:					
High	18.87	21.43	15.53		9.90
Low	15.47	18.90	10.89		7.00
Average	17.12	20.11	12.06		7.50
Average Margin	2.41	1.67	1.86		1.05

Source: 1988 Trader Survey
* Scale: 1 = good, 2 = average, 3 = bad, 4 = very bad.
** Only retailers that restrict themselves to maize purchases and sales of grain only.
  Others that are omitted from this table are.

	DSM	Mwanza	Arusha	Mbeya	Songea
1) purchases and sells flour:	2	4	8	0	0
2) purchases grain and sells flour:	0	2	2	0	3

Table VI.11: 1988 Average Purchase and Sale Prices of Maize by Level of Trade and Town

	DSM	Mwanza	Arusha	Mbeya	Songea
MOBILE INTERMEDIARIES					
Sale Price/Kg	15.00	21.05		19.23*	17.75
Purchase Price/Kg	11.50	13.25		11.00	7.00
Margin	3.50	7.80		8.23	10.75
STATIONARY TOWN WHOLESALERS					
Sale Price/Kg	15.63	18.58			
Purchase Price/Kg	13.38	16.38			
Margin	2.25	2.20			
RETAILERS					
Sale Price/Kg	17.12	20.11	12.06		7.50
Purchase Price/Kg	14.71	18.44	10.20		6.45
Margin	2.41	1.67	1.86		1.05

Source: 1988 Trader Survey
* All maize sales of intermediaries were made at Chunya (Lupa goldmines) rather than Mbeya.

Table VI.12: Revised Calculation of Maize Margins Based on Survey Traders' Purchase Prices by Town

	OPEN MARKET					OFFICIAL MARKET
	DSM	Mwanza	Arusha	Mbeya	Songea	National
Intermediary purchase	9.25*	13.30		10.80	7.00	
Intermediary Margin	4.15	3.10				
Wholesale purchase	13.40	16.40				
Wholesale Margin	1.30	2.00				
Retail purchase	14.70	8.40	10.20		6.50	
Retail Margin	2.40	2.70	1.90		1.00	
Retail sale price	17.10	21.10	12.10		7.50	17.00
MDB PUBLISHED PRICE DATA (November 1988)						
Open Market						
Retail Price/Kg	17.65	20.29	15.00**	14.41	8.09	

	OPEN MARKET					OFFICIAL MARKET
Producer purchase price***	11.50	13.25	10.00	11.00	7.00	9.00
Retail sale price	17.10	21.10	12.10		7.50	17.00
% of Sale Price accruing to Farmer	67%	63%	83%		93%	53%

Source: 1988 Trader Survey
* Due to the small size of the sample of DSM intermediary traders their purchase price was averaged with that of Songea intermediary traders whose primary destination is DSM.
** The large discrepancy between the survey and MDB Arusha retail sale prices relates to the fact that there is a very large gap between the sale price charged in the Central Market (TSh. 14.71/kg) at the time of the survey versus the price charged at the bus stand (TSh. 10.59/kg) where so many sales take place. MDB's figures are undoubtedly based on the Central Market price.
*** Prices that traders reported paying directly to producers at farmgate or in district market.

Table VI.13: Rice/Paddy Traders' Volume of Operations by Town (Kg)

Volume of Rice/Paddy Traded	DSM	Mwanza	Arusha	Mbeya	Songea	TOTAL
ALL TRADERS						
Last year:						
No. of traders	69	32	30	30	35	196
Average procurement (kg)	138083	2374	2950	1884	489	49825.7
Range: Low	0	0	0	0	0	0
High	2737500	40000	35000	26000	5000	2737500
This year:						
No. of traders	69	32	30	30	35	196
Average procurement (kg)	141810	3314	3833	2085	671	51489.6
Range: Low	0	0	0	0	0	0
High	2591500	32500	40000	26000	7000	2591500
Last week's aver. procurement	4775	107	75	651	37	1816.2
RICE/PADDY TRADERS ONLY						
Last year:						
No. of traders: TOTAL	31	12	14	13	11	81
RICE TRADERS	31	12	14	9	11	77
PADDY TRADERS	0	1	0	4	0	5
Average procurement (kg)	271713	5741	6321	4203	1555	106817.7
Range: Low	2400	400	600	200	400	200
High	2737500	40000	35000	26000	5000	2737500
Tonnage handled: TOTAL	8423100	68900	88500	54635	17105	8652240
RICE	8423100	68900	88500	14400	17105	8612005
PADDY	0	0	0	40235	0	40235
Traders' assessment of year+	1.4	2.1	2.5	1.1	2.6	1.8
This year:						
No. of traders: TOTAL	38	16	15	13	12	94
RICE TRADERS	38	15	15	9	12	89
PADDY TRADERS	0	1	0	4	0	5
Average procurement (kg)	246302	5800	7667	4650	1958	102672.6
Range: Low	400	400	600	200	700	200
High	2591500	32500	40000	26000	7000	2591500
Last week's aver. procurement	9278	298	151	651	144	3933.9
Tonnage handled: TOTAL	9359500	92800	115000	60450	23496	9651246
RICE	9359500	60300	115000	17095	23496	9575391
PADDY	0	32500	0	43355	0	75855

Source: 1988 Trader Survey
+ Scale: 1 = good, 2 = average, 3 = bad, 4 = very bad.

Table VI.14: Profile of Rice Traders by Type of Trader and Town

A. MOBILE INTERMEDIARIES

		DSM	Mwanza	Arusha	Mbeya	
					Mbeya–Chunya	Rural Paddy–Mbeya Rice
Number		3	5	0	2	4
Sex ratio		3:0	5:0		2:0	0:4
Average age		28	26		42	37
Years trading		8	4		9	6
% selling other food commodities		66%	80%		50%	0%
PROCUREMENT: (TONS)						
Last year	High	520.0	40.0		3.0	26.0
	Low	45.0	2.0		3.0	1.6
	Average	221.7	11.9		3.0	10.1
This year	High	700.0	32.5		5.0	26.0
	Low	50.0	1.5		3.0	2.1
	Average	276.7	13.1		4.0	10.8
Last week	High	20.0	1.0		0.2	2.6
	Low	0.0	0.0		0.0	0.5
	Average	6.7	0.3		0.1	1.2
Assessment of Previous Year's Trade*		1.7	2.0		1.0	1.0
1988 PURCHASE PRICE/KG.:						
	High	49.00	33.98		62.50	31.73
	Low	37.70	29.35		40.00	25.13
	Average	43.83	31.73		50.00	28.82
1988 SALE PRICE/KG:						
	High	61.00	51.25		125.00	70.00
	Low	51.65	43.75		75.00	52.00
	Average	55.57	47.50		90.00	60.50
Average Margin		11.74	15.77		40.00	31.68**

B. STATIONARY TOWN WHOLESALERS

		DSM	Mwanza	Arusha	Mbeya	Songea
Number		4	0	0	0	0
Sex ratio		4:0				
Average age		34				
Years trading		8				
% selling other food commodities		0%				
PROCUREMENT: (TONS)						
Last year	High	2737.5				
	Low	80.0				
	Average	1602.3				
This year	High	2591.5				
	Low	90.0				
	Average	1510.8				

Table VI.14 Cont: Profile of Rice Traders by Type of Trader and Town

		DSM	Mwanza	Arusha	Mbeya	Songea
Last week	High	52.5				
	Low	2.0				
	Average	28.3				
Assessment of Previous Year's Trade*		1.8				
1988 PURCHASE PRICE/KG:						
	High	53.50				
	Low	47.00				
	Average	49.25				
1988 SALE PRICE/KG:						
	High	57.25				
	Low	49.50				
	Average	52.50				
Average Margin/Kg:		3.25				

C. TOWN RETAILERS

		DSM	Mwanza	Arusha	Mbeya	Songea
Number		35	14	15	8	12
Sex ratio		35:0	11:3	13:2	8:0	12:0
Average age		33	27	31	37	30
Years trading		7	4	8	4	4
% selling other food commodities		51%	71%	67%	0%	8%
PROCUREMENT:						
Last year	High	652.3	6.0	35.0	3.5	5.0
	Low	0.0	0.0	0.0	0.2	0.0
	Average	50.0	1.8	5.9	1.2	1.4
This year	High	857.5	3.0	40.0	3.5	7.0
	Low	0.0	0.4	0.6	0.2	0.7
	Average	79.0	2.5	7.7	1.3	2.0
Last week	High	145.0	0.4	0.4	0.2	0.2
	Low	0.0	0.0	0.1	0.0	0.0
	Average	5.6	0.2	0.2	0.1	0.1
Assessment of Previous Year's Trade*		1.3	2.2	2.5	1.2	2.6
PURCHASE PRICE:						
	High	58.40	41.78	54.73	55.71	53.73
	Low	54.00	35.22	45.27	43.57	42.82
	Average	56.20	38.50	50.00	49.64	48.28
SALE PRICE						
	High	63.81	49.44	63.80	64.29	70.00
	Low	57.13	43.33	52.47	47.86	58.00
	Average	60.47	46.39	58.13	56.08	64.00
Average Margin		4.27	7.89	8.13	6.44	15.72

Source: 1988 Trader Survey
 * Scale: 1 = good, 2 = average, 3 = bad, 4 = very bad.
** Includes milling charges.

Table VI.15: 1988 Average Purchase and Sale Prices of Rice by Level of Trade and Town

	DSM	Mwanza	Arusha	Mbeya	Songea
MOBILE INTERMEDIARIES					
Paddy:					
Sale Price/Kg				60.50	
Purchase Price/Kg				28.82	
Margin				31.68	
Rice:					
Sale Price/Kg	55.57	47.50		90.00	
Purchase Price/Kg	43.83	31.73		50.00	
Margin	11.74	15.77		40.00	
STATIONARY TOWN WHOLESALERS					
Sale Price/Kg	52.50				
Purchase Price/Kg	49.25				
Margin	3.25				
RETAILERS					
Sale Price/Kg	60.42	46.75	57.87	54.29	64.00
Purchase Price/Kg	56.14	39.25	47.00	48.69	47.86
Margin	4.28	7.50	10.87	5.60	16.14

Source: 1988 Trader Survey

Table VI.16: Revised Calculation of Margins Based on Survey Traders' Rice Purchase Prices by Town

	OPEN MARKET					OFFICIAL MARKET
	DSM	Mwanza	Arusha	Mbeya	Songea	National
Intermediary purchase	43.00	31.73		50.00		
Intermediary Margin	5.50	7.60				
Wholesale purchase	49.30					
Wholesale Margin	6.80					
Retail purchase	56.10	39.30	47.00*	48.70	47.90*	
Retail Margin	4.30	7.50	10.90	5.60	16.91	
Retail sale price	60.40	46.80	57.90	54.30	64.00	59.70

MDB PUBLISHED PRICE DATA (November 1988)
Open Market Rice

	DSM	Mwanza	Arusha	Mbeya	Songea	National
Retail Price/Kg	62.50	58.75	67.50	40.00	83.57	

	OPEN MARKET					OFFICIAL MARKET
Producer purchase price*	40.75	29.70		28.80**	41.67	17.30
Retail sale price	60.40	46.80		54.30	64.00	59.70
% of Sale Price accruing to Farmer	67%	63%		53%***	65%	29%

Source: 1988 Trader Survey

* Prices that traders reported paying directly to producers at farmgate or in district market.
** Paddy price.
*** Includes a paddy milling charge.

Table VI.17: Dar es Salaam Open Market Maize Consumer Prices and Harvests, 1983/84–1988/89 ('000 Metric Tons)

Market Year	VALUES Nominal Price (TSh.) *	Real Price (TSh.) **	National Harvest	Population Adjusted Harvest[†]	Harvest Retention[§]	National Marketed Surplus
1983/84	6.51	15.64	1549	1549	1450	99
1984/85	6.16	10.87	1939	1886	1450	436
1985/86	13.75	18.21	2093	1982	1450	532
1986/87	14.59	14.59	2210	2034	1450	584
1987/88	18.06	13.90	2359	2112	1450	662
1988/89	20.28	11.90	2339	2037	1450	587
Average	13.23	14.18	2081.5	1933.3	1450	483

Market Year	INDICES National Consumer Price Index	Nominal Price Index *	Real Price Index **	National Harvest	Population Adjusted Harvest[†]	National Marketed Surplus
1983/84	42	45	107	70	76	17
1984/85	57	42	75	88	93	75
1985/86	76	94	125	95	97	91
1986/87	100	100	100	100	100	100
1987/88	130	124	95	107	104	113
1988/89	170	139	82	106	100	101
Average	96	91	97	94	95	83

* When open market maize was not available, a dummy value was calculated on the basis of prices in the preceding and subsequent years.
** Deflated by the National Consumer Price Index.
† Removal of the increase of production related to the 2.8% rate of population growth.
§ Assumes 75% of maize produced is retained for household consumption (MDB estimate).

Sources: 1) MDB Open Market Prices
         2) National Consumer Price Index see Table VII.1
         3) Harvest estimates in FAO/Kilimo, *Food Security Bulletin for June 1988*

Table VI.18: Mwanza Open Market Maize Consumer Prices and Harvests, 1983/84–1988/89 ('000 Metric Tons)

Market Year	VALUES Nominal Price (TSh.) *	Real Price (TSh.) **	Local Harvest	Population Adjusted Harvest[†]	Harvest Retention[§]	Local Marketed Surplus
1983/84	11.82	28.39	102	102	78	24
1984/85	16.79	29.63	47	46	78	−32
1985/86	11.58	15.33	78	74	78	−4
1986/87	9.60	9.60	107	98	78	20
1987/88	17.45	13.43	118	106	78	28
1988/89	23.86	14.00	106	92	78	14
Average	15.18	18.40	92.9	86.3	78	8

Market Year	INDICES National Consumer Price Index	Nominal Price Index *	Real Price Index **	Local Harvest	Population Adjusted Harvest[†]	Local Marketed Surplus
1983/84	42	123	296	95	104	119
1984/85	57	175	309	44	46	−158
1985/86	76	121	160	73	75	−20
1986/87	100	100	100	100	100	100
1987/88	130	182	140	110	107	135
1988/89	170	249	146	99	93	68
Average	96	158	192	87	88	41

* When open market maize was not available, a dummy value was calculated on the basis of prices in the preceding and subsequent years.

** Deflated by the National Consumer Price Index.

[†] Removal of the increase of production related to the 2.8% rate of population growth.

[§] Due to the maize deficit position of Mwanza region, it is assumed that 90% of maize produced is retained for household consumption.

Sources: 1) MDB Open Market Prices

2) National Consumer Price Index see Table VII.1

3) Harvest estimates in FAO/Kilimo, *Food Security Bulletin for June 1988*

Table VI.19: Arusha Open Market Maize Consumer Prices and Harvests, 1983/84–1988/89 ('000 Metric Tons)

Market Year	VALUES Nominal Price (TSh.) *	Real Price (TSh.) **	Local Harvest	Population Adjusted Harvest†	Harvest Retention§	Local Marketed Surplus
1983/84	12.73	30.58	87	87	93	–6
1984/85	16.36	28.88	97	94	93	1
1985/86	10.69	14.16	129	122	93	29
1986/87	11.59	11.59	198	182	93	89
1987/88	17.18	13.22	265	238	93	144
1988/89	18.31	10.74	242	211	93	117
Average	14.48	18.19	169.7	155.7	93	62

Market Year	INDICES National Consumer Price Index	Nominal Price Index *	Real Price Index **	Local Harvest	Population Adjusted Harvest†	Local Marketed Surplus
1983/84	42	110	264	44	48	–7
1984/85	57	141	249	49	52	1
1985/86	76	92	122	65	67	32
1986/87	100	100	100	100	100	100
1987/88	130	148	114	134	130	162
1988/89	170	158	93	122	116	132
Average	96	125	157	86	85	70

* When open market maize was not available, a dummy value was calculated on the basis of prices in the preceding and subsequent years.
** Deflated by the National Consumer Price Index.
† Removal of the increase of production related to the 2.8% rate of population growth.
§ Due to the importance of maize as a cashcrop it is assumed that 60% of maize produced is retained for household consumption.

Sources: 1) MDB Open Market Prices
2) National Consumer Price Index see Table VII.1
3) Harvest estimates in FAO/Kilimo, *Food Security Bulletin for June 1988*

Table VI.20: Mbeya Open Market Maize Consumer Prices and Harvests, 1983/84–1988/89 ('000 Metric Tons)

Market Year	VALUES Nominal Price (TSh.) *	Real Price (TSh.) **	Local Harvest	Population Adjusted Harvest†	Harvest Retention§	Local Marketed Surplus
1983/84	11.96	28.73	143	143	139	4
1984/85	6.90	12.18	287	279	139	140
1985/86	8.56	11.34	240	227	139	88
1986/87	8.73	8.73	232	214	139	75
1987/88	13.10	10.08	262	234	139	95
1988/89	15.44	9.06	336	293	139	154
Average	10.78	13.35	249.9	231.6	139	93

Market Year	INDICES National Consumer Price Index	Nominal Price Index *	Real Price Index **	Local Harvest	Population Adjusted Harvest†	Local Marketed Surplus
1983/84	42	137	329	62	67	5
1984/85	57	79	140	124	131	188
1985/86	76	98	130	103	106	118
1986/87	100	100	100	100	100	100
1987/88	130	150	115	113	110	128
1988/89	170	177	104	145	137	206
Average	96	124	153	108	108	124

* When open market maize was not available, a dummy value was calculated on the basis of prices in the preceding and subsequent years.

** Deflated by the National Consumer Price Index.

† Removal of the increase of production related to the 2.8% rate of population growth.

§ Due to the importance of maize as a cashcrop it is assumed that 60% of maize produced is retained for household consumption.

Sources: 1) MDB Open Market Prices

2) National Consumer Price Index see Table VII.1

3) Harvest estimates in FAO/Kilimo, *Food Security Bulletin for June 1988*

Table VI.21: Songea Open Market Maize Consumer Prices and Harvests, 1983/84–1988/89 ('000 Metric Tons)

Market Year	VALUES Nominal Price (TSh.) *	Real Price (TSh.) **	Local Harvest	Population Adjusted Harvest[†]	Harvest Retention[§]	Local Marketed Surplus
1983/84	3.81	9.15	115	115	110	5
1984/85	4.53	8.00	194	189	110	78
1985/86	5.33	7.06	144	136	110	26
1986/87	6.22	6.22	206	190	110	79
1987/88	8.50	6.54	296	265	110	155
1988/89	9.68	5.68	241	210	110	99
Average	6.35	7.11	199.3	184.1	110	74

Market Year	INDICES National Consumer Price Index	Nominal Price Index *	Real Price Index **	Local Harvest	Population Adjusted Harvest[†]	Local Marketed Surplus
1983/84	42	61	147	56	61	6
1984/85	57	73	129	94	100	99
1985/86	76	86	113	70	72	33
1986/87	100	100	100	100	100	100
1987/88	130	137	105	144	140	195
1988/89	170	156	91	117	111	126
Average	96	102	114	97	97	93

* When open market maize was not available, a dummy value was calculated on the basis of prices in the preceding and subsequent years.
** Deflated by the National Consumer Price Index.
† Removal of the increase of production related to the 2.8% rate of population growth.
§ Due to the importance of maize as a cashcrop it is assumed that 60% of maize produced is retained for household consumption.

Sources: 1) MDB Open Market Prices
2) National Consumer Price Index see Table VII.1
3) Harvest estimates in FAO/Kilimo, *Food Security Bulletin for June 1988*

Table VI.22: Dar es Salaam Open Market Rice Consumer Prices and Paddy Harvests, 1983/84–1988/89 ('000 Metric Tons)

Market Year	VALUES Nominal Price (TSh.) *	Real Price (TSh.) **	National Harvest	Population Adjusted Harvest[†]	Harvest Retention[§]	National Marketed Surplus
1983/84	26.60	63.90	379	379	229	151
1984/85	37.92	66.93	356	346	229	118
1985/86	48.33	64.00	427	404	229	176
1986/87	40.21	40.21	547	504	229	275
1987/88	54.19	41.70	644	577	229	348
1988/89	66.67	39.11	615	535	229	307
Average	45.65	52.64	518	457	229	229

Market Year	INDICES National Consumer Price Index	Nominal Price Index *	Real Price Index **	National Harvest	Population Adjusted Harvest[†]	National Marketed Surplus
1983/84	42	66	159	69	75	55
1984/85	57	94	166	65	69	43
1985/86	76	120	159	78	80	64
1986/87	100	100	100	100	100	100
1987/88	130	135	104	118	115	127
1988/89	170	166	97	112	106	112
Average	96	114	131	90	91	83

* When open market rice was not available, a dummy value was calculated on the basis of prices in the preceding and subsequent years.
** Deflated by the National Consumer Price Index.
† Removal of the increase of production related to the 2.8% rate of population growth.
§ Assumes 50% of rice produced is retained for household consumption (MDB estimate).

Sources: 1) MDB Open Market Prices
2) National Consumer Price Index see Table VII.1
3) Harvest estimates in FAO/Kilimo, *Food Security Bulletin for June 1988*

Table VI.23: Mwanza Open Market Rice Consumer Prices and Paddy Harvests, 1983/84–1988/89 ('000 Metric Tons)

Market Year	VALUES Nominal Price (TSh.) *	Real Price (TSh.) **	Local Harvest	Population Adjusted Harvest†	Harvest Retention§	Local Marketed Surplus
1983/84	26.83	64.45	36	36	36	0
1984/85	39.56	69.82	24	23	36	−12
1985/86	30.20	39.99	38	36	36	0
1986/87	31.65	31.65	86	79	36	43
1987/88	44.79	34.47	107	96	36	61
1988/89	61.01	35.79	181	158	36	122
Average	39.01	46.03	79	71	36	36

Market Year	INDICES National Consumer Price Index	Nominal Price Index *	Real Price Index **	Local Harvest	Population Adjusted Harvest†	Local Marketed Surplus
1983/84	42	85	204	42	45	1
1984/85	57	125	221	28	29	−28
1985/86	76	95	126	44	45	1
1986/87	100	100	100	100	100	100
1987/88	130	142	109	125	122	139
1988/89	170	193	113	211	199	281
Average	96	123	145	92	90	82

* When open market rice was not available, a dummy value was calculated on the basis of prices in the preceding and subsequent years.
** Deflated by the National Consumer Price Index.
† Removal of the increase of production related to the 2.8% rate of population growth.
§ Assumes 50% of rice produced is retained for household consumption (MDB estimate).

Sources: 1) MDB Open Market Prices
2) National Consumer Price Index see Table VII.1
3) Harvest estimates in FAO/Kilimo, *Food Security Bulletin for June 1988*

Table VI.24: Mbeya Open Market Rice Consumer Prices and Paddy Harvests, 1983/84–1988/89 (*'000 Metric Tons*)

Market Year	VALUES Nominal Price (TSh.) *	Real Price (TSh.) **	Local Harvest	Population Adjusted Harvest[†]	Harvest Retention[§]	Local Marketed Surplus
1983/84	27.07	65.03	96	96	27	69
1984/85	41.20	72.72	56	54	27	28
1985/86	37.50	49.66	48	45	27	19
1986/87	33.54	33.54	37	34	27	7
1987/88	35.10	27.01	59	53	27	26
1988/89	41.88	24.57	45	39	27	13
Average	36.05	45.42	49	54	27	27

Market Year	INDICES National Consumer Price Index	Nominal Price Index *	Real Price Index **	Local Harvest	Population Adjusted Harvest[†]	Local Marketed Surplus
1983/84	42	81	194	259	282	960
1984/85	57	123	217	151	160	384
1985/86	76	112	148	130	133	258
1986/87	100	100	100	100	100	100
1987/88	130	105	81	160	155	362
1988/89	170	125	73	122	116	175
Average	96	107	135	154	158	373

* When open market rice was not available, a dummy value was calculated on the basis of prices in the preceding and subsequent years.
** Deflated by the National Consumer Price Index.
† Removal of the increase of production related to the 2.8% rate of population growth.
§ Assumes 50% of rice produced is retained for household consumption (MDB estimate).

Sources: 1) MDB Open Market Prices
2) National Consumer Price Index see Table VII.1
3) Harvest estimates in FAO/Kilimo, *Food Security Bulletin for June 1988*

Table VI.25: *Cooperative Purchases and Producer Prices of Maize and Paddy, 1985/86–1988/89*

MAIZE

Cooperative Union	1985/86 Purchases (Tonnes)	% of Nat'l Coop Total	% of Marketed Surplus*	1986/87 Purchases (Tonnes)	% of Nat'l Coop Total	% of Marketed Surplus*	Open/ Official Price Ratio**	Open Market Producer Price	1987/88 Purchases (Tonnes)	% of Nat'l Coop Total	% of Marketed Surplus^	Open/ Official Price Ratio**	Open Market Producer Price
Mwanza (NYANZA)	39	0.0	-1.0	581	0.3	2.9	2.05	8.61	–			3.78	15.87
Arusha (ARCU)	39249	20.1	135.3	49967	24.4	56.1	1.38	8.70	68072	25.4	47.3	1.72	14.07
Ruvuma (RCU)	38663	19.8	148.7	35211	17.2	44.6	0.95	5.97	28566	10.7	36.2	1.23	10.06
Mbeya	13370	6.8	15.2	7996	3.9	10.7	1.05	6.61	15737	5.9	16.6	1.54	12.62
MBECU				[7902]					[15431]				
KYERECU				[94]					[306]				
NATIONAL TOTAL	195633	46.7	36.8	204449	45.9	35.0			267749	42.0	40.4		
Official Producer Price (TSh.)													
Premium	5.25			6.30					8.20				
Non-Premium	3.50			4.20					4.20				

PADDY

Cooperative Union	1985/86 Purchases (Tonnes)	% of Nat'l Coop Total	% of Marketed Surplus^	1986/87 Purchases (Tonnes)	% of Coop Total	% of Marketed Surplus^	Open/ Official Price Ratio^^	Open Market Producer Price	1987/88 Purchases (Tonnes)	% of Nat'l Coop Total	% of Marketed Surplus^	Open/ Official Price Ratio^^	Open Market Producer Price
Mwanza (NYANZA)	2096	16.7	–	–			1.18	11.29	14124	19.4	23.2	0.92	13.28
Arusha (ARCU)	–			–			1.15	11.06	28	0.0	–	1.46	21.05
Ruvuma (RCU)	–			231	2.3		1.44	13.84	1902	2.6		1.22	17.62
Mbeya	3892	31.0	20.5	2795	28.2	39.9	1.67	16.02	12145	16.7	46.7	1.55	22.29
MBECU				[1636]					[11521]				
KYERECU				[159]					[624]				
NATIONAL TOTAL	12538	47.8	7.1	9910	30.5	3.6			72282	38.7	20.9		
Official Producer Price (TSh.)													
Premium	8.00			9.60					14.40				
Non-Premium	5.50			6.05					14.40				

Sources: Tanzania, Marketing Development Bureau, *Annual Review of Maize, Rice and Wheat*, 1987 and 1988
FAO/KILIMO, *Food Security Bulletins*, 1986–1988

* See Tables VI.17–24

** Based on regional monthly producer prices collected by the Marketing Development Bureau.

Table VI.26: Comparative Results of Grain Price Correlations Among Pairs of Markets,* Dec. 82–Dec. 85 and Jan.86–Jan. 89

Correlation Coefficient**	Cumulative Total of Coefficients				
	Maize: 1982–85	1986–89	Rice: 1982–85	1986–89	
0.65–0.69			.004		
0.60–0.64		.002	.008		
0.55–0.59	.003	.007	.012	.020	
0.50–0.54	.027	.007	.016	.024	
0.45–0.49	.034	.025	.028	.059	
0.40–0.44	.027	.042	.036	.059	
0.35–0.39	.057	.052	.051	.059	
0.30–0.34	.054	.059	.091	.091	1st Quartile
0.25–0.29	.091	091	.067	.138	
0.20–0.24	.086	.111	.115	.119	2nd Quartile
0.15–0.19	.101	.106	.146	.111	
0.10–0.14	.106	.096	.079	.087	3rd Quartile
0.05–0.09	.094	.111	.119	.095	
0.00–0.04	.081	.074	.067	.036	
−0.04–0.00	.076	.074	.055	.016	
−0.09–0.05	.049	.054	.063	.028	
−0.14–0.10	.044	.039	.016	.032	
−0.19–0.15	.037	.025	.024	.008	
−0.24–0.20	.022	.012	.004	.020	
−0.29–0.25	.003	.010			
−0.34–0.30	.005				
−0.39–0.35	.003	.002			
Total	.999	.999	1.001	1.002	
No. of markets	29	29	23	23	
No. of pairs	406	406	253	253	
1st quartile	.25–.29	.25–.29	.25–.29	.30–.34	
2nd quartile	.10–.14	.15–.19	.15–.19	.20–.24	

Source: Compiled from Tanzania, MDB, *Monthly Market Bulletin*, Dec.1982–Jan.1989

* Maize markets: Arusha, Bukoba, DSM, Dodoma, Gonja, Iringa, Kigoma, Lindi, Lushoto, Maswa, Mbeya, Mbulu, Morogoro, Moshi, Mpwapwa, Mtwara, Musoma, Mwanza, Njombe, Sengerema, Shinyanga, Singida, Songea, Sumbawanga, Tabora, Tanga, Tarime, Tunduru, Urambo

Rice markets: Arusha, Bukoba, DSM, Dodoma, Iringa, Kigoma, Lindi, Lushoto, Mbeya, Mbulu, Morogoro, Moshi, Mpwapwa, Mtwara, Musoma, Mwanza, Njombe, Shinyanga, Singida, Songea, Tabora, Tanga, Urambo

** See Table V.3 for an explanation of the date handling procedure

Table VI.27: Official and Open Maize Retail Prices, 1982/83–1988/89 (TSh./Kg)*

	OFFICIAL	OPEN MARKET DSM		Mwanza		Mbeya		Arusha		Songea		5-Town Unweighted Average Mean	UNOFFICIAL/ OFFICIAL PRICE RATIO
		Mean	c.v.	Mean	c.v.	Mean	c.v.	Mean	c.v.	Mean	c.v.		
1982/83[1]	3.35	6.86	.247	6.62	.061	4.41	.077	3.88	.069	2.92	196	4.94	1.47
1983/84[2]	4.39	6.51	–	11.82	.428	11.96	.403	12.73	.670	3.81	.456	9.37	2.13
1984/85[2]	5.40	6.16	.084	16.79	.311	6.90	.161	16.36	.161	4.53	.097	10.15	1.88
1985/86[2]	7.60	13.75	.175	11.58	.207	8.56	.210	10.69	.235	5.33	.210	9.98	1.31
1986/87[2]	12.20	14.59	.181	9.60	.102	8.73	.118	11.59	.108	6.22	.189	10.15	0.83
1987/88[2]	12.20	18.06	.247	17.45	.304	13.10	.282	17.18	.353	8.50	.270	14.86	1.22
1988/89[2]	17.00	20.28	.162	23.86	.192	15.44	.161	18.31	.143	9.68	.163	17.51	1.03
Weighted Mean	9.15	12.59	.179	14.33	.238	10.14	.208	13.42	.257	6.00	.227	11.30	1.23

Source: Marketing Development Bureau, Ministry of Agriculture
* Calculated on the basis 1 debe = 17 kg
[1] November 1982–June 1983
[2] July–June

Table VI.28: Official and Open Rice Retail Prices, 1982/83–1988/89 (TSh./kg)

| | OFFICIAL | OPEN MARKET | | | | | | | | | | 5-Town Unweighted Average Mean | UNOFFICIAL/ OFFICIAL PRICE RATIO |
| | | DSM | | Mwanza | | Mbeya | | Arusha | | Songea | | | |
		Mean	c.v.	Mean	c.v.	Mean	c.v.	Mean	c.v.	Mean	c.v.		
1982/83[1]	5.35	15.27	.384	14.10	.096	13.33	.194	23.21	.168	16.42	.071	16.47	3.08
1983/84[2]	7.20	26.60	—	26.83	—	27.07	.418	33.45	.316	22.43	.133	27.28	3.79
1984/85[2]	13.40	37.92	.040	39.56	.223	41.20	.360	47.31	.143	28.81	.211	38.96	2.91
1985/86[2]	14.50	48.33	.244	30.20	.270	37.50	.306	45.63	.215	35.91	.233	39.51	2.72
1986/87[2]	19.00	40.21	.319	31.65	.092	33.54	.168	44.79	.085	37.89	.146	37.62	1.98
1987/88[2]	32.00	54.19	.054	44.79	.299	35.10	.108	51.93	.102	47.48	.253	46.68	1.46
1988/89[2]	59.70	66.67	.182	61.01	.177	41.88	.188	68.86	.121	73.63	.244	62.41	1.05
Weighted Mean	22.41	42.62	.193	36.52	.199	33.78	.252	46.12	.164	38.56	.190	39.52	1.76

Source: Marketing Development Bureau, Ministry of Agriculture
[1] November 1982–June 1983
[2] July–June

Table VII.1: National Consumer Price Index for Urban Areas, 1970–1988

Year	NOMINAL (1970=100)			REAL INDICES (1970=100)*			NOMINAL % CHANGE			REAL % CHANGE		
	Non-Food	Food	General	Non-Food	Food	General	Non-Food	Food	General	Non-Food	Food	General
70	100.0	100.0	100.0	100.0	100.0	100.0						
71	103.8	105.7	104.7	103.8	105.7	104.7	3.8	5.7	4.7	3.8	5.7	4.7
72	110.4	115.3	112.7	78.3	81.8	79.9	6.6	9.6	8.0	-25.5	-23.9	-24.8
73	120.8	128.7	124.5	85.7	91.3	88.3	10.4	13.4	11.8	7.4	9.5	8.4
74	126.0	173.7	148.4	63.0	86.9	74.2	5.2	45.0	23.9	-22.7	-4.4	-14.1
75	152.9	226.9	187.7	68.3	101.3	83.8	26.9	53.2	39.3	5.3	14.4	9.6
76	155.6	251.4	200.6	69.5	112.2	89.6	2.7	24.5	12.9	1.2	10.9	5.8
77	193.6	257.8	223.8	86.4	115.1	99.9	38.0	6.4	23.2	17.0	2.9	10.4
78	206.6	297.5	249.3	92.2	132.8	111.3	13.0	39.7	25.5	5.8	17.7	11.4
79	238.7	334.2	283.6	106.6	149.2	126.6	32.1	36.7	34.3	14.3	16.4	15.3
80	319.9	425.2	369.4	113.4	150.8	131.0	81.2	91.0	85.8	6.9	1.6	4.4
81	410.0	525.1	464.1	145.4	186.2	164.6	90.1	99.9	94.7	32.0	35.4	33.6
82	508.9	697.0	597.3	144.2	197.5	169.2	98.9	171.9	133.2	-1.2	11.2	4.6
83	648.3	886.6	760.3	183.7	251.2	215.4	139.4	189.6	163.0	39.5	53.7	46.2
84	803.3	1163.9	1034.8	168.8	244.5	217.4	155.0	277.3	274.5	-14.9	-6.6	2.0
85	1070.6	1551.3	1879.2	224.9	325.9	289.7	267.3	387.4	344.4	56.2	81.4	72.4
86	1417.7	2054.3	1826.4	297.8	431.6	383.7	347.1	503.0	447.2	72.9	105.7	93.9
87	1842.2	2669.6	2373.4	387.0	560.8	498.6	424.5	615.3	547.0	89.2	129.3	114.9
88	2416.8	3502.0	3113.5	326.2	472.6	420.2	574.6	832.4	740.1	-60.9	-88.2	-78.4

Sources:
1) Bank of Tanzania, Economic and Operations Report (June 1984), 89
2) Tanzania, Hali ya Uchumi wa Taifa katika Mwaka 1986 (DSM, Government Printers)
3) Tanzania Economic Trends 1(1) and 1(4) 1989, 54
4) Jackson, D., The Disappearance of Strikes in Tanzania: Incomes Policy and Industrial Democracy', Journal of Modern African Studies 17(2), 1979
5) Jamal, V., 'The Political Economy of Devaluation in Tanzania', ILO, Addis Ababa (1984), 32
6) Daily News 15/6/84
* Deflated by the Minimum Wage Index (see Table II.7).

Table VII.2: Proportion of Rural and Urban Households' Staple Food Supply by Weight arising from Non-Monetary Sources (%)

Food Items*	Household Expenditure Groups (TSh.)									
	0–999	1000–1999	2000–3999	4000–5999	6000–7999	8000–9999	10000–24999	25000–39999	40000+	TOTAL
URBAN HOUSEHOLDS										
Cereals	87.4	78.5	54.7	31.5	16.8	7.9	7.0	3.1	18.8	30.6
Maize	82.1	69.1	54.2	35.5	20.9	8.6	9.2	4.5	54.4	31.4
Rice	48.0	55.3	22.6	17.0	8.6	5.4	3.4	2.4	1.6	9.9
Starchy Roots	95.9	87.9	65.9	37.0	23.9	16.5	7.8	4.1	32.3	43.3
RURAL HOUSEHOLDS										
Cereals	94.7	93.2	82.4	78.8	73.0	63.5	69.0	69.8	70.7	84.7
Maize	94.6	94.1	82.9	81.3	74.1	68.3	77.5	78.3	90.0	86.1
Rice	83.7	84.3	59.4	39.0	50.0	26.4	35.1	57.1	35.5	62.3
Starchy Roots	98.4	96.8	92.5	81.9	81.5	81.0	88.9	22.9	91.6	91.7

Source: Tanzania, Household Budget Survey 1976/77

* 'Cereals' include maize, rice, millet, sorghum, wheat, barley, oats and miscellaneous cereals.
   'Starchy Roots' include cassava, sweet potatoes, yam, cocoyam, potatoes, cooking bananas and plantains.

Table VII.3: Household Economic Position (%)

Household Economic Position	Town DSM	Mwanza	Arusha	Mbeya	Songea	TOTAL
No. Assessed	61	27	30	30	35	183
1–Very Poor	3.3	0.0	0.0	6.7	0.0	2.2
2–Moderately Poor	9.8	33.3	16.7	16.7	20.0	17.5
3–Lower Middle	24.6	25.9	26.7	33.3	37.1	29.0
4–Middle	27.9	7.4	26.7	20.0	31.4	24.0
5–Upper Middle	21.3	22.2	20.0	13.3	5.7	16.9
6–Moderately Wealthy	13.1	7.4	10.0	10.0	5.7	9.8
7–Very Wealthy	0.0	3.7	0.0	0.0	0.0	0.5
Total	100.0	100.0	100.0	100.0	100.0	100.0
Mean Average	3.9	3.6	3.8	3.5	3.4	3.7
Coefficient of Variation	0.33	0.43	0.33	0.40	0.31	0.35
CUMULATIVE TOTAL						
Very Poor	3.3	0.0	0.0	6.7	0.0	2.2
≤ Moderately Poor	13.1	33.3	16.7	23.4	20.0	19.7
≤ Lower Middle	37.7	59.2	43.4	56.7	57.1	48.7
≤ Middle	65.6	66.6	70.1	76.7	88.5	72.7
≤ Upper Middle	86.9	88.8	90.1	90.0	94.2	89.6
≤ Moderately Wealthy	100.0	96.2	100.1	100.0	99.9	99.4
≤ Very Wealthy	100.0	99.9	100.1	100.0	99.9	99.9

Source: 1988 Household Survey

Table VII.4: Households by Region of Birth of Interviewee and Town (%)

Region of Birth	Town DSM	Mwanza	Arusha	Mbeya	Songea	TOTAL
No. Replied	64	27	30	30	35	186
Arusha	15.6	0.0	20.0	0.0	5.7	9.7
Coast	3.1	0.0	0.0	0.0	0.0	1.1
DSM	9.4	0.0	0.0	0.0	0.0	3.2
Dodoma	6.3	0.0	3.3	3.3	0.0	3.2
Iringa	6.3	0.0	0.0	13.3	11.4	6.5
Kagera	7.8	11.1	13.3	0.0	0.0	6.5
Kigoma	3.1	0.0	0.0	0.0	0.0	1.1
Kilimanjaro	15.6	0.0	30.0	3.3	2.9	11.3
Lindi	1.6	0.0	0.0	0.0	0.0	0.5
Mara	3.1	3.7	0.0	0.0	2.9	2.2
Mbeya	4.7	0.0	10.0	70.0	5.7	15.6
Morogoro	4.7	0.0	6.7	3.3	0.0	3.2
Mtwara	1.6	0.0	0.0	0.0	2.9	1.1
Mwanza	6.3	66.7	0.0	0.0	0.0	11.8
Rukwa	3.1	0.0	0.0	0.0	0.0	1.1
Ruvuma	3.1	0.0	0.0	0.0	68.6	14.0
Shinyanga	0.0	11.1	0.0	0.0	0.0	1.6
Singida	1.6	0.0	6.7	0.0	0.0	1.6
Tabora	0.0	7.4	0.0	0.0	0.0	1.1
Tanga	3.1	0.0	10.0	0.0	0.0	2.7
KENYA	0.0	0.0	0.0	3.3	0.0	0.5
UGANDA	0.0	0.0	0.0	3.3	0.0	0.5
Total	100.0	100.0	100.0	100.0	100.0	100.0

Source: 1988 Household Survey

Table VII.5: Households by Household Size and Town (%)

No. of HH Members	Town DSM	Mwanza	Arusha	Mbeya	Songea	TOTAL
No. Replied	64	29	30	30	35	188
1–2	0.0	6.9	16.7	6.7	5.7	6.9
3–4	12.5	13.8	13.3	26.7	5.7	13.8
5–6	34.4	24.1	23.3	50.0	17.1	30.3
7–8	32.8	24.1	36.7	10.0	34.3	28.7
9–10	10.9	24.1	10.0	6.7	20.0	13.8
11–12	4.7	6.9	0.0	0.0	5.7	3.7
13–14	0.0	0.0	0.0	0.0	8.6	1.6
15–16	1.6	0.0	0.0	0.0	2.9	1.1
Total	100.0	100.0	100.0	100.0	100.0	100.0

Source: 1988 Household Survey

Table VII.6: Household Head's Occupation by Town (%)

Household Head's Occupation	Town DSM	Mwanza	Arusha	Mbeya	Songea	TOTAL
No. Replied	64	29	30	30	35	188
Formally Employed – High Level	37.5	34.5	33.3	13.3	17.1	28.7
Self-employed Professional	0.0	0.0	3.3	0.0	0.0	0.5
Administrator	12.5	6.9	16.7	0.0	0.0	8.0
Govt Officer	7.8	20.7	10.0	13.3	14.3	12.2
Professional	9.4	6.9	3.3	0.0	2.9	5.3
Manager	7.8	0.0	0.0	0.0	0.0	2.7
Formally Employed – Junior Level	14.1	17.2	26.7	3.3	22.9	16.5
Skilled Technician	7.8	6.9	16.7	0.0	0.0	6.4
Govt Employee	1.6	0.0	3.3	0.0	0.0	1.1
Non-government Employee	4.7	10.3	6.7	3.3	22.9	9.0
Service Employees	21.9	10.3	20.0	3.3	5.7	13.8
Educator	9.4	6.9	16.7	3.3	5.7	8.5
University Employees	9.4	0.0	0.0	0.0	0.0	3.2
Soldier/Policeman	3.1	3.4	0.0	0.0	0.0	1.6
Party Functionary	0.0	0.0	3.3	0.0	0.0	0.5
Self-Employed	26.6	37.9	20.0	80.0	54.3	41.0
Skilled Self-employed	6.3	13.8	3.3	16.7	11.4	9.6
Petty Trader	3.1	3.4	3.3	6.7	5.7	4.3
Retail Trader	0.0	0.0	3.3	0.0	0.0	0.5
Businessman	12.5	17.2	0.0	23.3	5.7	11.7
Driver/Transporter	0.0	0.0	3.3	10.0	0.0	2.1
Casual Labourer	3.1	0.0	3.3	3.3	2.9	2.7
Farmer	0.0	3.4	0.0	16.7	25.7	8.0
Retired	1.6	0.0	3.3	3.3	2.9	2.1
Total	100.0	100.0	100.0	100.0	100.0	100.0

Source: 1988 Household Survey

Table VII.7: Households by Number of Members who Farm and Town (%)

No. of Farmers in Household	Town DSM	Mwanza	Arusha	Mbeya	Songea	TOTAL
No. Replied	64	29	30	30	35	188
None	84.4	86.2	73.3	73.3	25.7	70.2
One	14.1	10.3	13.3	20.0	22.9	16.0
Two	1.6	0.0	6.7	6.7	2.9	3.2
Three	0.0	0.0	3.3	0.0	17.1	3.7
Four	0.0	3.4	3.3	0.0	17.1	4.3
Five	0.0	0.0	0.0	0.0	8.6	1.6
Six	0.0	0.0	0.0	0.0	2.9	0.5
Seven	0.0	0.0	0.0	0.0	2.9	0.5
Total	100.0	100.0	100.0	100.0	100.0	100.0

Source: 1988 Household Survey

Table VII.8: Households by Main Staple Consumed and Town (%)

Household's Main Staple	Town DSM	Mwanza	Arusha	Mbeya	Songea	TOTAL
No. Replied	64	29	30	30	35	188
Maize	75.0	82.8	60.0	80.0	97.1	78.7
Rice	20.3	17.2	23.3	13.3	0.0	15.4
Bananas	4.7	0.0	16.7	3.3	0.0	4.8
Cassava	0.0	0.0	0.0	0.0	2.9	0.5
Wheat	0.0	0.0	0.0	3.3	0.0	0.5
Total	100.0	100.0	100.0	100.0	100.0	100.0

Source: 1988 Household Survey

Table VII.9: Households by % of Household Food Farmed and Town (%)

% of HH Food Farmed	Town DSM	Mwanza	Arusha	Mbeya	Songea	TOTAL
No. Replied	64	29	30	30	35	188
None	79.7	58.6	70.0	43.3	17.1	57.4
0.1–10.0	9.4	13.8	13.3	0.0	0.0	7.4
10.1–20.0	1.6	3.4	0.0	6.7	2.9	2.7
20.1–30.0	3.1	6.9	0.0	3.3	0.0	2.7
30.1–40.0	0.0	0.0	0.0	13.3	2.9	2.7
40.1–50.0	4.7	6.9	3.3	6.7	5.7	5.3
50.1–60.0	0.0	0.0	6.7	3.3	2.9	2.1
60.1–70.0	0.0	0.0	0.0	0.0	11.4	2.1
70.1–80.0	1.6	6.9	3.3	16.7	22.9	9.0
80.1–90.0	0.0	0.0	3.3	6.7	22.9	5.9
90.1–100.0	0.0	3.4	0.0	0.0	11.4	2.7
Total	100.0	100.0	100.0	100.0	100.0	100.0
Average	5.2	15.2	12.2	30.1	62.7	22.5

Source: 1988 Household Survey

Table VII.10: Households by No. of Cultivators in Household and Town (%)

No. of Cultivators in Household	Town DSM	Mwanza	Arusha	Mbeya	Songea	TOTAL
No. Replied	62	25	30	30	35	182
None	74.2	60.0	60.0	43.3	17.1	53.8
One	22.6	16.0	13.3	30.0	14.3	19.8
Two	3.2	12.0	10.0	26.7	11.4	11.0
Three	0.0	8.0	13.3	0.0	20.0	7.1
Four	0.0	0.0	3.3	0.0	17.1	3.8
Five	0.0	4.0	0.0	0.0	14.3	3.3
Six	0.0	0.0	0.0	0.0	2.9	0.5
Seven	0.0	0.0	0.0	0.0	2.9	0.5
Total	100.0	100.0	100.0	100.0	100.0	100.0

Source: 1988 Household Survey

Table VII.11: Households by Town and Cultivating Household Members (%)

Cultivator's Relationship to HH Head	Town DSM	Mwanza	Arusha	Mbeya	Songea	TOTAL
No. Replied	27	23	25	25	76	176
Male HH Head	48.1	30.4	12.0	56.0	35.5	36.4
Female HH Head	3.7	8.7	4.0	12.0	2.6	5.1
Wife	14.8	13.0	40.0	24.0	30.3	26.1
Sons	0.0	4.3	4.0	0.0	2.6	2.3
Daughters	0.0	0.0	12.0	4.0	2.6	3.4
Sons and Daughters	0.0	4.3	8.0	0.0	10.5	6.3
Resident Relation	0.0	13.0	8.0	0.0	14.5	9.1
Employed Workers	33.3	26.1	4.0	4.0	1.3	10.2
Housegirl	0.0	0.0	8.0	0.0	0.0	1.1
Total	100.0	100.0	100.0	100.0	100.0	100.0

Source: 1988 Household Survey

Table VII.12: Households by Size of Household Acreages and Town (%)

Total Household Acreage	Town DSM	Mwanza	Arusha	Mbeya	Songea	TOTAL
No. Replied	62	29	30	30	35	186
% without Land	74.2	51.7	60.0	43.3	17.1	52.7
% with Land	25.8	48.3	40.0	56.7	82.9	47.3
SIZE OF ACREAGE						
90.1–100.0	6.3	0.0	0.0	0.0	0.0	1.1
>30.0	12.5	0.0	0.0	0.0	0.0	2.3
>20.0	18.8	0.0	0.0	0.0	0.0	3.4
>10.0	18.8	0.0	16.7	0.0	3.4	6.8
>8.0	25.0	0.0	16.7	0.0	10.3	10.2
>6.0	25.0	7.1	16.7	11.8	20.7	17.0
>4.0	43.8	14.3	25.0	41.2	41.4	35.2
>3.0	50.0	14.3	33.3	47.1	44.8	39.8
>2.0	68.8	35.7	41.7	64.7	75.9	61.4
>1.0	93.8	71.4	50.0	82.4	93.1	81.8
>0.0	100.0	100.0	100.0	100.0	100.0	100.0
Aver. Acreage	13.1	2.3	3.5	3.7	4.2	6.1
Adjusted Aver.*	7.1	2.3	3.5	3.7	4.2	3.8

Source: 1988 Household Survey
* Removal of the DSM household that has a farm of 100 acres.

Table VII.13: Households by Acreage per Household Member and Town (%)

Acreage per HH Member	Town DSM	Mwanza	Arusha	Mbeya	Songea	TOTAL
No. Replied	62	29	30	30	35	186
% without Land	74.2	51.7	60.0	43.3	17.1	52.7
% with Land	25.8	48.3	40.0	56.7	82.9	47.3
Size of Acreage						
>15	6.3	0.0	0.0	0.0	0.0	1.1
> 4	12.5	0.0	0.0	0.0	0.0	2.3
> 3	18.8	0.0	0.0	0.0	0.0	3.4
> 2	25.0	0.0	8.3	0.0	6.9	8.0
> 1	31.3	7.1	25.0	35.3	10.3	20.5
> 0.75	43.8	7.1	25.0	47.1	24.1	29.5
> 0.50	50.0	14.3	33.3	64.7	51.7	45.5
> 0.25	75.0	42.9	50.0	88.2	89.7	73.9
> 0	100.0	100.0	100.0	100.0	100.0	100.0
Aver. Acreage	2.12	0.35	0.61	0.79	0.67	0.90
Adjusted Aver.*	1.08	0.35	0.61	0.79	0.67	0.71

Source: 1988 Household Survey
* Removal of the DSM household with a farm of 100 acres.

Table VII.14: Landholding Households by Type of Landholding and Town (%)

Type of Household Landholding	Town DSM	Mwanza	Arusha	Mbeya	Songea	Total
No. Replied	15	12	10	17	29	83
Adjacent to Residence	6.7	0.0	40.0	0.0	0.0	6.0
Purchased	73.3	16.7	10.0	17.6	6.9	22.9
Family Holding	20.0	58.3	50.0	58.8	34.5	42.2
Family and Purchased	0.0	0.0	0.0	0.0	3.4	1.2
Borrowed	0.0	0.0	0.0	23.5	55.2	24.1
Attached to Workplace	0.0	8.3	0.0	0.0	0.0	1.2
Rented	0.0	16.7	0.0	0.0	0.0	2.4
Total	100.0	100.0	100.0	100.0	100.0	100.0

Source: 1988 Household Survey

Table VII.15: Households by Non-Purchased Household Staple Food from Extra-Household Sources and Town (%)

% of HH Food from Non-Purchased Extra-HH Sources	Town DSM	Mwanza	Arusha	Mbeya	Songea	TOTAL
No. Replied	64	29	30	30	35	188
None	65.6	69.0	40.0	46.7	80.0	61.7
0.1– 0.5	12.5	17.2	23.3	16.7	14.3	16.0
5.1–10.0	9.4	0.0	13.3	16.7	2.9	8.5
10.1–15.0	0.0	0.0	10.0	6.7	0.0	2.7
15.1–20.0	4.7	0.0	3.3	0.0	0.0	2.1
20.1–25.0	0.0	6.9	3.3	0.0	2.9	2.1
25.1–30.0	1.6	0.0	0.0	3.3	0.0	1.1
30.1–35.0	0.0	3.4	0.0	6.7	0.0	1.6
35.1–40.0	1.6	0.0	0.0	3.3	0.0	1.1
40.1–45.0	0.0	0.0	0.0	0.0	0.0	0.0
45.1–50.0	1.6	3.4	6.7	0.0	0.0	2.1
50.1–55.0	0.0	0.0	0.0	0.0	0.0	0.0
55.1–60.0	1.6	0.0	0.0	0.0	0.0	0.5
60.1–65.0	1.6	0.0	0.0	0.0	0.0	0.5
65.1–100.0	0.0	0.0	0.0	0.0	0.0	0.0
Total	100.0	100.0	100.0	100.0	100.0	100.0
Average	6.0	5.0	8.3	7.5	1.2	5.6

Source: 1988 Household Survey

Table VII.16: Households by Non-Purchased Food Items Received and Town (%)

Food Items Received	Town DSM	Mwanza	Arusha	Mbeya	Songea	TOTAL
No. Replied	63	29	30	30	35	187
HH not Receiving	66.7	69.0	40.0	46.7	80.0	62.0
HH Receiving	33.3	31.0	60.0	53.3	20.0	38.0
COMPOSITION OF FOOD RECEIVED						
Maize	46.9	35.7	31.0	14.8	27.3	31.9
Rice	25.0	35.7	17.2	18.5	45.5	24.8
Bananas	15.6	0.0	31.0	40.7	9.1	23.0
Beans	6.3	0.0	20.7	3.7	9.1	8.8
Cassava	3.1	14.3	0.0	0.0	9.1	3.5
Potatoes	0.0	14.3	0.0	11.1	0.0	4.4
Wheat	3.1	0.0	0.0	3.7	0.0	1.8
Sweet Potatoes	0.0	0.0	0.0	3.7	0.0	0.9
Cocoyams	0.0	0.0	0.0	3.7	0.0	0.9
Total	100.0	100.0	100.0	100.0	100.0	100.0

Source: 1988 Household Survey

Table VII.17: Households by % of Purchased Staple Food Consumption and Town (%)

% Purchased Food	Town DSM	Mwanza	Arusha	Mbeya	Songea	TOTAL
Total	64	28	30	30	35	187
None	1.6	3.6	0.0	0.0	2.9	1.6
0.1–5.0	0.0	0.0	0.0	0.0	8.6	1.6
5.1–10.0	0.0	0.0	0.0	0.0	8.6	1.6
10.1–15.0	0.0	0.0	3.3	10.0	14.3	4.8
15.1–20.0	0.0	0.0	3.3	10.0	11.4	4.3
20.1–25.0	0.0	7.1	0.0	6.7	11.4	4.3
25.1–30.0	0.0	0.0	3.3	0.0	11.4	2.7
30.1–35.0	0.0	0.0	0.0	0.0	0.0	0.0
35.1–40.0	3.1	0.0	3.3	3.3	0.0	2.1
40.1–45.0	1.6	0.0	3.3	3.3	2.9	2.1
45.1–50.0	4.7	10.7	6.7	6.7	2.9	5.9
50.1–55.0	0.0	0.0	0.0	0.0	0.0	0.0
55.1–60.0	0.0	0.0	0.0	6.7	2.9	1.6
60.1–65.0	1.6	3.6	0.0	6.7	2.9	2.7
65.1–70.0	3.1	3.6	3.3	3.3	0.0	2.7
70.1–75.0	3.1	10.7	3.3	3.3	2.9	4.3
75.1–80.0	3.1	3.6	3.3	0.0	2.9	2.7
80.1–85.0	0.0	0.0	6.7	0.0	0.0	1.1
85.1–90.0	10.9	0.0	10.0	3.3	0.0	5.9
90.1–95.0	4.7	7.1	16.7	13.3	0.0	7.5
95.1–100.0	62.5	50.0	33.3	23.3	14.3	40.6
Total	100.0	100.0	100.0	100.0	100.0	100.0
Average	88.8	79.1	79.3	62.2	36.1	71.7

Source: 1988 Household Survey

Table VII.18: Households by % of Maize Purchases Originating in the Open Market and Town (%)

% of HH Maize Purchases made in Open Market	Town DSM	Mwanza	Arusha	Mbeya	Songea	TOTAL
No. Replied	43	23	19	14	8	112
None	9.3	3.8	0.0	7.1	12.5	6.3
0.1–10.0	2.3	0.0	0.0	0.0	0.0	0.9
10.1–20.0	2.3	0.0	0.0	0.0	0.0	0.9
20.1–30.0	2.3	7.7	0.0	0.0	0.0	2.7
30.1–40.0	0.0	0.0	0.0	0.0	0.0	0.0
40.1–50.0	11.6	0.0	0.0	0.0	0.0	4.5
50.1–60.0	0.0	0.0	0.0	0.0	0.0	0.0
60.1–70.0	0.0	0.0	0.0	0.0	0.0	0.0
70.1–80.0	2.3	0.0	0.0	7.1	0.0	1.8
80.1–90.0	4.7	0.0	5.0	7.1	0.0	3.6
90.1–100.0	65.1	88.5	95.0	78.6	87.5	79.3
Total	100.0	100.0	100.0	100.0	100.0	100.0
Average	77.9	90.4	99.5	84.7	87.5	82.2

Source: 1988 Household Survey

Table VII.19: Monthly Expenditure on Staple Foodstuffs per Capita by Town (%)

HH Staple Food Expenditure per Capita (TSh.)	Town DSM	Mwanza	Arusha	Mbeya	Songea	TOTAL
No. Replied	62	27	30	26	35	180
PERCENTAGE						
0.0	1.6	3.7	0.0	0.0	2.9	1.7
0.1–100.0	0.0	0.0	3.3	0.0	17.1	3.9
100.1–200.0	3.2	3.7	3.3	3.8	20.0	6.7
200.1–300.0	9.7	14.8	16.7	7.7	14.3	12.2
300.1–400.0	9.7	7.4	3.3	11.5	8.6	8.3
400.1–500.0	11.3	29.6	20.0	15.4	8.6	15.6
500.1–600.0	8.1	22.2	13.3	11.5	11.4	12.2
600.1–700.0	4.8	3.7	16.7	7.7	0.0	6.1
700.1–800.0	8.1	0.0	6.7	7.7	8.6	6.7
800.1–900.0	8.1	3.7	0.0	3.8	2.9	4.4
900.1–1000.0	9.7	0.0	10.0	3.8	5.7	6.7
1000.1–1100.0	1.6	0.0	3.3	3.8	0.0	1.7
1100.1–1200.0	4.8	0.0	0.0	0.0	0.0	1.7
1200.1–1300.0	3.2	7.4	0.0	3.8	0.0	2.8
1300.1–1400.0	1.6	0.0	0.0	7.7	0.0	1.7
1400.1–1500.0	4.8	0.0	0.0	0.0	0.0	1.7
1500.1–1600.0	1.6	3.7	3.3	3.8	0.0	2.2
1600.1–1700.0	3.2	0.0	0.0	0.0	0.0	1.1
1700.1–1800.0	0.0	0.0	0.0	3.8	0.0	0.6
1800.1–1900.0	0.0	0.0	0.0	0.0	0.0	0.0
1900.1–2000.0.	3.2	0.0	0.0	3.8	0.0	1.7
>2000.0	1.6	0.0	0.0	0.0	0.0	0.6
Total	100.0	100.0	100.0	100.0	100.0	100.0
CUMULATIVE PERCENTAGE						
0.0	1.6	3.7	0.0	0.0	2.9	1.7
≤ 100.0	1.6	3.7	3.3	0.0	20.0	5.6
≤ 200.0	4.8	7.4	6.7	3.8	40.0	12.2
≤ 300.0	14.5	22.2	23.3	11.5	54.3	24.4
≤ 400.0	24.2	29.6	26.7	23.1	62.9	32.8
≤ 500.0	35.5	59.3	46.7	38.5	71.4	48.3
≤ 600.0	43.5	81.5	60.0	50.0	82.9	60.6
≤ 700.0	48.4	85.2	76.7	57.7	82.9	66.7
≤ 800.0	56.5	85.2	83.3	65.4	91.4	73.3
≤ 900.0	64.5	88.9	83.3	69.2	94.3	77.8
≤ 1000.0	74.2	88.9	93.3	73.1	100.0	84.4
≤ 1100.0	75.8	88.9	96.7	76.9	100.0	86.1
≤ 1200.0	80.6	88.9	96.7	76.9	100.0	87.8
≤ 1300.0	83.9	96.3	96.7	80.8	100.0	90.6
≤ 1400.0	85.5	96.3	96.7	88.5	100.0	92.2
≤ 1500.0	90.3	96.3	96.7	88.5	100.0	93.9
≤ 1600.0	91.9	100.0	100.0	92.3	100.0	96.1
≤ 1700.0	95.2	100.0	100.0	92.3	100.0	97.2
≤ 1800.0	95.2	100.0	100.0	96.2	100.0	97.8
≤ 1900.0	95.2	100.0	100.0	96.2	100.0	97.8
≤ 2000.0.	98.4	100.0	100.0	100.0	100.0	99.4
> 2000.0	100.0	100.0	100.0	100.0	100.0	100.0
Average cost	836.72	540.37	581.42	795.88	360.31	651.18

Source: 1988 Household Survey

Table VII.20: Estimated Household Monthly Income per Capita (%)

Income Range (TSh.)	Town DSM	Mwanza	Arusha	Mbeya	Songea	TOTAL
No. Replied	60	2	30	25	34	151
PERCENTAGE						
300– 499	3.3	0.0	0.0	0.0	8.8	3.3
500– 999	18.3	0.0	46.7	8.0	38.2	26.5
1000– 1499	23.3	0.0	20.0	24.0	17.6	21.2
1500– 1999	8.3	0.0	16.7	8.0	20.6	12.6
2000– 2499	11.7	0.0	0.0	12.0	0.0	6.6
2500– 2999	5.0	0.0	6.7	16.0	0.0	6.0
3000– 3499	3.3	50.0	6.7	4.0	5.9	5.3
3500– 3999	0.0	50.0	0.0	4.0	0.0	1.3
4000– 4499	6.7	0.0	0.0	8.0	2.9	4.6
4500– 4999	3.3	0.0	0.0	0.0	2.9	2.0
5000– 5999	1.7	0.0	0.0	4.0	0.0	1.3
6000– 6999	1.7	0.0	3.3	0.0	0.0	1.3
7000– 7999	1.7	0.0	0.0	0.0	0.0	0.7
8000– 8999	1.7	0.0	0.0	4.0	0.0	1.3
9000– 9999	1.7	0.0	0.0	0.0	0.0	0.7
10000–14999	0.0	0.0	0.0	8.0	0.0	1.3
15000–19999	1.7	0.0	0.0	0.0	0.0	0.7
20000–24999	1.7	0.0	0.0	0.0	2.9	1.3
25000–49999	1.7	0.0	0.0	0.0	0.0	0.7
50000–74999	1.7	0.0	0.0	0.0	0.0	0.7
≥75000	1.7	0.0	0.0	0.0	0.0	0.7
Total	100.2	100.0	100.1	100.0	99.8	100.1
CUMULATIVE PERCENTAGE						
<500	3.3	0.0	0.0	0.0	8.8	3.3
<1000	21.6	0.0	46.7	8.0	47.0	29.8
<1500	44.9	0.0	66.7	32.0	64.6	51.0
<2000	53.2	0.0	83.4	40.0	85.2	63.6
<2500	64.9	0.0	83.4	52.0	85.2	70.2
<3000	69.9	0.0	90.1	68.0	85.2	76.2
<3500	73.2	50.0	96.8	72.0	91.1	81.5
<4000	73.2	100.0	96.8	76.0	91.1	82.8
<4500	79.9	100.0	96.8	84.0	94.0	87.4
<5000	83.2	100.0	96.8	84.0	96.9	89.4
<6000	84.9	100.0	96.8	88.0	96.9	90.7
<7000	86.6	100.0	100.0	88.0	96.9	92.0
<8000	88.3	100.0	100.0	88.0	96.9	92.7
<9000	90.0	100.0	100.0	92.0	96.9	94.0
<10000	91.7	100.0	100.0	92.0	96.9	94.7
<15000	91.7	100.0	100.0	100.0	96.9	96.0
<20000	93.4	100.0	100.0	100.0	96.9	96.7
<25000	95.1	100.0	100.0	100.0	100.0	98.0
<50000	96.8	100.0	100.0	100.0	100.0	98.7
<75000	98.5	100.0	100.0	100.0	100.0	99.4
≥75000	100.0	100.0	100.0	100.0	100.0	100.0
Average (TSh.)	5960	3375	1473	3106	2011	3673

Source: 1988 Household Survey

Table VII.21: Households by Town and % of Income Spent on Staple Food

% of Income Spent on Staple Food	Town DSM	Mwanza	Arusha	Mbeya	Songea	TOTAL
No. Replied	62	5	30	27	34	158
PERCENTAGE						
0.1–10.0	11.3	0.0	6.7	14.8	17.6	12.0
10.1–20.0	11.3	0.0	3.3	14.8	38.2	15.8
20.1–30.0	22.6	0.0	26.7	22.2	5.9	19.0
30.1–40.0	12.9	40.0	6.7	7.4	5.9	10.1
40.1–50.0	24.2	40.0	16.7	25.9	17.6	22.2
50.1–60.0	8.1	0.0	20.0	11.1	8.8	10.8
60.1–70.0	9.7	0.0	13.3	0.0	2.9	7.0
70.1–80.0	0.0	20.0	0.0	3.7	2.9	1.9
80.1–90.0	0.0	0.0	6.7	0.0	0.0	1.3
Total	100.0	100.0	100.0	100.0	100.0	100.0
CUMULATIVE PERCENTAGE						
≤10.0	11.3	0.0	6.7	14.8	17.6	12.0
≤20.0	22.6	0.0	10.0	29.6	55.9	27.8
≤30.0	45.2	0.0	36.7	51.9	61.8	46.8
≤40.0	58.1	40.0	43.3	59.3	67.6	57.0
≤50.0	82.3	80.0	60.0	85.2	85.3	79.1
≤60.0	90.3	80.0	80.0	96.3	94.1	89.9
≤70.0	100.0	80.0	93.3	96.3	97.1	96.8
≤80.0	100.0	100.0	93.3	100.0	100.0	98.7
≤90.0	100.0	100.0	100.0	100.0	100.0	100.0
Average	36.8	40.3	46.2	35.5	27.4	36.5

TOTAL FOOD EXPENDITURE AS % OF INCOME

	DSM	Mwanza	Arusha	Mbeya	Songea	TOTAL
Average	65.0	84.0	81.9	64.4	59.9	67.6

STAPLE FOOD EXPENDITURE AS % OF TOTAL FOOD EXPENDITURE

	DSM	Mwanza	Arusha	Mbeya	Songea	TOTAL
Average	56.6	48.0	56.4	55.1	45.7	54.0

Source: 1988 Household Survey

Table VII.22: Households by Incidence of Maize and Rice Bulk Purchase and Town (%)

Household Bulk Purchase	Town DSM		Mwanza		Arusha		Mbeya		Songea		TOTAL	
	Maize	Rice	Maize	Rice	Maize	Rice	Maize	Rice	Maize	Rice	Maize	Rice
INCIDENCE OF BULK PURCHASE												
No. Replied	64	64	28	28	30	30	30	30	35	35	187	187
No	56.3	67.2	57.1	75.0	36.7	46.7	70.0	70.0	88.6	80.0	61.5	67.9
Yes	43.8	32.8	42.9	25.0	63.3	53.3	30.0	30.0	11.4	20.0	38.5	32.1
Total	100.0	100.0	100.0	100.0	100.0	100.0	100.0	100.0	100.0	100.0	100.0	100.0
LOCATION OF PURCHASE												
No. Replied	28	21	12	7	19	16	9	9	4	7	72	60
Farm	0.0	0.0	0.0	0.0	0.0	0.0	22.2	11.1	50.0	57.1	5.6	8.3
District Bus Stand	0.0	0.0	8.3	14.3	0.0	0.0	0.0	0.0	0.0	0.0	1.4	1.7
Town Bus Stand	0.0	0.0	0.0	0.0	21.1	6.3	0.0	11.1	0.0	0.0	5.6	3.3
Town Market	85.7	76.2	41.7	57.1	73.7	81.3	44.4	44.4	50.0	14.3	68.1	63.3
Producer in Town Perimeter	0.0	0.0	0.0	0.0	5.3	6.3	0.0	0.0	0.0	0.0	1.4	1.7
Local Rural Markets	3.6	19.0	25.0	28.6	0.0	0.0	11.1	22.2	0.0	28.6	6.9	16.7
State Farm	0.0	0.0	0.0	0.0	0.0	0.0	11.1	0.0	0.0	0.0	1.4	0.0
NMC	10.7	4.8	16.7	0.0	0.0	0.0	11.1	0.0	0.0	0.0	8.3	1.7
Cooperative Union	0.0	0.0	0.0	0.0	0.0	0.0	0.0	11.1	0.0	0.0	0.0	1.7
Not Answered	0.0	0.0	8.3	0.0	0.0	6.3	0.0	0.0	0.0	0.0	1.4	1.7
Total	100.0	100.0	100.0	100.0	100.0	100.0	100.0	100.0	100.0	100.0	100.0	100.0
FORM OF MAIZE BULK TRANSPORT												
No. Replied	28	21	12	7	19	16	9	9	4	7	72	60
Hired Pickup	17.9	9.5	8.3	0.0	21.1	6.3	0.0	11.1	0.0	0.0	13.9	6.7
Hired Handcart	7.1	0.0	0.0	0.0	52.6	50.0	0.0	0.0	25.0	14.3	18.1	15.0
Own Car/Pickup	17.9	28.6	8.3	14.3	5.3	6.3	0.0	22.2	0.0	0.0	9.7	16.7
Hired Porter	3.6	4.8	0.0	0.0	10.5	12.5	0.0	0.0	0.0	0.0	4.2	5.0
Hired Taxi	0.0	0.0	0.0	0.0	10.5	12.5	0.0	0.0	0.0	0.0	2.8	3.3
Bus	25.0	14.3	0.0	0.0	0.0	0.0	33.3	33.3	0.0	14.3	13.9	11.7

Table VII.22 Cont.: Households by Incidence of Maize and Rice Bulk Purchase and Town (%)

Household Bulk Purchase	DSM Maize	DSM Rice	Mwanza Maize	Mwanza Rice	Arusha Maize	Arusha Rice	Mbeya Maize	Mbeya Rice	Songea Maize	Songea Rice	TOTAL Maize	TOTAL Rice
Office Transport	7.1	23.8	8.3	14.3	0.0	0.0	11.1	0.0	0.0	28.6	5.6	13.3
By Foot	10.7	14.3	0.0	0.0	0.0	6.3	33.3	22.2	25.0	0.0	9.7	10.0
Lorry	0.0	0.0	0.0	0.0	0.0	0.0	0.0	0.0	50.0	42.9	2.8	5.0
Ox Cart	0.0	0.0	0.0	0.0	0.0	0.0	11.1	11.1	0.0	0.0	1.4	1.7
Borrowed Vehicle	0.0	0.0	0.0	0.0	0.0	0.0	11.1	0.0	0.0	0.0	1.4	0.0
Relations' Vehicle	3.6	0.0	0.0	0.0	0.0	0.0	0.0	0.0	0.0	0.0	1.4	0.0
Bicycle	3.6	0.0	0.0	0.0	0.0	0.0	0.0	0.0	0.0	0.0	1.4	0.0
Not Answered	3.6	4.8	75.0	71.4	0.0	6.3	0.0	0.0	0.0	0.0	13.9	11.7
Total	100.0	100.0	100.0	100.0	100.0	100.0	100.0	100.0	100.0	100.0	100.0	100.0

Source: 1988 Household Survey

Table VII.23: Percentage of Households Experiencing Food Supply Difficulties by Year and Town

Year	Town DSM	Mwanza	Arusha	Mbeya	Songea	TOTAL
No. Replied	64	26	29	26	30	175
1979	14.1	15.4	13.8	7.7	0.0	10.9
1980	34.4	15.4	0.0	11.5	0.0	16.6
1981	45.3	15.4	0.0	15.4	0.0	21.1
1982	67.2	19.2	3.4	23.1	0.0	31.4
1983	73.4	30.8	0.0	26.9	0.0	35.4
1984	76.6	76.9	86.2	19.2	90.0	72.0
1985	29.7	26.9	0.0	7.7	0.0	16.0
1986	6.3	3.8	3.4	7.7	3.3	5.1
1987	0.0	3.8	0.0	0.0	10.0	2.3
1988	1.6	3.8	0.0	0.0	3.3	1.7
Average	34.8	21.2	10.7	11.9	10.7	21.3

Source: 1988 Household Survey

Table VII.24: Households by Type of Food Supply Difficulties Experienced During Past Year and Town (%)

Food Supply Difficulties	Town DSM	Mwanza	Arusha	Mbeya	Songea	TOTAL
No. Replied	63	29	30	30	35	187
WHETHER HOUSEHOLD EXPERIENCED ANY FOOD SUPPLY DIFFICULTIES						
No	49.2	48.3	20.0	66.7	42.9	46.0
Yes	50.8	51.7	80.0	33.3	57.1	54.0
Total	100.0	100.0	100.0	100.0	100.0	100.0
TYPE OF FOOD SUPPLY DIFFICULTIES EXPERIENCED						
No. of Replies	45	15	35	14	30	139
1) *Market Supply*	68.9	0.0	40.0	35.7	13.3	38.8
Maize Shortage	6.7	0.0	0.0	0.0	0.0	2.2
Rice Shortage	42.2	0.0	14.3	14.3	10.0	20.9
Bean Shortage	6.7	0.0	5.7	7.1	3.3	5.0
Banana Shortage	0.0	0.0	2.9	7.1	0.0	1.4
Unstable Supply	8.9	0.0	17.1	7.1	0.0	7.9
Inadequate Formal Supply	4.4	0.0	0.0	0.0	0.0	1.4
2) *Prices*	28.9	86.7	60.0	50.0	33.3	46.0
High Prices	28.9	86.7	60.0	50.0	23.3	43.9
Can't Afford Non-Staple Foods	0.0	0.0	0.0	0.0	10.0	2.2
3) *Food Quality/Diversity*	2.2	0.0	0.0	0.0	3.3	1.4
Monotonous Supply	0.0	0.0	0.0	0.0	3.3	0.7
Poor Food Quality	2.2	0.0	0.0	0.0	0.0	0.7
4) *Direct Farm Supply*	0.0	13.3	0.0	14.3	50.0	13.7
Rainy Season Shortages	0.0	0.0	0.0	0.0	16.7	3.6
Insufficient Own Farm Harvest	0.0	0.0	0.0	0.0	16.7	3.6
Over-Sold Harvest	0.0	0.0	0.0	0.0	6.7	1.4
Transport Difficulties for Own Farm Supply	0.0	6.7	0.0	0.0	0.0	0.7
Unable to Cultivate this year	0.0	0.0	0.0	0.0	6.7	1.4
No Own Farm	0.0	0.0	0.0	7.1	0.0	0.7
No Land for Cultivating	0.0	6.7	0.0	0.0	0.0	0.7
Difficult as Non-Native Resident	0.0	0.0	0.0	7.1	3.3	1.4
Total	100.0	100.0	100.0	100.0	100.0	100.0

Source: 1988 Household Survey

Table VII.25: Household Measures in Years of Difficult Food Supply by Town (%)

Household Food Crisis Measures	Town DSM	Mwanza	Arusha	Mbeya	Songea	TOTAL
No. Replied	61	24	30	17	30	162
HOUSEHOLD ACTION						
None	3.3	3.3	3.3	3.3	3.3	3.3
Don't Remember	0.0	0.0	0.0	0.0	0.0	0.0
Reactive Measures	96.7	96.7	96.7	96.7	96.7	96.7
Total	100.0	100.0	100.0	100.0	100.0	100.0
TYPES OF REACTIVE MEASURES						
No. of Replies	92	33	26	28	47	226
1) *Food Substitution*	25.0	12.1	23.1	17.9	21.3	21.2
Substitute Starchy Roots	23.9	12.1	19.2	3.6	19.1	18.1
Changed to Available Foodstuffs*	0.0	0.0	3.8	14.3	2.1	2.7
Ate Poorer Quality Food	1.1	0.0	0.0	0.0	0.0	0.4
2) *Regulated Consumption*	8.7	12.1	11.5	3.6	2.1	7.5
Reduced Consumption	7.6	0.0	0.0	3.6	2.1	4.0
Reduced HH Membership	1.1	0.0	0.0	0.0	0.0	0.4
Avoided having Dependents	0.0	12.1	11.5	0.0	0.0	3.1
3) *Increased Food Expenditure*	9.8	6.1	0.0	10.7	31.9	12.8
Increased % of Income spent on Food	9.8	6.1	0.0	10.7	31.9	12.8
4) *Increased Household Income*	6.5	18.2	15.4	7.1	2.1	8.4
Family Member starts Trading	2.2	3.0	3.8	0.0	0.0	1.8
Increased Work in Trade	2.2	12.1	3.8	0.0	0.0	3.1
Started Intermediary Trade in Food	0.0	0.0	0.0	0.0	2.1	0.4
Started Side-line Business	1.1	3.0	0.0	3.6	0.0	1.3
Sale of Own Garden Produce	1.1	0.0	7.7	3.6	0.0	1.8
5) *Official Urban Supply*	6.5	9.1	23.1	7.1	4.3	8.4
Depend on NMC Supply	0.0	0.0	19.2	0.0	2.1	2.7
Depended on Govt Ration Shops	2.2	3.0	3.8	7.1	0.0	2.7
Queuing	4.3	6.1	0.0	0.0	2.1	3.1
6) *Urban Clientage Sources*	3.3	6.1	0.0	0.0	2.1	2.7
Used Connections to get Food from NMC	0.0	6.1	0.0	0.0	0.0	0.9
Lobbied to get Food from NMC	1.1	0.0	0.0	0.0	0.0	0.4
'Scouting Around'	2.2	0.0	0.0	0.0	2.1	1.3
7) *Urban Parallel Market*	22.8	3.0	0.0	0.0	0.0	9.7
Purchased in 'Black' Market	22.8	0.0	0.0	0.0	0.0	9.3
Depended on Trader Relations	0.0	3.0	0.0	0.0	0.0	0.4
8) *Direct Rural Market Sources*	3.3	3.0	19.2	25.0	4.3	8.0
Purchased from Rural Area	1.1	3.0	19.2	10.7	0.0	4.4
Purchased Food from Distant Regions	2.2	0.0	0.0	7.1	2.1	2.2
Bartered with Peasants	0.0	0.0	0.0	0.0	2.1	0.4
Purchased from State Farm	0.0	0.0	0.0	7.1	0.0	0.9
9) *Supply from Extended Family*	4.3	9.1	7.7	10.7	2.1	5.8
Relied on Relations	4.3	9.1	3.8	10.7	2.1	5.3
Air Shipment from Another Region	0.0	0.0	3.8	0.0	0.0	0.4
10) *Household Farm Supply*	9.8	21.2	0.0	17.9	29.8	15.5
Bought Farm	3.3	0.0	0.0	0.0	0.0	1.3
Started/Extended HH Farming	4.3	18.2	0.0	10.7	2.1	6.2
Sent Wife to Home Area to Cultivate	1.1	0.0	0.0	0.0	0.0	0.4
Went to Village to Cultivate	0.0	3.0	0.0	0.0	0.0	0.4
Depended on HH Stores	1.1	0.0	0.0	0.0	0.0	0.4
More Careful Usage of HH Stores	0.0	0.0	0.0	7.1	27.7	6.6
Total	100.0	100.0	100.0	100.0	100.0	100.0

Source: 1988 Household Survey * refers to potatoes and bananas.

Table VII.26: Household Respondents' Suggestions for Improving their Town's Food Supply (%)

Suggestions	Town DSM	Mwanza	Arusha	Mbeya	Songea	TOTAL
No. Replied	36	26	16	10	1	89
No. of Responses	47	36	23	11	1	118
1) *Nothing*	2.1	0.0	0.0	9.1	100.0	2.5
2) *Market Liberalization*	42.6	8.3	0.0	0.0	0.0	19.5
More Market Liberalization	42.6	8.3	0.0	0.0	0.0	19.5
3) *Government Intervention*	10.6	19.4	21.7	18.2	0.0	16.1
More Efficient Distribution	8.5	5.6	21.7	0.0	0.0	9.3
Eliminate Middlemen	2.1	0.0	0.0	0.0	0.0	0.8
Eliminate Black Market	0.0	0.0	0.0	9.1	0.0	0.8
Producer Shops in Town	0.0	0.0	0.0	9.1	0.0	0.8
Decrease/Stabilize Consumer Prices	0.0	11.1	0.0	0.0	0.0	3.4
Reduce Beer Brewing*	0.0	2.8	0.0	0.0	0.0	0.8
4) *Market Infrastructure*	17.0	8.3	8.7	9.1	0.0	11.9
Transport Improvements	17.0	8.3	8.7	9.1	0.0	11.9
5) *Agricultural Production*	27.7	63.9	69.6	63.6	0.0	50.0
Increase Incentives to Peasants	2.1	0.0	0.0	0.0	0.0	0.8
Increase Production	19.1	47.2	56.5	27.3	0.0	35.6
Peasants Work Harder	0.0	0.0	8.7	0.0	0.0	1.7
Need More Agricultural Land	2.1	0.0	0.0	0.0	0.0	0.8
Scientific Agriculture	2.1	2.8	0.0	9.1	0.0	2.5
Increase Investment in Agriculture	2.1	0.0	0.0	0.0	0.0	0.8
Everyone should Farm	0.0	13.9	4.3	27.3	0.0	7.6
Total	100.0	100.0	100.0	100.0	100.0	100.0

Source: 1988 Household Survey
* Decrease usage of grain for beer brewing.

Table VII.27: Household Respondents' Suggestions for Government Measures to Improve Their Town's Food Supply (%)

Suggestions	Town DSM	Mwanza	Arusha	Mbeya	Songea	TOTAL
No. Replied	63	28	30	25	35	181
No. of Responses	117	48	48	44	57	314
1) *Pro private farming*	0.9	6.3	0.0	2.3	0.0	1.6
Allow private farming	0.9	0.0	0.0	0.0	0.0	0.3
Govt should sell land	0.0	2.1	0.0	0.0	0.0	0.3
Mobilize everyone to farm	0.0	4.2	0.0	2.3	0.0	1.0
2) *Govt market liberalization*	37.6	14.6	6.3	4.5	1.8	18.2
Nothing	0.0	0.0	0.0	2.3	0.0	0.3
More market liberalization	23.9	8.3	2.1	2.3	1.8	11.1
Get rid of NMC	1.7	0.0	2.1	0.0	0.0	1.0
Allow by-pass of cooperative union	0.9	0.0	0.0	0.0	0.0	0.3
Remove road barriers	6.0	0.0	0.0	0.0	0.0	2.2
Give traders' loans and market premises	1.7	4.2	0.0	0.0	0.0	1.3
Decrease traders' taxation	0.9	2.1	2.1	0.0	0.0	1.0
Build more produce markets	1.7	0.0	0.0	0.0	0.0	0.6
Encourage inter-regional trade	0.9	0.0	0.0	0.0	0.0	0.3

Table VII.27 Cont.: Household Respondents' Suggestions for Government Measures to Improve Their Town's Food Supply (%)

Suggestions	DSM	Mwanza	Arusha	Mbeya	Songea	TOTAL
3) *Mixed marketing*	4.3	0.0	0.0	0.0	21.1	5.4
Allow govt & open market operations	3.4	0.0	0.0	0.0	0.0	1.3
NMC provide reserves & stabilize prices	0.9	0.0	0.0	0.0	17.5	3.5
Resolve price policy one way or another	0.0	0.0	0.0	0.0	3.5	0.6
4) *Increase govt market control*	7.7	20.8	16.7	52.3	19.3	19.4
Stop border smuggling	0.9	0.0	6.3	0.0	0.0	1.3
Restrict grain movement out of region	0.0	0.0	0.0	0.0	3.5	0.6
Give grain market monopoly to coops	0.0	0.0	0.0	6.8	0.0	1.0
Make NMC sole marketing agency	0.0	0.0	2.1	0.0	0.0	0.3
Stop NMC sales to traders	0.0	2.1	0.0	0.0	0.0	0.3
Open NMC retail shops	0.0	0.0	0.0	4.5	0.0	0.6
NMC give food assist. during scarcity	0.0	2.1	0.0	2.3	0.0	0.6
More price regulation	1.7	14.6	6.3	27.3	14.0	10.2
Flood market to control prices	0.9	0.0	0.0	0.0	0.0	0.3
Subsidize consumer prices	0.0	0.0	0.0	0.0	1.8	0.3
Eliminate middlemen	3.4	2.1	2.1	9.1	0.0	3.2
Enforce use of weighing machines	0.0	0.0	0.0	2.3	0.0	0.3
Improve quality of staple foodstuffs	0.9	0.0	0.0	0.0	0.0	0.3
5) *Improve official market system*	16.2	18.8	22.9	13.6	24.6	18.8
Timely coop crop purchase	0.9	0.0	12.5	0.0	5.3	3.2
Coop should pay cash for crops	0.9	0.0	0.0	0.0	1.8	0.6
Eliminate coop union corruption	0.0	0.0	0.0	0.0	1.8	0.3
Coops should take over from NMC	0.0	2.1	0.0	0.0	0.0	0.3
Ensure efficiency in food distribution	1.7	0.0	8.3	0.0	0.0	1.9
Make coop and NMC more efficient	0.0	2.1	0.0	0.0	7.0	1.6
Improve rice supply	0.0	0.0	0.0	0.0	3.5	0.6
Increase producer prices & incentives	10.3	14.6	2.1	13.6	0.0	8.3
Improve public grain storage & fumigation	1.7	0.0	0.0	0.0	5.3	1.6
Ensure adequate grain importation	0.9	0.0	0.0	0.0	0.0	0.3
6) *Govt market infrastructure*	17.9	14.6	20.8	9.1	8.8	15.0
Improve transport	17.9	14.6	20.8	4.5	8.8	14.3
Control transport charges	0.0	0.0	0.0	2.3	0.0	0.3
Start govt transport fleets	0.0	0.0	0.0	2.3	0.0	0.3
7) *Improve peasant production*	14.5	18.8	31.3	11.4	22.8	18.8
Improve farmer input supply	9.4	14.6	22.9	6.8	19.3	13.7
Strengthen agricultural extension	2.6	2.1	2.1	2.3	0.0	1.9
Mechanize agriculture & irrigation	1.7	2.1	4.2	2.3	0.0	1.9
Improve peasant crop storage	0.9	0.0	2.1	0.0	3.5	1.3
8) *Pro state farming*	0.0	0.0	0.0	4.5	1.8	1.0
More state farming	0.0	0.0	0.0	2.3	1.8	0.6
Encourage private transporters	0.0	0.0	0.0	2.3	0.0	0.3
9) *Govt benefits to urban dwellers*	0.9	6.3	2.1	2.3	0.0	1.9
Increase salaries in line w/ fd price rise	0.0	2.1	0.0	0.0	0.0	0.3
Give plots to civil servants & others	0.9	4.2	2.1	2.3	0.0	1.6
Total	100.0	100.0	100.0	100.0	100.0	100.0

Source: 1988 Household Survey

Table VII.28: Household Respondents' Suggestions for Traders' Action to Improve Their Town's Food Supply (%)

Suggestions	Town DSM	Mwanza	Arusha	Mbeya	Songea	TOTAL
No. Replied	58	21	19	19	33	150
No. of Responses	73	31	20	24	39	187
1) *Nothing*	4.1	3.2	5.0	12.5	10.3	6.4
2) *Favourable opinion of traders*	0.0	6.5	0.0	4.2	20.5	5.9
Considered to be useful	0.0	6.5	0.0	0.0	7.7	2.7
Considered to be 'saviours'	0.0	0.0	0.0	0.0	12.8	2.7
Considered at mercy of transport costs	0.0	0.0	0.0	4.2	0.0	0.5
3) *Expansion of trader activity*	39.7	3.2	5.0	8.3	30.8	24.1
Get more market liberalization	1.4	0.0	0.0	0.0	0.0	0.5
Buy more from farmers & bring to town	2.7	0.0	0.0	0.0	20.5	5.3
Increase supply	8.2	0.0	0.0	0.0	0.0	3.2
Bring rice from other regions	0.0	0.0	0.0	0.0	10.3	2.1
Don't buy from NMC	0.0	0.0	5.0	0.0	0.0	0.5
Increase number of food traders	1.4	0.0	0.0	0.0	0.0	0.5
Be more competitive	4.1	0.0	0.0	0.0	0.0	1.6
Open more retail outlets	2.7	0.0	0.0	8.3	0.0	2.1
Increase specialization in food trade	1.4	0.0	0.0	0.0	0.0	0.5
Improve storage facilities	6.8	0.0	0.0	0.0	0.0	2.7
Package in affordable quantitites	1.4	0.0	0.0	0.0	0.0	0.5
Provide transport from source to market	2.7	0.0	0.0	0.0	0.0	1.1
Advertise in radio & newspaper	1.4	0.0	0.0	0.0	0.0	0.5
Use credit facilities	2.7	0.0	0.0	0.0	0.0	1.1
Form pressure group organizations	2.7	3.2	0.0	0.0	0.0	1.6
4) *Unfavourable opinion of traders*	0.0	0.0	0.0	8.3	2.6	1.6
Considered to be detrimental	0.0	0.0	0.0	4.2	2.6	1.1
Responsive only to supply & demand	0.0	0.0	0.0	4.2	0.0	0.5
5) *Reform of trader activity*	56.2	87.1	90.0	66.7	35.9	62.0
Eliminate traders	0.0	0.0	5.0	0.0	2.6	1.1
Reduce middlemen – buy direct from producers	15.1	0.0	30.0	4.2	0.0	9.6
Stop hawking – have permanent stalls	2.7	3.2	0.0	4.2	0.0	2.1
Adhere to price control	5.5	19.4	55.0	0.0	2.6	11.8
Reduce prices to reasonable level	9.6	41.9	0.0	0.0	5.1	11.8
Reduce profit seeking	9.6	19.4	0.0	25.0	12.8	12.8
Don't cause shortages	1.4	0.0	0.0	0.0	7.7	2.1
Don't hoard	1.4	0.0	0.0	4.2	2.6	1.6
Even out supply	1.4	0.0	0.0	0.0	2.6	1.1
Don't underweigh	0.0	0.0	0.0	8.3	0.0	1.1
Be honest	6.8	0.0	0.0	0.0	0.0	2.7
Be more humane	1.4	0.0	0.0	0.0	0.0	0.5
Buy from cooperatives	1.4	0.0	0.0	0.0	0.0	0.5
Start traders' coops	0.0	3.2	0.0	4.2	0.0	1.1
Traders should farm	0.0	0.0	0.0	16.7	0.0	2.1
Total	100.0	100.0	100.0	100.0	100.0	100.0

Source: 1988 Household Survey

Table VII.29: Annual Price and Marketed Surplus Index Changes for Maize by Town,
1983/84–1988/89 (1986/87 = 100)

| Town | Index Percentage Point Differences between Years: | | | | | |
	1983/4– 1984/5	1984/5– 1985/6	1985/6– 1986/7	1986/7– 1987/8	1987/8– 1988/9	Average
Dar es Salaam						
Price	−32.67	50.28	−24.80	−4.74	−13.72	−5.13
Surplus	57.70	16.44	8.90	13.36	−12.84	16.71
Ratio	−0.57	3.06	−2.79	−0.36	1.07	−0.31
Mwanza						
Price	12.92	−148.95	−59.74	3985.00	5.92	−30.00
Surplus	−276.30	137.07	120.45	35.19	−66.88	−10.09
Ratio	−0.05	−1.09	−0.50	1.13	−0.09	2.97
Arusha						
Price	−14.71	−127.00	−22.14	14.07	−21.40	−34.24
Surplus	8.28	31.18	67.73	62.42	−30.61	27.80
Ratio	−1.78	−4.07	−0.33	0.23	0.70	−1.23
Mbeya						
Price	−189.60	−9.65	−29.85	15.47	−11.73	−45.07
Surplus	182.62	−69.84	−18.17	28.02	77.90	40.11
Ratio	−1.04	0.14	1.64	0.55	−0.15	−1.12
Songea						
Price	−18.60	−15.07	−13.48	5.16	−13.87	−11.17
Surplus	93.12	−66.26	67.40	95.27	−69.63	23.98
Ratio	−0.20	0.23	−0.20	0.05	0.20	−0.47

Source: See Tables VI.17–21 and Figure VII.1

Table VII.30: Annual Price and Marketed Surplus Index Changes for Paddy by Town,
1983/84–1988/89 (1986/87 = 100)

| Town | Index Percentage Point Differences between Years | | | | | |
	1983/4– 1984/5	1984/5– 1985/6	1985/6– 1986/7	1986/7– 1987/8	1987/8– 1988/9	Average
Dar es Salaam						
Price	7.53	−7.28	−59.17	3.71	−6.45	−12.33
Surplus	−11.89	21.00	36.16	26.61	−15.00	11.38
Ratio	−0.63	−0.35	−1.64	0.14	0.43	−1.08
Mwanza						
Price	16.97	−94.25	−26.36	8.9	4.18	−18.11
Surplus	−29.11	29.02	99.41	39.23	141.56	56.02
Ratio	−0.58	−3.25	−0.27	0.23	0.03	−0.32
Mbeya						
Price	22.93	−68.75	−48.06	−19.47	−7.28	−24.13
Surplus	−576.83	−125.77	−157.84	261.75	−186.75	−157.1
Ratio	−0.04	0.55	0.3	−0.07	0.04	0.15

Source: See Tables VI.22–24 and Figure VII.2

Figure III.2: Simplified Marketing Chain for Grain Sale Under Private Trade, 1957–1962

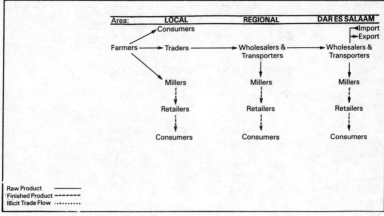

Price Control: None
Licensing: Transporters, Wheat Millers and Retailers

Source: Kriesel, H.C. *et al.*, *Agricultural Marketing in Tanzania: Background Research and Policy Proposals* (East Lansing, Michigan State University, 1970), 22.

Figure III.3: Simplified Marketing Chain for Grain Sale Under the National Agricultural Production Board, 1963–1972

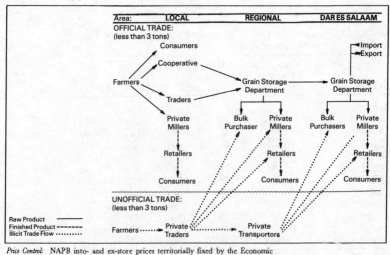

Price Control: NAPB into- and ex-store prices territorially fixed by the Economic Commission of the Cabinet; retail prices locally fixed by the Regional and Area Commissioners under the authority of the Price Controller
Licensing: Transporters' licences issued by the Transport Licensing Authority; millers' licences issued by the NAPB with recommendation from the Area Commissioner for Cooperatives; retailers' licences issued by Town and District Councils

Figure III.1: Simplified Marketing Chain for Grain Sale Under the Grain Storage Department, 1949–1956

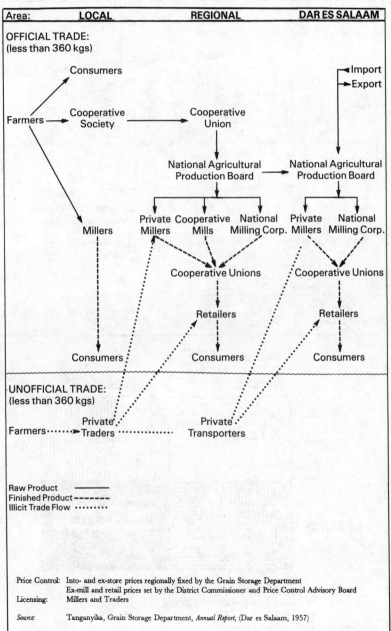

Price Control: Into- and ex-store prices regionally fixed by the Grain Storage Department
Ex-mill and retail prices set by the District Commissioner and Price Control Advisory Board
Licensing: Millers and Traders

Source: Tanganyika, Grain Storage Department, *Annual Report*, (Dar es Salaam, 1957)

Figure V.1: Types of 'Black' Markets

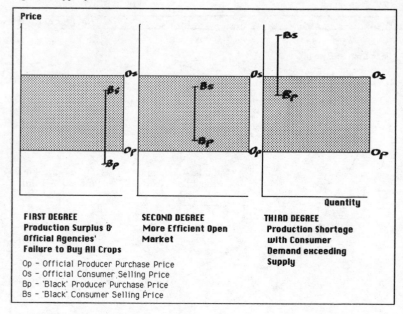

FIRST DEGREE
Production Surplus &
Official Agencies'
Failure to Buy All Crops

SECOND DEGREE
More Efficient Open
Market

THIRD DEGREE
Production Shortage
with Consumer
Demand exceeding
Supply

Op – Official Producer Purchase Price
Os – Official Consumer Selling Price
Bp – 'Black' Producer Purchase Price
Bs – 'Black' Consumer Selling Price

Figure VI.1: Types of 'Open' Urban Staple Food Markets

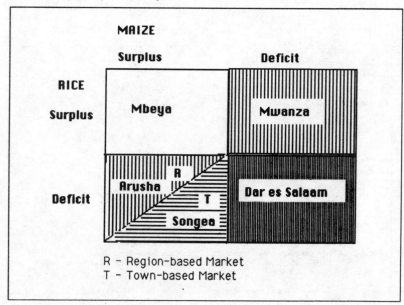

R – Region-based Market
T – Town-based Market

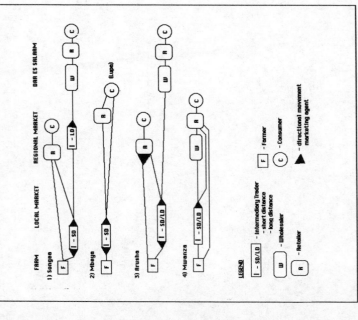

Figure VI.3: Schematic Open Market Chain for Rice by Town, 1985–88

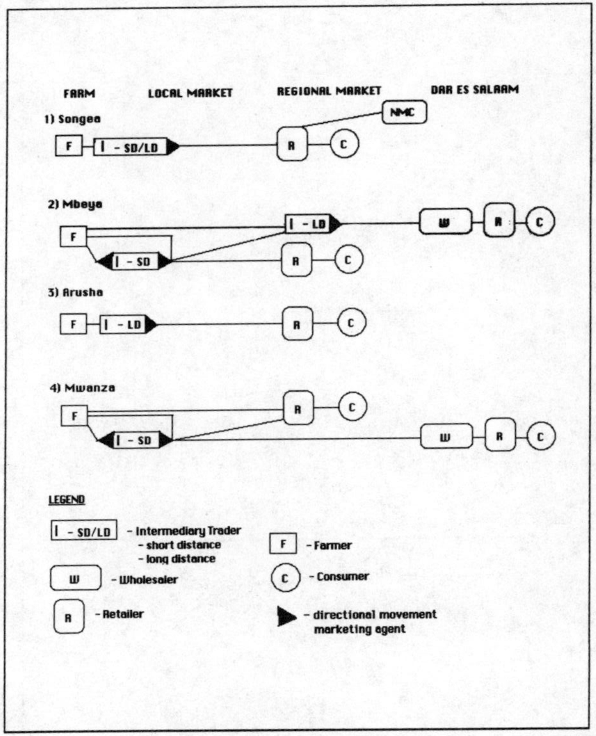

Figure VI.2: Schematic Open Market Chain for Maize by Town, 1985–88

Figure VII.1: Indices of Maize Marketed Surplus and Open Market Real Consumer Prices by Region, 1983/84–1988/89 (1986/87 = 100)

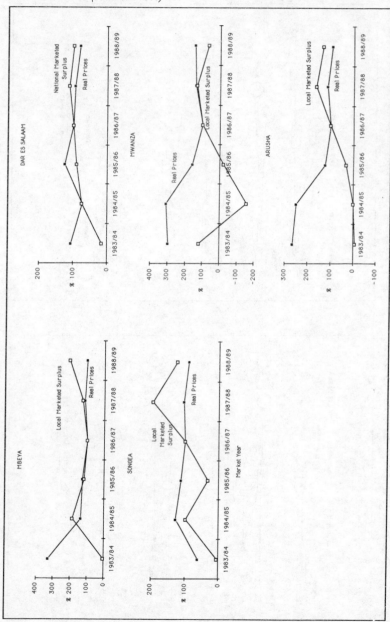

Figure VII.2: Indices of Paddy Marketed Surplus and Open Market Real Rice Consumer Prices by Region, 1983/84–1988/89 (1986/87 = 100)

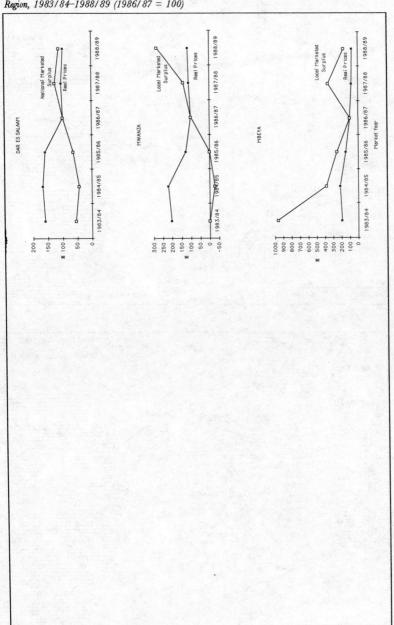

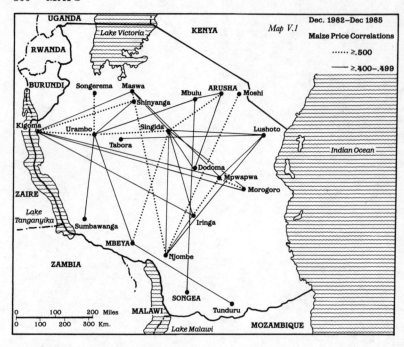

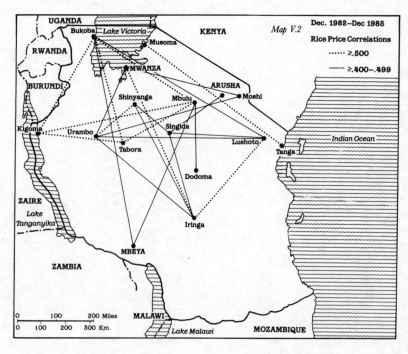

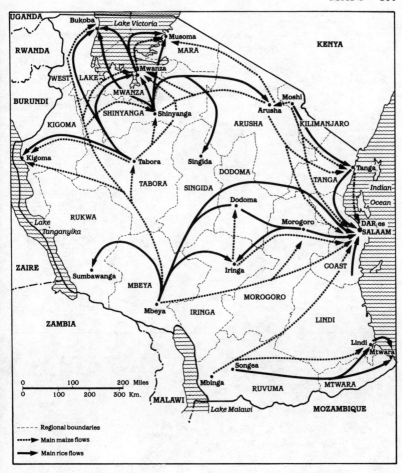

Map VI.1: Origin and Destinations of Open Market Maize and Rice Flows

Source: MDB, 'Aspects of the Open Market for Food Commodities in Mainland Tanzania' (DSM, June 1986)

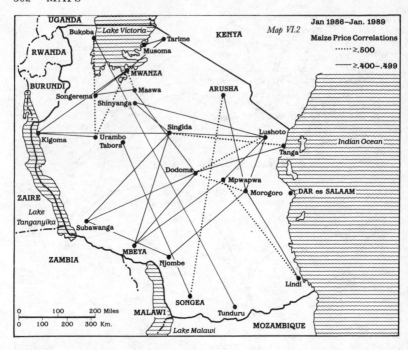

UGANDA
Bukoba Lake Victoria Tarime KENYA *Map VI.2*
RWANDA Musoma Jan 1986–Jan. 1989
Maize Price Correlations
BURUNDI MWANZA .... ≥.500
Songerema Maswa ARUSHA ———— ≥.400–.499
Shinyanga
Singida Lushoto
Kigoma Urambo Indian Ocean
Tabora Tanga
Dodoma
ZAIRE Mpwapwa
Lake Morogoro DAR es SALAAM
Tanganyika
Subawanga
MBEYA Lindi
ZAMBIA Njombe
0   100   200 Miles
0 100 200 300 Km. SONGEA
MALAWI Tunduru
Lake Malawi MOZAMBIQUE

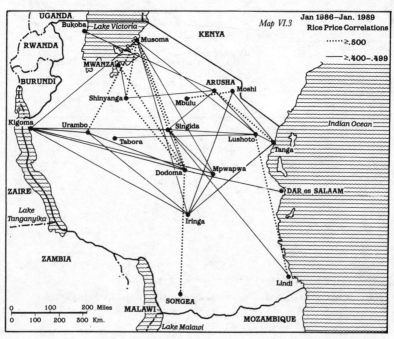

UGANDA
Bukoba Lake Victoria Musoma *Map VI.3*
KENYA Jan 1986–Jan. 1989
RWANDA Rice Price Correlations
MWANZA .... ≥.500
BURUNDI ARUSHA Moshi ———— ≥.400–.499
Shinyanga Mbulu
Kigoma Urambo Singida Indian Ocean
Tabora Lushoto
Dodoma Mpwapwa Tanga
ZAIRE
Lake DAR es SALAAM
Tanganyika Iringa
ZAMBIA Lindi
0   100   200 Miles
0 100 200 300 Km. SONGEA
MALAWI
Lake Malawi MOZAMBIQUE

Index